Second Edition

Being
and
Caring

Second Edition

Being and Caring

A Psychology For Living

Victor Daniels
Laurence J. Horowitz
Sonoma State University

WAVELAND
PRESS, INC.
Long Grove, Illinois

For information about this book, contact:
Waveland Press, Inc.
4180 IL Route 83, Suite 101
Long Grove, IL 60047-9580
(847) 634-0081
info@waveland.com
www.waveland.com

The authors thank the following copyright holders for permission to reprint material in this book:

Ric Masten, for an excerpt from "Even as We Speak" by Ric Masten, published by Sunflower Ink, Palo Colorado Rd., Carmel, CA 93923. Reprinted with permission.

Pergamon Press, for T. H. Holmes and R. H. Rahe, "The Social Readjustment Scale," from *Journal of Psychosomatic Research, 11* (1967), p. 216. Copyright © 1967, Pergamon Press Ltd.

Real People Press, for quotations from Frederick S. Perls, *Gestalt Therapy Verbatim* (Moab, UT, 1969); and Perls, *In and Out of the Garbage Pail* (Moab, UT, 1972); and lines from "My Life Measured Out in Abandoned Words" by Robert Hall, in *Gestalt Is*, ed. John O. Stevens. Reprinted with permission of Real People Press.

Contents

Exercises

Preface

We all write, direct, and act the parts we play in the theaters of our lives. These roles grow out of how we feel about ourselves, how we want the world to see us, and the constraints of our environments. We are sometimes terribly tragic, sometimes hilariously funny, and sometimes exquisitely absurd. Within these contexts, each of us has the option of finding ways to live that help us to feel good and know ourselves more deeply—to create and flow and to stretch and reach. As Rabbi Hillel said, "If I'm not for me, who will be? If I'm only for myself, what am I? And if not now, when?" In that spirit, we hope this book will help you in your quest for increased understanding.

In recent years, many psychological understandings and techniques have come into popular use. Each has the advantage of originality and the disadvantage of being partial, of overemphasizing one part of the personality. We have synthesized these understandings—the wisdom of such writers as Freud, Rogers, Perls, Jung, Skinner, and Reich—and developed an approach that involves the systematic development of each part of the personality. Readers of *Being and Caring* will find ways to move beyond limiting attitudes and assumptions, use inner resources more effectively, make outer relationships more rewarding, and live their lives more consciously than before.

Being and Caring speaks directly to the reader's past, present, and future life. Instead of talking about issues, it penetrates to the heart of students' concerns about them. Rather than presenting knowledge that is here today but gone after the exam, it provides practical information and skills that can be put to immediate use. Through its exercises, it provides an ongoing workshop in learning to confront dilemmas of existence that every person faces.

For student and teacher alike, we have tried both to inform and to demystify. What others have stated in complicated ways, we have sought to say simply and directly. The resources we draw upon for understanding range from the research laboratory to psychological clinics and consulting rooms; from the writings of philosophers to the observations of sages and spiritual teachers; from the ideas of colleagues and friends to a wealth of insights and incidents from our clients and students. We're happiest when we have hard scientific data, but we've tried to avoid relying on facts and figures at the expense of experience and insights.

As we wrote, we found ourselves wanting to pull together our experiences and viewpoints so that "I" statements could be made and be true to both of us. Although some of the tales in these pages are from Larry's life and some from Victor's, we tell them all in the first person. It doesn't matter which is which. We call this narrator the "generic I."

We intend no "more conscious than thou" statements—there's much more in these pages than we've integrated into our own lives. As an older brother said after reading the text, "You know all this stuff—how come you're still such a schmuck?"

CHANGES FROM THE FIRST EDITION

The entire book has been rewritten, from the first paragraph to the last, retaining what was best in the first edition and adding much more. The new edition preserves the warm, personal tone of the earlier one, but the writing is clearer and sharper, with a smoother flow, greater dignity, and more coherent organization.

There is a wealth of valuable new information: The areas of emotion and cognition are treated in greater depth and detail, with special attention to such crucial areas as emotional complexes, fear and anxiety, anger and aggression, cognitive restructuring or "reframing," attribution processes, and altered states of consciousness. A chapter on somatic psychology provides a practical approach to stress and then explores the dynamics of "body armoring" and its relation to the total personality. The new chapters on sexuality, assertion training, and conflict are both enlightening and useful. The revised "Talking and Listening" chapter is a virtual communication handbook. And this new edition includes so much material on intimacy, love, relationships, and families that the book can easily be used in a course on marriage and the family.

OUR POINT OF VIEW

Much of our early training was behavioristic: It focused on understanding people's observable actions. Over the years we have broadened our ways of working and understanding to include psychoanalytic, person-centered, Jungian, and other approaches that emphasize subjective experience. We practice and teach Gestalt therapy and family therapy.

Our present outlook is an "existential" one—but it's different from the old European existentialism, which was preoccupied with despair, loneliness, and alienation. Those states of being seem to us no more central to an existential view than caring, sharing, involvement, and joy—along with the enduring issues of how to be true to oneself and live responsibly and with integrity. The word *existential* refers in part to what *exists*—what *is*. Behaviorists are interested in knowing what *is*. Zen masters are interested in knowing what *is*. In this sense, both are existentialists, their outlooks grounded in an empiricism that encompasses both observable actions and subjective experience. Our focus is not on positions, but on processes. This emphasis helps make the book the unique and effective learning tool that it is.

HOW TO USE THIS BOOK EFFECTIVELY

You can use this book by yourself, with another person, or with a group. We encourage you to question, challenge, and think about what rings true for you rather than uncritically accepting anything we say.

The book's organization makes it easy for a classroom instructor to tailor the sequence of presentation in a way that makes maximum use of what is relevant to students in *this* course. A class with a behavioral emphasis, for example, might read Part Four and Chapters 10 and 12 early in the semester, so that they can use that information as a basis for behavior change projects that may last throughout the term. A class with a human relations emphasis might proceed from Part Two immediately to Part Six.

The exercises help build a bridge between student interests and an instructor's curricular goals. They provide a way for the theoretical content to be personally understood, allowing learning to go on through both left-brain and right-brain processes, with the goal sometimes of fuller comprehension and sometimes of developing specific skills. Learners can enrich their understanding by sharing the feelings, events, and experiences called to mind by the text and exercises. This can lead to an exciting process-oriented class in which participants deeply examine important personal events and consider new possibilities for themselves. (Be aware that a sure way to deaden such a group is to offer opinions rather than exchange experiences, to analyze and theorize rather than hear and understand.)

Many students and general readers alike who read the first edition actively applied the material to themselves, reading not just with their heads but with their feelings and senses as well. We've received letters from people who keep the first edition beside the bed and in the evening open it up at random to read, or use the index to find passages relevant to particular issues.

If you're not reading the book in connection with a class, you might arrange to have a group sponsored by your community center, church or temple, or other neighborhood institution. Or you an put up a notice on the bulletin board at work or at your laundromat announcing that you'd like to meet with other people who are also reading the book. This is called a "wash and dry self-directed learning group."

HOW THIS BOOK IS ORGANIZED

Being and Caring begins, in Part One, by setting out some guiding principles:

Learn to appreciate and enjoy yourself, your life, and other people, rather than depreciatively judging all these.

Live in a self-determining, authentic way that's based primarily on who you are rather than on what others want you to be.

Develop the neglected sides of who you are and become a more fully integrated person.

Increase your freedom and power by accepting responsibility for your behavior.

Sharpen your ability to be aware of events both within and outside yourself.

Part Two presents skills and information about interacting with other people. Parts Three, Four, and Five, which comprise the heart of the text, consider emotion (Part Three), cognition (Part Four), and overt behavior (Part Five). The order is psychological: Emotional clarity facilitates clear thinking, and both feeling and thinking affect our actions. Part Six returns to our connections with others with an emphasis on intimate and other long-term relationships.

ACKNOWLEDGMENTS

This book is dedicated to our families, friends, colleagues, and students, with whom we continue to live and learn. Virginia Horowitz and Kooch Nasser Daniels provided indispensable ideas, suggestions, support, and gourmet dining. Many of our colleagues at Sonoma State University gave us useful ideas and perspectives, including Gordon Tappan, David Van Nuys, Stash Geurtsen, Hobart Thomas, Bernd Jager, Don Isaac, and David Peri, all of whom we quoted directly. We deeply appreciate the assistance of Sam Shapiro and Abe Arkoff at the University of Hawaii and of family therapist Gene Alexander, in San Francisco, who generously allowed us to borrow directly from his own unpublished material. Sally Jean Nelson and Don Isbell at Kaiser Foundation Hospital in San Diego contributed much to our understanding of stress.

In addition, we are grateful for the indispensable critiques and perspectives provided by reviewers who read and reread our various drafts: James O. Davis of Southwest Missouri State University, Carl L. Denti of Dutchess Community College, and Mel Moyer of Glassboro State College. We offer very special thanks to reviewer John Peters of San Diego Mesa College, who not only made extremely detailed comments and suggestions on every draft, but also provided additional material. Criticisms of the first edition by John C. Condry Jr. at Cornell also proved useful.

We remain indebted to our principal mentors, whose influence is both explicit and implicit in theses pages: Fritz Perls, founder of Gestalt therapy; Harold H. Kelley and Bertram H. Raven at UCLA; and Albert Bandura, John Krumboltz, and Arthur Coladarci at Stanford.

In closing, we want to acknowledge the invaluable support and perseverance of our editors throughout the writing and production processes: Franklin C. Graham, Victoria Nelson, Pat Herbst, Liz Currie, and Judy Ziajka; and, in the first edition, Lansing Hays, Lieselotte Hofmann, and Marge Bader. We are very grateful to our many students who contributed personal stories that have found their way into these pages and to Judith Wright, Mary Mitchell, and others who read and critiqued the first edition and various chapters of the second. We thank John Stevens at Real People Press for allowing us to quote extensively from Gestalt Therapy Verbatim. And, of course, Paul and Neena Horowitz and Tara and Lila (Kid Rainbow) Daniels provided their inevitable small miracles.

Victor Daniels
Laurence J. Horowitz

Part One

FOUNDATIONS

Personal Evolution

*L*ook in the mirror: What tales do the lines in your own face tell? Or if your face is still unlined, what do the expressions into which you mold your features say about who you are, and who you wish to be? In our first few years, we all live with the faces we were born with. After that, we start wearing the faces and living the lives we've created for ourselves.

Events of our earliest years establish patterns of thinking, feeling, and acting that influence us for a lifetime. An observant parent, for example, can watch a child develop an enduring sense of trust or mistrust toward the world during its earliest months.

Yet those old learnings are only part of who we are. Each of us has also learned to compensate, innovate, adapt, and go beyond. Since some of our old patterns are lifelong habits, learning new ones to take their place will take time. But as we develop more effective attitudes and behaviors, unwanted old responses become a lesser part of our being.

Each of us becomes more of who we can be in part by being fully who we are now. "Don't push the river," said Fritz Perls, founder of Gestalt therapy, "it flows by itself." So often, to fit our ideas about who we should or could be, we stop ourselves from acknowledging who we *are*. We don't have to rush headlong into changing ourselves, nor feel unhappy about who we are today to evolve in constructive ways. As we recognize our complexities—our diverse parts that interact, conflict, demand, and counterdemand—we're more likely to appreciate our processes, purposes, and actions.

An old Indian named Pota-lamo sold onions in a shady corner of one of Mexico City's great markets. Asked how much he'd accept for all his strings of onions, Pota-lamo said he would not sell them all. "Why not?" the customer asked. "Aren't you here to sell your onions?" The Indian replied:

"No, I am here to live my life. I love this marketplace—the crowds . . . the sunlight and the waving palmettoes. I love to have Pedro and Luis come by and say: 'Buenos Dias,' and talk. . . . But if I sell all my onions to one customer, then is my day ended. I have lost my life that I love—and that I will not do." (Seton & Seton, 1966, pp. 76–77)

Finding ways to enjoy and appreciate ourselves, those around us, and our interactions with the circumstances of our lives is part of what might be called personal wisdom—something as unique as your fingerprints, signature, or way of laughing. Such wisdom includes actively seeking choices and alternatives rather than passively playing the role of a "victim of circumstances." There's the story of a king's longstanding advisor who overstepped his role and was condemned to death. The king, in a gesture of compassion, allowed him to choose how he was to die. The advisor saw his opening: "I wish, your Majesty, to die by old age!" In similar fashion, you can confront your reality creatively rather than accepting other people's solutions and limitations.

Now, here is a glance at some recent history that places our quest for understanding in a larger context.

THE EMERGING YEARS OF "PEOPLE PSYCHOLOGY"

Amid the material growth and prosperity that followed World War II, visions of abundance dominated the national consciousness. Opinion polls carried out from the late 1930s through the 1960s show that most Americans shared a belief in hard work—even at a boring job—more and bigger material possessions, a fairly large family, a sexual division of labor that placed the husband at work and the wife in the kitchen, and strict, well-defined sexual codes. The men who ran the nation's government and businesses were viewed by the naive majority as reliable and trustworthy (Yankelovich, 1981, pp. 43, 60).

Most of us took it for granted that an unhappy person was "poorly adjusted" to what was obviously good for him or her and needed to "become better adjusted" to his or her surroundings. Unhappiness was seen as a defect in a life of all possible goods. A popular textbook from the forties and fifties comments that a "maladjusted" person was often viewed as morally "bad" or "wrong": "A worrying girl is told to 'snap out of it' and advised that her difficulties exist 'only in her imagination' " (Schaffer & Shoben, 2nd ed., 1956, p. 7).

Adjustment textbooks, valuable to many readers though they were, suffered from two significant limitations. First, the goal was some abstraction called "normality." *Webster's New World Dictionary* (1966) defines *normal* as ". . . an accepted standard, model, or pattern; especially corresponding to the median or average." (No recent dictionary contains as unequivocal a statement; later definitions of *normal* are much more relativistic.) The old "adjustment psychology" sought to help troubled people become *like everyone else* instead of accepting their own uniqueness.

Second, most of the values and conditions to which a person was asked to "adjust" were unquestioned. Alternatively, we can ask, "What if the environment damages the well-being of the people in it?"

Even in the fifties, "adjustment" had its critics, among them the noted psychiatrist Robert Lindner. In *Prescription for Rebellion*, first published in 1952, he wrote:

> This concept [of adjustment] enjoins men to conform, to passivity and resignation. . . . The method is . . . to distort subtly the sense of great teachers, prophets, and educators so that words and ideas which have been designed to be flaming legends upon the banners of humanity's progress are twisted . . . to bank the fires of protest. (1962, chap. 1)

During the sixties, as if in response to Lindner, black Americans took hold of their power in the civil rights movement and previously docile students shocked placid campuses with civil rights and Vietnam War protests. Today, protest in various forms continues as a positive contribution people are making. Like it or not, our personal lives have a political dimension: Decisions made in Washington and corporate executive suites intimately affect our lives.

Fritz Perls (1947) argued that in the context of a society changing as rapidly as ours, it's not clear just what we're supposed to adjust to. He held that the demand to adjust can interfere with the self-reliance that maturity requires. To adjust blindly, he asserted, is to participate in the collective madness inherent in some aspects of our society.

Jungian analyst James Hillman goes a step farther, pointing out that the "manic consumerism and overtiredness and deep depressions" of many clients in therapy today reflect the environments in which they live:

> The distortions of communication, the sense of alienation and harassment, the deprivations of intimacy, feeling of false value, inner worthlessness . . . [are] realistic . . . in relation to external realities. . . . My practice tells me that I can no longer distinguish clearly between neurosis of self and neurosis of world. . . . (1980)

We need, states Hillman, to develop a psychopathology of civilization. As we discover how our culture is crazy, we can conceive of saner, wiser ways to redirect it.

The Mystique of Self-Fulfillment

Psychological theorists like Carl Rogers, Fritz Perls, and Abraham Maslow have each contributed to what has come to be known as the *humanistic* orientation in psychology. Rogers emphasizes a person's capacity to define the central issues of his or her life. Perls identified the fragmented nature of many people's experience and the need to move toward a sense of integration and wholeness. Maslow described needs common to all of us as we seek both to be our unique selves and to understand the ways of the world we live in. Their perspectives can help each of us participate creatively in our world without being consumed by it.

The self-fulfillment ethic appears to have three different roots. One is the emergence of a psychology that aims at helping people discover themselves at a deep level, use themselves creatively, and achieve a full, happy life that doesn't depend entirely on possessions and status. A second is our historic attitude of commitment to individualism. A third is our consumption-oriented economic system that relentlessly exhorts people to buy everything they want—*today!*

Is the quest for self-fulfillment an unmixed blessing? Some think not. "You're obsessed with your own fulfillment but you don't help others with theirs," such criticism runs. "There's no cooperative glue there, no shared effort of the kind that's needed to build a mutually nourishing society."

In their movement toward greater self-knowledge, people go through stages of development. Some of these are much like the stages typical of long-term counseling. During this process, we permit ourselves to acknowledge long-denied areas inside us, including grief about remembered childhood abuses and possibly anger at parents, a spouse, or others who punished or hurt us. Such development includes a period of focusing on "what *I* feel, what *I* think, what *I* want to do." I want to be aware of and not determined by what others want or expect me to do.

At the next stage, however, a hard-earned maturity begins to set in. For instance, a woman who for thirty years feared her rage toward her overbearing mother finds herself finished with it and now experiences a deep acceptance and a caring for her mother such as she never felt before. Her stages of growth mirror a similar movement in the psychological profession from placing the primary emphasis on individual growth to helping people appreciate their own processes in the lived-in world of relationships to their families, communities, and society. The next step beyond self-fulfillment is to take our more fulfilled selves into mutually enriching social relationships with others.

Beyond Conformity and the "Me Generation"—Being for Me and Caring about You

From birth until death, a person can grow in his or her ability to be with other people in mutually fulfilling ways. *At the same time,* the person is developing an ability to be independent, separate, and unique. Thus contemporary theorists speak of an interplay between two motives: *individuation* and *relatedness* (Boszormenyi-Nagy, 1965; Mahler, 1975). At every point, both are active. I watch my three year old—choosing, refusing, pushing me away as she says, "I want to do it myself," then two minutes later coming over and saying, "Pick me up—hold me."

Unless development is blocked in some way, these two tendencies not only coexist but support each other. The more I know and the better I feel about myself, the more supportive, challenging, and caring I can be in my relationship with you. And vice versa. This interplay represents the guiding perspective of this book.

When I've learned to stand on my own feet, I'm ready to move toward you and with you. It's then that I discover what *synergy* means: self-interest enlightened by appreciative awareness of myself in your existence and of your participation in my world. We do for each other in ways that enrich us, too, and do for ourselves in ways that enrich each other.

An ancient Chinese text called the *I Ching* states:

> If a well is being lined with stone, it cannot be used while the work is going on. But the work is not in vain; the result is that the water stays clear. . . . A man must put himself in order. During such a time he can do nothing for others, but . . . by enhancing his powers and abilities through inner develop-

ment, he can accomplish all the more later on. (Wilhelm & Baynes, 1967, pp. 187–188)

The medicine pole of the North American Plains Indians is a forked pole in which the two forks represent contrasting sides of our own nature. These forks can also be viewed as the Self and the Other Person, showing that the Other Person is not only outside but also within us. When we make our peace with the Other, the medicine pole suggests, we can most easily make peace with ourselves.

Here's an experience that can help you appreciate your unique qualities and those you share with others:

Something in My Pocket

This is an exercise for people who are reading this book in the context of a class or group. Imagine that you have something in your pocket that makes an important statement about who you are. You can magically shrink your object to make it fit your pocket.

Now, each member of the group, one at a time, takes a couple of minutes to describe what's in his or her pocket and say a little about it. Others may ask questions if they wish. (If the group is large, break into small groups.)

When everyone has spoken, take a few minutes more to describe what you felt and experienced as you listened to the others. *Focus on sharing your own feelings and experiences—stay away from stating opinions and making theories.* You can help each other with this.

Anyone who objects to participating in this or any other group experience has the option of quietly sitting it out.

LIVING BY OUR REAL CONCERNS

Each of us has issues that seem essential, some in common with many other people, some less so:

"I want to be important and respected."
"I want a job I can depend on, my own house, and a car that isn't falling apart."
"I want to stop avoiding and sabotaging myself."
"I want to believe in myself."

Taking Time for Assessment

Taking stock of our lives—whether in psychotherapy, in meditation, or on an extended fishing trip—is something 99 percent of us need to do more, claims Bugenthal (1981). "Next year," we think. "When my schedule lightens up." And next year we put it off until the next—ad infinitum.

Occasionally I need to take time to assess how my important themes and concerns have and haven't changed, and how my life today does and doesn't respond to them. If too much of my energy goes toward matters that are secondary, I rightly begin to feel that something's "not quite right" in my life—even if I can't quite put my finger on what it is.

Living and discovering in ways that embody my life themes may require important redirections of my energy. These may involve changes within my life. My deep concerns are found both in the far future and in how I do what I do each day. The "something" that's "not quite right" may be what I'm doing with my circumstances, rather than the circumstances themselves.

I may find that taking care of such essentials as food, rent, clothing, and transportation requires spending more energy than I like doing things I don't enjoy. I need to find a way to feel all right about what I do. This doesn't mean, "Chin up, and put a sunny face on what's nasty and uncomfortable." Rather, it means that if I've examined how I use my time and energy and find no more effective alternative, I may need to go easier on myself, and recognize that, all things considered, I'm doing the best I can for me and those important to me. None of this means denying the existence of difficult and disagreeable situations: There's a bottom line that says, "No matter how existential I get, handling the feces distributorship for my neighborhood won't put much 'wow' in my now."

Clarifying Our Directions

Evolving toward ways of living that demonstrate our own values and priorities involves a self-determination that's more than just rebellion against others' expectations. It's an active process of redefining what we want to do with who we know ourselves to be. How do I know if the direction I choose is a productive one? *If it leads me to make better use of who I am, I'm willing to call it growth.*

What You Need for Yourself Now

Relax your posture and muscles, close your eyes, and imagine the following:

You are walking along a country path. Look around you and discover what kind of place you're walking through.

Then you come to some kind of barrier. Notice everything you can about the barrier; then find a way to get past it.

On the other side of the barrier, you'll come to a place that provides something you need and tells you something about your life now. Don't try to "make yourself imagine" certain things, but allow whatever comes spontaneously to come, especially if it's strange or unexpected.

After you've finished, think about your fantasy. What kind of barrier did you create? Did your way of getting past it tell you something about your way of handling obstacles? Did what you found on the other side provide a message about something you're ignoring?

If you're with another person, tell about your fantasies and what they mean to you. Then, if you're in a group, each of you tell what you learned about yourself and the other person.

A new way of being, or of doing something, may feel unusual in the beginning, just as a new method of throwing a ball or holding a tennis racquet may seem odd at first. With continued use or practice, it comes to seem more usual. But while the feeling of unusualness lasts, you get something extra: It's easier to be aware of what's going on inside you when you're first learning something new, before it comes to be routine. That intense awareness can be a rich event.

Something new that you try might seem small. Remember Lao-tzu's comment that "big things of the world can only be achieved by attending to their small beginnings. . . . A tower nine stories high begins with a heap of earth" (1961, p. 91). I can distrust my ability to accomplish anything when I focus only on the finished product, and forget that the process of creating something can be as rewarding as completing it. When I'm afraid I'll never make it, I don't even start. Perhaps if we pay attention to the ways we frighten ourselves, that act will be a start toward what we want to accomplish.

ETHICS AND WISDOM

Explicitly or implicitly, any book of practical psychology includes ethics. The direction of our evolution is influenced by the nature of our ethics. Our approach is this: to experience our acts in terms of *how helpful or harmful they are—how useful or counterproductive—to whom or what, how, under what circumstances*. With anything I think of doing, I can ask, "What are the consequences of my behaviors and attitudes?" This includes the effect of what I do on me, as one of the beings involved.

In the movie *Honeysuckle Rose*, Willie Nelson has an affair with an attractive twenty-two year old who is singing and playing guitar in his band. When Willie's wife finds out, everything turns to pain. The punch line comes when the twenty-two year old, choked with tears, pays a call on Willie's wife, apologizes, and says, "Anything that hurts this many people this much must be wrong."

In events themselves, independent of their consequences, we find no "right" or "wrong," no "good" and "evil." The event simply *is*. The ethics lies in the present and future effect on me, on you, and on the other beings involved. If an act has no helpful or harmful effect, then it doesn't involve ethics.

Wisdom is an underused word these days: It's not a central item in our culture's value system—but it's a major currency for getting along well with others and attaining peace of mind.

An old Zen saying declares, "When an ordinary man attains knowledge, he is a sage; when a sage attains understanding, he is an ordinary man" (Miura and Sasaki, 1965, p. 121).

Our knowing process becomes distorted when we're required to learn large amounts of information in which we find little meaning or value. As Erich Fromm describes it, "Time and energy are taken up by learning more and more facts so there is little left for thinking. . . . 'Information' alone can be just as much of an obstacle to thinking as the lack of it" (1971, p. 248). Thus we challenge the increased emphasis on technologically derived information as inevitably good.

As I come to see how the facts in my life relate to each other, I begin to develop *understanding*. Understanding is seeing relationships among facts that are important to me. As I develop understanding, I become able to use my knowledge.

Wisdom goes beyond understanding. Solomon is said to have asked God for the capacity to distinguish between good and bad, and God responded,

> "Behold . . . I have given you a wise and understanding heart; so that there was none like thee before thee . . . neither after thee shall any arise like unto thee" . . . and the Lord gave Solomon wisdom. (2 Chronicles 1:9–10)

Wisdom is the knowledge of the spirit. We tend to expect a different kind of knowing from our spirituality than from our heads—a very personal integration of knowing, feeling, sensing, and doing. *I'm likely to act wisely to the degree that I strive consciously to understand how each situation in my life can be nourishing for me and others there.* When I so define and use myself that I survive, grow, and assist others to do likewise, I'm finding ways to use my wisdom—and my ethics, which is the code by which I direct the use of my wisdom. Such wisdom is not grave and ponderous: It includes a sense of humor and an ability to see oneself in perspective.

We're wiser when we draw on both our conscious and our intuitive faculties of knowing. In my conscious reasoning, I can explicitly take account of both means and purposes. In my intuitive knowing, I have available, as Eugene Gendlin (1978) calls it, my "felt sense" of things—the messages from my physical self as well as from my mental self. Yet when I'm listening for the many-faceted wisdom of my organism, there's still the problem of how to tell the difference between blind impulse and inspired, wise intuition. Learning how to make that distinction is what much of this book is about.

2

Enjoying Life:
From Judgment to Appreciation

We all have the capacity to enjoy life. But instead we may act out old habits that darken our days and sabotage our hopes.

The admonition to "keep a stiff upper lip," for instance, can make it hard to smile easily. Achievement, serious demeanor, and worthiness are equated and people who readily laugh or smile are not to be taken seriously. In this view, if a task isn't at least a little unpleasant, we must be doing it wrong. This "be serious" attitude is pervasive in our working world.

If we don't want to live that way, we *can* find ways to enjoy what we do. A light touch feels especially good when we're dealing with matters of gravity. It helps us develop a sense of perspective and contributes to the creativity that's so needed in problem solving and decision making.

As a clergyman observed when he told his congregation of his decision to switch from "fire and brimstone" sermons to those that celebrate the bountiful gifts that the Lord has bestowed upon us, "There are over eight hundred 'happy texts' in the Bible. If God said that many times to be glad and rejoice, he must surely have meant it." Learning to celebrate our existence in work, play, and relationships is both a religious and a spiritual charge.

Unless I'm living in a way that pleases me, my actions and projects are unlikely to nourish others. Consider an unhappy, embittered mother who "sacrifices herself to give her daughter everything." The gifts her daughter carries with her are the mother's unhappiness and bitterness—and her guilt. On the other hand, if you enjoy your own existence, your actions and undertakings are more likely to help others enrich their lives, too. It may take time—but what else have we got to do that's more important than learning how to be good to ourselves—and to those around us?

SELF-ESTEEM

How fully we enjoy our lives is dependent on our *self-esteem:* how we feel about ourselves and perceive our value to others. High self-esteem, an attitude that includes self-respect and good feelings about ourselves, makes it easy to enjoy life. Low self-esteem, an attitude that includes feelings that we're somehow wrong, bad, or inadequate, makes it harder.

A tragic irony is that if my own self-esteem is low, I may depreciate others so I can feel good by comparison: "At least I'm not as bad as *you.* " In doing that, I challenge their self-esteem.

Thus, self-esteem is a learned process that emerges from our social interactions. To a significant degree, it's an estimate of how I perceive the people in my environment valuing me.

Arthur, an X-ray technician, has only recently begun to raise his self-esteem. He comments, "When I was a child, everything I did was criticized or punished, often in front of company. I felt inadequate. My stepfather didn't think me good enough to eat the same food he did. Once for a month and a half he didn't speak to me, look at me, or in any way recognize that I existed. At eighteen, unknown to my family, I changed my name, gathered up every picture ever taken of me, and burned them all. Now I see this picture burning as a statement of how much I had come to hate and despise myself."

We can start to deal with such feelings in ourselves and avoid passing them on to future generations. A child who has been abused—physically or emotionally—is often a child abuser as an adult.

My three-year-old daughter just came in from the other room and said, "You have to stop typing so it will be quiet. Mama's trying to put the baby to sleep." I went in and checked with my wife: "No," she said, "You're not too noisy. I didn't say anything."

I could have chided my daughter, "You mustn't interrupt me—and with lies, too!" She would have felt bad, wrong, and unworthy. I would have contributed to lowering her self-esteem.

Instead, I sensed what was going on. With my wife putting the baby to sleep and me busy typing, my daughter was left to herself. "You want me to stop typing and be with you for a while?"

"Yes, that's right." I hope she learned that her feelings were valued and that she's worth my responding to.

Here's something useful to try:

The Self-Esteem Estimator

For one full day, notice what happens to your feelings about yourself each time a person speaks to you. You're likely to find that sometimes the simplest statements contribute to your feeling valued or devalued, depending on the tone of voice, the facial expression, and the timing (did it support you, or serve as a way of ignoring something you said?).

Also listen to what you say to others. Does your comment seem to make the other person feel better or worse about himself or herself?

What do his or her words, facial expression, or gestures communicate? How does your own body language or voice convey some message you weren't aware of?

THE NATURE OF JUDGMENT

We all know the feeling many American Indians call "bitterness in our hearts." When I feel this way, I tend to pass harsh judgment on whomever or whatever comes my way. As I pass judgment, I separate myself from others.

Sometimes such a judgment is loud and clear enough for everyone to hear. At other times it's subtle—just an instant of tightness, a flash of thought that's almost gone before I notice it. All these are *depreciative judgments*.

Evaluation, Preference, and Judgment

Our own judgments about what we do and don't value provide us needed life-orientation and guidance. Constructive criticism of our ideas and undertakings gives us feedback about what's useful and what isn't. But we don't have to transform the need for constructive appraisal into habitual rejection through judgment that can pervade our lives, interfere with our appreciation of ourselves, and demean the beauty in our world.

To clarify that distinction, when I have to make decisions or choose among alternatives, I call it *evaluation*. "Yes, this one is better for my purposes than the other one." Evaluation is considering the *effects* of something: Is it helpful or harmful? To whom, how, under what circumstances? If you prefer the terms *criticism* or *judgment* for such appraisal, thinking in terms of *evaluative judgment* or *evaluative criticism* can help avoid confusion with depreciative judgment.

Liking or disliking, by contrast, is primarily a feeling process. I *enjoy* this more than that. My likes and dislikes are partly the result of helpful learning that protects me and keeps me out of trouble, and partly the result of accidental learning and old conditioned responses that once were appropriate but now are confining habits. When I pay attention to what I actually prefer now, I'm likely to respond more openly instead of staying locked into old habits.

I may be hesitant to admit some of my likes and dislikes. If I'm uneasy about some preference, or afraid I'll have to defend or justify it, I'm likely to disguise it as a judgment. Instead of saying, "I don't like Brian," I say, "Brian's a jerk" (he is, you know). Instead of stating my own feelings, I pretend, even to myself, that I'm responding to "the way things are."

I use the term *projective judgments* for these feelings disguised as judgments. I assign my own feelings to some aspect of the person, thing, or event I'm judging instead of recognizing that they come from me. Not acknowledging that *I feel hostile* toward you, I label *your action* as stupid or ridiculous. Thus I define you in terms of what's happening in me.

Effects of Depreciative Judgment

Accusations, condemnations, and rejection contribute to low self-esteem in others and, when directed inward, maintain it in ourselves. The weighing, anticipating, withholding, and limiting they involve stop me from being open and giving. When I let go of judgment in this sense, I open myself to a broader canvas of experience. An old Hasidic story has it that a poor rabbi gave his last few pennies to the town ne'er-do-well. In response to his critics he said, "Shall I be more finicky than God, who gave it to me?"

Habitual judging makes life brittle. Few things steal more vitality, or cast a chillier, darker mood, than the habit of criticizing and condemning.

Being a habitual critic also affects the quality of friendships. Even though, when I put someone down, others might say, "Yeah, you really said it to him!" after that they're on guard against being my next victim. And I cut myself off from hearing others. If I heard you, I'd hear your pain at what I say and do to you. So I reduce the contact we might have had. In important relationships, I can't nourish myself by poisoning you. A chronic critic in time becomes harder, more hostile, more egotistical. Since several popular writers have glorified "one-upmanship," it's important to remember that champion one-uppers leave their victims one down. They may evoke others' admiration and fear, but seldom their affection.

We can think about the counsel Jesus offered:

> Pass no judgment, and you will not be judged; do not condemn, and you will not be condemned; acquit, and you will be acquitted; give, and gifts will be given you . . . for whatever measure you deal out to others will be dealt to you in return. (Luke 6:37–38, New English Bible)

Roman Emperor Marcus Aurelius commented, "Men exist for the sake of one another. Teach them or bear with them" (1937, p. 264). When I feel an impulse to criticize people, I might first ask myself, *"Am I willing to take the time to show them a better way* and do it nonjudgmentally so they'll be willing to hear? Do I know a better way—really?"

Discovering What's beneath Our Judgments

When I'm clear with myself, my words and attitudes describe things "as I see them." I don't pretend to call them "as they are." So instead of saying, "It's good," I say, "I like it." Instead of "It's bad," I say, "I don't like it."

Doing this isn't easy, for my old habits are strong. When, for instance, I'm angry at what someone does, I'm tempted to (and sometimes do) yell, "You idiot!" or something more colorful. When I do that I'm labeling the person, not the behavior, as wrong, and the odds are the person will get angry at me in return. He or she wants to feel in the right, and the only way to do that is to have me in the wrong.

Similarly, I don't have to respond to another's anger at me by depreciatively judging him or her—a usual sure-fire ticket to escalation. Recently I slowly backed up my truck—into the car behind me. It was only a small bump, but the man came out of the car very angry, saying, "Well, now, what do you call *that?*" My response was, "A dumb move on my part." He was so defused that after we found that his car was all right, he ended up saying, "Well, I'm glad everything turned out okay," and we shook hands, smiled at each other, and left. When we don't feel impelled to respond to hostility with hostility, we're apt to make better contact with people and resolve issues more effectively.

At first I may have a hard time telling the difference between evaluation and depreciation. But with continued attention, I can learn to discriminate between them.

If I'm insecure enough, I may take your evaluative comment as a demeaning judgment regardless of your manner. Still, I'm more likely to hear you when you *tell me your feelings,* or when you *describe how you react to what I do,* than when your words or voice imply that you're better and I'm worse.

It is important that we acknowledge our humanity: *I don't have to pretend to be nonjudgmental about things I really do judge.* For example, when we lose a close friend or loved one through circumstances that might have been avoided, forgiving those responsible may seem like too much to ask. As you feel the bitterness that lingers on in you, be gentle with yourself. If you forgive no one else, at least forgive yourself. Nietzsche had a word for us: "I know of the hatred and envy of your hearts. You are not great enough not to know hatred and envy. Be great enough, then, not to be ashamed of them" (1954, pp. 158–159).

DISCOUNTING OURSELVES

Many people (not just those who chronically feel bad about themselves) disparage themselves, as much as—or even more than—they put down others. Of course, most of us are more likely to discount ourselves when we already feel down and blue.

Here's a way to explore your condemnatory judgments of yourself:

"The Trouble with You"

Sit back, relax, and close your eyes.

Now say to yourself, "The trouble with you is . . . ," "What's wrong with you is . . . ," "You should . . . ," "You shouldn't . . . ," and so on. Bring out all the criticisms of yourself you can think of.

Stay aware of your physical sensations as you do this. Pause occasionally to listen to your own words. How does your condemning voice sound? Do you recognize anyone besides yourself in that voice?

Now change places in your mind and become the you who has just been criticized. How do you respond to these criticisms and admonitions? Do your replies follow any consistent pattern?

Now, if you're in a group, get together with the other members and share your experiences. Talk in the first person present tense: "As my critic, I say . . . ," and so on (adapted from Stevens, 1971, pp. 60–61).

The "I'm Not Okay" Pattern

When I was a child, if adults told me how deficient and defective I was, after a while I began to believe it. I *introjected* that message—took it into myself uncritically, without chewing it through and evaluating it. So now I disparage myself in many areas of my life. I feel that I'm "not okay" (Harris, 1973). All these pangs of annoyance and uptightness about myself add up to too many dark hours. When I'm out in the world feeling this way, other people reflect back these dark feelings, making my world grayer still. To some degree, this has happened to most of us.

How many times a day, in small ways or large ones, do you feel inferior? But ask yourself, inferior compared to what? Compared to what you might realistically expect to be and do, given your background and the breaks you've had? Of course not. That way you'd come out right where you are.

Every person has an easy time with some things and a hard time with others, even though it may *seem* as if some people are "good at everything." You can relax some of your self-judgment and appreciate that you're different from anyone else. You're not just this or that—like each of us, you're a whole collection of abilities and potential ways of being . . . what a gift!

You can improve your skill at doing almost anything, once you get rid of your image of yourself as "no good at it." If you're weak in one thing, you're potentially strong in a complementary area. I'm not so good at cocktail parties, but I can be a delight person to person.

Some people think that being down on themselves helps them change. It does just the opposite. My mind can play all kinds of tricks to keep me from noticing when I act in a way I don't like, making me work twice as hard to be aware of what I'm doing than when I feel all right about my actions. Acknowledging what I'm doing makes awareness of it easier.

Here is one of the most important statements in this book: At this point in your life, at this moment in time, *however you are, it's all right for you to be that way*. To feel what you feel, to think what you think, to do what you do. What is, is. What you are, you are. Recognizing that can make it easier to begin moving today in directions that will help you feel better about your life tomorrow.

"Shoulds"

Every depreciative judgment about myself has a "should" at its center. I "should" be a certain way, and if I'm not, I'm defective.

In the course of a day I may get mad at myself because I didn't do what I think I "should" have done. Similarly, sometimes I get angry at others because they didn't do what *I* think they "should" have done.

"Should," as it's widely used, carries a quality of absoluteness. The things I "should" do are RIGHT, and the things I "shouldn't" do are WRONG. And that's that. Many of these are old messages from other times and situations—some are appropriate now and some aren't.

In my life, I do what I do. My action brings certain consequences. If I don't confuse myself by thinking, "I should have done something else," I can see those consequences and learn from them. When my mind is filled with what I "should" have done, ordinarily I don't find out as much about what happened as a result of what I *did*.

None of this means that we shouldn't have "shoulds." We all have "shoulds." If you try not to have any, you'll blind yourself to the ones you do have. When you pay attention to your "shoulds" and "should nots," you can notice especially the impossible "shoulds," such as "what I should have done." As you learn which "shoulds" have real value for you and which ones don't, you can let the latter find their place among the old photographs and memories of your yesterdays.

WORKING WITH JUDGMENTS

Monitoring depreciative judgments can decrease their frequency and intensity.

The most reliable way to monitor your judgments is to *count* them. If there's a golf course nearby, you can get a golf score counter at the pro shop. Some sporting goods stores also carry them. Worn on the wrist, they look almost but not quite like a watch.

Counting Judgments

In this exercise you'll learn to pay attention to your judgments of yourself or of anyone or anything else. Notice instances of judging and criticizing, whether aloud or silent.

If you say to yourself, "What an awful dress she has on"—notice as you do it. Each time you condemn anything, punch your wrist counter once.

At first maybe you'll even be self-critical when you notice yourself being critical. Forget that; more of the same you don't need. Use the attitude of "noticing" yourself, not "catching" yourself. It's the difference between "Oho! There I go again!" and "Damn! Will I never learn?" In the latter case, you would punch your counter twice—the second time for putting yourself down for judging.

At the end of each day, record your total and draw a line that represents your daily total on a chart. Keep the chart for several weeks. At first the total may even increase from day to day: Don't despair. This simply shows that you're developing greater awareness of what you've been doing all along. Persevere and your tally will probably start to drop.*

After a while, you and your fault finding will be on more familiar terms. You'll find it easier to hear yourself when you judge. You'll be aware of tightness in your jaws and stomach, your shallow breathing, and the narrowness in your voice. Monitoring judgments can also serve as a channel of self-knowledge through our self-observations of our motives and desires as we judge. These can help us find our underlying positive intent, as described on the next page.

---

*For about one person in twenty, this process doesn't work. Some people just get more and more self-critical. If this is true of you, you can either (a) see a psychologist or counselor or (b) forget it for now, work with other processes in this book that you can get a better handle on, and perhaps come back to this later. The general principle is: *Work on what you find value in working on now.*

SAYING "YES" TO OURSELVES

There are several alternatives to depreciative judgment. One is positive judgment. I declare a person or event right, good, or as it should be. The hazard here is that I'm still operating from a judgmental framework and can easily slip over into negative or depreciative judgment.

Another alternative is to appreciate something for what it is, without judging it as either good or bad. You might try this:

Appreciating Yourself

Do this in your imagination.

Take five minutes to brag about yourself. Mention every good thing you know about yourself. Overdo it. Describe all the things about you that make you wonderful.

The key is not to generalize but to stay very specific. How am I such a superb person? In what particular ways?

As you do this, listen to how you hedge and qualify your appreciation of yourself. Where do you have a hard time giving yourself credit? What is easier for you: appreciating yourself or putting yourself down?

If you were less appreciative than you were judgmental in "The Trouble with You," how did you sabotage yourself? By having a hard time thinking of your virtues? By disowning the appreciation you and others give you—"I don't deserve that, I'm really not that good"?—or . . . ?

Carol had her parents sit in at her counseling session. Her father opened by saying, "Carol, I'm really happy with the way I've seen you develop this past year." He intended to give her a positive, supportive statement. She responded to his comment with, "You're judging and evaluating me." The counselor's response was to identify the positive function Carol's defensiveness served for her: She wanted to stand on her own feet and evaluate herself rather than depending on her parents for even well-intended direction and evaluation.

The Theory of Positive Intent

Family therapists Shirley Luthman and Martin Kirshenbaum describe the perspective that guided Carol's counselor:

> In every piece of behavior, no matter how destructive . . . , there is some kernel of an intent to grow. . . . The theory of positive intent involves finding that pure kernel of growth intent, labeling the growth process, nourishing it and enabling the individual to find ways of expressing [it] that are self-enhancing, not self-destructive. (1974, p. 5)

They cite the example of a wife who learned as a little girl that she would be seen as weak and would be depreciated if she expressed hurt. Now, instead of telling her husband when she feels hurt by something he does, she starts calling him names. He feels put down, gets angry at her, attacks back, and the cycle escalates. Luthman and Kirshenbaum take due note of the destructive behaviors emitted by each of the spouses and then go beneath them to point out that *the woman's positive intent is that she hopes for understanding and appreciation of her feelings.*

So appreciating what's going on involves two steps:

1. Recognizing what it is in our behavior that drives away the very response we want from others or that defeats us in other ways.
2. Recognizing that we don't defeat ourselves because we're bad, sick, stupid, or crazy, but when we don't recognize and honor our own positive intent, nor that of others (1974, p. 6).

The theory of positive intent helps us take an apparently negative, destructive behavior and use it as a starting point for growth. The process of *reframing,* described in Chapter 17, provides a practical way of doing this.

The Perfection in What Is

Perfection has two very different meanings. One is the gradual change from being "imperfect" to being "perfect." The other is the perfection of each thing that exists, just as it is right now.

One day as I sat by a creek listening to its voices, I reached into the water and scooped up a handful of stones. I looked at them glistening and realized that every stone was perfect. Some had intricate designs. One was a nice shape for throwing. A few were poetic in their ordinary grayness. There weren't "good stones" or "bad stones." Every stone was absolutely perfect. As an old Chinese poem points out:

> In the landscape of spring
> there is neither better nor worse;
> The flowering branches grow naturally,
> some long, some short.

It's the same with people. Here and now, I'm a perfect me, and you're a perfect you. No one in the world can be as perfect a You as You are. Listen to one of James Bugenthal's clients:

> Mom and Dad were trying so hard but they were so scared. And I was scared too. . . . And what were we frightened of? Just of being ourselves! . . . (She is weeping hot, quiet tears as she talks.) And that's what I've been running from: by being so bright or pretty or popular or successful or all the other things I've tried to be. I've been trying to be those things instead of just being me. (1965, p. 274)

None of this means that we need to tolerate troublesome conditions in our lives that we can change. Instead, the task is to get in touch with exactly how things are not okay, and set out to remedy that. Saint Theresa of Avila said it beautifully: "Lord, grant me the serenity to accept the things I cannot change, the courage to change the things I can, and the wisdom to know the difference."

Since I have some choice about how I feel, I can feel hostile, angry, and bitter as I work to change harmful conditions, or I can feel full, alive, and in contact with myself and my world. I find that I'm at least as effective in the latter case as in the former. Art Hoppe, my favorite newspaper columnist, wrote one day, "If we all celebrated life, who could oppress or kill or hate his fellow man?"

3

Self-Determination and Authenticity

*O*ur culture has taught us to value being *self-determining:* making our own choices about important events in our lives rather than having those choices made for us by others. That value is expressed in our desire to be *authentic:* to speak and act as who we truly are rather than shaping all our responses to fit other people's expectations. Self-determination and authenticity are different sides of the same issue: Each requires the other for its full expression.

At some point in our lives, many of us have turned away from people or pursuits we cared about to keep the security and love we needed. Chet recalls, "When I was about six, blacks and Mexicans had just started to move into our South Los Angeles neighborhood, and I used to play with them. When Mother found out, she got very upset, told me 'how awful they were,' and forbade me to play with them again. I remember how sad I was. They were my friends. Even so, for many years after that I avoided members of minority groups as potential friends."

Each of us can learn to trust our own sense of what means most to us and accept it as our guide as we seek to find our own direction. The Hasidic Rabbi Zusya is said to have commented before his death that in the hereafter he didn't expect to be asked, "Why were you not like Moses?" but rather "Why were you not like Zusya?"

Relying upon anyone's advice as to what you "should" or "shouldn't" do will have you living borrowed pieces of other people's lives instead of being responsible for your own life. And that includes this advice! No one is more suited to be you for you than you are. Nietzsche's Zarathustra says, "This is my way; where is yours?—thus I answered those who asked me 'the way.' For *the* way—that does not exist" (1954, p. 307).

When we act in ways that are different from what our parents, spouses, lovers, or friends expect, those important others may interpret our moves toward self-determination as rebellion against them. Teenagers often aggravate bad feelings by seeming to flaunt their necessary moves toward self-determination in ways their parents find hurtful. Even though that may feel like a natural response to the parents' oppressive abundance of instructions about how to be, it can decrease trust and escalate the power struggle.

When others respond with mistrust to my choices and actions, I can describe in the most caring way I know that I do appreciate their concerns and suggestions, but that as part of my own growth I have to be accountable to myself and to make certain decisions for myself. That may not "make everything all right," but at least it opens the door to dialogue—especially when demonstrating my respect for them may help them to demonstrate greater respect for me.

AUTHENTICITY

When a nineteenth-century Danish youth named Sören Kierkegaard gave up his study for the priesthood to become one of the first existential philosophers, it was not because he underwent a change of heart, but because in his church he found no opening to follow his own direction (Wild, 1955, p. 27). The Church, he concluded—and in our day we can easily add other powerful organizations and prevailing social "norms"—had begun to interfere with people's capacity to be true to themselves. It did this, Kierkegaard stated, by reinforcing prevailing attitudes and platitudes instead of supporting each person's right and obligation to an inward search. Another existentialist, Martin Heidegger, added that when we take refuge in the decisions of others it is not long before we think what others think, feel what others feel, and do what others do.

Kierkegaard used the term *authenticity* to refer to being in touch with our inner selves and acting from that full contact with who we are. To be authentic means to be true to myself. I cannot be authentic and put up a false front before others at the same time.

Being True to Ourselves

In each area of my life, I can ask, "How much room do I have to *be myself* in this situation? How much of the room I have do I use?"

It's possible to be authentic when I'm not happy or comfortable as well as when I'm feeling good. When I'm lonely, for example, I don't need to pretend that I'm not. If I reveal my loneliness to you, there's at least a chance that we'll touch each other in a way that has meaning for both of us. Even if we don't, my attempt to communicate has intrinsic value. But if I keep silent when I want to tell you how I feel, we probably *won't* make contact in more than a superficial way.

I don't have to demand that I always do what I intended, or what I'd have liked. After all, I don't always correctly anticipate outside events, how other people will react, or even how I'll react. I have both the strength to achieve and the human capacity to fail. What I don't want to do is kid myself. And somewhere along the line, I want to get to a point where I don't have to kid you, either.

Jungian analyst Ira Progoff suggests a way of working with our life history to gain a deeper sense of who we are. "Under the pressure of events," he writes, "our lives become hard packed like soil that has not been tilled for many years. One experience is added to another so rapidly that . . . we do not have time . . . to establish an inner relationship to them." But, he suggests, imaginatively reexperiencing the "steppingstones" of our past can loosen the soil of our lives so that new insights can emerge and nurture the tender shoots of new possibilities (1975, pp. 98–100).

Steppingstones are significant turning points or periods in our lives—pleasant, painful, or neither—that brought us where we are today. They can help us recognize the "deeper than conscious" directions in which we move with our life currents.

Steppingstones

Have paper and pencil with you. If possible, dim the lights. Relax your body, close your eyes, and sit silently. Don't try to make something specific happen—just be receptive and let events in your life emerge before your mind's eye. Don't try to edit or screen them—accept whatever comes.

When you're ready, list your steppingstones: the events and circumstances that, as you think of them now, seem especially important in your process of becoming who you are today. Put down at least eight but no more than twelve. Let these come to you in whatever order they do; you can number them in chronological order when you're done. A brief phrase, or even a single word, is enough to denote each one.

Got your list? Now recall what feelings stirred in you as you wrote it. Record these, too. Then return to a contemplative state of mind, reread your list, and jot down any additional thoughts or emotions that come to you.

If you're working in a group, members may wish to share their steppingstones. *Just read the list itself*—not your elaborations and reflections. Then leave a minute or so for people to think about what you read, before the next person reads. (For more details, refer to Progoff, 1975, pp. 98–118.)

Being authentic requires self-trust. Sometimes we find ourselves in conflict: I value you and myself and I want to please us both. To do what I want to, instead of what you want me to, I've got to be willing to approve of myself even when you don't approve of me.

Being open with others can be frightening, for it increases my vulnerability and lessens my options for manipulation. In a way, I'm safer when you're mystified by my cloaks, masks, and shadows, for then you seldom know just who or where I am.

If you and I are authentic with each other, we may become very close. On the other hand, we may find that our authentic ways of being clash so sharply that we can't get along without pretending. Moving toward authenticity may be painful. It may mean making major changes in what we ask of, accept from, and give to each other. Sometimes it may even mean modifying old relationships or developing new ones. But the general principle is clear: To express yourself as you are, with minimal pretense, allows for a less stressful and more satisfying life.

Personal and Social Selves

Newborn infants have no roles to play. They just *are,* completely true to themselves. We could say that a newborn is entirely a *personal self.*

Conflict with and response to others lead to the beginnings of a *social self.* This early social self includes all of the personal self. Thus integrated, there's nothing that the infant is unwilling to reveal to others.

Before long, we act in certain ways that meet other people's expectations and not in other ways that bring disapproval. Much of the personal self is expressed but parts of it are less shared—the personal self is secondary to the social self. The child has learned that punishment is likely when those parts are seen. Thus the social self, or *persona* as Jung called it—a word that comes from the masks ancient Greek actors wore to symbolize the roles they played—serves two purposes: to make a specific impression on other people, and to conceal the inner self.

Children allowed to express most of who they are are likely to be lively, spontaneous youngsters. By contrast, when the behavior deemed acceptable is severely circumscribed, the personal and social selves lose much of their common ground. When people identify heavily with the persona and deny the rest of who they are, psychiatrist R. D. Laing (1969) speaks of a *divided self.*

We may stay locked into certain roles out of habit. Virginia Satir speaks of the *parental cloak:* A person who "forgets to take it off" becomes so identified with the role of being a parent that he or she forgets to be with his or her children in a more spontaneous, personal way (1972, p. 208).

Each of us has the option to present ourselves in our social roles in ways that move closer to who we are inside, so that our personal and social selves overlap more.

Acting as If

When I'm being authentic, I'm voicing my real wants and needs. When I'm concealing and manipulating, I'm testing you.

Marie says she wants a lasting relationship. She has a habit of taking up with men who hang around for a while and then wander on their way. She can't understand why this happens again and again.

Marie's style of approaching men is cool and offhand, as if she doesn't put much commitment into anything. Her double message is "I want you—I don't care about you." But once she and a man get into a relationship, she begins acting the way she genuinely feels, which means putting out a lot of caring and expecting the same in return.

No wonder she never gets it. Her as-if presentation of herself as cool and offhand attracts men who are looking for a temporary, casual relationship. They give her what she seems to be asking for. Coming on cool is easier for her than saying "I like you a lot." There's less risk of rejection. But Marie will probably do better if somewhere along the line she learns to take the risk of expressing her feelings.

When I trust you to deal with me as I am, I communicate clearly who I am and what I want. When I act from the part of my social self that's different from my personal self, I speak and act *as if* I'm thinking and feeling something other than I am.

During my day, I choose how much I'm willing to meet the demands and expectations of each person I encounter. Sometimes I choose to present my personal self in as-if ways: Contradictory as it sounds, being authentic sometimes can involve pretending. You may want me to go to a fancy cocktail party with you and act as if I enjoy that, even though I don't. Because it's important to you and I care for you, I go with you and find some way to enjoy the event. I feel all right about this, as long as you don't ask me to pretend too often or too much. In such ways, I can be authentically willing to give to or receive from you on your terms as well as on my own.

In certain situations, however, I can easily fall into my as-if ways even though I'd rather not. In restaurants, I used to be too embarrassed to ask to see a menu to see if I could afford what was on it before I sat down. And after I sat down, I was too embarrassed to get up and walk out if the items cost too much. So sometimes I paid more than I could afford by acting as if I were loaded. Now, if I'm in a restaurant and everyone else at my table is ordering the expensive items, I sometimes think I should order high too. But by dropping my as-ifery, I can order what I want, even if it's inexpensive.

I resent my as-ifs when I feel that I have no choice. A man who is to appear in court may find that he not only has to pay for a lawyer but also has to buy a new suit. His lawyer tells him, "When you walk in wearing a dark suit, shirt, and tie, you immediately reduce your sentence. Your clothes are saying, 'I'm like you, Judge.' " The price of not making that as-if statement is too high.

When I constantly work at fitting your expectations, I lose touch with my experience and lessen my ability to take care of myself. When I'm stating clearly what I want, I'm likely to be decisive and direct. I'm in touch with my strength—and so are you.

Hypocrisy is a particular kind of as-ifery. It means being phony, presenting a public front of seeming to act in the service of higher principles than I really am. If I tell people I'm doing something because I want to help my community, or because it's "the American Way," when in fact my reason is because it helps my business or gives me a tax writeoff, I'm being hypocritical.

The Script

Psychiatrist Eric Berne speaks of the parental instructions we've received about how to act and be, and what to do with our lives, as our *scripts* (1961). These programs in our heads serve to justify actions that are script-determined and cause us to question those that are not.

Our scripts are also our own doing. As I grew up, I rewrote the script others gave me so that it fit me better. Then I conveniently "forgot" that I did the editing and the rewrite job so that I could blame others when I didn't like my actions, explaining away my behavior instead of acknowledging my power to do something about it.

Here's a way to explore your old scripts and what you did with them:

Reviewing Your Scripts

You'll need a pen and a piece of paper. Divide the paper into halves with a vertical line from top to bottom, then draw four horizontal lines spaced equal distances apart, making ten rectangles. Above the lefthand column write, "Script given to me." Above the righthand column write, "What I did with it." Then label your horizontal divisions "0–4 years," "5–8 years," "9–12 years," "13–16 years," and "17–present." (Depending on your age, you may drop the last category or add another.)

Then, for each life stage you've just labeled, imagine that one of your parents (or whoever was the important adult in your life then) hands you a script. Now look at it and see a one-sentence statement of how to be (underneath it may be more specific instructions). Write down that one-line statement in the appropriate place on your page. If you recall any other scripts from that time in your life, jot them down, too.

Then in the corresponding spaces in the righthand column, write your responses to those scripts. Did you do as instructed? Did you say "no" and choose some other way? Did you say "yes" but resolve to act some other way?

Done? Now with each prescription you accepted, imagine a way you can negate it. Then you can go one step farther and consider how you can find your own way—a way that suits you but that may not exactly either agree with or rebel against the prescription.

If you're doing this in a class or group, take about fifteen minutes to do all but the last paragraph above by yourself. Then get together with two other people. Each of you takes ten minutes to talk about what you've written and to reflect on the questions in the previous paragraph. The other two people listen, asking relevant questions.

If you're doing this exercise by yourself, within the next day after you've done the written part, mention it in the course of conversation to an acquaintance or friend. "That reminds me of something I did last night in connection with this great book I'm reading. . . ." Highlight what you wrote down and what it brought up in you, and then just talk with the person about it for a while, listening to what it evokes in him or her.

Until I realize that I'm acting out an obsolete script, I may be stuck with some ineffective, unproductive, or even self-destructive behavior. Long ago, for instance, I may have received a script that said, "Good boys and girls never say 'no.'" Most children in that situation rewrite their scripts: "I don't dare *say* 'no,' but I can *behave* 'no.'" I may still do that: "Okay, I'll be right there." Hours later . . .

In Japan, where confrontation is studiously avoided, saying 'no' by saying 'yes' extremely weakly—for instance, "I'll see what can be done"—is common practice, but there everyone knows that a weak yes may mean no. Similarly, the Chinese say, "We will consider it for discussion." But since we don't have such a shared understanding here, we communicate better when we say what we mean.

When I follow a script that no longer fits me, I expend a lot of energy trying to bottle up the spontaneous flow of my life force. I don't have to waste my energy in stopping myself. I can judiciously appraise where I have room to be myself in a fuller way and where I don't.

HOW WE BECOME STRANGERS TO OURSELVES

British psychiatrist R. D. Laing displays a keen appreciation of dilemmas faced by some people who are diagnosed as "schizophrenic." He provides the example of a boy who keeps his distance rather than running up to hug his mother. "Hello, Mom," he says.

"Don't you want to hug me?" she asks. "Don't you love your Mummy?"

"No."

"But Mummy knows you do, darling. You're just saying that. I know you don't really feel that way." Whereupon she grabs him and smothers him in a big hug (1971, p. 153). In so doing, she disconfirms, or denies, his report of what he's experiencing.

Disconfirmation, Confirmation, and Pseudoconfirmation

Through my responses to what you do and say, I *confirm* or *disconfirm* your sense of who you are. Those parts of our being about which we're least secure, notes Laing, need confirmation more than others—and we need confirmation more at some times than at others.

If significant others validate what you think, feel, and do, you're encouraged to develop a secure, reliable sense of yourself. If you get feedback that reinforces your own impressions, you learn to trust your ability to discern what's going on around you. You're likely to develop a clear sense of *contact*—of where you leave off and other people begin, rather than becoming enmeshed in the sticky web of what Perls terms *confluence*, where you're not sure of your boundaries.

But when others act in ways that deny your actions and your perceptions of yourself and your world, you may become confused and uncertain about your identity. In order to keep the love and protection of significant others, you may choose to repress your questions and misgivings and agree with their insistence that they know you better than you know yourself.

What's different about words and actions that confirm and those that disconfirm? A confirmatory response, says Laing, *acknowledges* your action—though it doesn't necessarily agree with it. Disconfirmation, by contrast, has a *tangential* quality. My response appears to deal with your concern, but actually it deals with an aspect of the matter that concerns me—not the one that concerns you. For example, my wife walks in saying, "Look at the beautiful new blouse I found this morning. It matches my red skirt."

"How much did it cost?" I reply. "You know our budget can't handle any unnecessary expenses."

I ignored her happiness and her feelings about the worth of the new blouse. My thoughts and feelings may be valid, but they're valid in addition to and not instead of hers. Besides, she bought it at the Goodwill.

An especially subtle and fascinating process is that of *pseudoconfirmation*. This is a pretense at confirmation, giving the appearance of it without the substance. *I tell you who you are, then I confirm my definition of you.* The real you that differs from my image of you is not acknowledged. I induce you to accept my ideas about you, then confirm your attempts to apply them to yourself.

For example, Lisa, a reasonably attractive, somewhat shy high school girl who's interested in art and biology, is in the kitchen with her father and her boyfriend Jack.

"Lisa," says her father, holding up the paper—"Look! They're having tryouts for cheerleader at school next week."

Lisa (cringing slightly):   Dad, I don't think . . .

Father (cutting her off):   You're a natural! With your personality, looks, and coordination, you can't lose! You'll love it!

Jack (enthusiastically):   Yeah, he's right! Listen, can't you just see us at the junior prom! Great idea!

Lisa (doubtfully):   Well, maybe . . .

Father: Great! It's settled then I know it'll be wonderful for you. I'll have your mother take you tomorrow to get some clothes for the tryouts.

Introjection and Induction

All of us, during adulthood as well as childhood, are sometimes asked to "swallow whole" the ways that significant others—or our larger social environment—prescribe for us. Such *introjection* is at the root of our difficulties in being true to ourselves and finding our own ways. I may introject the idea that I should be or will be an undertaker, a Republican, a sex maniac, or a bum. To undo my introjections, I may have to reexamine and "chew through" the way of being that I've "swallowed whole."

Laing astutely noted that parents have a way of getting children to comply with their expectations that's much subtler than telling them what to do: They tell them who and how they *are*. He calls this form of pseudoconfirmation *induction*—we induce each other to take on particular roles. For instance, "A naughty child is a role in a particular family drama. . . . His parents tell him he *is* naughty, because he does not do what they tell him. . . . [Since] they define what he does *as* naughty . . . he learns . . . *how* to be naughty in his particular family" (1972, pp. 78–90).

Induction goes a step beyond projection. "Projection," writes Laing, "is done by one person as his *own* experience of the other. *Induction* is done by one person to *the other's* experience" (1972, p. 119). See Chapter 8 for more about projection.

Mystification

A kid who hears, "You don't like chocolate, you like vanilla!" enough times may start believing it. Actually the child is hearing the grownup say not only "You like vanilla," but also *I want you to like vanilla*.

As the adult, my straight message is, "I want you to like vanilla, and I'll approve of you if you do." When I say that, you have room to reply, "I know you want me to like vanilla, but I prefer chocolate, thank you."

But if I say, "You know you prefer vanilla," I'm giving you a double message: "You have no choice—you're going to get vanilla" and "I want you to *feel that you have a choice*, even though I'm choosing for you."

To describe this process, Laing (1971) borrowed the term *mystification* from Karl Marx, who defined it as "a plausible misrepresentation of what the exploiters do to the exploited to make them feel at one with the exploiters." Mystification (which can include disconfirmation) clouds, masks, and obscures. To an adolescent: "You can't be unhappy—we've given you everything. You wouldn't say what you just said if you weren't ill." Ultimately, both the mystified and the mystifier are confused.

RESPECTING OTHERS' AUTHENTICITY

Someone once remarked, "A friend is a person who leaves you with all your freedom intact but obliges you to be fully what you are." In that spirit, in being authentic, I don't want to intrude on your authenticity. If I give you a lot of warmth and caring, for example, I might consider whether I demand warmth and caring from you in return, whether you feel it right then or not.

And when I'm extremely helpful, I might ask myself, "How much of my helpfulness is a demand that you be helpless?" When my caretaking is excessive, it may keep you from learning to do things for yourself. I can stunt your growth by giving you too much. All of us need some frustration in order to learn to stand on our own feet. Consider this story:

> The student Tokusan used to come to the master Ryutan in the evenings to talk and to listen. One night it was very late before he finished asking questions.
> "Why don't you go to bed?" asked Ryutan. Tokusan bowed, and lifted the screen to go out. "The hall is very dark," he said.
> "Here, take this candle," said Ryutan, lighting one for the student.
> Tokusan reached out his hand, and took the candle.
> Ryutan leaned forward, and blew it out. (Peter Pauper Press, 1959)

I do well to remember that in many cases you can tune me out completely. This is illustrated literally by one of my relatives who was deaf from birth. As a youngster he had a hearing aid that could be turned up and down. Imagine his mother's frustration when she would start yelling at him and see him turn the hearing aid down. "What am I supposed to do," she said, "tell him to turn it up so he can listen to me scream?"

We all have the option this deaf child had. He had to tune out observably. We can do it on the sly. *We only have to listen when we want to.* If you're impervious to my needs, I may be deaf to your demands.

A traditional Navajo, declares anthropologist Dorothy Lee, seldom speaks for another person. A father who is offered a good price for his child's bow and arrow will let the boy decide what to do and respect the boy's decision not to sell even though the child may need the clothing the money would buy.

A traditional Navajo mother allows her child to make his or her own mistakes, to suffer pain or grief or joy and learn from experience. She teaches not by giving orders but by pointing out cause-and-effect relationships. She knows that the freedom to choose, and to learn from what happens, is an important step in developing self-reliance (1959, pp. 8–13). I call it the *if-then principle: If* you do this, *then* that will happen. It's one way to reduce the power struggles involved in living together. For example, to my young daughter: "*If* you pick your things up off the floor, *then* I'll take you for a walk." I'm reducing the threat and increasing her autonomy. She has the option to say "no" and remain to some degree in charge of her own existence.

To use the if-then formula, I have to abide by her decision—including leaving the junk there. I also have to follow through on the consequences: If she picks it up, we go for a walk; if she doesn't, we don't. Using this principle even intermittently seems to have improved the peace and harmony of our family life. I'll let you know more in the next edition.

Carl Rogers describes an attitude that he terms "unconditional positive regard," which he defines as "an atmosphere which . . . demonstrates 'I care'; not 'I care for you *if* you behave thus and so' " (1961). This kind of acceptance is not so easy. It can take hard work to set aside my goals for you—what I want for you and what I think would be good for you—and leave you room to be yourself. But it opens the way for me to know you as you are.

4

Integration and Fragmentation: Pulling Ourselves Together

*T*he old German word *Gestalt*, passed on to us by the Gestalt psychologists early in this century, means "form, pattern, whole, configuration." It has to do with how the parts of something fit together as a consistent whole—or fail to do so.

Similarly, if I've found ways for the elements of my personality to live together comfortably, in a relatively "integrated" fashion, I can know the different parts of me and have them available when I need them. Otherwise I'm somewhat "disintegrated," likely to keep parts of myself out of my awareness and to work hard to avoid perceiving how my different sides conflict.

BECOMING A WHOLE PERSON

There are two ways to view being whole. In one, we are all by definition whole: Somewhere in this mind-body-spirit being that I call "me," everything that's part of me exists, available to me when I find a way to get to it.

To the degree that I'm in contact with all of myself, I am whole in the second sense of the word: I have the many sides of me available when I need them.

Most of us are a mixture of old elements and new ones that we've only partly assimilated. Some parts of ourselves don't fit together too well. Some don't talk to each other at all. In both our older and newer parts, there are places where we don't let our life energy flow: thoughts we stop ourselves from thinking, emotions we stop ourselves from feeling, and actions we stop ourselves from taking. Perls spoke of those places as "holes in the personality," aspects of ourselves that we don't allow ourselves to recognize or experience. Each contains a dimension of myself that's lost to me as long as I keep that part of me "off limits" (1969a, pp. 36–37).

I might, for example, view myself as a helpless victim of circumstances and other people's actions, being "the nice guy no matter what." To experience life from a victim's framework, I tell myself that "I'm not *doing* anything—it's just *happening* to me." Thereby I give up contact with the part of me that actively charts my way and responsibly makes my decisions. When I feel powerless, part of me is missing.

My personal power and inner richness becomes available as I reopen and "reown" the disowned parts of myself. An important element of this is *having and using alternatives*—diverse ways to deal with myself, people, and events. Such alternatives emerge, in part, from recognizing my most habitual way of responding. That awareness opens other possibilities.

EGO PROCESSES

Freud drew attention to a process that functions like an "internal executive" to determine which parts of us can express themselves when, and how. It "tests reality"—checking out what's real and what isn't, so we don't make unnecessary mistakes.

This is *ego* function, not to be confused with the pop usage of the word in which we say someone "has a big ego" or "is egotistical," meaning the person thinks himself or herself more important or "better" than other people.

Freud used ego as one of the principal actors in his psychic drama. There is *id*, or the processes of responding to hunger, thirst, aggression, and sexuality; *ego*, which serves as the mediator between id forces and the restraints and constraints of outside reality; and *superego*, a conscience that "includes . . . the rules and precepts handed down by parents and authorities and the 'ego ideal' fashioned by the individual, i.e., the kind of person he or she aspires to become. . . . Like ego, the superego is but partly conscious" (Hampden-Turner, 1981, p. 42).

These three functions of id, ego, and superego were not meant to be taken as real "things" with an actual physical existence, as some have misunderstood them, but as metaphors, as processes.

When it's working well, ego function is a guiding faculty that helps the different parts of us communicate with one another. Freud wrote:

> The aim of . . . treatment is to . . . bring about the most far-reaching unification and strengthening of [a person's] ego, to enable him to save the mental energy which he is expending upon internal conflicts. (1959, Vol. 5, p. 126)

Now let's return to the other meaning of ego, where as Alfred Adler declared, "Man is but a drop of water . . . but a very conceited drop" (in Way, 1950, p. 167). There are different elements of this kind of ego: *Infantile ego* is my process of saying, "Am I getting enough?" A "no" response leads me to demand, "Me! Me! Me!" *Image-based ego* is my process of asking, "Am I good enough?" It isn't present in early life but develops as the social self grows out of our perception of other people's evaluations of us. One side of image-based ego is *self-glorification*. This is telling myself and others, and wanting others to tell me, how marvelous I am—as in this story:

Four pupils of the Tendai school of Zen promised to observe seven days of meditative silence.

On the first day all were quiet, but when night came and the oil lamps grew dim, one of the pupils exclaimed to a servant: "Fix those lamps."

The second pupil was surprised to hear the first one talk. "We are not supposed to say a word," he said.

"You two are stupid. Why did you talk?" added the third.

"I am the only one who has not talked," declared the fourth.

The other side of image-based ego is *self-depreciation:* telling myself how worthless I am and imagining that others see me that way too. Self-glorification and self-depreciation both grow out of my anxieties about my value, lovableness, or competence.

Feeling separate and isolated is an important part of infantile and image-based ego. I see how you and I are different, and how you may want to hurt me, but I have a hard time seeing how we are the same and how you care.

Even following a religious path, I may still be running my same infantile ego trips in a disguised form: "*I* must be the one who is saved; *I* am more spiritual than you are." In the Talmud, a *mitzvah* is an act of goodness that assures me my place in heaven. But there's a catch: If I do the mitzvah out of concern for you, I score; if I do the mitzvah thinking, "More gold stars to get me into heaven," it doesn't count.

When I see that I have a choice of doing or not doing something that serves and strengthens my infantile or image-based ego, I can choose not to do it. For instance, when I find myself trying hard to think of something clever to say, a good thing to do is to say nothing. The Chinese philosophy of the Tao says, "Not so fast," to one who is becoming too clever, too witty, too skillful.

As I learn to take better care of my emotional needs and to value myself as I am, I feel less need to put others down, "win," or seem "important"—and I more easily give what others need and get what I want.

THE SHADOW

According to mythology and superstition, a person without a shadow is the Devil himself—or herself. Even today, most people are cautious with someone who seems "too good to be true" (Fordham, 1966, p. 50). Knowing who we are involves facing our shadowy sides as well as our sunny ones.

Jung used the term *shadow* for our unacceptable and unacknowledged sides. Like Freud's ego, shadow is not a "thing" but a process, a useful metaphor. It refers to the parts of us that we hide from our conscious mind—including desirable qualities that we've learned to think of as "not part of us"—and the ways we hide them. As a guideline, the narrower the standards and definitions that govern our life, the more powerful our shadow side.

Sam comments, "In my family, I took on the 'good boy' role and my brother, the 'bad boy' role. I pushed my 'bad boy' into my shadow side, while my brother pushed his 'good boy' into his shadow. He got attention by being bad. When he was good, the family treated him as if he were invisible. Now we're both beginning to reown the parts of us that we suppressed."

In dreams the shadow may appear as dark, primitive, threatening, hostile figures. There, in the dream theater of our secret selves, we find unacknowledged parts of us, parts that hold energy and vitality we've disowned. So the shy, mild-mannered person who never raises his or her voice dreams of bold adventures, while the sexually repressed person's dreams are enlivened with lust. Paradoxically, when material from the shadow is allowed into consciousness, it loses much of its frightening nature.

Coming to terms with my aggressive, hostile impulses is a crucial task. While shadow tendencies remain hidden, suggests Fordham (1966), they grow in strength and vigor, and when they burst through they may overwhelm the rest of the personality. "One Half of you must understand the Other Half or you will tear yourself apart," says American Indian Yellow Robe in *Seven Arrows*. "It is the same with the Other Half of any people who live together. . . . Both Halves must try to understand" (Storm, 1972, pp. 124–125).

Refusal to face myself can keep me stuck in repetitive, self-defeating patterns, since unconsciously I disavow other possibilities. My shadow is likely to be a large one, as in this fragment from Robert Hall's poem:

> *My popcorn is gone*
> *The seats are half-empty (the cartoon is over)*
> *I've seen the feature several times before*
> *I'm afraid of the dark*
> *And it's time to go home. (1975, p. 219)*

But I can learn to acknowledge my aliveness in the "dark side" of my own nature.

Suppose, for instance, that I've viewed myself as "someone who's always happy," and I always try to keep a smiling face. I can begin to recognize that sometimes sadness and grief are appropriate, that there are various ways of experiencing and handling those emotions, and that most people who care about me will still accept me even if I don't always look happy. It's not uncommon for a client in the depths of pain and despair to detail personal disaster with a broad smile in the initial counseling session. Integration of feelings and form becomes the first order of business.

OUR INTERIOR DRAMA

The philosopher Martin Buber declared that wholeness depends on the quality of an individual's dialogue with himself or herself (1971). Such a dialogue involves coming to know the "partial personalities" that exist in each of us. Consider these statements:

> "I have no idea why I did it—something just came over me."
> "I'm not myself at all today."
> "Often I do things I don't really want to, but I can't seem to help myself."
> "I want so many different things I don't know *what* I want."

These comments show that we are each multiple, complex, and interdependent, like a collection of different people, or "characters," living together in one body. We may be communicating well or poorly with these various parts of ourselves.

When one of my characters has great energy, I may commit an act that has long-term effects that are not what I want, but have to live with. When I can examine my mistakes from the place in me where I feel centered and whole, I'm less likely to repeat them.

One of my own characters is my "performer"—juggling firebrands and eating apples at the same time. Another is my talkative character. Then there's my "pusher," who can push me to work very hard for long hours and give me no rest. And my loose, easygoing self who's into having a good time now. And my quiet, listening, intuitive self who's tuned in to what's happening with other people. What does your inventory (playbill) look like?

Recognizing Your Characters

Look through an old magazine that you don't want anymore. Each time you see a picture that touches you strongly in some way—attracts you, repels you, arouses your curiosity, etc.—cut it out. When you have fifteen or twenty pictures, lay them out on the floor. Let each one represent a side of you. Some of these may be parts of you that were important in the past; others are parts that you are struggling with or trying to express now. Many of these are likely to be characters that are important parts of your life. Give each a one-line title.

Arrange your pictures so that the nearness of certain ones to others shows which parts of you are most clearly in contact.

Now check whether you've omitted any important dimensions of who you are. If so, find another picture—or even a trinket or other object.

If you're doing this exercise in a group—three to eight people works best—after about half an hour, when all have finished, everyone will gather around to look at your creation. As you describe it, tell how each picture or item is you and say something about what's happening in that area of your life. Others can ask you questions.

When you're done, listen to each other person's self-description through his or her pictures. (If there are more than about eight of you, separate into two or more groups so you don't take forever.)

After you've finished, you may want to take cardboard and glue and make your pictures into a collage. Watching how these change through time can be interesting.

When I have two of my characters fighting for control, I can both sabotage and torture myself: My easygoing character has me down at the beach to have a good time, but my compulsively responsible character keeps telling me about the work I need to be doing.

If I let them, some of my characters, or major roles, will fill up my existence and let none of the others in. Locked into one side of my personality, I lose my sense of perspective and my alternatives. When I get pigeonholed in one of my characters, if I recognize for even an instant that that's where I am, I can remember that *I am much more than that*—and then move into expressing one of those other dimensions of myself. As this happens, I develop multiple perspectives on events instead of having only one (Hillman, 1975). That allows me to choose another approach when my first impulse appears inappropriate or ineffective.

Sometimes when I'm extremely angry with my children, I close my eyes or turn my head away or look at the ceiling. That way I stay with only my anger. I'm less likely to see something in them that might touch other ways of feeling in me. My other option is to look at them while I talk to them. When I do that, I'm more likely to let in my compassion and love for them. I don't disown my anger, but I'm more available to work out with them what it means for me, and what I want from them.

DEVELOPING OUR UNDERDEVELOPED SIDES

Creativity exists when we find new ways of understanding relationships and relating to the world of things. It can occur at the easel, at the kitchen table, or at an insurance executive's desk. Creativity includes perceiving and responding to the world anew, out of the "sense of wonder"—the ability to enter a situation and see it "as if for the first time."

We can begin such exploration by finding out what's already highly developed in us, and what's less so. And therein lies a fascinating tale.

Jung's "Psychological Types"

During his long association with Sigmund Freud and Alfred Adler, Carl Jung became intrigued with how three psychologists studying the same phenomena chose to explain them in such different ways. Freud explained most things in terms of biological impulses and a child's family relationships. Adler focused on the feeling of powerlessness and a wish to feel strong and successful. Jung himself was most interested in people's interior worlds of fantasy and imagination. At length, Jung deduced that the different approaches grew out of the three men's differing personalities. Freud, he arguably concluded, was an *extravert*, while he and Adler were *introverts* (Bennett, 1967, pp. 43–51). Extraverts are outgoing, interested in other people and external things, while introverts are usually more reserved, reflective, and concerned with the personal meanings they find in events. Introverts are likely to neglect the outward-going parts of themselves, just as extraverts often neglect the development of their inner resources.

But Jung was still puzzled. He and Adler, both introverts, were nonetheless very different from each other. After ten more years of reflection, he formulated his now-famous typology of functions—thinking, feeling, sensing, and intuiting.

Jung saw each person as having a *superior* or well-developed mode and an *inferior* or minimally developed mode. In his view, if thinking is superior in a person, feeling will be inferior, and vice versa. If intuiting is superior, sensing will be inferior, and again vice versa—like this:

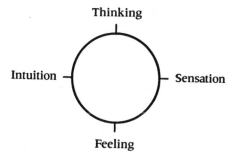

How does it happen that most of us have a superior function and an inferior one? Jung suggests that from the beginning, each of us has a temperament that predisposes us in certain ways. We all tend to do first what we do well and to put off what we do poorly. This increases the one-sidedness of our development, which in turn gets further reinforcement from the tendency of family and friends to confirm a person's "gifts" and disconfirm his or her other sides.

Marie Louise von Franz suggests that when you try to discover your type, you should not ask yourself what "matters most" to you; rather consider what you *habitually do* most. That points to your superior function. Then consider where your greatest difficulty lies. Where do you often feel frustrated—and end up pounding your head against the wall? Where are you most sensitive to criticism? These are clues to your inferior function (1979, pp. 3, 16, 87).

A question to remember, in contemplating the sides of yourself you seldom express, is: "What's trying to get through? What new perspective that wasn't there before?"

A danger in Jung's theory of types, suggests Tappan (1980), is that when used uncritically, it can be narrow and limiting—people think they know what they're all about before they've genuinely investigated themselves. If you view yourself as a thinking type, for example, you may conclude that your feelings tend to be primitive and undeveloped. This rightly describes the caricatured extreme, but not most human beings. Everyone has some areas of feeling and thinking that are primitive and others that are sophisticated. So instead of "What's my type?" we can ask, "What does the types model tell me about who I am?"

Anima and Animus

Opening to a fuller sense of who we are is opening to what animates us—what attracts and repels us. Jung gave the names *anima* and *animus* to two groups of qualities that exist in the unconscious—*anima* in men and *animus* in women. The Adam and Eve story, he suggested, points to such a splitting-apart, and then to the continuing effort to find one's other half and achieve again the primal unity we knew in the beginning.

Jung used the term *anima* for the presence in the male personality of a group of qualities often considered "feminine": receptive, nurturing, soft, intuitive, drawing on the depths of the inner world and the unconscious. For men, anima brings personal meanings into events, and contributes to a sense of an interior life. Hillman comments,

> We meet [anima] as waters without whom we dry, . . . as Lady of the Beasts riding our passions, . . . a nurse . . . and a serving maid. . . . And she is also . . . wisdom . . . compassion . . . and destruction. . . . She . . . makes possible experiencing through images, for she embodies the reflective, reacting, mirroring activity of consciousness. (1975, pp. 42–43)

A man who integrates these *anima* qualities can remain strong and masculine yet be powerfully gentle and sensitive. When he is closed to the latter qualities, insisting on being only hard and masculine, the suppressed "anima energy" is likely to break through in such forms as "waspish, poisonous remarks by which he devalues everything" (von Franz, 1968, p. 190). He may feel irritable and depressed, insecure and touchy. We see these characteristics in adolescent males who are "fighting with their anima" to fit our cultural image of supermasculinity. Can you imagine any of the characters John Wayne built ever crying?

Jung called another constellation of traits, those that often are part of a woman's unconscious side, the *animus:* assertive, achieving, rational, problem solving, outgoing. When unrecognized, this energy can be hard, judgmental, and self-righteous—dominating us with ideas about how things "ought to be" and luring us away from sensitive contact in human relationships. "Even in a woman who is outwardly very feminine an animus can be a hard, inexorable power," writes von Franz, "obstinate, cold, and completely inaccessible" (1968, p. 207).

When recognized, animus qualities can help a woman build a bridge to her deeper self through creative activity. They help her develop initiative, courage, and a capacity for planned action. They contribute to an inner strength that complements her outer softness.

In a balanced personality, "masculine" and "feminine" elements intertwine. This process cannot be stereotyped by sex. For instance, some "animus-dominated women" have developed only their ambitious, assertive, achievement-oriented qualities and now face the task of opening up to the traditionally feminine sides of themselves.

As I begin opening to the less developed area, notes Tappan (1980), I can start letting go of the anima and animus metaphors and remind myself that there aren't really "two sides" at all, but a multiplicity of qualities that occur naturally in both men and women. I'm a many-sided being—and I need all of me.

Berne's "Parent, Adult, and Child"

Psychiatrist Eric Berne (1961) described another polarity in each of us, which he calls our *parent ego state* and *child ego state.* As children, we were influenced to varying degrees by one or more adults. At the same time we were children, with childlike qualities. Today some of both those ways of being continue on. At times I act like a four year old; sometimes in the past I acted like a parent even before I became one. We may invest most of our behavior in one side, but the other is also there.

Berne distinguishes three dimensions of our inner child: the "natural child," the "little professor," and the "adapted child."

As children, we are all impulsive, expressive, and full of wonder. We have few "shoulds." I think here of Gene Kelly in the movie *Singin' in the Rain*. Singing and dancing, he jumps, skips, and splashes through the water in the gutter with a child's absolute delight. When we remain in touch with that spontaneity, we can still be playful and childlike, even as adults. This is our *natural child*.

As my *little professor*, I figure out how things work and how to get what I want. I'm curious about and interested in everything. My guesses about the world are often wrong, but through them I learn, and sometimes they contain great wisdom.

My *adapted child* has learned ways to avoid punishment and get rewards. I may go along with the demands on me or run away from them: I turn into a "withdrawn child" who is distant and unresponsive; a "rebellious child" who says "no" to almost everything; or a "compliant child"—a "good boy" or "good girl" who does everything I'm told to.

With our "inner parent" as with our "inner child," we make choices about how we do and don't want to act. Out of the range of behaviors our parents present us, we select some to imitate. For instance, Robin's mother always talks in a loud, harsh voice. From her earliest years, Robin has disliked that voice and has chosen to speak more quietly.

If my parent nurtured and cared for me with great love and concern, my "parental" care-taking is likely to have some of those same qualities. We might call this my *nurturing parent*. If my parent gave many orders, punished me often, and was cold and distant, then I may express some of those qualities. We can call this my *judgmental parent*. Or if my parent smothered me with so much affection and protectiveness that I had a hard time learning to stand on my own feet, I may try to do too much for you and not encourage your self-determination. This is my *overprotective parent*.

Whatever my past, in my present I can move toward being less judgmental, less overprotective, more nurturing in taking care of myself as well as my children.

In the exercise that follows, don't try to be any particular way in either of the roles you play. Its purpose is to explore rather than to modify the ways you are.

Parent and Child

This requires at least four people, works best with ten or more, and can be done with any larger number.

First pair up. In each pair, decide which of you will be the "parent" and which the "child."

You have fifteen minutes to interact with all the other parents and children in the room. Each of you has complete freedom to do as you wish, so long as you stay within the roles of parent and child and do nothing to hurt anyone in the room. Naturally, each parent has responsibility for his or her own child.

After fifteen minutes, reverse roles. Everyone who was a child becomes a parent, and vice versa.

When fifteen minutes more have passed, get together with the whole group to discuss what happened. What were your styles of being a parent? Did any forgotten childhood qualities come to the fore? What different ways of handling these roles did others in the group display? What roles felt good to you?

Berne identifies the *adult* as growing out of my experience with my world when I'm not so anxious that it interferes with thinking clearly and acting effectively. This inner adult lets me learn by experiencing the consequences of what I do. It appears to have two parts: My *rational adult* is the part of me that has learned to deal with myself and my world as effectively as I can based on the information I have available. My *emotional adult* is the part of me that has learned to appreciate and live with my feelings. With freedom to feel as we do, and appropriate guidance, the emotional adult develops along with the rational adult.

THE MEDICINE WHEEL

The Cheyenne, Crow, and Sioux tribes of Plains Indians guided their lives by the ancient teaching of the medicine wheel. In his compelling and beautiful book, *Seven Arrows*, Hyemeyohsts Storm writes,

> To the North on the Medicine Wheel is found Wisdom. . . . The South is the place of Innocence and Trust, and for perceiving closely our nature of heart. . . . The West is the Looks-Within place, which speaks of the introspective nature of man. . . . The East . . . is the place of Illumination, where we can see things clearly far and wide. . . .
>
> To Touch and Feel is to Experience. Many people live out their entire lives without ever really Touching and being Touched by anything. These people live within a world of mind and imagination that may move them sometimes to joy, tears, happiness or sorrow. But [they] do not live and become one with life. . . .
>
> Each person is a unique Living Medicine Wheel, powerful beyond imagination, that has been . . . placed upon this earth to Touch, Experience and Learn. (1972, pp. 6–7)

Each of us has a "Beginning Gift"—a customary way of being—that corresponds to one of the directions of the wheel. As we visit the other places on the wheel and learn what each offers, we become able to make our decisions within the Balance of the Four Directions. We become whole.

Compare Jung's typology with the medicine wheel (see the illustration "Two Models of Wholeness" on page 41). Their intriguing similarities remind us that the quest for wholeness can occupy us for a lifetime. Wholeness is not something we can

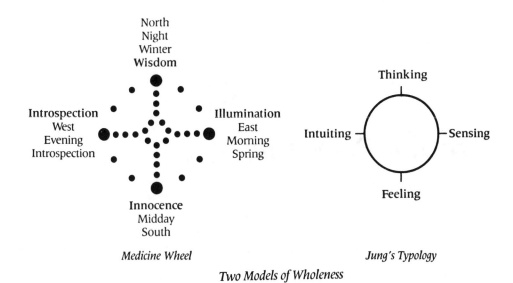

Medicine Wheel   *Jung's Typology*

Two Models of Wholeness

"get" in a "Know Yourself Forever One-Weekend Workshop." There are always further destinations. If I revisit a place on the wheel where I've been before, my perspective is different, and it's no longer the same place it was.

5

Choice and Responsibility

When I pay attention to how my actions affect other people, I open the door to making the world around me more agreeable and a little more benevolently disposed toward me.

When I handle an encounter with another person—be it in business, romance, parenting, or anything else—in a way that leaves him or her feeling belittled, cheated, or deceived, I'm likely to meet mistrust and trouble.

In this form of recycling, each of us is touched by the effects of almost everything we do. We create a web of opportunities and obstacles for ourselves. Our temperaments, early learnings, and environments provide materials, but we ourselves are the architects, general contractors, carpenters, and stonemasons of our lives. We choose what to build and how to build it—as local representatives of the Karmic Construction Company.

RESPONSIBILITY AND SELF-SUPPORT

Ordinarily the word *responsibility* is synonymous with "accountability." But there's another equally important meaning. Perls (1969a, p. 100) separates the word into two parts: *response-ability*. In this often forgotten dimension, it means the ability to respond, to be alive, to feel, to be sensitive. It doesn't just mean "obligation," or "duty"—especially not in the sense of something I've been directed to do without involvement, so that I do it automatically, without thinking—like a robot rather than a person. Growth in these terms is a move from letting others be responsible for me to taking responsibility for myself.

Beyond Dependency

In our adult lives, as we discover how we still hang on to some of our helpless childhood ways so that the people around us will do things for us, we move from manipulating others for support toward developing self-support. This shift is a central element in maturity.

A relationship is enriching and satisfying when both people share the responsibility for clearly stating what they want and sharing what they have to give. Dependency in such a relationship—where one person is always in charge and the other is always passive—may be a turn-on in some instances, but it seldom provides a basis for long-term satisfaction. This is an especially important issue for women who occupy roles commonly viewed as "dependent." Husbands "let" their wives do things, and the wives give their husbands the power to regulate large areas of their lives.

Keeping a person dependent can cause hostility—especially when double messages are involved. I may say, for instance, "I want you to go out and do something on your own," while my actions tell you loudly that I want you to depend on me, and, what's more, I'll give you lots of approval if you do depend on me. We observe this process frequently between parent and child, employer and employee, husband and wife, and in other ongoing relationships.

When I assign the cause of my behavior to you, to my "unconscious," to my parents or my past, I make it difficult for me to change. If my parents did it to me, they're the ones who must undo it if it's to be undone. If they're gone out of my life, presumably I'm stuck with what they did: "It's all their fault."

Recognizing my responsibility for myself doesn't mean I have to give up being any way I am, or doing anything I do. It does mean that I need to stop believing that I act in these ways only because of my ancient history. Each day I choose to act in the ways I do.

Responsibility and Authenticity

Responsibility and freedom are related to self-determination and authenticity. I can be authentic only to the degree that I make my own choices about who I am and what I do—including choosing those times when I'm willing to go along with what others want from me.

Choosing the path of least resistance—the one laid out by others and circumstances—is a choice, too. Actually, even when I'm following orders, *I decide* whether I'll do as ordered or risk doing otherwise. As Sartre pointed out, "What is not possible is not to choose. . . . If I do not choose, I am still choosing" (1967, p. 54).

To forget that I discover, create, and maintain the conditions of my life leads to alienation—the feeling that I have no control over my own destiny, that I'm a pawn moved by the hands of the unseen "They" who sit in seats of power. But as I regain my sense of being the doer, the thinker, the feeler, my life becomes my own and I reclaim the power that is rightfully my own.

The Effects of Our Social Environments

Each of us is born into a historical period, a race, a culture, a rich family or a poor one, and a neighborhood. No matter what personal transformations we undergo, these elements are part of our personal history.

But there is a difference between speaking of responsibility for our *life situation* and responsibility for *how we are in our life situation*. In some cases there may not be much I can do about my situation at this moment. But even in that case, I have choices about *how I wish to be* in that situation. Within the limits set by my environment, I can choose how I let the forces around me influence me. Deliberately or by default, I can select the way I am wherever I am.

When I'm in New York City, I begin to talk and move a little faster than when I'm in the country. The very vibrations of the city affect me. Still, I stay true to myself. When I was growing up in New York, I chose never to rush for a subway train; after all, another train would pull in soon. As I walked down the station steps, people invariably pushed by me to get to *that* train. But I knew that I didn't have to let the rhythm of the subway become the rhythm of my life.

If, however, like Hermann Hesse's Siddhartha, I live by an ageless, ever-flowing river and choose to live *with* that river, I can let its voices slowly seep into my being. The river can be the flow of the lives of the people around me, and *their* voices can seep into my being.

Some elements of my world open doors to fuller, richer ways of living and experiencing, while others close them. Next time you watch TV, be sensitive to how the program or commercial manipulates your thoughts and feelings. Much of that is intentional, with objectives different from your own. You're making all those things you watch, read, and listen to part of your existence. With them, and with other places where you spend your time, you can ask yourself, *"Do I want to make that part of me?"* This question has both a personal and a political aspect: "How am I affected by my environment?" and "What's in it for my environment to have me accept the messages it's giving me?"

Many of our social institutions seem to want me to be available for ready manipulation. If I feel inadequate about making my own decisions, I give up my power, my responsibility, and my right to define who I am to big business, the media, government agencies, and other influential groups. As I discover how my social environment wants me to be, and why, I can more wisely choose which of its elements I want to incorporate into my life and which I don't.

This Is My Existence

In the course of an ordinary day, take five or ten minutes for this exercise in each place that is part of your day, including where you are right now.

During that time, get fully in touch with what's going on. Pay attention to people and things and events that you're usually not aware of, as well as those you usually notice.

As you slowly and carefully touch and look and listen, ask yourself, "Who here is like me? Who here is not? What in this location is like me, and what is not? *How* are these people and things like me? How are they alien to who I am?"

You might find it useful to do this throughout the coming week.

Does this evaluation suggest any changes you want to make in how you arrange your environment, or in where you spend your time?

ACTIONS AND EXPERIENCE

To others, I am what I do and say. My acts, and how others view them, define me in my world. To myself, I am also what I think and feel—my intentions and urges that determine my actions.

I Am What I Do

At the height of a battle, a soldier runs out into the line of fire to help his wounded buddy. The next day, he sits in his shelter all day long. From moment to moment and day to day, he chooses whether to act in a way called "brave."

That same soldier is six feet tall. He was six feet tall yesterday and he'll be six feet tall tomorrow. He can't choose to be five feet seven instead. In the same way, a table is a table and can't choose to become something else.

This illustrates Jean-Paul Sartre's distinction between an *action* and an *attribute*. "Six feet tallness" and "tableness" are attributes. They can't be changed. "Bravery" is different. It's based on actions. There's no such thing as "a brave man," declares Sartre. If a man usually acts bravely, that's all we can say. To others, his acts define him: "Man is . . . nothing else than the ensemble of his acts, nothing else than his life" (Sartre, 1967, p. 47).

Suppose I'm in a heated argument with a member of my family and then the phone rings. When I pick up the receiver, it's a friend with good news. My whole mood changes. Instead of being angry, suddenly I can become agreeable.

What happened? *I allowed myself to be angry. Then I made myself agreeable.* I choose how I want to be. My authenticity depends on it.

When I live with the idea that I'm "a sad person" or "a coward" or whatever, I blind myself to the fact that *I create* these ways of thinking and feeling about myself. As I recognize that I could discover other ways to act and feel, I gain a greater measure of choice.

Here's a way to pay attention to how you create and maintain your ways of feeling and behaving. As you are going through a day, you are constantly describing yourself to others and to yourself. Notice how you do this. What favorite stories do you reel off again and again, and what do they tell you about who you are? Who talks to you about their feelings, and which of those feelings sound like your own? How is the music you listen to like you? How much of the information you select helps keep you where you are, and how much of it helps you move on?

Sometimes our self-images are statements of who and what we "are" that help us avoid facing what our actions paint us as. If I'm trying to be my illusion of who I am, I may not want to be aware of who I actually am. "I cut out my silhouette of illusion with sharp scissors of denial," commented my colleague Dean Taylor. The Scrooge in me may rationalize, "My deeds don't represent me. I'm 'good at heart' and that's what counts." But no matter how I may claim that my deeds don't represent me, in fact they do. Though I may claim that I can't act otherwise, in fact I can.

I Am What I Experience

To hear from you how your world is for you can be very different from defining how you are in my terms. Such a knowing opens dialogue and provides new access to each other.

"Suppose there is a depressed woman standing here beside me," comments my colleague Bernd Jager (1975). "To her, your faces might look like closed doors. The room seems narrow and repressive. People are like a blur—gray and uninviting. She's in this room in a way different from the way I'm here. If we assume that she and I are in the same room, we make a mistake."

Being sensitive to another's experience is especially important with children. Unless I truly hear my child's concerns, joys, hopes, and fears, in his or her terms, I'm likely to misunderstand and respond inappropriately. For example, George A. Kelly and his colleagues studied "laziness" in school children:

> [We asked] the teacher what the child would do if she did not try to motivate him. Often the teacher would insist that the child would do nothing—absolutely nothing—just sit! . . . We would ask her to observe how he went about "just sitting." Invariably the teacher would be able to report some extremely interesting goings-on . . . some teachers found that their laziest pupils were those who could produce the most novel ideas, others that the term "laziness" had been applied to activities that they had simply been unable to understand or appreciate (1964, pp. 345–354).

Both our observable actions and our inner experiences are related to other currents in our personalities, conscious and unconscious, to which we now turn.

Intention and Volition

With our intentions we formulate our values, construct our behavior, and define our ways of approaching or withdrawing to get or be what we want. In their *theory of positive intent*, Luthman and Kirshenbaum point to a deep level of intentionality in which we want to be secure, to feel good, to love and be loved, and to express ourselves in our own ways (1974, pp. 5–7).

But if I've been chastised for expressing my deep desires or convictions, or have been rewarded for words or actions that contradicted them, I may learn to behave in ways that subvert essential personal truths. This accounts for many of the self-defeating, self-negating patterns that seem so inexplicable.

Diane, for instance, has many good ideas, but when the time comes to speak up, she stays silent. Her surface intention—to speak up—is sabotaged by the habits she learned as a child, when the message she got was, "Be quiet. Family time is a time for the adults to talk." Her middle-level intention is to avoid being punished for speaking up: After all these years, she is still using Daddy's wrath to silence herself. Her deeper intention is to maintain family harmony and win her father's approval. Her middle-level intention interferes with that deep intention as well as her surface one, for it impedes the success in school and work that would please both her and her father.

As social psychologist Harold H. Kelley (1979) points out, we all recognize that various intentions may underlie what others do. As described in detail in Chapter 8, our responses depend on the intentions we attribute to other people. I may feel upset, indifferent, or pleased about something you do, depending on why I think you did it. The same is true in our assessment of our own behavior. This doesn't contradict the fact that many actions have predictable effects regardless of the intentions that led to them.

It's useful to distinguish the act of forming an intention from the act of carrying it out. How commonly we say of someone, "He has good intentions, but . . . " So I define *intention* as conceiving of, at some level of awareness, what I wish to do; and *volition* as mobilizing the energy to carry out an intention and doing so.

Unconscious Choices and Intentions

The term *unconscious*, writes Rollo May, refers to conscious material denied, re-pressed, or forgotten; to underlying "irrational" impulses and "spontaneous" urges; to possibilities that we somehow sense or experience only in a vague way (1967, p. 46).

Recognizing that our unconscious as well as our conscious life is at some level intentional implies that we can no longer use "I did it unconsciously" to excuse our behavior. In a similar vein, Sartre declares, "The existentialist . . . will never agree that a sweeping passion is a ravaging torrent which fatally leads a [person] to certain acts and is therefore an excuse" (1967, pp. 41, 57).

When my intentions and volitions derive from a fuller dialogue with myself, I'm less likely to do things today that I'll regret tomorrow. I'm more likely to do things that are in accord with my own nature—and that are responsive to the needs of others in my world. Then my subconscious me and my conscious me start to talk to each other, get along better, and use each other's resources.

WHAT'S DONE TO ME AND WHAT I DO

Do you promise yourself that "someday" you'll work on things you need to work on in your life? Do you expect someone else—a psychologist, social worker, friend, or minister—to solve your problems for you? Do you let the expectations of people in your past define what you can and can't do for yourself today?

What do you need to do to be good to yourself? How do you avoid asking yourself that question? Once you've asked it, how do you answer? By avoidance, or by doing something for yourself? How is avoidance a way of doing something for yourself?

I can readily describe how things are done to me that change my life. Viewing myself as though I were an object, I feel manipulated and powerless, as if my life is determined by outside events and others' expectations.

Here's a way to explore that:

Subject and Object

Sit comfortably and close your eyes. Imagine yourself as an object. Don't "decide" what object to be, but rather be receptive to whatever appears. Experience yourself as this object for several minutes. Notice what happens to you, what things are done to you, and how you feel about them.

Then after a few minutes, when this first fantasy has played itself out, have a new fantasy. In this one you're the subject and doer, the controller, the creator. Again allow what you're going to be to appear in your mind "on its own" rather than consciously trying to "force" yourself to be a certain thing. Take at least five minutes to observe, discover, and feel, in the theater of your imagination, what you do and what you experience.

Stop reading now to have your fantasies. Then continue.

Now, looking at your fantasies, ask yourself, "How do I allow myself to get done to? What kinds of things do I allow myself to imagine? What kinds of power do I allow myself when I'm the doer?

If you're in a group, get together with three other people to share your experiences and answer these questions. Then return to the larger group to compare experiences.

Steve Gaskin writes, "I used to drink and drive a lot, and . . . get in a lot of wrecks. . . . I began to figure out that it wasn't like an accident at all, you know, it was something that I bought, asking for it" (1970).

When I trace my problems back to their source, it almost always turns out that, in some way, *I chose them.* If I apologize for being alive, people will treat me as though I have no right to be here. And if I ask for something as though I don't expect to get it, the chances are I won't:

"You wouldn't possibly be willing to . . . ?" "I don't suppose I might . . . ?"

The way I ask a question tells the other person what kind of answer I expect. I can ask for something in a way that makes it easy to reply, "No" or "I don't know," or in a way that leads to "Yes" or "Sure, I will."

I might say: "It's all right if I . . . isn't it?" or "What can you tell me about . . . ?" Or "Do you have any . . . ?" or "Do you know . . . ?" *Whether I get a yes or a no often depends on which response I ask for.* In my daily life, I can give myself at least as much consideration as I give others. I don't have to set myself up to be a victim.

When I was asked to move to another counseling office, I said to myself, "I better check the new place." Then I thought, "No, the man who's asking me to move knows what I need." I made one feeble attempt to get a key, didn't get it, and gave up trying.

After the movers had moved my things, I finally saw the office. It was terrible—so noisy I couldn't carry on a conversation. I'd been done to, and I was angry, just as angry at allowing myself to *get* done to as at *getting* done to.

That was just one event—and ultimately I got a satisfactory office. Some people, however, live a major share of their lives committed to the victim position. LaVonne, for instance, recently began to recognize how much of her life she had been defining in terms of being done to, and how little she allowed herself to feel her own power. "I felt constantly victimized," she writes. "My relationships were dominated by my self-fulfilling prophecy that no one could ever love me. Without realizing it, I was very successful at manipulating people into rejecting me. I didn't realize that I *chose* to feel hurt and dominated, and that I invited others to victimize me. Now I'm working to change that, and I've stopped blinding myself with self-pity."

Whatever I'm doing, I'm creating a whole mood, whether it be a vigorous, lively one, or a shoulder-slumping droopiness. If I look pugnacious, I'll probably intimidate some people and get into fights with others. If I come on like a doormat, I'm likely to get walked on. My way of presenting myself creates the context for my relationships.

Blaming Others

How often and how automatically many of us place responsibility outside ourselves when something goes wrong: "It wasn't my fault!" "I couldn't help it!" Democrats and Republicans do it all the time.

It's easy to see how it all gets started: "But Billy did it first," Johnny protests, or "It was Suzie's idea." Understanding Parent (UP) replies, "Oh, okay—but behave yourself next time." By accepting that excuse, UP is *teaching him to believe that he doesn't have to be responsible for what he does.*

Blame, on the other hand, breeds resentment. "It's your fault!" is a red flag phrase that invites defensiveness and argument. The hook in blame is lodged in that smidgen of truth in what you said or implied. I can seldom say, "I had absolutely nothing to do with it." When a person's blamer goes to work, it's very canny. It knows exactly where to go *zap*, where to pick out that nasty kernel of truth, however tiny it may be. A talented putdown artist is expert at zeroing in on where you feel inadequate and making you feel even smaller there.

As long as I defend where you attack and blame, you control the action. I'm on the defensive. But I can protect myself against your blaming, and others', by remembering that *I am not obliged to accept anyone else's evaluation of me.* As counselor Norman Brice points out, *When I depend on what others think of me, I'm vulnerable to being made to feel bad by every ill-dispositioned person I happen to meet.* "There are few of us," says Brice, "who have the presence of mind to say, 'Oh, no! That's *your* truth. That's not *the* truth!'"

To let go of longstanding habits of blaming is no easy task. As my wife will readily attest, I've been working on it for years. The bright spot is that I don't blame as much as I used to, and I often recognize that I'm blaming or about to start, stop short, and do something else instead.

I'm especially suspicious of my "Why did you . . . ?" or "Why did you say . . . ?" questions. These are *usually* a way of attacking and blaming. They almost always evoke resentment. They put you in the position of having to explain yourself or your actions or admit to being bad or some kind of a fool. Few of us welcome that choice, especially when that smidgen of truth is still floating around.

Blaming is hard to give up, partly because it often serves as a distraction. I can blame you in order to divert attention from an issue you've raised, or to distract myself from my own concerns that I'm uneasy about dealing with. For example, I blame you for leaving your dirty dishes on the table when my real issue is how I'm feeling exploited and not cared about, and I don't feel safe telling you how I feel.

It's such a touchy area. Even when I tell you in a clean, nonblaming way how I feel in response to something you did, sometimes you'll probably still feel blamed. Also, when I'm angry, I can be doing my best not to blame you and still sound as if I'm blaming. I'll do no one any good by blaming myself for blaming you. But I can stay as aware as I can of what I'm doing, and as open as I can to how you feel in response.

Self-Blame

I'm apt to blame myself most heavily in those areas where I feel the least adequate: "I'm such a nerd that there's nothing I can do. I'm helpless." Using pseudo-self-blame in this way is a device to avoid responsibility. I'm not blaming myself—I'm blaming the circumstances or people in my past that made me as I am.

When I acknowledge some of my responsibility for my own troubles, I can no longer use my presumed "helplessness" or "inadequacy" to distract myself from doing anything to change. I can tell myself, *"I got into this; now I can get out of it and into a situation I'll feel better about."*

Theresa has yet to take that step. She describes herself as a total failure socially. When people see her coming, they walk away. She admits that she does nothing to involve herself with others, but uses that to say, "You see how inadequate I am?" This self-fulfilling statement of her helplessness is a way of saying to herself and her world, "See? I'm incapable of doing otherwise."

But I don't have to let my self-blame stop me cold. When my teenage daughter saved her money for a minibike, I said, "I don't like them, they're noisy, etc., etc., but if that's what you want, I'm not going to stop you." Then I heard myself throwing roadblock after roadblock in her path. I thought, "That's a dirty trick. I don't want you to have the bike, but I don't want you to think I'm stopping you. So I try to manipulate you into thinking it's too much bother and you didn't really want it anyway."

I went through the process of blaming myself. I had a choice there. I could have said, "Too bad. I'm so defective I can't do anything about it." Instead I said, "I don't want to leave it there." I talked with her again and changed things, clearly taking responsibility for what I'd done. (But, oh, how I hate minibikes!)

We seldom know enough to be sure what's going to happen as a result of what we do. We can only guess, assume, and hope. At this moment, under these circumstances, with the knowledge I have now, I make my choice. I live with its results.

Mistakes are familiar mice in everybody's cornfield. If I think as clearly and act as honestly and wisely as I can, that's enough. We can decrease our self-aggravation and suffering by learning to take our mistakes, failures, and half-successes as a "texture" in our lives. My "errors" and "defeats" sometimes teach me more than my successes. In that important sense they aren't failures at all.

What's Yours and What's Mine

Some years ago I arranged the purchase of 145 acres of forest land. I bought a plot for myself, and friends bought the rest in parcels of 10 to 15 acres each. Had I not set up the deal, none of us would live there now. That responsibility was mine. But since then we've each "done our own thing." Some of us have built simple dwellings, others expensive ones. One person uses his land for a rhododendron nursery. If I wished, I could view the whole thing as my doing. In fact, it's not.

In most cases, what happens between you and me results from what we both do. You *anger yourself, feel hurt, feel good,* etc., in response to my words and actions. I can't, all by myself, make you angry, hurt your feelings, or make you feel good. You've got to be willing to use my input to go to one of those places. Usually, the most I can do is *create the situation.*

Yet try this: For the next ten seconds *don't think about watermelons.*

See what's happening? Anything I say or do has the potential to set up a train of associations in your mind. If I know you well enough to be pretty sure where you'll go in response to what I say, and I go ahead and say it, I'm sending you there.

In the many instances when I don't know how you'll respond to what I say or do, however, I take responsibility only for my wants and actions. I have no responsibility for—or control over—your response.

Likewise, how *I* feel in response to what *you* do is my own doing—not yours. Even when I have to deal with difficulties you cause me, it's within my power to maintain a creative state of mind. I don't have to get in my own way by making myself miserable and thereby making life even harder.

ONLY I CAN DO IT

A monk asked: "How does one get emancipated?"
The master said: "Who has ever put you in bondage?"
—D. T. Suzuki

We often say, "I can't," when the truth is, "I won't." "I can't quit injuring myself . . . can't stop abusing other people . . . can't cut down my spending," and so on. It's a handy dodge. This "can't" seems to make life easier, fixing things so I don't need to put out as much effort. I'm not responsible—"I can't do it, that's all."

Owning Your "Won'ts"

Be on the alert for those moments when you are about to say, "I can't." Each time you hear your "I can't" coming up, substitute "I won't." (If that's too hard a statement for you, say, "I can't right now.") Instead of "I'm not able to," say, "I'm not willing to." Instead of "I'm unable to," "I'm unwilling to." As you practice this, you'll start to detect when we use "I can't" to cover up what's really happening with us or to disown responsibility.

"I try" can be another copout. Often, if I want something badly enough, I can do it. On the face of it, "I tried" means I did everything I could, but didn't succeed. It implies, "I can't." Actually, it more often helps me to disown my responsibility for not putting out the energy and commitment it takes to accomplish the objective in question. Perhaps I didn't want to do it badly enough to do it, but I don't want to admit that.

In this regard, the Spanish language reaches a delightfully absurd point. The English sentence, "I missed the bus," for instance, translates into Spanish as, "The bus left me": "*El camión me dejó.*" Or if I don't manage to succeed at something, in Spanish I might remark, "The project didn't get itself off the ground": "*El proyecto no se levantó.*"

I can't fix you up. Neither can your counselor. Your door of opportunity doesn't open with an electric eye. Some people have more handicaps than others, but everyone has at least a few.

I think here of my friend and colleague Anne. Anne was born with severe cerebral palsy. Her distorted words came slowly and with difficulty. She moved her limbs in spasmodic jerks. During her early years she was considered severely mentally retarded. Her parents put her in an institution, but she refused to stay. Brought home, she insisted on going to school. So Anne—who was not a pretty girl—went to school and suffered many jibes and jokes, but also got support and appreciation for her strength. She went through high school and college. I met her when she asked to be an intern at the school for handicapped children I directed. Her internship included psychometrics, psychological testing, curriculum design, and parent consultation. She was one of my best interns.

In ways that we may not even recognize, most of us contribute to larger events of this world. I uphold or confront the law as I pay or withold my taxes. I help maintain our society by being the consumer I am. I abdicate my power by withdrawing completely into my private concerns and avoiding involvement in my community, or exercise it by working for issues I think are important and for candidates of integrity who support them.

6

The Structure of Awareness

My awareness is my life. It is the source of my survival. My lack of awareness is my limit, and could mean my end.

Developing our awareness means learning to live in contact with our own experience. We can easily be so caught up in *what* we're doing that we don't realize *how* we're doing it. "The question at stake," declared Epictetus, "is this: Are we in our senses, or are we not?" (1937, p. 144).

As with any capacity, increasing our awareness takes time and effort. In this chapter we explore the elements of awareness and examine methods of becoming more perceptive.

WHAT AWARENESS IS—AND ISN'T

Awareness is the sensing of what exists, how it exists, and where and when it exists—its internal and external context. In contrast to knowledge, which is a file cabinet of information we learned in the past, awareness involves present sensing, along with thinking about how present events connect with other aspects of our lives. Just as our direct experience becomes more meaningful when we connect it with the rest of what we know, many educators now are realizing that we learn much more when our thinking occurs in a context of experiencing.

Zen teachers speak of developing a *mirror mind* that can reflect whatever image falls upon it clearly and without distortion or interpretation. This isn't easy to learn. For example, Nadine, a college junior, fell into a trap that's a common one for undergraduate students in psychology. She comments, "When I started taking psychology courses, I kept myself busy asking 'why' about everything I saw in myself and others. I thought I was gaining understanding by all that questioning, but I ended up more confused than ever. I was getting knowledge without awareness."

With awareness, often you don't need to "figure out" why something is happening. Instead, as you become more aware of your actions and reactions, you begin to discover answers to some of your questions. The events inside you may just need time to emerge.

Although awareness often leads to a re-viewing, it doesn't always go in an expected direction. When a couple undergoing therapy become more aware of their problems, for example, they may improve their relationship or they may split up. What happens with awareness is unpredictable. That's both the delight and the frustration of discovery.

Motivation influences our awareness. "When pride and memory argue," the old saying goes, "pride wins." I may want things to be different than they are, so I conveniently rewrite my personal history book, then forget that I rewrote it. Or I distract myself from noticing what I don't what to see or hear, then conclude that things are as I wanted them to be. So a useful way to start expanding my awareness is to *assume that I'm not so aware of what I do,* and to assume that there are areas of myself that I do not know well. I'm wise to assume that some of my thoughts, emotions, and even overt actions escape the scrutiny of my "attending mind." *For if I assume total knowledge of myself, I close myself to discovering anything except what I already think I know.* I become impervious to new discoveries.

Full awareness is possible only when seeing, hearing, or grasping the truth is more important than getting something else I want. Otherwise I distort my awareness in the service of my wants.

It's important to note that *self-awareness is totally different from "self-consciousness."* In self-consciousness, as the term is popularly used, a small bit of my attention goes to noticing what I'm doing or how I look. Mostly I'm worrying about what others are thinking about me. Mark Twain observed that others do very little of that kind of thinking, so relax. Just note that if you start to feel self-conscious, it's a signal to pull your attention out of projective thinking and into active observing. We'll talk more about self-consciousness in Chapter 8.

DEVELOPING OUR AWARENESS

Developing our awareness involves learning to observe the process rather than getting lost in directing it. Otherwise we end up repeating again and again the same old cycles of thought, emotion, or behavior. But as we learn to strengthen and focus our awareness, we begin to watch ourselves unfold, and we experience our world more vividly. Awareness by and in itself can be constructive. When we become aware, we can rely on the wisdom of our organism.

A Basic Tool

The following exercise provides a fundamental tool for developing awareness:

The Awareness Continuum

Describe what you are aware of from moment to moment, either out loud to another person, or quietly to yourself.

Begin each sentence with "Now I am aware. . . " For example, "Now I am aware that the sun is shining on the floor. Now I am aware that my mind keeps going back to something that happened to me yesterday. Now I am aware of feeling a pain just below my left shoulder blade," and so on.

As you describe what you are aware of, pay special attention to *specific details* of what's going on. Avoid generalities. Instead of "I'm aware of the way I'm sitting," you might say, "Now I'm aware of sitting with my left foot up on the couch and my body slumped sideways."

You may find yourself thinking, "The things I'm aware of in the now are so simple, trite, and obvious." That's the point. *There's essential value in learning to be aware of the obvious.*

If you're talking to another person, he or she can help you stay in the present. When you say something that isn't an awareness of a present event, the listener says, in a nonjudgmental way, "You've wandered."

If you're doing this with another person, after five or ten minutes, switch so that the other person talks and you listen.

With a class or group, everyone sits in a large circle and one person at a time speaks for a minute or two. Each person has only one turn, and if some time passes while no one wishes to speak, no one speaks. If there's a skilled guide, he or she begins by modeling the process and while it's going on can gently point out departures from reporting present awareness. While others are speaking, continue to pay attention to your own awareness continuum—notice what you're feeling and what you're otherwise experiencing as you listen to others report their awareness. (Adapted from Perls, Hefferline & Goodman, 1965, pp. 31–32, 82–83)

When you first try the awareness continuum, you may begin to daydream. You may notice that your present experience includes your thoughts: "Now I am wondering who will win the election," and so on. Then bring your attention back to sensing, with "Now I am aware . . . " and continue.

"Saying 'Now I am aware of—' often seems tedious, repetitious, and unnecessary at first," comments Gestalt therapist Barry Stevens, "but this slows me down, and helps me to focus on something *now*. Without this, I tend to scan, moving rapidly from this to that. . . . Fritz called it the Supermarket Approach or grasshopper awareness—seeing this, that, and the other and not being really aware of any of it" (1975, p. 187).

The full value of the awareness continuum surfaces when you begin using it in everyday life. It serves to let us know about important areas of our experience that we haven't been attending to. Beth describes how it proved valuable to her:

After a relaxed weekend away, I arrived home and instantly felt terrible. I noticed several things: My muscles tensed and my voice sounded angry. My energy dropped to zero and my mind went from alert to sluggish. I didn't want to be home.

For the next week I carried on the awareness continuum. I tried to be aware of how my body responded to different situations. At school I was relaxed and comfortable. At home I tensed up and I felt heavy expectations.

When finally I drummed up the courage to talk to Ken about it, I felt a flood of relief. Then we talked out my feelings one by one. It turned out that the rigid expectations I thought he had about me were just in my mind.

Awareness and Self-Acceptance

Awareness and self-acceptance are reciprocal. In my fullest awareness I am seeing, hearing, and feeling what is . . . including my judging of people, events, and things as "bad" or "wrong," which usually colors or tints my awareness.

So there is a crucially important connection: *When I observe and I accept what I do, think, and feel as the way I am now, including my judging behavior as "right" or "wrong," I can perceive what I'm doing most clearly. Only when I'm aware of what I'm doing do I have the option of doing something else.* The exciting paradox is that by accepting and acknowledging myself as completely all right just as I am now, at this instant in my life, new discoveries and directions become available. Gestalt therapist Stella Resnick elaborates on this process:

> When people first start out in therapy . . . frequently . . . they are afraid to see themselves because they think they won't like what they see. They are judging themselves, and this judging is experienced with pain. . . . Witnessing without judging . . . [reduces] internal conflict and self-victimization. . . . Growth comes not through goals of unrealistic perfection, but out of a place of inner support and self-love. (1975, pp. 227–228)

You can begin moving into a *growth circle*. Doing less depreciative judging allows you to be more aware. Increased awareness helps you be alert to when you judge. There is no good awareness or bad awareness—no "my awareness is better than yours." The important event is your observation of what you're doing, on the inside and the outside, whatever that is.

Observing Awareness

The purpose of the following exercise is to encourage you to become aware of the spontaneous movement of your waking consciousness, without restricting your attention to the present. It's a relaxing experience—a useful thing to do when you feel overburdened and can use a few quiet minutes to recoup your energy.

The Ebb and Flow of Awareness

Lie down on your back—or if there's nowhere you can lie down, sit comfortably. Allow yourself to open or close your eyes whenever you wish. Let your mind drift freely wherever it wants.

Then start to notice, wnen you remember to, whatever fills your consciousness at that moment. You may find, as you do this, that sometimes you're noticing the sounds, sights, or smells of your immediate surroundings, other times you're attending to events in your body, and still other times your consciousness is filled with fantasies and daydreams, thoughts and images, memories and anticipations, and conversations with yourself.

Get a sense of this natural ebb and flow of what you do with your consciousness from one moment to the next. Don't try to *change* anything. Just *notice* what *is*—what the natural process of your own mind, as it now exists, involves. Take whatever time you want to give yourself. Be generous.

When you've finished "The Ebb and Flow of Awareness," we suggest that you find a pencil and a piece of paper and then go right on to "The Editor's Exercise" that follows. It's a continuation of what you just did, with an additional dimension.

The Editor's Exercise

With pencil and paper by your side, continue what you were doing in "The Ebb and Flow of Awareness," with one change: Each time something new comes into your awareness, jot down one or two words that will allow you to remember it later. Do this for at least ten minutes, right now. Then continue reading.

Now, keeping before you your list of what has just passed through your mind, take another sheet of paper. Imagine that you are a newspaper editor. *Lay out a front page that reflects the content of your own awareness.* Draw lines to mark out the columns, and indicate how much space each story gets in accord with the amount of time it occupied your attention. Then write a one-line headline for each "story"—don't bother with the details.

If you're doing this with others, and there's something you wouldn't want to mention aloud, the article headline might be something like, "Censorship is Big Story," or "X-Rated Story Deemed Too Hot to Handle."

Finished? Now look over your front page. What's your big headline? What are the major issues? What brief news flashes came into your awareness? What do you use for fillers?

What does this say about where the biggest share of your attention goes? Which news sources do you favor to the exclusion of which others? Are you most attuned to sensations in your body, to sights and sounds around you, to thoughts about the past, or to daydreams and future fantasies?

If you're doing this with others, compare your front page with theirs to discover the different ways each of you tends to focus consciousness.

ATTENTION AND DISTRACTION

Attention is focused awareness. *Bare attention* is attention focused on here-and-now events. It involves two elements: an ability to concentrate—to focus my attention where I want it—and an attentiveness to what is happening in the moment.

Zen masters speak of *one-pointed attention*—focusing on just one thing at a time. For instance, when I watch a sunset, I'm just watching the sunset, not doing anything else. Our ordinary consciousness, however, is *many pointed.* As I watch the sunset, my attention darts back and forth between first this thought and then that one. Indeed, most of my attention may go into mental processes that keep me *out* of my here-and-now sunset.

Gestalt psychologists speak of the *figure-ground phenomenon.* I can drive down a street many times and never notice a certain mailbox. It's just part of the background or "ground" against which other things stand out. But suppose I want to mail a letter. Now the mailbox leaps out at me. Suddenly it is the "figure," and everything else becomes the "ground."

Whatever I focus on becomes the figure, and other things fade into the less clearly defined background. One day I notice the sun, the breeze, the trees, the flowers. The next day in my busy schedule I'm oblivious to all but pen, paper, and appointments.

As If for the First Time

Familiarity leads to fading into the background. Here's a way to rediscover the richness in events that long acquaintance so often leads us to overlook.

As I continue to live on a street, I begin to see less of what's there.

Walk down a street you've never walked down before. Get a sense of how you pay attention to what's there.

Then return to your own old street with this same alertness. Deliberately find things you've never seen before—both large things and small details. See how much you can discover that you never noticed before, or that you once saw but now no longer see.

Interest and Attention

What I'm aware of depends not only on what's happening, but also on what I choose to pay attention to. Perls comments, "The pictures or sounds of the world do not enter us automatically, but *selectively.* We don't see; we *look for, search, scan* for something. We don't hear all the sounds of the world, we *listen*" (1969b).

I'm likely to become fragmented and out of touch with myself if I habitually respond to the stimuli that bid for my attention, instead of listening and searching. I stay more centered and more in touch with my aliveness when I actively choose what I attend to. My interest creates the meaning I find in a situation. A mother may have a hearing loss and be sleeping three rooms away from her baby, but should the baby make an unusual cry, the mother is likely to awaken. The other night my wife woke me up to point this out.

Distraction

I used to pay scant attention to people when they talked with me. Time after time I'd realize that my mind had drifted away. Frequently I'd have to ask the other person to repeat something. If I didn't ask for a recap, I had to reconcile myself to missing part of what was said and try to "fake it" to continue the conversation.

I'm still sometimes surprised at how much I've missed when I listen to a tape recording of a conversation between another person and me. I'm not always an accurate judge of how well I'm paying attention. If I want to make sure I'm hearing you, or that I'm being heard, I'd better double-check: "If I heard you right, you said . . . ," or "Tell me what you heard me say, will you? I feel like I didn't say it very clearly."

I want to feel free to ask you to repeat what you said if I didn't quite understand it. And I want you to ask me to rephrase if you didn't hear what I said. If we agree on these two things, we'll hear each other more often. More about this in Chapter 9.

When my daughter was two years old, she frequently used to say something five or six times while my wife or I were attending to something else. By the fifth or sixth repetition, she often got upset and her voice started to turn into a shrieky whine. The problem, we realized, was that our daughter needed to learn to get a person's attention before she started to talk. She started speaking as if we were listening while we were still attending to something else. In a few weeks she learned to *get a person's attention* before starting to talk. "Mama, listen for a minute!" "Papa, I want to show you something!" She also learned that calling people by their names was a powerful way to get their attention. These days she has no hesitation about making such requests.

When I have something to gain, I have little trouble paying attention. Observe yourself: How easily are you distracted from an unpleasant task? From an enjoyable one?

One morning as I was administering an important exam, some workmen started drilling outside. Many students complained, so we gave another form of the exam under quieter conditions. The result: There was no significant difference between the two test scores for any student. Though disturbed by the noise, the students were not distracted. The test was too crucial to them. The encouraging implication is that when it's important enough to us to do so, we all have substantial ability to focus and direct our attention.

Here's a technique for calming yourself and focusing your attention right here in this moment when you feel scattered or hurried.

Just One Thing at a Time

Sometimes I notice that I'm hurrying, and not here with what I'm doing now. At such times, my mind and body are tense.

When I realize that I'm doing that, I stop what I'm doing and breathe deeply and slowly a few times.

Then I return to what I was doing but allow myself only one movement at a time.

With my momentary stop after each movement, to see and feel where I am and note the next thing I'm going to do, I stop my hurried, automatic way of acting. Doing things this way may feel strange to you at first, but the strangeness wears off as you learn to focus your attention on each moment and movement.

Try this. Get up and do one simple thing, like taking something out of your pocket. Do this in your usual way and at your usual pace.

Now review in your mind what you just did.

Then perform exactly the same sequence of actions over again, *just one thing at a time.*

Attention in Everyday Tasks

In his intriguing book *Zen and the Art of Motorcycle Maintenance* (1976), Robert M. Pirsig describes how several principles of awareness and attention can be applied to exacting, demanding jobs. He uses working on a motorcycle as a model. There are six principles we'll mention here.

First, *assume an attitude of modesty.* The higher your opinion of yourself, Pirsig says, the less likely you are to admit that you've goofed on something and the more likely you are to ignore facts that turn up." A mechanic who has a big ego to defend is at a terrific disadvantage." If modesty does not come easy to you, fake it (1976, p. 308).

Pirsig's second principle is for those whose anxiety stops them from getting started. Read every book and magazine you can about how to do the repair job, he suggests. "Remember, too, that you're after peace of mind—not just a fixed machine. And think the job through before you start to work: You can save time and trouble later by listing everything you're going to do on little slips of paper and then organizing and reorganizing the sequence as you think about the job" (1976, p. 309).

The third principle is: When you're bored, *stop.* Boredom means your mind is wandering elsewhere. That's when we make mistakes. We also make them when we're tired. Pirsig turns jobs that bore him most, like greasing and oil changing, into a ritual, paying attention to the ordinary, finding in simple things a beauty that is often overlooked.

Pirsig's fourth principle has proven especially valuable to me. *Impatience* is a great cause of mistakes. One cause of impatience, Pirsig suggests, is *underestimating how long the job will take.* Pirsig's solution is to *allow an indefinite time for the job* and to double the allotted time when circumstances force time planning.

A fifth Pirsig principle is that "overall goals must be scaled down in importance and immediate goals must be scaled up." That can help avoid making Big Mistakes.

Finally, the sixth useful Pirsig principle is called "mechanic's feel." Many people try to screw bolts on as tight as they'll go and treat other aspects of a job the same way. Mechanic's feel involves attending carefully to the material I'm working with—it's softness or hardness, its elasticity, and what it tells me about how it wants to be handled. It will let me know just how far to turn the bolt, how much pressure is just enough and not too much (p. 317).

Boredom

Boredom is a deenergizing of my attention. It can function as a useful statement about what I'm doing. It can identify something I don't want to hear. In any event, it can be a way I torture myself and deaden my life.

I most often feel bored when I try to pay attention to something that doesn't interest me right then. My options may include finding something interesting in it, changing what's happening, drifting off into my own world of thoughts and fantasies, or leaving. I don't have to poison myself by staying bored.

That "poison" can be real and deadly. For instance, you've probably known old people who died not long after retiring, or who died shortly after their spouses. Others in similar situations find interests that nourish and sustain them.

When you and I are talking, if I'm not interested in what's happening, I can change it. I do you no favor by pretending that I'm interested in what you're saying when I'm not. That poisons us both. When I'm listening because I think I "should," I feel dead or resentful, and you and I make little contact.

If I'm bored, you may not be vitally interested either. We can probably find something else to do or talk about that we'd both prefer. I can say, "I'm not with this right now. Can we come back to it later, and talk about something now that I feel involved in too?" Or I can suggest doing something else entirely.

When I give you that kind of feedback, in a nonjudgmental way, I'm saying that I care about you and that we can have many good times with each other. But if you reply, "You don't care about me, because you're bored with what I'm saying," you're telling me you don't want to know when I'm interested and when I'm not. Or you may be telling me you don't feel my caring for you, so I need to let you know I care.

In a group, when I say I'm bored, it opens the way for other people to say how they feel, too. If enough of us are bored, we can all do something else. If I'm the only one, or almost the only one, then either I find a way to enjoy some aspect of what's going on or I leave.

I find some things inherently more interesting than others. Yet I can interest myself more or less in anything or anyone. People who are not like those I usually spend my time with are especially interesting to me when I open myself to hearing what they have to say. As I develop my ability to be interested in wherever I am and whomever I'm with, I'm less at the mercy of circumstances and I have less need to be "entertained."

EMPTINESS

Our capacity to be aware is hindered if our minds are too full. We need some spaces between our activities and our thoughts. Here is a classic story that makes that point:

> The master Nan-in had a visitor who came to inquire about Zen. But instead of listening, the visitor kept talking. . . .
> After a while, Nan-in served tea. He poured tea into his visitor's cup until it was full, then he kept on pouring.
> Finally, the visitor could not restrain himself.

"Don't you see it's full?" he said. "You can't get any more in!"

"Just so," replied Nan-in, stopping at last. "And like this cup, you are filled with your own ideas. How can you expect me to give you Zen unless you offer me an empty cup?" (Peter Pauper Press, 1959)

Dave does not offer an empty cup. An engineer, he fills up every moment with activity, never giving himself a quiet moment to be with his thoughts and feelings. When the TV goes off, he picks up a newspaper or starts talking with anyone available. When he goes out, he keeps his portable radio, with earphones, on constantly—he might stumble on some unfilled time.

Our culture encourages us to be too busy—to fill our consciousness with as many things and activities as we can. Space that isn't filled with things and time that isn't filled with action can seem threatening.

People in counseling often deal with such feelings. Sometimes clients report sensing a sort of frightening black hole or deep pit inside them. So they grab for whatever they can, hanging on desperately so they won't "fall in."

Fritz Perls encouraged people who experience such feelings to *let go*—to go ahead and plunge into the darkness, being attentive to what they observe and feel. Again and again people find that when they get past their panic, they attain a valuable experience of their interior worlds. Perls (1969b) spoke of the emptiness that we sometimes so fear as a *fertile void* that holds important keys to change. He also spoke of "holes in the personality." These places where we don't allow our energy to flow may make themselves known to us in fantasies and dreams: Someone who seldom reaches out to others dreams of a man with no arms; someone who perennially leans on others for support instead of providing for herself dreams of having no feet. Such a hole in the personality points to a way we can reown and develop a disowned capacity.

Among his patients, reports psychologist Wilson Van Dusen, "I discovered a world of tiny holes. . . . In severely disturbed patients, the holes appeared as defects: blankness, . . . failure of concentration . . . these holes appear in all persons to a greater or lesser extent" (1975, p. 88).

Van Dusen tells of a thirty-year-old schizophrenic who had been hospitalized nine years:

> He accepts this as a black, hole-like world. In this black hole he can't think or remember and this threatens him. . . . He feels the dull concern: "I must concentrate, hold my mind from drifting." . . .
>
> I ask him if he will let himself drift. . . . He complies. We are silent. In a moment some feeling breaks forth. He reddens and laughs. . . . I asked whether he wanted to climb out of the hole. He said . . . he would stay in it and see what else of interest might happen. . . . He had discovered that of itself the void filled up with new things. He didn't have to work so hard to fill it up. (1975, pp. 90–91)

When I try to flee from my emptiness, I'm hesitant about what aspects of myself I might discover—aspects of me that may be paired with memories of painful or punishing experiences.

There may be times when you feel the kind of frustrated emptiness in which nothing seems to have much meaning, and you get an uneasy feeling of something wrong because you lack defined activity or direction. At such times we need to remember that a pause in a person's life is seldom an accident. It can be a time of many possibilities. You have a greater degree of freedom when you're not locked tightly into undertakings and directions. Usually you create your pauses in some way, knowingly or not. Louis comments, "Sometimes I'll be walking along, and the need to pause is so strong, I stop dead still." The bind comes when you think you should be doing something else, instead of using the pause as a time for growth and exploration. When you have nothing to do is a good time to do your nothing.

Part Two

CONNECTING WITH OTHERS

Being Persons Together

7

*O*ur connections with other people can evoke our positive qualities and help us identify those areas of ourselves where we can evolve creatively and constructively. Being a unique and special person *and* being in close affiliation with others, however, is sometimes hard work.

Effective relationships include a measure of valuable frustration: They provoke us to confront our contradictions and develop beyond previous limitations. Even though they may be frustrating and painful, such confrontations can include a commitment to our mutual individual growth as collaborators rather than antagonists.

When I ask you to undo my feelings of low self-worth, however, or to reconstruct my life for me, I'm burdening you with more than you can do. No one else can *give* me happiness and inner peace. Expecting you to rectify the defects in my life is disowning my capacity for self-support. And it impairs my capacity to enjoy you as you are. Ken Keyes (1979) writes, "The opportunity to live with another human being is one of life's greatest gifts. You damage and bruise this gift by your expectations that the relationship make you happy."

Being with others and being with ourselves is an ebb and flow. There are life stages when it's valuable to be free of the stress of intense involvement with another person. Often, for instance, after a young person has moved away from home to share an apartment with friends or live in a college dorm, he or she begins to want to live separately for a time. Similarly, after the demise of a relationship, whether from divorce, death, or attrition, being alone is a useful time for redefining yourself.

"Don't be in too big a hurry to get involved with someone," counsels Keyes. "Work on yourself first. . . . Introduce yourself to the beautiful, capable and lovable you. Then let others discover you!"

The next section of this chapter addresses the difference between being alone and being lonely. Then three important elements of connecting with other people are presented in turn: mutuality, trust, and self-disclosure.

LONELINESS AND ALONENESS

Many—perhaps most—of us are a little awkward in the way we use some of our time alone. The term *alone* applies to being with myself and not being with other people. *Lonely,* by contrast, refers to *a state of mind and feeling*—feeling deprived of people's presence or the contact with them we'd like to have. It's a subjective state, not a situation itself. I can be alone without feeling lonely, and I can feel lonely amid a multitude.

Forms of Loneliness

Loneliness, paradoxically, is an experience we all share.* Each of us sometimes feels the "existential loneliness" of knowing that we are the only person who can feel our own life from the inside. We can't experience anyone else's life as they do. Existential lonelinesss includes facing the inevitability of things and people passing from my life, of others dying, and eventually of facing death.

Most of our loneliness, however, is of other kinds. One aspect of loneliness is interactional: wanting to be with someone who's not available. Another is intra-psychic: holding back from making contact even when people are available.

In the *loneliness of withholding myself,* I'm afraid of your disinterest or disapproval if I showed how I really feel. Perhaps I "shouldn't feel that way," so we stay safely on the surface and avoid contact. I may hesitate from fear that I would appear childish if I were to speak of my fear, my love, my doubt, my sorrow: I "should be able to handle it myself." Similarly, at times I want to feel your magic but may keep you at a distance when I need your magic most.

Lonely people often lack social skills. Do we start with a reclusive chicken, or an isolate of an egg? Loneliness can result from not knowing how to approach people I want to be with, or to say what I want to when I'm with them.

Notice how some people look straight ahead as they walk along, as if they had blinders on. They can pass people they know and seem not to see them—or in fact not see them. As a teenager and young adult I feared that others would be offended if I "intruded on their privacy." Each person lived inside a glass box, and I couldn't reach or look inside without permission. I enjoyed discovering that most people preferred a "hello" or a friendly nod to my "respect for their privacy." It wasn't respect at all, but my fear of reprisal for being intrusive.

Here's something you can explore. For a while, smile and nod at everyone you pass or meet, even strangers. Then, for a while, scowl or look away from everyone. What do you discover?

---

*Our thinking on this subject owes much to that of Clark Moustakas (1961b).

A variation of the loneliness of holding back is the *loneliness of estrangement,* when we hold back from a person we've been close to in the past. It can be painful to find few words to say when once we found so many.

The *loneliness of feeling rejected (and resentful)* results from reaching out and having the other person turn away. When I make a clear statement of wanting to make contact and get a "no" from you, I may feel rejected and resentful. I feel less than I was: exposed, vulnerable, and without supports.

The *loneliness of separation* can result from being away from people we care about when we haven't developed new friends to take their place. This often occurs in the passage from adolescence to adulthood. The highest rate of loneliness is found among people 18 to 25 years of age (Egan & Cowan, 1980, p. 198). This is the time when we move away from depending on our parents for emotional support and may physically move away from home. We vacillate between feeling mature self-support and feeling desolate and lost as we try to redefine our identity without the physical and emotional attachments we're accustomed to.

The *loneliness of physical isolation* is a variety of the loneliness of separation that involves being physically apart from other people, like someone alone in a room or a cell or at a kosher restaurant in Libya.

The *loneliness of alienation* is another variation of the loneliness of separation. You've probably experienced this: Perhaps as a child you moved into a new neighborhood where you knew no one, or where most other children were from a different racial, ethnic, social, or religious group and were outspoken about the difference. Hopefully, you *are* different—different from anyone around you.

Some Responses to Loneliness

I look for ways to survive my loneliness when my loss or weakening of attachments triggers my survival responses.

1. *Escape.* I can try to escape through alcohol, TV or other drugs or total commitment to play, work, or long-distance running. With such avoidance I learn nothing, so that next time will be just as painful as this time.
2. *Life projects.* I take my energy away from my swirling vortex of thoughts about my loneliness and invest it in activities and enterprises that transform my time alone from loneliness into enjoyable solitude.
3. *Reaching out directly.* This involves finding the kind of company I want: going places and presenting myself where otherwise I might hold back. I might also go to classes or community or church clubs and interest groups to develop social skills while being with others.
4. *Experiencing and observing my process.* I allow myself to feel my loneliness as it is and notice what I'm doing to create and maintain it. I attend to my internal dialogue: "I wish . . . ," watch the fantasies I play out on my inner screen, and notice when and where I tense and tighten. I acknowledge that I hold back from doing what could nourish and enrich me.
5. *Going into the center of my loneliness.* There's nothing wrong with letting myself go with the blues. Hearing what I'm telling me at such times can open me to what this episode of loneliness reveals about where I am in my life process. As I

experience my loneliness intensely and intentionally, I learn that I don't have to run away from it.

And sometimes I don't have to do anything with my blues at all. I don't have to find meaning, or purpose, or explore them. I just have to be with them. They're my Being for now.

Appreciating Aloneness and Solitude

Today aloneness enjoys new respectability. Census figures reveal that the number of people under 35 who live alone doubled between 1970 and 1980, and it's still rising. Sociologists have coined the new term *stable single* to define independent women and men who plan to stay single. The formerly married and the never married are buying homes, traveling alone, and establishing firm careers. They view marriage or living together as an option rather than as a necessity.

We may avoid aloneness in response to social pressure. Our culture values always having "companionship"—even if it's a transistor radio and headphones. Using solitude creatively does not mean that the alone person is unliked, unwanted, weird, or "not a team player."

In fact, my aloneness can hold a pleasure of its own. "I never found the companion that was so companionable as solitude," declared Thoreau. And Byron penned these lines:

> *There is a pleasure in the pathless woods,*
> *There is a rapture on the lonely shore,*
> *There is society, where none intrudes,*
> *By the deep Sea, and music in its roar.*
> —Childe Harold IV: clxxviii

Alone Times and Lonely Times

You'll need three sheets of paper and something to write with.

1. Write "Childhood" on page 1; "Growing Up" on page 2; "Today" on page 3. Divide each page in half, with "Aloneness" on one half and "Loneliness" on the other.

2. Taking one page (stage) at a time, recall times when you felt "alone" and list words that describe how you remember feeling at each time. Do the same for times when you felt "lonely." As words emerge, put them under the category that feels appropriate. Try to avoid using the same word in both places while working on any one page (stage). You may find, however, that you place words in different categories at different stages.

3. On each page, when you read the lists, notice what feelings come up that help you distinguish the two categories from each other.

4. If you're doing this with a class or group, discuss the way you and

others have experienced these states at different stages. Can you use other people's words to enrich your vocabulary in either category at any stage?

Time Alone in Relationships

People intensely involved in a close relationship need time to themselves as much as anyone. When I want to be alone, you may feel threatened, as if my need for solitude means I love you less, or because it might leave you alone.

Mary and Ed are in therapy because of this issue. Married four years, each cares deeply about the other. Now Mary is asking for some time by herself when she comes home from work. Ed has a hard time seeing that in any other light than as a lessening of her affection for him. For Ed, being alone is something you do at work and he dislikes it. His work is solitary, his contacts with people brief. Mary, by contrast, deals with people constantly in her job. Ed is struggling to appreciate that difference and to recognize not only Mary's need to be by herself, but also his own needs for time by himself away from work.

The constancy of family interactions intensifies the need for a respite. It's a gift to be able to tell the other parent, "I need me—I want to take a walk. Will you take over for a while?" Many single parents, who can be in an even tighter bind, participate in support networks of friends and neighbors they can call on. One group of families has an arrangement in which any child can "run away" to any other designated house for a few days. The parents, too, get vacations when their children "run away."

MUTUALITY

Our mutual responsibility is to help each other develop roots and wings. Roots offer a continuing, solid sense of being nourished. Wings are our ability to fly beyond the nest as a unique spirit. Only when I've defined my ground can I fly freely. Then I can soar and know where I can return.

Psychoanalyst Margaret Mahler (1975) observed the slow unfolding of our "psychological birth" to be a continuing interplay of our capacities for separateness and relatedness that continues throughout our lives.

Individuation and Relatedness

We differ in how clear a sense of ourselves as individuals each of us has. Jung called this process of developing a sense of personal uniqueness *individuation.* Many people rely on others for a sense of identity: Most of us know couples who "go everywhere and do everything together," and report not knowing how to act when alone. More individuated persons still experience some need to determine the other's response to validate their own. With still greater individuation, we become less reliant on, and more respectful of, the responses of others.

Family therapist Murray Bowen (1965, 1972) speaks of a newborn infant's coexisting with its family in an *undifferentiated ego-mass*—a relationship of reciprocal conformity in which the various members are lost in the others. With infants this is normal; with older children and adults it can lead to feeling immobilized, frustrated, and unhappy.

Gail comments, "When my brother got picked up by the cops for stealing, Mom acted like it was her crime instead of his. When one person did something wrong, we were all punished. So nobody developed a sense of personal responsibility, or really felt like a separate person."

Since each person depends on the conglomerate others for a sense of identity, emotional growth is slowed. When one person tries to step outside the accepted boundaries, the other(s) may decide the person is "sick!—What are you, anyway, crazy?" In fact, this "crazy" behavior may be the sanest thing that's happening in the family.

Bowen postulates that people tend to choose friends, partners, and spouses who are at about their own level of individuation. On this basis people growing up in EM (ego-mass) families create a new ego-mass (EM^2) in the couple they form.

To develop a sense of yourself as an individual in the face of such pressures toward conformity requires hard-working awareness:

> *Awareness of the system:*   Noticing how interlocking manipulations resist my efforts to develop as an individual and coerce me to support the system.
>
> *Awareness of myself:*   When I'm confused about how I feel or have no clear opinion, being able to notice my uncertainty—and allow myself that uncertainty.
>
> *Unhooking:*   Noticing when I feel guilty, ashamed or wrong for not being as my friends, mate, or family want me to be—and finding a way to inhibit that response (such as through positive reframing, described in Chapter 17).
>
> *Choosing:*   Identifying what choices I have and how I may want to risk being.
>
> *Communicating:*   Giving my friends, partner, or family clear and reassuring messages that I still care about them—assuming that I do—and that what I have to do is for me.

Each step involves deliberate moves to actively explore the alternatives available. Passive insight per se offers little.

Subject and Object Roles

Philosopher Martin Buber (1958) distinguished between an *I-it* relationship and an *I-Thou* relationship. When I relate to you as an *it*, I treat you as an object to serve my needs and interests. When I treat you as a *Thou*, I respect you. I care about you and what you want, as well as about me and what I want, and I anticipate enjoying being your *Thou*.

It is easy to treat a child as an object or *it* rather than as a person or *Thou*. I may pick up my child and put her down somewhere without warning, for instance, or grab her hand and pull her along with me without consulting her. Such actions don't help her feelings of security and self-esteem. In other ways, we also treat adults as *its*.

Ordinarily, everyone around a newborn infant functions, from the infant's perspective, to serve his or her needs for food, nurturing, and warmth. The infant is a *subject*, and others act as *objects* to provide for its needs (Boszormenyi-Nagy, 1965a).

As the infant becomes a child, it starts to take care of some of its own needs and to respond to those of others. For instance, my preschool daughter and a friend just came up to the cabin where I'm writing and asked for water. Perceiving the prospect of my afternoon writing time going down the drain, I laid down the law: "Here's the water. Now you can stay at the cabin only if you two play at the end away from my writing area. If you start asking for my attention, back home you go." They were acting as subjects in asking for water and play materials, and I filled the object role, providing what they wanted. But then I became subject, saying, "I need," asking them to be the objects—"Give me room to place my undivided attention on writing." This give-and-take is *mutuality*. The same principle holds where both persons participate in the same activity: In mutually fulfilling lovemaking, partners both offer themselves to the other's sexual needs and fulfill their own wants in the interaction.

Giving each other guidance and support when we want it and need it is part of an adult relationship. Perhaps I got involved with you because I thought you'd give me the kind of "parenting" I like and because I also acknowledge your childlike needs and provide the "parenting" you want. When I insist on locking you into either role, however, it can lead to a one-way relationship. We're not on equal terms. In *Learning to Love Again*, Mel Krantzler writes:

> I didn't give Laura space. . . . She wasn't a separate person, only an extension of my need to be taken care of. These weren't pleasant truths, they were true for my relationships with every women who was or had been important in my life. (1979, p. 12)

Someone who is always busy meeting others' needs has little time to discover who he or she is as an individual. On the other hand, the person who manipulates another into filling all his or her wants never develops self-support. Both tacitly contract to stop growing.

With children, from toddlers to young adults, I can provide an appropriate measure of guidance *about what to do but not about who to be*. My son Paul, for example, is a hard-working musician. His explorations in his early twenties included study and work that did not allow him the financial capacity to totally leave our home. He's in and out, like a swinging door. The family supports his explorations and his commitment to music, encouraging him to study, dream, work, and value himself in the process. We talk and argue through what we want, need, and expect from him, and he does the same with us. It takes work, but it happens. Our support and encouragement don't demand that he be dependent and don't require him to feel guilty and obligated in return—we hope.

Enjoying Differences

On *M.A.S.H.* the other evening, Hawkeye said to Hotlips something like, "Maybe our trouble, Margaret, is that we try to find made-to-order people in what in fact is an off-the-rack world." Accepting and respecting each other as we are can lead to enjoyment and satisfaction, celebration and admiration. Attempts to control how others should be breed resentment and distance.

Walter, looking back on his childrearing years, observed, "It's interesting how for years I trained my children to think for themselves and be independent, and then when they started going in their own directions I wanted them to 'stop rebelling' and act like good little robots." If I value your self-reliance, I have to be prepared for you to be self-reliant in your way. If I value your appreciation of your unique self, you're more likely to appreciate my unique self.

There's value in learning to see others' differences as exciting rather than threatening. My wife, for instance, tends to let plants grow aggressively when I would prune them. She allows our children greater latitude in certain matters where I tend to be narrower in my limits—and vice versa in other matters. She can be extremely expressive (wildly so, I sometimes grump to myself when I forget to prize our differences) in situations where I'm more restrained. Virginia Satir (1972) calls an attitude of welcoming and appreciating another's way of being-in-the-world a "reverence for life," observing that while we may attract one another because of our sameness, it is our differentness that keeps us interested. Thus a central issue facing each of us is *how to be with you as I am, and enjoy you as you are*.

The following exercise points up how unique each person is, even on a strictly physical level:

Matching Walking

Get together with someone more or less your own height. For five minutes, one of you will be the "walker" and the other will be the "matcher." Walk side by side, with the "walker" walking normally and the "matcher" walking as much like the walker as possible—your posture, the swing of your arms, how your feet contact the ground, everything. The walker can provide feedback—"slump forward just a little more, and don't swing your arms quite so much," and so on.

As matcher, you may want to comment to the walker about how you feel walking that way; aside from that, and the walker's specific feedback, don't talk. Get into feeling as fully as you can how it is to "be in the walker's body."

After five minutes, reverse roles and repeat the process. Then take a final five minutes to talk with your partner about what you experienced.

If you're doing this with a group, the pairs can describe their experiences to the others after you come back together.

"Love consists in this," declared German poet Rainer Maria Rilke,"—that two solitudes protect and touch and greet each other" (in Greenberg, 1967). To be with you as you are, I have to be willing to be most of myself and accept most of you. I can reach out to you only to the extent that I am willing to reach into myself.

TRUST

We most often use the word *trust* to mean "depend on positively." I feel that you'll help me, and won't hurt me—or hurt someone or something I care about.

Trust can also mean "predict." In the case of one couple, for twenty years the husband played around with other women and lied about it. "I can't trust him at all," the wife said. In fact, she could trust him totally—to consistently pursue other women. So when someone says, "I can't trust you," the meaning is sometimes, "I don't like what I can depend on." I can always trust another person *to do what seems to that person to be in his or her interest at the time*. The more I know about what's important to you, the more I know about what I can depend on you to do.

In the rest of this chapter, the word *trust* is used in the first of these two meanings. A trusting attitude in this sense can be a self-fulfilling prophecy. When I walk into a situation expecting a warm and friendly response, I'm likely to reach out to others and find that they respond just as I trusted they would.

Trusting other people happens when I have *become trustworthy*. If I don't trust myself, I won't trust others. As I learn to trust myself, I become better able to trust others, and anticipate what I can trust another person to do and what I can't.

Mistrust, while it is often a response to a real conflict in our objectives, can also occur in the absence of any such conflict. Social psychologist Theodore Newcomb speaks of *autistic hostility:* Imagining you to be hostile when you're not, I respond with hostility toward you, eliciting your antagonism in return (in Raven & Rubin, 1976, p. 445).

You might like to try the "trust walk," an old but perennially enjoyable exercise that's described here with a new twist:

The Trust Walk

With another person, decide who will lead and who will follow for the first fifteen minutes. The follower closes his or her eyes, and the two of you set off together on a fifteen-minute walk. As leader, lead your partner as if that person were indeed blind, guiding him or her to experience shapes, textures, even tastes—anything you wish, being careful to guide in a way that avoids any harm or danger.

If you see some especially attractive sight that you'd like your partner to see, you can position him or her to see it, stand out of the way, and tap the tops of both shoulders. Your partner may open his or her eyes until you tap again—no more than about twenty seconds. Emphasize the other senses, however, and use vision sparingly. During your turn to be "blind," enjoy the walk, and also notice your trusting and mistrusting thoughts and feelings. When your half hour is up, you and your partner can discuss these feelings.

How Trust Develops

Mary Salter Ainsworth of London's Tavistock Institute observes that "Whereas a sensitive mother seems constantly to be 'tuned in' to receive her baby's signals, [and] interpret and respond to them both promptly and appropriately, an insensitive mother will often not notice her baby's signals, will misinterpret them when she does notice them, and will then respond tardily, inappropriately, or not at all" (in Bowlby, 1979, pp. 110–112). The children with sensitive, "tuned-in" mothers appeared more likely to develop a stable self-reliance combined with trust in others. Erik Erikson calls this a sense of *basic trust* (1964, p. 249).

Trust in Enduring Relationships

Trust in enduring relationships develops gradually as the members experience mutuality. In time we trust each other and give to each other without "in-kind" or immediate reciprocity. "Instant trust lacks firmness," says clinical psychologist Martin Rosenman. "You don't know how it will stand up under pressure since it has not been tested.... As trust, caring, and respect grow, you can reveal more personal and embarrassing parts of yourself" (1979, pp. 50–51).

Trust is promoted by honesty, and nothing kills it faster than lying. If you catch me in a little lie, you're likely to suspect that I may be lying about bigger things, too. Lederer and Jackson note that in a close relationship, the attempts at deception are likely to be unsuccessful, for your mate is only deceived *if* he or she *wishes* to be" (1968, p. 108). One measure that can help us avoid getting caught in that cycle is to avoid putting the other person in the bind of: "Always be honest with me but don't ever hurt my feelings."

Trust requires the consistency of receiving the same message verbally and nonverbally. If my words say one thing while my voice, body, or actions say something else, I'm going to set off your red radar alert signal—unless you're committed to trusting me even when it means lying to yourself.

But a double message doesn't have to stop us cold. We can appreciate the nonverbal channels *as dependable ways of communicating*. As we learn each other's voice tones, postures, gestures, and facial expressions, we get better at reaching beyond the words and responding to the nonverbal message.

Compassion regarding each other's mistakes also encourages trust. "If the spouses can be truthful and open about themselves—for example, if a husband can admit he is afraid that he is failing at his job instead of attacking his wife for spending too much money—mutual support and helpfulness are possible" (Lederer & Jackson, p. 108). By contrast, it can be deadly for one person to tell the other something in confidence and then get it back later as an attack. Lynch (1980) provides the example of a man who tells his wife, "I was so depressed I couldn't go to work today. I walked along the beach crying." Two days later, his wife says harshly, "Well, what did you do today—go to the beach again?"

Lynch goes on to comment, "I like to say there are sixteen nails in the coffin of every relationship. An experience that shatters trust, like the one above, is one nail. When those 16 nails are used up, the relationship is dead, and there's nothing so dead as a dead relationship. You can't revive the magic. God knows we've all tried."

Trust between two people increases to the degree that we mutually give and receive without worrying about being exploited or "measuring" how much we get. When we do feel exploited, we can give each other clear statements about it without being afraid we'll be rejected or discounted. When we feel discounted or hurt, we can assume that the other's intention was not malicious and work to clear things up rather than seek revenge. Trust is also fostered when we feel able to acknowledge our misguided judgments, mistaken responses, and shaky feelings without fear of being punished.

Trust, Closeness, and Autonomy

At times, we fear getting too close to others. We might worry about our mobility, our freedom, or the responsibility for the other person's well-being. If I've learned to believe that being in a relationship requires diminishing my self-reliance, it's hard for me to reach out now, and tempting for me to sabotage a relationship when it threatens to get too deep.

Studies of especially well-functioning persons show that these people typically display a smoothly working balance of self-reliance and the ability to seek and offer help when the occasion demands. Most of those studied grew up in close families that consistently provided support and encouragement (Bowlby, 1979, pp. 107–109).

In some couples, both people operate as whole, separate people but don't commit much to the relationship. Sometimes this is mutual and sometimes one person is more involved in a couple while the other is more concerned with staying autonomous. Some couples and families function better with much closeness and less independence; others seem to need much independence and less closeness. Still others are endlessly working it out. Problems occur when you try to hide what you want from me, or hide your feelings when you feel that I'm not supporting your self-direction. In a mutual relationship, our self-reliant or self-focused action is complementary to our wanting to be together and our caring about each other. We help each other through hazards on which less mutually respectful and supportive relationships run aground.

Couples can drift apart or explode apart when one person's preoccupation with occupational success becomes so great that he or she invests little energy in being with the other or in enjoying their time together. The mate, closed out of the other's circle of commitment, is left with the symbols but not the substance of what matters most. It's taken me time to learn that my wife, though she thinks my writing and teaching have real value, doesn't love me for it or even care all that much about it. She cares that I spend quality time with her and the family, listen to her, and share my feelings with her. When I skimp on that contact, things deteriorate between us. I feel similarly resentful when she gets so involved in her work that she spends little time with me. In these times, being clear about what I feel and want is hazardous but essential.

SELF-DISCLOSURE*

It's easier to let ourselves be visible when we feel secure and comfortable. When a situation is threatening or painful, we may hide.

*The insights in this section draw heavily on Sidney Jourard's seminal thinking in this area (1968, 1971).

No one is completely closed or completely open. Each of us is closed in certain ways and open in others. In some contexts, closed can mean safe and protected, while open is vulnerable and risking. There are times when I need to be closed and times when I need to be open.

I don't want to give up my defenses. *I want to be able to use them when I need them.* I guard against poison, when that's what someone wants to give me. I close off from doing things I sometimes like to do, if I'm tired or just don't feel like doing them now: Disengaging can be a way I take care of myself and gather my energy for when I need it. I take the best care of myself when, paradoxically, I can retain an open awareness that helps me see *where and how* I want to be observable, and *where and how* I want to be concealed.

My level of openness affects the quality of the contact I make with others. In my teaching, I've discovered that the class that doesn't go well is usually the class in which I haven't opened myself to where the students are, to their needs and directions.

Sometimes the signals from my body fit the present situation and sometimes not. I may close up now in a situation that reminds me of something that was painful in the past, even though the present state of affairs isn't really threatening. At other times my body gives me useful information that my head can use.

When I feel another person being closed toward me, I tend to withhold myself, too. I can feel some of my muscles tense and tighten as my body seems to pull away and close up. Yet if I want to be in touch with that person, it may be up to me to make the first move. I can risk sharing myself. Open communication requires *self-disclosure*. We can do this cautiously at first, verbally and nonverbally with words and gestures, giving each other a measure of access into our interior worlds and implicitly stating our trust in the other's ability to appreciate our commitment.

Many people, says A. L. Scoresby, think they are doing their partner a favor by hiding worry or other intense feelings (1977, pp. 37–38). But most of us, when we share much time with someone, learn the nonverbal signs that something's not all right with the other person. So when I don't share my worries, my wife, sensing the worry, is likely to be mystified by it. "What's eating him, anyway?" By trying to protect her, I cause her to worry, too.

Difficult as it sometimes is, clear self-disclosure can be particularly valuable when we're disengaging from our involvement with someone. During the demise of a relationship in the years before I learned that, the normal confusion and hurt of such an event was compounded by my come-close/go-away double message: "I want to break up, but I don't." Years later, Sally and I, who had lived together for two years, sat looking at each other one autumn morning. As we looked into each other's eyes, both realizing that we were no longer giving each other what we needed, we were straightforward about what we wanted and weren't getting from each other, and what we were not willing to give. The normal pain of separation was not compounded by deception and withholding and now, many years later, we are still good friends.

Other Aspects of Disclosure

Self-disclosure doesn't just mean talking about intensely personal matters. Disclosing trivial but interesting bits of information about myself is one way to start a conversation. If I say too much about things that are deeply personal right at the beginning, you may feel that I'm "coming on too strong" and retreat.

Sometimes very early in a relationship, people may be deeply involved in certain areas. In a weekend romance where both people know they're not likely to see each other again, there isn't time to build up trust slowly. In fleeting conversations with strangers, people are sometimes remarkably candid. And in more normal situations, the "rules" by which we form our impressions of others and calculate our responses to them may be relaxed in exceptional circumstances—like when I am in emotional distress and badly need to talk about it.

Even complaints can be a form of disclosure. Looking back on a recent relationship, Juanita says, "I never told Ramón that it bothered me that he always talked about his ex-girlfriend. I believed that allowing him to talk freely about the situation would help him get over her and his guilt. Now I realize that I should have said how I felt because I just took my frustrations out in other ways."

Limits on Disclosure

If you've brought a lawsuit against me, I'm likely to disclose as little as I can, for your very act of bringing the suit is a statement that you have no faith in our ability to work things out through direct communication. Or if I'm dependent on you in some important way, and afraid you may leave me, fire me, or pass me over for promotion, I'm likely to very selective about my self-disclosure. I'll disclose only those facts that are consistent with the approval I want from you.

Even in my most intimate relationships I'm not always transparent to the people who love me, nor need they always be that completely open with me.

In an interesting study of a work group, one of the two least liked and most maladjusted members was the most secretive and undisclosing person in the group, while the other was the highest discloser (Jourard, 1971b). Those who were better liked and more effective had developed their ability to anticipate how much and what kind of disclosure is appropriate to a given situation.

8

Attribution and Projection

*O*nce I worked as a school psychologist in a community where an Aleutian family had recently arrived. The principal suggested that the boy's hair, which was cut in the traditional Eskimo style, be cut shorter. The father immediately cut off *all* the boy's hair. The next day, Eddie came into the classroom, put his head on his desk and his jacket over his head, and would not come out. This behavior was referred to me as a problem, with the child attached to it.

I made several assumptions about the boy's behavior, including castration fears associated with having his hair cut off and anthropologists' findings that some tribes cut off the hair of a person they are excommunicating. But I got nothing back from the boy that fit any of my interpretations. Finally I asked directly, "Eddie, why do you have your jacket over your head?" He peeked out from under his jacket and replied, "It's cold." When we gave him a knit cap to wear until his hair grew back, he was just fine.

Guessing at each other's thoughts, feelings, motives, and intentions, even when many of the facts are not in, is a universal—and useful—process. We need to predict each other's actions, determine the sequence of events, and make sense of our experience. All this guides our own behavior: In large measure I act toward you in ways that fit who I imagine you to be. I may not realize that my assumption or interpretation is a guess. I may conclude that it's a fact—and may have a strong commitment to viewing it as such. I could infer that things are as I want them to be, or as I'm afraid they are—without knowing that I'm doing that. Or I may apply habitual ways of responding to others from my past to you in the present.

Therein lies the central issue of the present chapter: how to recognize our biases in guessing others' motives, feelings, and intentions, and how to minimize them and become more accurate. Social psychologists call this the *correspondence* between our attributions—our assignment of meanings—and the events in others we hope they reflect. When correspondence is high, I'm on target. When it's low, I'm not (Jones & Davis, 1965).

ELEMENTS OF ATTRIBUTION

There are, notes social psychologist Harold H. Kelley (1967, 1972a, 1972b, 1973; Kelley & Michela, 1980), two different contexts in which we infer what's going on in others. I may observe you just once, in only one situation, or at different times in various situations. In the first case, says Kelley, I compare your behavior to the way I'd expect others to act in the same situation and base my conclusions largely on that comparison. In the second case, where we have a history of past experience with another person to base our predictions on, Kelley suggests that we look for unique circumstances—some situation or other person—that are present when a person behaves in a certain way and absent at other times. For example, you're occasionally depressed, and I worry that it's something I've done. Eventually I begin to realize that your depression almost always occurs just after you've talked to your ex-husband. Checking out that guess with you and finding that it's right, I stop worrying that it's something I've done.

There are three rules we often use in drawing conclusions about others. The first is *distinctiveness*. If Ellen is extremely friendly with several different people, I may conclude that she's affectionate by nature. If she's much friendlier with Derek than with others, I conclude that she feels something special for him.

Distinctive actions tell us more about someone than conventional ones. There are many reasons for acting conventionally, including social and environmental pressures. But someone who acts unexpectedly is almost certain to have some personal, internal reason. When someone acts out of role, for instance—like a general taking an antinuclear position—we're apt to think we know more about the person and to have more confidence in our conclusions (Jones, Gergen & Davis, 1962; Katz & Burnstein, 1973).

A second rule, *consensus*, states that if most people would act as you did, I'm likely to conclude that the situation had a powerful influence on you. This is recognized in court, where killing in self-defense has a special status: We assume that when one's life is threatened by another, anyone might do the same.

The consensus rule also suggests that I'll be more comfortable with my guesses about you if others have drawn the same conclusions—as when somebody says, "I was going to call you at home and the secretary said it would be all right."

The third rule, *consistency*, has to do with whether you act similarly in different situations or at different times.

We tend to organize our views of others so that all the elements fit together into a consistent pattern—even if accuracy suffers. In one study, six out of ten people who viewed a film ignored important scenes when they wrote descriptions of the major character, in order to portray her in a consistent way (Gollin, 1954). Norman Anderson (1978) adds that people seek not just logical consistency, but also *emotional consistency*, in their impressions of others. Apparently we prefer not to have mixed feelings.

In the service of consistency, we tend to *discount* other possible causes of someone's behavior once we've seized on a given cause as the likely one.

PROJECTION

I watch what you do, hear what you say, think about it, and weave all this into a guess about what's happening inside you. Then, like a film projector, I project my guess back onto you and assume that it fits your realities. This is attribution.

But when my guess is so strongly shaped by my own needs and motives that it has little to do with you and a great deal to do with what's going on in me, it takes on qualities that go beyond those involved in ordinary attribution. Often this includes attributing behavior and qualities to others that we're unwilling to perceive in ourselves, like the dishonest person who constantly suspects others of dishonesty, or the person who complains of being constantly victimized and proceeds to exploit everyone in sight. Sound familiar?

Freud called this process *projection*. Part of it has a magical giveaway quality: By projecting onto others something distasteful about me, I supposedly no longer have to deal with it in myself. "In projection," says Perls, "We shift the boundary between ourselves and the rest of the world a little too much in our favor—in a manner that makes it possible for us to disavow or disown . . . aspects of our personalities." He linked this process to introjection: When I've internalized some prohibition or "should" to please or appease another, I project the qualities that the introject forbids me to possess.

It's especially important to come to terms with aggressive, hostile impulses. Otherwise we project these impulses onto others and then try to destroy them there because *they* are "evil."

Perls and his coauthors suggest that you can guess what another person is like and *try on that way of being for yourself.* "Think yourself into the shoes of the aggressor, admirer, rejecter, foolhardy one," they suggest (1965, p. 222). How do you feel when you imagine yourself as that person? Do you connect with anything in yourself?

Projecting Our Shadow Sides

When I find myself intolerant of what another person does, I do well to look for ways I do the same, perhaps in a disguised or more sophisticated way. *The things I'm most intolerant of in others tend to be the things I'm most intolerant of in me.*

Karen Horney noted that even love can be projected. Elaborating on her observations, Perls writes: "If you are afraid to express 'I hate you,' you will soon imagine yourself being hated by the world, and likewise if you are too shy to say 'I love you,' you will find yourself expecting love from the world" (1947, p. 242).

I can use my imaginings about others to find out about myself. Often, what I imagine that you're thinking and feeling is what I would think and feel if I were in your place.

Here's something to try:

Projection onto Objects

Pick out an object around you—any ordinary item will do—and imagine you're that object. Think of as many aspects of being it as you can, or of one aspect in depth and detail. If you're with others who are doing the same, pair up with another person and share your experiences. If you're alone, you can conduct a written dialogue with the object to see what it tells you.

In your daily life, you can imagine being different objects at different times and see what common themes stand out.

When I project onto you what I disavow in myself and then judge you harshly for possessing that quality, I poison our relationship and hinder my own ability to grow. I find "proof" that what I see in you is really there by giving the smallest detail great significance. The projector is amazingly talented at elaborating, exaggerating, and dismissing contradictory evidence, and needs just one confirming instance to feel total certainty—"Aha! I knew it all the time!"

We also project what we admire. A woman who thinks she's weak, for instance, may see people she's attracted to as strong, whether they really are or not. As I find out what I'm projecting, I get in touch with strengths within myself that I've been unaware of.

Transference and Displacement

Without recognizing it, sometimes we act toward a person as though he or she were someone from our past—like a former spouse, lover, or parent. When I do that with you, I see mostly the image I project on you, and little of who you actually are. Freud called this process *transference*. I transfer my way of relating to someone else onto my relationship with you. A wife, for instance, may transfer some of her feelings toward her father onto her husband. Sexual feelings toward her husband get confused with sexual taboos involving her father, and she may experience some confusion regarding her own sexuality.

Transference can play a crucial role in counseling when, as often happens, a client transfers unresolved feelings toward a parent onto the counselor and then resolves them in that situation. Subsequently, the client comes to perceive the relationship with the parent more clearly and no longer needs to confuse others with him or her.

As adults, we may learn how we've misread our parents. As we discover how our projections influenced our "knowing," we can appreciate our parents as people in their own right.

No situation of later life is more like our childhood family than our intimate relationships—especially our connection with a mate and with children. Many of the patterns and dramas of our early years are likely to be rerun. In my present family, for example, I might throw a temper tantrum much as I did at the age of two—something I wouldn't do with my associates at work. And in certain ways, I expect my mate to care for me as my parents cared for me, evoking memories of comforting from long ago.

A certain amount of this feels all right to me. But if my "internal" experience of you—influenced by my adult experience as well as my recollection of childhood—is so strong that I can't see through it to contact you as you are, we're in for trouble. Then I'm likely to distort what I hear you say so that it sounds like what I expect you to say—*even when it's not what you're saying*—without realizing that I'm doing this. To the extent that I do this, I live in a world of imaginary people whose motives and intentions, feelings and messages I've changed in my mind to fit my historical expectations.

When I *overtly act* toward you in ways that were meant for someone else, it's called *displacement*. Displacement of aggression is especially common. I can't beat up father, but I can beat up little brother. I'm afraid to talk back to my boss, but I can be nasty to my mate. I do cruel things to you that are really meant for the big kids who used to torment me when I was small. Transference and displacement are often linked.

Self-Consciousness and Projection

When we feel self-conscious, suggests Perls, we act as if we have no eyes. I'm so anxious about what you think of me that I see almost nothing about you. I've projected my eyes onto you, and from there I look back at myself, criticizing and belittling what I see.

We can also act as if we have no ears, not hearing ourselves but worrying about how others hear us. In Perls's words, "People expect the ears to be outside and they talk and expect someone to listen. But who listens?" (1969a, pp. 36–37).

When I'm caught up in my own mind, I have little attention left to perceive what's outside me. Embarrassed about not knowing what's going on, I pretend. Then I become self-conscious because I'm faking my way through and I'm afraid someone might find me out.

Fortunately, this process is reversible. The more energy I put into observing what's going on, the less energy I divert into covering up. I can tell I'm coming out of one of the whirlpools in my mind when I begin to see and hear again.

With a group of people, try this:

Owning Your Projected Eyes

Clear a space so a person can walk all the way across the room. Half of the group stands on one side of the room, half on the opposite side.

One at a time, each of you walks from one end of the room to the other, stopping in the middle to say your name.

The others learn what they can about who you are by watching your walk and body language and listening to how you say your name.

Notice how you feel as you make this statement of yourself with all those eyes on you. When everyone has done this, take some time to discuss how you felt. Don't read on until you've finished your discussion.

Have you finished your discussion? Now each of you go back, walk across the room, and speak your name once more—with one difference.

This time, while you're walking look carefully at the other people standing there. See what they're doing, how they're standing, etc. Do you feel any different? How? Again share your feelings with the others.

Next time you walk into a room and feel self-conscious, stop, take a deep slow breath, and feel your breathing and your whole body. Then, really look at and listen to the other people there, *learning all you can about them.* As you do, your self-consciousness is likely to diminish.

Next time you start to worry about what someone else is thinking of you, stop and consider how much you've been observing that person. Have you been watching him or her closely? Probably not. You've been largely involved in your own concerns. The same is likely to be true of others around you. Each person is too busy wondering how he or she is coming across to have much time to pay attention to *you.*

Projection and Unmet Needs

Projections can grow out of unmet or unresolved needs for acceptance, affection, power, or other qualities. Remember those stencils you can trace letters or spray paint through? If I hold one up and look through it, I see only what's visible through the cutout letters. Boszormenyi-Nagy (1965a, p. 46) suggests that due to unmet needs, sometimes we act as if we're carrying around such a stencil, tacking it onto anyone we meet who's even vaguely appropriate. We perceive only what's visible through it. If I view others through a "paranoid" stencil, for instance, I tend to experience them as critical, punitive, dangerous, or "out to get me."

Projection is often involved when a person feels rejected. Unaware that I'm rejecting others—whether by keeping my distance, by pushing others away with putdowns and hostility, by talking only about surface trivia, or in yet other ways—I imagine that others are rejecting me. I may need contact and affection, but I'm afraid people would turn away if I reached out, smother me if they did respond, or hurt me even more deeply if I were to open up to some connection. But since I convince myself that the other person has "rejected me," I don't need to deal with any of those issues. If you think others don't want to be with you, *be attentive to how you withdraw and keep others away.*

The projection process, notes Boszormenyi-Nagy, is strongest in people who are doing a poor job of taking care of their own and each other's emotional needs. In an ongoing relationship, if my reality is not so nourishing, I may imagine you taking care of me as I was or wanted to be taken care of in the past. I still mourn the loss of idealized mothering and fathering figures of my childhood and fantasize that you can provide for me as I "remember" them doing—instead of working out mutually supportive behavior with the *real* you.

People sometimes expect a child to meet emotional needs that the spouse isn't meeting. To keep the parent's love and approval, the child may try to meet the parent's wish. Melody, for instance, was divorced the year after her younger daughter was born. Overindulged as a child, Melody treated her own children as "little adults" who could not only take care of her emotional needs, but some of her physical needs too. Her oldest daughter Heather became the one who washed the dishes, kept the house clean, made lunch for everyone, etc. Theodore Lidz (1963) calls this *crossing the generation boundaries*—Melody switched generational roles with her daughters. Now at eighteen, Heather reflects sadly, "I never had a chance to be a little kid. I was busy being responsible and taking care of Mom." In some ways she's still stuck emotionally at a child's level—just like Melody.

Another side of this issue is *resenting you for neglecting my needs* now just as they were neglected in the past—whether or not you're really neglecting me now. Sometimes this is explicit: "You're just like my father. How do I deserve not just one good-for-nothing male in one lifetime, but two?" Sometimes repressed hate and wishes for revenge toward a parent are displaced onto a spouse or child with violent and tragic consequences, as in child abuse.

If you and I behave as described here, our relationship is in large measure a shadow play of mutual projections, as we each serve as a stimulus to the other for replaying our old tapes. When we start to work at making present-day contact aimed at finding ways to meet our emotional needs in the present, we begin to be genuine companions for each other who can offer accommodation, acceptance, richness, and depth.

HOW OUR ATTRIBUTIONS GO ASTRAY

We can easily get stuck on assumptions that are distortions: "I know what you mean! . . . Don't try to tell me you didn't mean that! . . . You knew very well what I wanted!" If I hold to my mistaken assumption despite your protests, we're headed for trouble.

Among the things that can contribute to the distortions we sometimes cling to so tenaciously are these:

1. *Strong emotional needs* that are not necessarily in line with other people's realities. When our insecurities are strong enough, our attributions tend to be in directions that support or assuage them. Strong investment in our hopes or fears can also bias our inferences.

2. *"Mind reading" while neglecting to check out our conclusions.* People like to play "mind reader" . . . especially amateur psychologists. Reading meanings into what others say, we act on the basis of our interpretations. When our expectations are not fulfilled, we may identify those persons as being resistant, avoidant, or fixated. This is a good way to drive each other crazy.

Just as I may imagine that I'm unerring as I guess what's happening in you, I may expect you to be omniscient in your guesses about me—and take it as evidence of indifference if you're not.

"You should have *known!* You must not care for me very much if you didn't even know *that!*"

"But you never told me!"

"That doesn't *matter.* I shouldn't have to tell you a thing like that. You should just *understand!*"

You keep on refusing to tell me explicitly what you're thinking and feeling, and at the same time you feel hurt and angry because I don't understand how you feel or what you want. In fact, I can love you but not be able to read your subtle signals. If we both recognize that, you don't build up resentment about my misreading you, and I don't build up resentment about your not telling me what you're dealing with. When I want to know, I ask. When you want me to know what you're experiencing, you tell me—and vice versa.

3. *Preconceptions and expectations.* These can lead us to ignore or distort the evidence of our experience. In a dramatic experiment, Kelley (1950) gave students written descriptions of a person who was scheduled to present a guest lecture. The descriptions were identical except for one word: The speaker was characterized in some as "warm" and in others as "cold." Then the guest lecturer came in and led a class discussion. Afterwards, those told he was "warm" were much more approving than those told he was "cold," even though all had listened to the same person lead the same discussion!

4. *The "false consensus bias"* leads us to assume that most other people think, feel, and act pretty much as we do, and that those who behave differently are deviant. A parent who batters his or her child, for instance, is more likely than others to believe that such abuse is common. And students who agreed to wear a large "Eat at Joe's" sign around their college campus for thirty minutes were twice as likely to think most other students would agree to do the same as were students who refused. That's why the Deltas of the movie *Animal House* got into such trouble. Wouldn't everybody want to have a toga party (Goldstein, 1981; Ross, 1977; Ross, Greene & House, 1977)?

5. *The "self is positive, other is negative" bias.* To maintain our self-images and justify our actions, we tend to take credit for positive actions by us and others, but to hold others responsible for negative ones. Finger pointing becomes an act of self-purification.

6. *"Impression management" by the other person.* You may be playing a role and trying to lead me to believe it reflects who you are at a deeper level when in fact it doesn't—and you aren't (Goffman, 1959; Jones, 1964).

7. *Lack of crucial information.* I simply may not have the data I need to accurately infer how you're responding. My confusion may be a guide to my need for information yet interfere with my information gathering.

8. *The "availability bias."* The information most readily available about someone may influence us most, whether or not it's the most important or most accurate. "Primacy" and "recency" effects are relevant here: What I learned about you first and/or what I've found out most recently may affect my impressions more than the knowledge I've gathered in between.

9. *Distancing language.* This is a way I distort my attributions about *myself*—a way I project, and thereby disown, my power and responsibility. Fran, for example, says: "And then you notice that the years are going by and you have a hard time being in meaningful contact with other people and it's just like you're in a bad dream . . ." Substituting *I* for *you* changes the personal relevance of the statement. Fran really meant, "*I* notice; *I* have a hard time; it's like *I'm* in a bad dream." She was out of touch with herself as the doer of what she did.

One is usually also the projective form: "One thinks that . . ." protects me from my responsibility for "I think that . . ." and so on. And there's also, "Some people say . . ." and "Everybody knows that. . . ." We can likewise disown thoughts and feelings by using the word *it,* or an equivalent. My "temper" possesses me. My temper is an *it.* Instead, I can use "I-language" to reaffirm, at least in speech, my projected power and responsibility. So instead of "A compulsion to scream enters my mind," I say "*I feel like screaming.*" Instead of "A wall separates me from other people," I say "*I push people away.*"

HIGH-INTEREST INFERENCE CHECKING

Accurate attributions are derived from what we see, sense, and hear. People who are mistaken are usually those who close themselves to changing their ideas when new information comes along.

Suppose I meet someone I'd like to talk with, but she seems distant. If I assume it's because she doesn't like me, I may be right or wrong. Perhaps her car just died, and that's why she's distracted. By asking if something is bothering her, I'm less likely to misinterpret her response.

To check out an attribution directly, I ask you if what I'm assuming is so. I might say something like, "I think I'm hearing you say. . . ." Since I'm stating my inference out loud in a clear, accepting way, you may be less hesitant about responding. If my guess is wrong, clarify as you wish. Of course, such an exchange will be effective only if I seem responsive and available. If I sound intolerant or accusatory, if you're smart you'll stay closed.

Even in a longstanding relationship, *at almost any point I can start asking what's happening with you even though I haven't been asking up until now.* There's almost always room for a new beginning.

The way I ask can be very important. In a marriage counseling session, the husband became irate when his wife asked, "Where are you now?" He thought she was probing and poking, attacking him and implying, "You're being secretive."

"Is that how you feel?" I asked her.

"No," she replied. She began to look for a statement about herself that would reach her husband and came up with: "I need to hear you now."

He replied, "That feels good. I can respond to that and not feel probed at."

The same principle is equally important for parent and child, teacher and student.

Here's a valuable exercise to help you learn to distinguish what you see, sense, and hear from what you imagine and intuit. As you become able to tell the difference between what someone else sees you doing and what they guess about you, you'll be less easily sucked in by the misconceptions other people form about you.

 I See—I Imagine

Sit facing another person, no more than a couple of feet apart.

First, one of you takes five minutes to observe the other and state aloud what you observe and what you guess about him or her. Your observations are what you actually see and hear with your senses: for instance, "I see you scratching your face," "I hear your voice quivering," "I see that your shirt is worn and patched." Your guesses are what you imagine about your partner: "I imagine that your face itches," "I'm guessing that you're a little scared doing this," "I infer that you're living on a very low budget," "You look pleased—I'll 'own' that." These are your attributions, identified as such.

Your partner corrects you whenever you confuse imaginings with observations. For example, "I see that you're very tired." "No. You *see* my eyelids drooping and my body slumping, and you *guess* that I'm tired." While this is going on, your partner does not give feedback about whether your guesses are right, but just points out any guess that's stated as an *observation—even if the guess is correct.*

After you're confident that you can clearly and reliably distinguish between your direct observations on one hand and your imaginings, intuitings, and projections on the other, you might try intentionally "sliding by" guesses disguised as observations. See if you can trick the other person into accepting your guess as an observation: for example, "I see that you're happy right now." But if your partner is sharp, he or she will reply, "No, you *see* that I'm smiling, and from that you imagine that I'm happy."

After five minutes, switch roles and repeat the exercise. When you've both had your turn, you can talk about your experiences—and check on any guesses you're especially curious about.

Take the full five minutes each. If you feel awkward and uncomfortable, *just keep doing it* and it will start to get more comfortable. And don't worry; the most mundane and ordinary observations are profound.

Sometimes a person maintains that his or her feelings, actions, and intentions are different than I've concluded that they are. My experience is that *there is no value in trying to convince you that your inner events are as I say they are.*

Some people ask, "Won't checking out my attributions interfere with using my intuition?" No. Learning to distinguish between your actual sensory data and your inferences lets you avoid confusing your observations with your imaginings and helps you check out inferences based on your data rather than assuming that the inferences *are* the data. The better I get at checking out my attributions, the more I can rely on my intuitive intelligence. *My intuition is most trustworthy when I'm tuned into all the cues that might give me information.* Intuition includes both being sensitive to all the data another person provides and being adept at piecing it together into a multidimensional picture by drawing on faculties that are deeper and more mysterious than my conscious intelligence alone. I want to use my intuition when it serves me well and not enshrine it when I'm off the mark.

Another useful insight lies in Zajonc's (1960) contrast between *transmission tuning,* in which I expect to have to transmit my impression of someone to others, and *reception tuning,* in which I expect to receive more information about the person. Cohen (1964) found that people who were told to be ready to describe their impressions to others were more likely to form a consistent impression and ignore information that contradicted it. People instructed to be ready for more information were more receptive to data that didn't fit the impression they'd already formed. Apparently, when we're not under pressure to draw quick inferences, we're better off to withhold judgment and adopt an attitude of wanting to learn more.

9

Talking and Listening

*W*e hear more in the words that we and others use when we listen to the music as well as to the lyrics. The fullest and richest communication typically involves listening for the feelings, meanings, and intentions that underlie the words we hear (and checking out what we think we're hearing to avoid getting stuck in mind reading).

Communication theorists Richard Bandler and John Grinder distinguish between the *surface structure* (what's explicit) and the *deep structure* (what's hidden or latent) of our communication (1975, pp. 59–60). When you speak, the experiences your words evoke in me are to some degree *different from* the experiences that led you to form those words. In Bandler and Grinder's usage, *deep structure* refers not to the actual experiences that underlie our words, but to a *complete verbal description* of the main features of those experiences. Here we refer to that as the *verbal deep structure* and reserve the term *deep structure* for our memories and feelings themselves. They use *surface structure* just as it's used here: for our actual words. "I'm scared" may be the surface structure of an event that has as its verbal deep structure "I'm scared of my mate when we argue intensely and emotionally."

To recover the verbal deep structure from the surface structure, the basic question is, "What's left out?" For instance, suggest Bandler and Grinder, read the following sentence, then close your eyes and notice the visual image it calls up: "Mary hurt me."

Examine your image. What did you supply for "hurt"? Did you envision Mary slapping someone, or making a snide and sarcastic remark, or . . . ? What you saw in your mind was *something you added* to the surface structure. You supplied it because it was *deleted*—left out. Once you realize that *you don't know* what Mary did, you can ask the speaker to describe how, where, and when Mary hurt him. "Mary dropped her bowling ball on my toe" eliminates the previous ambiguity. Here are more examples of deletions:

Surface Structure	What's Missing
I'm fed up. Enough already.	With what or whom. When?
You're disturbing.	Disturbing whom? How?
My husband claimed he was frightened.	Claimed to whom? Frightened by whom? How? When?
Running away doesn't help.	From what? Help whom or what? Ever?

Much of the rest of this chapter is devoted to finding ways of coming closer to hearing other people's deep structures and of presenting our own more clearly.

TALKING

When I'm trying to say how I feel or what I want and you don't hear me, I may assume that you don't care about me and I feel hurt, distracted, or angry. In friendships, couples, families, workplaces, or classrooms, when people don't listen to each other's feelings, someone is likely to use cheating, drinking, running away, temper tantrums, bed wetting, playing sick, or hurting less powerful people to express the feelings that aren't being talked about. That's called *acting out* our emotions. We act out our feelings when we think we can't discuss them.

Talking with and Talking At

My tone of voice, rhythm of speech, lack of contact with your thoughts and feelings, or sense of your distractedness may tell me that I'm talking *at* you. At that point, I can listen to what you're saying verbally or nonverbally, make eye contact if I haven't been doing that, and start talking *with* you in a way that becomes our shared reality.

When you talk *at* me, by broadcasting loudly or mumbling so softly that I have to strain to hear you, I imagine that you're talking primarily for yourself and indirectly to me. If you talk *with* me and want me to hear you, I feel valued. You care.

One way I talk *at* you is by saying many of my words automatically, like programmed speeches off a tape. I may get center stage and a few nods or "uh-huhs" of appreciation while I'm playing my tape for the eleventh time.

Another way I talk *at* you is by trying to sell you my point of view. The real answer to the question, "Who are you trying to convince?" is often, "Myself."

Yet another way of talking *at* people is with sarcasm. I've sharply reduced my use of sarcasm since I noticed that people typically close up and become defensive in response to it. Like "playful teasing," sarcasm often hurts.

When three or more of us are together, speaking to anyone *about* someone else who's present is *gossiping*. Instead, I can make my statement *to* the person it's meant for. For instance, rather than saying, "Jean, I think Tim was unfair to you just then," I say, "Tim, I think that was unfair." This principle of *"no gossiping"* can increase directness and clarity.

We can talk *with* each other even in brief exchanges. Going through the checkout stand at the market, I might distractedly comment on the weather while I'm thinking about something else entirely. By contrast, if I take a moment to look clearly at the checker, I may perceive a little about him or her. Then I might say, "You look energetic," or "I like your necklace." If my words touch the other person, we have a moment of genuine contact and both feel good.

While you're speaking, I might think of something I "must" say and have a hard time holding back until I've heard you out. That can lead to statements like, "Sorry I interrupted you, but I was afraid I'd forget what I was going to say." I do well to remember that you're not hearing while I'm interfering.

Occasionally I get extremely annoyed when others interrupt me. I'm finding it easier these days to raise a finger and say, "Wait, I'm not done. I'd like to finish." or "I feel interrupted." I need, of course, to accept that kind of assertion from you, too, and to make my statement concise enough that others have time to speak. When I ramble on, I'm inviting interruption.

Questions and Statements

Substantive questions are attempts to get information and share communication. Effective questioning involves inquiry that leads to interested sharing.

There's a difference between *closed questions* and *open-ended* questions. A closed question can usually be answered in a word or two: "What time is it?" It does little to develop a conversation. An open-ended question invites a fuller reply: "What do you have planned for today?"

If a question is intended to convey your feelings or viewpoint, criticize another person's actions, or keep the other person talking and allow you to withdraw, it's not a true question but a *statement in disguise.* For instance, in the question, "Why did you spill that all over the kitchen floor?" the real message may be the statement, "I'm upset and angry that you spilled that."

Disguising my statement as a question allows me to cloud my own position. That makes me less vulnerable to attack. But there are unfortunate side effects. The most important of these is that *my real statement may never get across to you.* For example, Susan would like Frank to take her out to dinner. The "questions only" dialogue lets everybody play it "safe":

"Frank, do you want to go out to dinner tonight?"

Susan is really saying that she'd like to go out to dinner. Frank, not realizing that, replies,

"I don't know. Why don't we stay home and fix something here?"

"Why don't we ever go out anymore?" retorts Susan.

"What do you mean we never go out? Didn't we go out just last week?"

Susan's voice grows sharp: "Do you *really* think once a week is enough?"

Frank (irritated): "Does it *matter* if we go out to dinner or not?"

Susan (pouting): "Don't you *want* to take me out?"

If Susan had presented her statement as such, the exchange might have gone:

"I want to go out to dinner tonight."

"Okay, where would you like to go?"—or, "I'm not feeling up to it. I can make us something."

Questions disguised as statements often come across as attacks—especially "Why did you . . . ?" questions. As the other person defends, the conflict escalates.

Next time you're tempted to ask "why?" ask "how?" or "what?" instead. Rather than "Why do you think you do that?" ask, "Specifically, *what* do you do? *How* are you doing it?" Or even "When/where do you do it?" With these questions, notice how your experience is different than when you ask "why?"

My communication becomes clearer when I learn to make clear statements, to detect others' statements disguised as questions, and to *respond to the statements instead of getting hooked by the questions.* I can ignore the red herring question and say, "You sound upset. Is that right?" Or if the person is familiar with the idea of statements that hide beneath questions, "I think I hear a statement. What is it?"

Questions and Statements

This is a group exercise, but individuals can do Part A, perhaps writing two or three sentences of each kind instead of only one.

A. Divide into groups of three people. Using the topic of "Intimacy" as a starting point (or choosing any other topic that interests your group), each group is to write three sentences. These should include one real question, one real statement, and one statement disguised as a question. You'll have about ten minutes for this. When you're finished, each person in your group should possess a piece of paper bearing one of the three sentences.

B. When all groups have their three statements, get back together with the larger group. Now each person will read the sentence he or she holds: a statement, question, or statement disguised as a question. Others tell which of the three they think it is. The person who reads it agrees or disagrees. If a listener thinks a question masks a statement and the reader disagrees, the reader can ask the listener, "What do you think is the underlying statement?" An example: The apparent question, "Don't you think women have a greater need than men to share their feelings?" is hiding the statement, "I think. . . ."

(Some questions may be ambivalent, open to interpretation as either real questions or questions disguised as statements.)

Repetition

One way to make sure you hear me when I'm saying something I consider important is to repeat my own message as many times as necessary to make sure it gets across. For example, Jill enters the room where Andy is sitting morosely in the corner. "Andy, how are you?"

"Not so good. I'd like some time alone right now."

"It's good to see you. I'm sorry you haven't been well."

"I really don't feel like visiting now. I'd rather be alone."

"Of course. But first, let's get you nice and comfortable."

"Jill, let me say it again. I want to be alone."

"Just lie here and I'll go put on some hot water."

"Jill, perhaps you didn't hear me clearly. *I want to be alone.*"

"Oh, you want to be by yourself right now! Let me know when you're ready for company."

"Okay. That'll be great."

So repetition can sometimes help get a message across. And if we've agreed to give each other acknowledgments that "I hear you" or the equivalent once we've understood, we don't need to be afraid of boring each other with the repetition.

Clear and Concise—With Spice

Writer Rasa Gustaitis reports that, after trying unsuccessfully to engage Fritz Perls in chitchat, she said, "You're impossible to communicate with."

"Communicate what?" was his reply.

Many people never pause when they're talking. They run each sentence into the next, stringing them together with "ands," "buts," and "sos." I have a hard time staying with such a person's line of thought for long. I need a moment to let the image evoked by each statement form in my mind. Perls used to ask people who talk in run-on sentences to say "period" after each sentence, and then breathe before starting another one.

We can also get rid of *fillers* that can turn a simple comment into a torrent of words. Some fillers are short, like "You know," "I mean." Others are long: "Well, I guess if I were really to look at it from that angle, I could see where that might make some kind of genuine sense in the particular situation at hand." I could rephrase that sentence, "That makes sense to me," and lose nothing.

In addition, we can avoid gratuitous remarks that do nothing to improve communication but can make someone feel bad, like, "Ready at last? It's about time."

This is especially important in close relationships. Research has consistently shown that married people are ruder to each other than they are to strangers. They interrupt their spouses more, put them down more, and hurt their feelings more. Extending courtesy and graciousness in our close relationships, and "editing out" gratuitous insults, is a small measure that can go hand in hand with constructive assertion. For instance, as Ogden Nash succinctly states, "To keep your marriage brimming with love . . . when you're wrong, admit it; when you're right, shut up!"

HABITS THAT INTERFERE WITH LISTENING

> *When I ask you to listen to me*
> *and you start giving me advice,*
> *you have not done what I asked.*
> *When I ask you to listen to me*
> *and you begin to tell me why*
> *I shouldn't feel that way,*
> *you are trampling on my feelings.*
> *When I ask you to listen to me*
> *and you feel you have to do something*

to solve my problem,
you have failed me,
strange as that may seem.
Listen! All I asked was that you listen,
not to talk or do—just hear me . . .
And if you want to talk, wait a minute
for your turn—and I'll listen to you.
(Original source unknown)

Shifting the Spotlight

When I was younger, if I had something to say, I left little room for anyone else to speak. My voice was loud enough to ride over other people's comments and *I got my thing said.* In so doing, I defeated my purpose: People were so resentful that they didn't hear what I said.

The greatest obstacle to effective listening, I eventually discovered, is *getting caught in our own thoughts.* I hear your first sentence or two, then tune out and go into my own ideas and fantasies until your voice tells me you're about finished. Then I tune back in, so I can say my thing. Thus we talk back and forth past each other, each obsessed with our own concerns and hardly hearing the other person's.

The *challenge of listening* is to not take the focus off the other person. In listening, the other person's needs, feelings, and issues are central. When each of us keeps *shifting the spotlight* back to our own concerns, without responding directly to the other person's, I may be near you, but I don't hear you.

Invisibility

Making the other person invisible goes a step farther than "shifting the spotlight." It may involve changing the subject completely after you've said something as if you had never spoken. Or others in a group may make you invisible by ignoring your comments completely.

Snap Judgments

Once I make a snap judgment, I close myself to further information that might challenge it. I'm sure I'm right (so don't bother me with reality!).

I can stop listening by "knowing" what you're going to say before you say it, so I use my listening time preparing a reply instead of taking in your full meaning. Or I may cut you off and finish your sentences for you. When I let you finish them yourself, how different what you say often is from what I was anticipating. How dare you!!

Or I may dispute a detail that has little to do with your real meaning—getting "caught in the words" instead of listening for your meaning and intention.

Advising and Analyzing

One person seldom solves another's problems. No matter how sure I am about what you should do, or how much insight I think I have into your problems, ultimately you must make your own decisions . . . including whether to take my advice.

Psychiatrist Eric Berne (1978) describes the game "Why don't you—yes, but" in which someone asks for advice and then turns down every suggestion: "No, that won't work either, because . . ." The request for advice is actually a request for attention rather than an attempt to solve the problem.

A person may also seek advice as a way to avoid responsibility for his or her decisions. If I tell you what to do and things go wrong—well, it wasn't your responsibility. But if things go right, you miss out on developing the trust in yourself that comes from your own decision making and problem solving. Besides, *I* don't want the responsibility for your actions if you do what I tell you to. I can tell you what I do and that has its limited value. I may share information you lack to help you in your decision. Generally, what I earn as a sage is a minimum wage—very little payoff.

One or more of the reflective listening responses to be described shortly may be useful when someone seems to be asking for advice. It encourages a person to come up with his or her own answers.

When I still follow my old impulse to "make recommendations," the other person may fall silent, with a distant look that tells me I'm way off the mark. Surrendering my omniscience, I can acknowledge that perhaps I don't yet understand his or her situation, but want to. I feed back what I think I've heard, get a "yes" or a "no" and a clarification, and we go on from there. Even when my first reaction was insensitive, if I show that I care and want to understand, the other person usually responds.

When someone is wondering how to handle a disturbing matter, we can remember that people tend to deal with distressed feelings most effectively when those feelings are *recognized, voiced,* and then *heard* by a sympathetic listener (Livingston, 1979).

Analyzing another person rarely has value for anyone. Overzealous psychology students sometimes have a disconcerting tendency to constantly interpret your behavior and you're apt to get self-conscious. The more I dissect you, the less I'm likely to hear how your world is for you. When I'm not so busy analyzing you with my head, I can hear you with my heart.

Walt, a high-tech exec, kept encouraging Brenda to talk to him, but when she told him her feelings, he'd reply with a "That does not compute" attitude. After a while she began to give him only the kind of information he was asking for, which was thinking data he could handle through his computer. Through counseling, Walt learned that in his business as well as in his personal life, he can deal with his own and other people's feelings as well as with profit and loss.

EFFECTIVE LISTENING

People want to be listened to in matters important to *them.* When others know I'm hearing them fully, including the tone, the level of urgency, and what they want from me, they're usually more receptive to me in return.

The Role of Intentions in Listening

The meanings I respond to may not be the meanings you intend. As Karen recalls, "After an early trip to the post office, I bought some doughnuts on my way home. Ken got up, looked at the doughnuts, and asked, 'Is this supposed to be breakfast?' I heard, 'Is *this* supposed to be *breakfast?*' I went on a tirade: 'If you want a big breakfast, just say so instead of bitching about the doughnuts I was thoughtful enough to pick up,' etc. . . . He calmly explained that he thought maybe I'd bought them for my class at school and wanted to make sure they were for us."

Confusing one intention for another can lead to hurt and anger. When that happens, I can *clarify my intention,* as Ken did about the doughnuts: "What I wanted was. . . ." And checking on your intention before I get locked into a "position" pays off. "The message I got is . . . Is that what you meant?"

By noticing the kinds of mistakes in inferring intentions I consistently make, I can identify my areas of oversensitivity and "deafness."

Content and Relationship Messages. The essential point of a message may lie either in its explicit content or in some statement it makes, perhaps "between the lines," about the relationship between the speaker and the listener. Some people, point out Watzlawick, Beavin and Jackson (1967), take everything as a relationship message to the point where it interferes with hearing content. We're more likely to do this the more unsure we are—about ourselves or in the relationship. If you're busy and say "no" when I ask you to do the dishes, I don't have to assume that you don't love me. After all, since I sent you a content message, it's reasonable to assume that you're responding on the same level—that you're rejecting not me, but the dishes.

Hidden Agendas. Can you recall a recent discussion that seemed to restate the same problem without getting anywhere? Or one in which the other person seemed to be talking around something that was never quite said? Or one where you had a deeper concern that you didn't mention? An important issue that remains beneath the surface is called a *hidden agenda.* For example, a couple talks of Michelangelo as the hour grows late, though the main event for both of them is heated hormones.

Gottman and colleagues (1976, pp. 83–104) describe some common hidden agendas. The first is *caring:* Whatever the content of a statement, the other person infers a relationship message of "my partner feels . . . toward me." The hidden meaning in the statement, "There's a piece of pie in your lunch bag," might be, "I love you and want to make you happy" . . . or the reverse may be true, fatso.

A second hidden agenda involves *responsiveness* or *interest:* My partner isn't interested in me and doesn't make room for us to spend enough time together. A mate's sharp "I don't know" when asked where the paper is might mean, "I wish you'd talk with me more and read the paper less."

A third common hidden agenda involves *power:* "I'm in control," or "I have no voice in decisions." A child might correctly or incorrectly translate the parent's message, "I wish we could keep the house a little cleaner," as, "I expect you to do what I tell you to."

A fourth hidden agenda involves *identity:* statements of self-definition that somehow declare, "I want you to recognize who I am."

The hidden agenda may be as real as the observed or working agenda. If powerful enough, it can stop progress in any other area until it's dealt with. When I suspect that you have a hidden agenda, I want to check it out and, if possible, make it an open agenda.

Reflective Listening Skills

Carl Rogers has suggested several listening skills that are extremely useful. These *reflective listening* techniques involve stating the other person's ideas and feelings as you hear them.

If I'm unclear about what you said, I can ask you to repeat it before I try reflection. For example, "I didn't quite get that. Will you please repeat it?" And if I still don't understand, I say, "I still didn't get it. Try it again in different words."

Sometimes when a message comes through jumbled, the speaker may not want it to be clear. Maybe the real message is, "I promised the job to somebody else, but I don't want to say so."

Or: "No, I don't want to go out with you again, but I'm embarrassed to just tell you that."

In those cases, it's as if the message has a lot of wrapping paper around it. At that point, I can peel away the paper and repeat back to you what I think your message is. I might say, "I think you just said you have someone else in mind for the job." Or in the other example, "I think you just said you feel like we don't quite connect, and you don't want to make a date with me." If I say this in a way that lets you know I can hear the message without falling apart, it gives you the options of confirming, denying, changing the message, or not replying—and I find out what I needed to know.

The best introduction to the reflective listening process is to try it out:

Reflective Listening

Pair up with another person. For fifteen minutes, one of you will talk about some matter of personal interest and the other will listen. The listener will respond in three different ways, for five minutes each.

Part 1: Reflecting back explicit content. As the listener, for the first five minutes you do nothing but reflect back verbal meanings. After every few sentences, *repeat back what you heard the talker say*—in your own words or some of the same words the talker used. If the talker doesn't pause for you to reflect, interrupt: "Wait, that's enough! I think you just said . . ." and so on. As soon as the talker is satisfied that you understand, he or she continues. If this exercise feels stiff and unnatural, it's because you're using just one response over and over, rather than alternating it with others. Nonetheless, stay with it *for the full five minutes.*

Part 2: Reflecting back underlying feelings. For the second five minutes, as the talker continues, you as listener will switch to *noticing the emotional meaning that seems to underlie the talker's words.* Reflect this underlying feeling back to the person: "I'm hearing that you seem to feel hurt and angry about what happened." Or, "You sound delighted."

When uncertain about the feeling coming through, you can use the pattern described in Chapter 8: "I'm guessing you feel. . . ." Again the talker confirms or corrects your impression.

Part 3: Responding with your own feelings. In the final five minutes, instead of reflecting back the other person's statements or feelings, you will describe the feelings that the other person's comments evoke in you: "I feel overwhelmed as you tell me that." Remember that *the spotlight is still on the other person.* You're describing your response to what the other person says and does—including what he or she does right now: "I feel myself closing up as you speak in that loud, sharp voice." Actually use the words "I feel" in each response and stay clear of "I feel *that,*" which almost always means you're expressing an idea or opinion rather than a feeling.

After this final five minutes, take a few minutes to discuss what you experienced during your fifteen-minute conversation. Then switch roles. For fifteen minutes you talk, while your partner responds in each of the three ways just described.

Reflection can be an effective response to anger—especially when used to acknowledge the anger as it masks feelings of fear or hurt. Communications consultant Pat Livingston tells a touching story that shows how.

One day at home, I went out front and found a man with a very red face yelling and waving his finger at my son. As I approached, he shouted at me,
"Are you this kid's mother?"
"Yes."
"He's gone to hell in a handbasket and you're not a fit mother," he said. I was about to start shouting back when a voice in my head told me to suppress that impulse. Instead, through clenched teeth I reflected back, "You seem to have some concern about my son."
With just those words, the man started sobbing: "I thought I killed him. He hit my car with a stick as I went around a corner and I thought I'd hit him." . . . We had a long talk, and now from time to time he rides by and waves at the kids. (1979)

A word of caution about reflection: When I'm angry at another person, or feeling critical or hostile, it's hazardous to focus on reflecting that person's feelings. What I need to deal with then is *my* feelings.

My emotions can interfere with my ability to listen or they can help me listen. If I'm afraid or anxious, I may have a hard time hearing much. If I want you to like me, I may worry so much about how you're responding to me that I'm almost deaf to what you say. Or your words may touch off my anger or anxiety even though you intend no offense or threat.

But when I attend to what I feel as you talk, and try to discover how I'm triggering those feelings, I'm using my emotional responses to become more sensitive to what's going on with both of us.

Sometimes I want to make sure *you* hear something *I'm* saying. Then I might say, "I'm not sure I said that very well. Tell me what you hear me saying." I'm *getting you to reflect back what I said* to find out if I'm clear.

I may also say, "I tune out when I listen sometimes, and it's important to me that you hear me, so if you tune out while I'm talking, let me know and I'll repeat it." The key to this is letting you know I respect wherever you are.

The Tribal Council and the Go-Around

The *tribal council,* an ancient social institution used by North American Indian peoples to deal with important problems, gives everyone a chance to hear the others. It makes it less likely that anyone can dominate the conversation by his or her ability to shout others down.

The Tribal Council

Everyone sits in a circle and the ceremonial pipe is lighted and passed around. (A cup of herb tea or a ceremonial stick or other object can be used instead of a pipe.)

One person says, "I will speak," and begins. No one else may speak until this person ends with the words "I have spoken." Even if the speaker falls silent for several minutes in the middle of a statement, no one interrupts. This guarantees each speaker time to contact his or her feelings without others butting in.

When a person has finished, the pipe or other ceremonial object goes around the circle. No one speaks. Everyone reflects.

Another person says, "I will speak," and makes his or her statement.

No one may speak a second time until everyone has spoken once.

Often only one statement from each person is needed to reach a decision. (In a variation that moves more quickly but provides less time for reflection, each speaker holds the ceremonial object while speaking and then passes it to the next speaker, but it does not move around the circle each time.)

A simpler relative of the tribal council is the *go-around.* It can be a good way to start off a meeting: Everyone makes contact and hears what other people are thinking and feeling. Each person in the circle says how he or she is feeling right now, tells of a recent important experience, or speaks to an issue. Then the person sitting to his or her right or left speaks, and so on around the circle. This can go quickly, while the tribal council often takes a long time. In the go-around, each person may be limited to a minute or two. (Be careful not to get so caught up in rehearsing your statement that you don't hear what others say. An alternate procedure that minimizes rehearsal is to have each speaker choose the person who will speak next.)

We Don't Always Have to Listen

Listening is a more active process than hearing. Of the many things I hear, I choose a few to listen to. When I'm unwilling to listen, I may indulge in "selective deafness" in which I don't hear what I don't want to hear.

We don't have to be good listeners all the time, or communicate well with everyone. Some of the people I meet aren't going to hear me no matter how well I speak. And there are times when I need to be with myself.

I can stay in touch with what I want to listen to and what I don't. I can ask myself, "What am I learning—or enjoying?" "Does the other person really need me as a listener now?" I can more easily be there for you when you want me to if I don't waste my energy listening to things neither of us cares about.

I don't need to make listening into a hard job. My presence alone, when I'm truly there for the other person, is nourishing and helpful. Often a person can tell just by the way I sit, by eye contact, and by other signs whether I'm present and interested or not. When I'm not, all the listening techniques in the world won't help. When I'm tuned in, I may not need to say anything at all for the other person to feel heard. That's *active silence.*

SOUND AND SILENCE

The ability to be silent when appropriate is an important dimension of self-mastery. When in a group, some people are uncomfortable with silence. If half a minute passes with no one talking, someone will comment to fill the space. This leaves people little time to sit with their thoughts.

As I discover my own silence, my consciousness undergoes a change. I begin to hear the quiet around me that's punctuated by the occasional sounds and the spaces between the words when others talk to me.

Inner and outer silence go together. After you read this paragraph, stop reading and listen to your own inner talking—to its rhythm and sound and the kinds of words and phrases you use. Whom are you talking to? Do you badger and nag? Are you figuring something out, or just babbling on (Perls, Hefferline & Goodman, 1965, p. 108)?

Now listen as another person talks. The speaker's cadence or rhythm carries a message. What is it?

As you keep listening to his or her voice, begin to imagine music playing in the background. It may be rock, country music, jazz, baroque chamber music, symphonic, or whatever else fits the sound of that voice right now. Next, try to think of a song title that fits the music. Your title may be the statement the person is making.

As you yourself talk, does your voice fit your message? If not, can you make it do so? Listen in your mind as Perls (1969b) describes some of the things he hears in people's voices:

> *Do you sing, or do you saw?*
> *Do you stroke, or do you rasp?*
> *Is your voice dead, or soaked in tears?*

*Are you machine-gunning me with the rapidity and explosiveness of each of
  your words? . . .*
Do you torture me with mumbling low sounds? . . .
Is your voice boomingly filling the room, leaving no place for anyone else? . . .
*Or are you engulfing me in loving sound vibrations, melting me and turning
  on lush, embracing fantasies? . . .*
The sound is true—
Poison or nourishment.
And I dance to your music or I run away.
I cringe, or am attracted.

Double messages—saying two contradictory things at the same time—are sent via a contradiction between my words and the sound of my voice. A loud, aggressive "I am not angry" is a double message. So is a tense, tight "I feel fine." When I notice that I'm sending a double message, I can label what I'm doing: "I guess I'm saying two different things at once. On one hand I'd like to let you use the tools, and on the other hand I'm concerned that they might get broken."

I can respond to your double message in a similar way: "Let's see if I'm hearing you. You seem to be saying two things . . ."

Double messages occur when we have hidden rules about what we can discuss, or when some important feeling isn't getting mentioned. They're common when we have hidden agendas. They're not something "bad" or "wrong" that we need to respond to moralistically, but rather a source of confusion and mistrust that we need to clear up.

 ### Double Messages

Face another person. Deliberately send one message verbally and a contradictory message nonverbally, through your tone of voice, body language, gesture, timing, etc. (Example, "I want you to look me in the eye." Turn your head and look away while you say this.) Then the other person replies, doing the same thing. The nonverbal message might reflect a hidden agenda. Continue until each of you has sent three double messages. Then briefly discuss your experience.

HANDLING COMPLAINTS AND DISAGREEMENTS

In ongoing relationships, we can prevent ourselves from saying things we need to say because we're "waiting for the appropriate time." As these many small things build up, we get a big storehouse of "things that haven't been said," each with anxiety and resentment attached. By saying them as they occur, we avoid that buildup.

The unsaid feeling may be simple, like "I love you," "I wish you wouldn't make the tea so hot," or "I don't want you to put your fingers in the peanut butter jar."

When you tell someone how you feel about what he or she says or does, it's crucial to *specify the particular behavior your feelings are a response to.* This specificity distinguishes helpful feedback from useless or even harmful feedback. If I say, "I feel closed off toward you right now," I *haven't mentioned any action on your part that I'm responding to*. But if I say, "I feel angry at you for criticizing Frank," or "I love being hugged like that," I'm telling you how I feel about *something you do* that makes a difference to me.

If I'm on the receiving end of your complaint or request, after I've edited out my likely response of snapping back—or after I've snapped back and apologized—my best response may be that of *collecting more information*—finding out in a more detailed way what you want to change and how it's affecting you. That reassures you of my receptivity and goodwill, and orients both of us toward finding a mutually acceptable solution (Scoresby, 1977, p. 42).

It's usually more helpful to tell you what I *can* do and *want* to do, than what I *can't* and *won't do*. If my wife asks me to pick up some things at the store and my day is already almost full—but I'm willing to do what shopping I can in the time I have left—instead of saying, "I've got a million things to do today. I have to . . ." and so on, I can say, "I've got an hour free when I can do some shopping, but only after three o'clock" (Gottman et al., p. 48).

Completing the Transaction

In an *incomplete transaction,* things are left hanging. A decision is left unmade. An issue gets talked around without a conclusion. I've watched this go on in administrative meetings as well as with couples and families. It's very draining, as the backlog of things left undone and undecided builds up.

Lederer and Jackson (1968, pp. 213–219) point out that incomplete transactions are especially frustrating when a person who uses this tactic appears courteous, considerate, thoughtful, and patient—and insists with a hurt, misunderstood air that he or she is "only interested in your welfare."

They suggest two steps to handle incomplete transactions: (1) Ask for precise clarification of cloudy communications; (2) *firmly insist on a substantive (if tentative) outcome*—don't leave a matter undecided.

Avoiding Cross-Complaints

A *cross-complaint* is a special variety of incomplete transaction. One person voices a complaint; the other, instead of dealing with it, responds with a different complaint of his or her own. In politics this is known as "dragging a red herring across the trail." The smell of the herring is so powerful that the dog forgets what it was tracking—until it's too late. Nothing gets settled, and frustration and resentment result.

We can eliminate cross-complaining by following this crucial principle: *Don't argue with me on my own time.* First we deal with your complaint until we reach closure. *Then* I can bring up a different complaint (Lederer & Jackson, 1968, pp. 243–244).

Argument and Exploration

The word *argument* has two meanings. One refers to two people talking back and forth with raised tempers and voices, each trying to prove the other wrong. While at times this is exciting, it seldom resolves disagreements.

An argument also refers to a reasoned line of thought: "I find three relevant arguments for what I want." Presenting such arguments, and testing them to see if they hold up, is a useful process. The arguments that give us trouble are the other kind.

It's important, however, to avoid overpowering a child with "reason." I can usually give a child a very logical, coherent argument about why he or she should do what I want, and the child is unlikely to be able to come up with nearly as good an argument in reply. In that case, my reasoning isn't honest reasoning—it's a mystifying exercise in power and oppression.

Watzlawick et al. (1967, pp. 54–58) describe the issue in many arguments as one of *punctuation: who gets the comma and who gets the period.* Compare these sentences: "She nags, he withdraws." "She nags, he withdraws, she nags." The person who gets the period "wins."

Barbara and Phil, a couple in their late thirties, had moved out of suburbia and "onto the land." They argued incessantly, and each tried hard to win. Barbara could win certain arguments by pointing out to Phil what he'd done wrong on the land, and Phil could win others by reminding her of how inadequate she was at "roughing it." The "loser" (both of them) often felt hurt, angry, and resentful.

With a counselor's help, they realized that one person could make a point without this meaning that he or she "won" and the other person "lost." Phil could agree to help Barbara lay a piece of flooring without feeling that he "gave in." They also learned to appreciate what the other had learned to do and focus on what needed to be done, instead of blaming the other for not doing it better or sooner.

What makes this area especially tricky is that many of us resist perceiving how we presently respond. It was an eye-opener for me when a number of years ago a friend said, "You know, you really don't like being contradicted." My self-image had been that I was open-minded and ready to listen to anything.

In almost every argument, our underlying feelings are the most important events. When I argue that I'm "just being logical," *it's almost never true.* If I'm being "logical," then you must be either stupid or stubbornly self-centered. That message is unlikely to elicit your goodwill.

Once I stop attacking you and start listening, *we can move from argument toward exploration.* We explore our interests with feelings, ideas, and values. We're more likely to look at various alternatives and to tell our relevant stories as well as our positions and opinions. And we're more apt to find something positive in the other person's perspective or approach.

If, on the other hand, we forget to mention the things we appreciate, we may end up like the dour old Scotsman who looked down at his wife's grave and said, "Aye, she was a good woman and I nearly told her so once" (Scoresby, 1977, p. 44).

10

Power and Assertion

*I*n power lies the freedom to make decisions and choose our directions. We express our power in our work, our relationships, and our creativity. Yet, notes Rollo May, we also view power with suspicion. "They" use it to dominate others, and us, when they get the chance. "*They* are power driven, but *we* are motivated only by benevolence, reason, and morality" (1972, p. 20). We hesitate to confront issues of power partly because if we did we would come face to face with our own sense of powerlessness—our struggle to affect what happens in important areas of our lives.

Violence is often a conclusion of power hunger. Some of the people in our prisons are those who, after years or decades of unsuccessful attempts to overcome social and economic discrimination, finally explode into antisocial behavior. Behind some (not all) violent acts is an impotent cry for help, a desperate exercise of some kind of power somewhere that will have an impact on someone, somehow—however counterproductive.

When I feel powerful, I'm more confident and more optimistic. But power can also mask insecurity, so that people who feel inadequate may compensate by pursuing power over others. And If I feel ineffectual, getting hold of power may help me ward off threats. The contradiction is that I'm still insecure, not dealing effectively with what I most need to deal with. In addition, my attempts to dominate others are likely to lead them to retaliate or otherwise resist my influence, which both feeds my insecurity and distracts me from feeling and facing it.

DIMENSIONS OF POWER

This chapter is about the use of power in assertive ways that encourage and respect others' rights. Power includes self-determination, having observable influence in matters important to us, and possessing authority commensurate with our responsibility. Ideally, Carl Rogers would guide us to trust our own power, to feel no need to have "power over," and to exercise our power in a cooperative rather than competitive way (1977, xii). The socially and economically oppressed would applaud these goals and their own participation in realizing them.

Power and Control

Power, as defined here, is a capacity to energize, to move. *Control* is a statement of direction. Imagine that you and I are at a control panel inside a vehicle. Each of us has charge of certain instruments and levers. You're responsible for control and I'm responsible for power. You decide where we go and the route we take; I decide how much energy we have to get there: if and when we move and how fast we go.

I can use my control in at least two ways. *Compulsive control* is a clamping down that channels energy in a narrow way. I push and squeeze all my power into those directions. *Centered control* comes from a deeper contact with myself, in which I trust my directions and my use of my power. When I'm in touch with what I need for me and what others around me need for them, I can focus energy in directions that meet these needs. (There is also *compulsive uncontrol:* actively refusing to exercise any guidance or direction.)

The paradox is that *the more compulsively I control, the more likely I am to go out of control* and be less able to spontaneously meet my needs and the needs of those around me.

"Power doesn't mean," points out editor and writer Michael Korda, "winning every argument, or resorting to verbal or physical violence. It means . . . standing up for yourself in what matters to you . . . It means compromising where you can live with the compromise, expressing your desires, feelings and needs openly—in short, behaving like an adult, equal human being *and being treated like one*" (1981, pp. 69–70).

Sources of Social Power

Social psychologists John French and Bertram Raven (1959), who define power as *potential influence*, identified six different sources of power:

> *Informational power* is exercised through providing new information or a new perspective. Its principle value is an expanded view.
> *Reward power* involves the ability to give others something they want if they do what I want them to. Chapter 22 discusses the process of reward power in great detail.
> *Coercive power* involves the capacity to punish others when they don't do as I wish. In that role I may be feared, resented, or disliked.
> *Expert power* differs from informational power in that the expert continues to be a needed resource. For example, my doctor and my mechanic are experts.

Referent power exists when we're members of the same group, like a minister who acts as he thinks a minister should. Referent (role-designated) power is also involved when we identify with ("refer to") someone we admire, as when a person dresses like a favorite celebrity. *Negative referent influence* occurs when we react against thinking, looking, or acting like someone we dislike. Rectangular small moustaches under the nose have gone out of style.

Legitimate power is accepted authority. "Legitimate power is evident in . . . military units, industrial organizations, governmental agencies—where . . . it is clear who has power over whom" (Raven & Rubin, 1976, p. 217). There's also the *legitimate power of the powerless,* like a blind person asking for assistance. Even if I'm in a hurry, probably I'll do what's asked.

Power in Ongoing Relationships

In some relationships there is a continuing uneven distribution of power, where one person (the initiator) makes most of the decisions and the other (the participator) goes along with them. In other relationships there is an *apparent* unevenness: The apparently less powerful person actually finds ways to exercise power, too. Much of this chapter explores ways we can articulate our wants and be heard.

People—adults and children, men and women—feel devalued when they're expected to give in and seek veiled ways to exercise power. One way to do that is from the position of "victim," by using guilt. Another way is to develop a handicap or symptom that others have to make allowance for.

Clinical psychologist Jay Haley (1978), who views many symptoms as tactics, points out that often a symptom is an unconscious way of resolving a power struggle. This is often the case with compulsions. "It's a compulsion—I can't control it." One woman was given to compulsive hand washing in response to an extremely controlling husband. He forbade her to wash her hands, but to no avail because it was an "involuntary compulsion"—and she could use it to oppose him on almost any issue.

There's always a price for yielding our power and our rights—or for usurping those of others. I may adopt an "underdog" position in which, even though I don't get what I want, I make sure you won't either, by finding subtle ways to sabotage your undertakings.

Control that assumes direction for another person's life sometimes is disguised. In a "pseudobenevolent dictatorship," for example, I give you what I've decided you want and then applaud myself for being so generous. If you're not equally appreciative, you should be ashamed of yourself for your ingratitude (Lederer & Jackson, 1968).

One way you can handle my phony benevolence is by thanking me but firmly stating that you prefer to determine the nature of my gift or favor: "It's so thoughtful of you to give me the food processor. Monday I'll exchange it for season tickets to the theater." If I'm really trying to please you rather than control you, I'll accept the change. Otherwise my dictatorial ways stand unmasked.

WHAT ASSERTION IS—AND ISN'T

How do you ask for what you want? Do you sit around hoping someone will know what you want and give it to you? Do you hug someone when you want an embrace? Or do you stand there afraid to ask for a hug, or to give one?

When I'm not willing to ask directly for what I want, I seldom get it. When I ask, I may get it or I may not, but I've established my caring for myself and my trust in others by asking.

I can ask myself, "How am I stopping myself from getting what I want, and how can I be good to myself now?" I might feel afraid that if I assert myself by saying that I'd like to share some time with you, you'll "reject" me. If I feel worthless and you turn me down, clearly I'm not good enough. The worse I feel about myself, the more susceptible I am to feeling rejected. I may, of course, have a stake in feeling worthless: It's a great way to avoid having either of us expect anything from me.

No one can reject me unless I buy into feeling rejected. If a person wants to do something other than be with me, that's a statement about *him or her*. I can go right on feeling good about *me*.

Years ago when I was a single man, one evening I was sitting in a cafe with a lovely woman. We were getting tired and ready to go home. I said, "I'll gladly come home with you if you invite me." She laughed and said, "No, thanks, but I'm glad you asked," and we both felt good as we parted. My statement was phrased so that we could both feel at ease with whatever reply she wanted to make. We can make our statements in ways that fit us and leave others room to reply in ways that fit them.

When I speak clearly and directly, others usually respect me and often feel attracted to me. By contrast, to be "self-sacrificing" when I don't want to is no service to others, because I feel resentful toward them and resentful toward me when I do that. Once I was visiting a hospital ward when a badly burned child who'd been there a long time was calling the nurse. She was busy with another patient, had been going at a hectic pace, and obviously needed a few moments by herself. Hearing the child call, she looked at him, saw that he was in no pain or danger, and said, "Georgie, *I need me now.*" The boy understood.

I've always got something that I can give myself, if I'm willing to do it. I hate getting stuck in traffic and sometimes get angry when I do. But I also know that wherever I am—even in a morass of concrete and steel—it's a chance to listen to music or watch people in the cars around me. I still resent getting stuck in traffic, but I can do something for myself while I'm there.

Nonassertion and Aggression

If I'm so timid that I seldom get what I want, or so aggressive and belligerent that I offend people and turn them off, I can learn to express myself more effectively. Asserting myself is asking for what I want, or acting to get what I want, in a way that respects both of us. As Alberti and Emmons (1982) point out, it's the middle way between timid holding back and inconsiderate tromping on other people's toes. I respect myself by asking for what I want. I respect you by recognizing your right to fulfill or not fulfill my request.

Respect doesn't imply automatic approval of what you say or do. Automatic agreement and unquestioning approval are forms of *deference*. I may defer to you when I'm only mildly invested in the issue, or when I appease you to avoid conflict no matter what. At times, deference may be appropriate, but only if it doesn't involve sacrificing my self-respect. Assertion is an antidote to such holding back, in which I want to reach out or to ask for what I want but I'm hesistant to, as in shyness.

Assertion also differs from aggression. When I forget that assertion involves respect for your desires and rights as well as mine, I may become aggressive, perhaps not recognizing your right to refuse my request or to ask me for what you want. "The purposes of aggression," write Nelson and Isbell (1978), "are domination . . . and intimidation." Aggression degrades, belittles or humiliates the other person. It may be direct, or indirect—as with deception, seduction, or manipulation. "The basic message," add Arthur Lange and Patricia Jakubowski, "is: This is what I think— you're stupid for believing differently. This is what I want—what you want isn't important. This is what I feel—your feelings don't count" (1976, p. 10).

Fear and Shyness in Nonassertion and Aggression

Paradoxically, both nonassertive and aggressive requests and refusals frequently are based on fear. People who demand or refuse aggressively are apt to be afraid that otherwise they won't get what they want. Aggressive people fear being vulnerable or losing control of events if they present themselves differently. So aggression may cover an underlying uncertainty—and in some cases it even masks shyness.

The fears that underlie nonassertion are more obvious. I may be afraid you'll turn me down if I ask for what I want, so I don't ask. I may fear the pain of getting close to another person and then having the relationship end, or I may be afraid to get close at all. Such fears play a crucial role in shyness, declares social psychologist Philip Zimbardo (1978). I may also be afraid that you'll get angry or retaliate if I refuse your request, or that I'll be aggressive if I try to be assertive.

Shyness, Zimbardo points out, is widespread. More than eight out of ten people he surveyed reported that they were shy at some point in their lives. Four out of ten said they were presently shy. "Since most shy people have a low sense of self-esteem," writes Zimbardo, " . . . they learn to avoid any situation that may be potentially embarrassing, thereby further isolating themselves from other people" (1978, pp. 25, 43).

Shyness involves not only fears of being embarrassed or humiliated in front of others, but also a deficiency in social skills that make contacts with others easier. Becoming more assertive can include developing appropriate social skills.

The Nature of Assertion

When I'm assertive, I'm offering myself to you as clearly and honestly as I know how, without dominating, manipulating, judging, or ridiculing you. I'm hoping to level with you in a way you can hear—one that doesn't trigger your defensiveness. Lange and Jakubowski write, "The basic message in assertion is: This is what I think.

This is what I feel. This is how I see the situation" (1976, p. 7). Examples are: "I'll need some time to think that over before I give you an answer"; "Wait, I want to finish what I'm saying"; and "Sorry, but I won't be able to do that tomorrow."

In aspiring to become more assertive, however, we confront a contradiction: Honesty is valued as an ultimate good and tact is valued as an ultimate achievement of maturity. *Tact* is a way of stating what I want with the wisdom of grace and good taste; I change the shading but not the color of what I say.

While tact is often necessary and appropriate, it need not subvert my ability to make the statements I need to make. I can assert myself directly, and I can be tactfully assertive, when each is called for.

Much of my movement toward effectively assertive communication depends on how well I integrate the following necessary if risky attitudes:

1. This is how I feel—logical, reasonable, or not.
2. I may change my mind, be confused, or even be making a mistake; if so, I don't need to punish me or you.
3. Though I appreciate "applause," it's not critical now.
4. I am responsible for my doings, feelings, and to some extent the outcomes of my interactions with others.
5. I can assess the degree to which other people's issues and problems are also my responsibility.

FORMS OF ASSERTIVENESS

This section describes different kinds of assertive responses, and the next section deals with how to practice and use them.

Direct Statements of Wants and Feelings

"I Want" Statements.   These are just what they sound like. "I want" statements include both "I want to . . ." and "I want you to . . . ," using language that fits your own style: "I'd appreciate a call if you're going to be late." Even if you refuse my request, I'm relieved of the conflict of wanting, being afraid to ask, and worrying about how you'll respond.

People sometimes misinterpret statements of wants or preferences as nonnegotiable demands. Jakubowski and Lange (1978, p. 158) suggest three ways to reduce the likelihood of this happening. First, I can also ask about your preferences, or your willingness to do what I ask: "I'd like to see *Star Wars.* How do you feel about going?" or "Would you be willing to get together for half an hour this afternoon?" Second, I can "quantify" my wants on a scale of slight to intense: "I badly need to stay home and rest tonight," or "I lean slightly toward staying home tonight." Third, I can explicitly state what my "I want" statement does and doesn't mean: "I'd rather go to Florida this Christmas than to visit your parents in North Dakota. That's a preference—not an ultimatum."

"I Feel" Statements. First I *describe some specific behavior of yours* and then tell you how I feel about it. "When you touch me and talk to me the way you did this morning, my love for you just bubbles over."

Mixed Feelings Statements. When I have ambivalent feelings about something, I can describe them both simultaneously, or mention my strong feelings about something first, let that sink in, and then describe my qualifying feelings. In some cases, when I lump them together, my strong feelings can seem invalidated by my modified ones. At other times it's important to state them together: "It was a wonderful evening, I enjoyed your company immensely, and I would feel sleazy going to bed with my best friend's husband," she said.

"I feel" and "mixed feelings" statements are *self-disclosing assertions:* I tell you something about events inside me that provide the basis for my response.

Empathic Assertion

Empathic assertion, a term coined by Patricia Jakubowski, is a way I can show some sensitivity to you at the same time that I'm making my request. It includes two parts: first, recognition of your situation, feelings, wants, or beliefs; and second, a statement of my own. For instance, "I appreciate your desire to have me along, and yet I need to make my own decision" (Jakubowski & Lange, 1978, p. 162).

Saying "No"

Saying "no" is a way we protect ourselves against excessive demands, differentiate our own priorities from other people's, and define our identity. Many of a two year old's "nos" translate as, "I am a separate person—please respect that," as the youngster evolves a sense of self. My saying "no" to you may reflect my need to say "yes" to me.

Here's an experience that will help you explore various dimensions of making and responding to requests.

Asking and Refusing

Sit facing another person—ideally, someone you do not know well. Think of a request that's difficult for you to make of someone else. If possible, set up the present situation like the actual situation in which you'd make that request and try to get the other person to agree to what you ask. Be aware of the level of self-disclosure involved in the request you choose to make.

The other person must refuse at least three times, regardless of anything you say or do. After each refusal, ask again, in any assertive way you think might get the other person to say "yes." After the third refusal, the other person may continue to refuse, may refuse definitely and finally, or may agree to your request.

(A less threatening variation: Ask the other person for something, or to do something, simple and commonplace—like telling you the time.)

After you've had a chance to discuss your experiences, reverse roles.

What is your style of asking? Which ways of assertion came easily to you? What did you stay away from and avoid using? How were you manipulative?

In responding to the other person, was it easier for you to say "no" or "yes"? What did the other person do that was most effective with you? What was the least effective? How did you feel in response to the various tactics used?

A fully assertive refusal is a direct refusal. "I'm not going to do that." The strength of a direct refusal is that it gives you no handle to manipulate me and it's honest, because I don't give you a defensive excuse.

Confrontation*

Confrontation is appropriate when a *discrepancy* exists—between your words and deeds, or between your actions and my legitimate expectations. To many people, the word *confrontation* suggests *attack*. Sometimes that's so, but only in aggressive confrontation, which involves accusing and trying to intimidate or manipulate others.

Assertive confrontation, by contrast, involves my *describing your behavior* and *describing its effects*—on you, me, and others—and, where appropriate, asking for what I want. "Dale, your twenty-minute coffee breaks have been averaging three quarters of an hour. I find myself thinking dark thoughts about you. If you need more time on one break, I'd like you to keep a written record of it and make it up on another break." Such a confrontation clears the air when it's specific. Vagueness here is a form of withholding and creates a new set of issues.

Where the discrepancy is between your words and actions, assertive confrontation includes *describing what you said you'd do*. "Trudy, you said you'd keep Friday evenings clear for us to spend together, but 'something else came up' twice this month. I feel frustrated and neglected. I'd like you to stick by our agreement or renegotiate it."

Confrontation can involve giving someone information he or she doesn't seem to have, or to grasp fully. Here I confront the discrepancy between what you think the results of your actions are and what the information you don't have shows them to be. "Ted, the city comptroller says that if the tax bill you're supporting passes, the school's finances will be hurt so badly that our kids will have to go across town to Parkside. Do you think it's worth it?"

Another kind of confrontation involves letting you know when I experience you differently from the way I hear you envisioning yourself. I ask you to consider another point of view. "Ellen, you may think the cold way you told off Joe showed everybody he's beneath you, but I like your gentler, caring side much better."

Egan describes two other situations in which confrontation is appropriate. He calls one of them *strength confrontation*—pointing out abilities a person has but doesn't

*We are indebted to Gerard Egan's (1977) thinking here.

recognize. "Sam, you keep saying you wish you had more 'personality.' I see you as the best-liked guy in the shop." The other side of that is *weakness confrontation:* identifying what someone doesn't do or is doing poorly. "Gina, I'd like to hear you more often in meetings. Your excellent ideas are useless if you don't mention them."

Confrontation is most likely to be effective when it is based on understanding the other person's interests. Confrontation alone doesn't settle things but rather identifies what needs to be settled, and we may need to negotiate how to do that. At that point, advance your token to Chapter 27.

Managing Criticism and Putdowns

There are two kinds of criticism. One is useful evaluative criticism that says, "You're not doing that terribly well. Here's a more effective way." The other type is the judgmental putdown. When we offer evaluation in a caring rather than a punishing, competitive, or depreciative way, we increase its constructive value and decrease the recipient's defensiveness.

Both in giving evaluative criticism and in receiving it gracefully, suggest Nelson and Isbell (1978, pp. 18, 21), "The heart and soul [of the matter] is recognizing our relationship and/or common goals with the other person. Doing this dissolves defensiveness. We change an 'adversary relationship' to a 'caring relationship.' " They suggest these options for responding to criticism:

1. *Set limits.* Stop an attack if it continues: "I am feeling attacked." This is an appropriate time for direct assertion and stating your feelings.
2. *Accept the criticism.* When a criticism is legitimate, outright acceptance of it is an assertive response.
3. *Disagree and self-affirm* when the criticism is based on false information, is a broad generalization, or involves value judgments with which you disagree.
4. *Delay your response.* Ask for time to think the message over and sort out your feelings about it.

Handling Putdowns.   Sometimes it's important to unmask a depreciative judgment by reflecting back the feeling, as, "I'm hearing you as feeling hostile this afternoon."

Or I can confront your statement head on by responding with my own feelings: "I don't like that term and I'd like you to stop using it with me," or, "When you address me that way, I feel angry and want nothing to do with you."

There are also subtler ways of handling putdowns. One is *requesting clarification,* an approach developed by Manuel J. Smith (1975), who called it *negative inquiry.*

"You don't really *like* that outfit, do you?" says Margaret.

"I don't understand. What don't *you* like about it?" replies Beth. (That's *requesting clarification.* Notice that Beth shifts the focus by identifying Margaret's feelings as such.)

Margaret: "It's last year's style."

"Oh? What don't *you* like about wearing older clothing that's still serviceable?" *(requesting clarification)*

"Most of the women I know like to keep up with the latest fashion."

"I see that having stylish clothing is very important to you." *(reflection)*

So requesting clarification involves repeating, "I don't understand. What's wrong with that?" until the critic has no effective reply left. It may even turn a nasty remark into a useful suggestion.

Agreeing with the grain of truth is another way to defuse criticism developed by Smith, who called it *fogging*. You find something in the criticism to agree with and then side with the critic. At Judy's party, Al says, "You've sure got a dull crowd here tonight."

"The party *is* getting off to a slow start," replies Judy.

"You haven't been any sparkler tonight yourself."

"You're right. I'm kind of tired and I haven't really *been here.*"

"Well, I guess I'm a little tired, too." Al's criticism is acknowledged and no one gets upset.

These two approaches are effective when they're used together. To use them effectively, you may have to relax your concern about your self-image at the very point where the critic is asking you to be sensitive about it. Now to try them out:

Requesting Clarification and Agreeing with the Grain of Truth

With a partner, preferably someone you feel at ease with, one of you criticizes the other. Begin with trivial things, such as the other's clothing. Then go on to things closer to home, based on your observations of the other's behavior. The person being criticized assumes a physical posture that is at once centered and relaxed, breathes fully, and responds by "agreeing with the grain of truth." Do this for about three minutes.

. . .

Now reverse roles and continue for three more minutes.

. . .

Now the critic continues criticizing, but the other person, "requests clarification." Again continue for three minutes and then reverse roles.

. . .

Finally, each of you has one more turn to engage in criticism, and this time the person criticized has three responses available: the two just described and "reflecting underlying feelings." Respond first with one, then with another, to keep the critic from controlling events.

A different approach is to *dismiss and redirect.* Jakubowski and Lange (1978, p. 238) write, "[This] involves denying the relevance of a putdown or irrelevant comment . . . and redirecting the discussion to the main issue. . . . 'How much I paid for the mower isn't the point.' (dismiss) 'The point is that it shouldn't have stopped working in a week.' (redirect)"

Other assertive processes include *repetition,* described in Chapter 9, and *exposing faulty logic,* described in Chapter 16.

Expressing and Accepting Positive Feelings

Giving and accepting appreciation, praise, and compliments is difficult for many of us. On either end of the exchange, we tend to get embarrassed and uncomfortable.

Much of this embarrassment occurs when we "save up" the good things we want to say until the statement we want to make seems overwhelming. It's usually easier to give many small strokes instead—those that refer to some specific act: "I loved the gentle way you responded to Mark's confusion this morning." When small appreciations like that are offered and received, they're less likely to embarrass either person.

Defusing Others' Defensiveness

Your assertion may provoke a defensive reponse. You can deal with that, suggests Livingston (1979), by reflecting it. For example, to the defensive response of "You're getting pretty uptight about a fairly small matter, aren't you?" you might reply:

"You think it's ridiculous for me to be concerned about this matter that seems trivial to you?"

"Yes."

In most cases the reflection calms the other person down. Then it becomes possible to reassert:

"I can understand that it seems like a small thing to you. Even so, it's very important to me that you tell me when you won't be able to finish something on time."

DEVELOPING ASSERTIVENESS

A method widely used in assertion training is *behavior rehearsal*, a form of role playing meant to develop specific skills. It requires a group of four to fifteen people. The description of the process below is based on the valuable suggestions of Liberman, King, De Risi, and McCann (1975).

Behavior Rehearsal

The training process incorporates three stages.

The first stage. Select one or more other people from the group to help you enact the situation in which you'd like to be more assertive. Choose an issue you feel comfortable disclosing to the group. Notice the level of risk you choose to take. Select people who in the same way remind you of the person or people in the real situation. Arrange the environment to represent the real one, tell each person briefly what his or her role is to be, and then position each appropriately on the "stage." The incident chosen for enactment should be either a recent or a forthcoming event. Each actor has a detailed description of his or her role and script. Analyzing "why" you or the others in the situation act as they do is taboo—the object here is to act out, not talk about. Now you and the others actually act out the situation.

Group members have a chance to comment on what they observed. Comments focus on what you did and how the group members feel personally about the situation. Special attention is given to body language and voice, including whether you seem timid, confident, aggressive, etc.

The second stage. Another group member volunteers to assume your role, modeling behavior that might prove more effective. Ideally, several different people will do this so that you can watch, listen, and choose from a number of alternatives. Group members give each model appreciation and recognition for their modeling, regardless of how it turns out.

The third stage. Describe to the group what elements of the modeled alternative behaviors you intend to try out. Then play yourself again as the scene is reenacted, this time practicing the new response. If you forget to do something you said you intended to, the director can prompt you with a word or two.

Afterward, group members provide immediate positive feedback for anything you said or did that was more assertive, and may point out any ways in which you still came across as timid or aggressive.

A frequent obstacle to assertiveness is the habit of talking very quietly. Liberman et al. suggest the tactic of standing ten or twenty feet from the other person or people in the scene and replaying it from that distance, so that you have to talk fairly loudly to be heard at all.

The technique of *in vivo* desensitization, described in Chapter 12, is another effective way to strengthen assertive behavior.

Part Three

LIVING WITH FEELING

11

Our Emotional Nature

Our emotions just may have been the first "language" by which we communicated with ourselves and others. I doubt that primitive people were terribly involved with small talk and chitchat. Cocktail parties, brunches, and gourmet cooking had not yet been introduced as essential for survival, so most events were recognized as noteworthy when they provoked an emotional response: "Hey, those teeth are heading for me!"

Sometimes our emotions seem so powerful that we feel helpless in their grasp. Then we can easily forget that emotions are also the way we experience our wonder and delight, our excitement, and our aliveness.

How to handle our emotions effectively and appropriately is a tough issue for many of us. I may feel loving toward you but reluctant to tell you so, or outraged at something you've done but afraid to let you know that. Or I may convey my anger or disappointment in a way that attacks your self-esteem and drives a wedge between us.

Experts disagree on how to handle our emotions most effectively. Some advocate "emotional control"—learning to hold in "inappropriate" expressions of feelings and channel that emotional energy in other ways. Some have emphasized letting out what has been held in, to release emotional blocks. Others have developed ways to substitute rational thoughts that lead to feeling good for irrational thoughts that lead to feeling bad.

All these approaches are useful. All are partial. Today some psychologists advocate a more integrated approach that includes elements of all of them. Such an approach is presented later in this chapter and applied in greater detail to specific emotional states in chapters that follow.

GETTING TO KNOW OUR EMOTIONS

Most of us know how to reason relatively well, but our ability to do so is frequently sabotaged by the distracting hard work of screening feelings and censoring emotions. As naturally expressive children, we sought to find ways to keep our feelings available to us, but too often we learned to deny them and block them out of our awareness. Thus, before I became aware of the richness that lay buried in my ability to feel my life, I wanted to become "more rational." Subsequently I worked hard to learn that in order to *think more clearly,* I also had to learn to *feel more clearly.*

To act effectively, the ability to *identify our level of arousal and then determine how we want to regulate it* is an important one. Within limits, we can develop that ability.

Joseph Wood Krutch (1966) tells of a duck who was frantic in protecting her young. She flew into a flurry even at well-meaning human friends who had cared for her for years. If they kept coming close, she'd forget what she was disturbed about and even attack her ducklings.

Similarly, when I'm upset I can lose my sense of what's important. When I have to make a big decision and I feel overwhelmed and "unbalanced," I want to wait until I've regained my sense of perspective. Yet so often when I'm in that state, the decision itself is what I'm upset about. Even so, just taking a few minutes to relax my muscles, breathe, and center myself (see Chapter 20) can help.

My emotions are sensitive instruments for living, alerting me to important events in and around me long before my rational mind has figured out what's happening. Even though we may have learned to numb ourselves to them, all the feelings we've ever experienced are there and available for us to experience directly again. We don't lose our capacity to feel—we just put it in cold storage.

Try this:

Checking Your Feel-o-Meter

Walk into a room. Look around. Listen to the sounds. Smell the smells. Notice all the sensory events you can.

Now pay attention to the feelings inside you. How do you feel in that room?

Next, if there are people in the room, tune in to them one at a time and see what kind of feeling you experience.

Now, so far as you can, notice what it is about the room and about each person that triggers the feelings you experience.

The Flow of Feeling

I need my laughter, and I need my tears. I need my anger, and I need my love. And I want them all!

Sometimes I lash out at you or at myself. Then, when I've spent my anger, and I know you've heard me or I've heard myself clearly, I am free to let that go and move on. Likewise, when I cry, I wash away the poison of the past and free myself to be open to another way of feeling.

As I have cried, so I can laugh and dance, and play and love. When I feel deeply and express my feelings as they are, I'm in touch with who I am and I see more clearly who you are. Learning to trust my flow of feelings follows hard, deliberate work.

Sometimes our feelings come and go in an easy progression. Other times we seem to hang on to them beyond their time. One morning Bob and his son David had a heated argument. Bob ended up shouting at David and went off to work red-faced and angry. His memory of the incident stayed with him all day. David forgot it. Bob came home that night feeling upset and tried to "deal with" the morning encounter. David, in a cheerful mood, could hardly remember the issue or the event and was surprised that his father mentioned it.

We need to leave some space for each other's different rates of speed in getting in touch with feelings and in moving from one feeling to another. I don't want to tell you that you shouldn't still feel sad because I don't feel sad any more. On the other hand, when you get over your sadness or anger faster than I do, it doesn't mean that you're insensitive or that you don't care about me.

I can hang onto any feeling. Hanging onto anger is especially common, because I can use my "justifiable" anger to punish you, even when the circumstances that triggered it are long past. When I keep hanging onto a feeling, it cuts me off from having other feelings as new events occur. When I get up on the wrong side of the bed, I don't have to stay there all day. When I insist on staying there, it's a signal that I need to look and see what source of discontent in my life I'm not dealing with.

I don't always need to deeply experience all ways of feeling, but I want to be careful: Am I consistently avoiding the same areas? Am I always giving myself the same kinds of reasons for avoiding those dimensions of myself? For my own growth, I need times of trial and challenge as well as times of rest and easy sailing.

Subtleties of Feeling

Every moment of a person's life has a feeling tone. Even when I think, "I don't feel anything," if I pay close attention some feeling will emerge. Perhaps I'm bored, impatient, or anesthetized. Those are feelings. Or I may feel bold, flustered, optimistic, sexy, vulnerable, wary, or zany. All these are part of emotional life. They may lack the power and passion of intense love, grief, or anger, but they're among the feeling tones that color most of our hours and days.

Gestalt therapist Miriam Polster (1982), talking to a young woman who said, "I don't feel anything right now," referred to the amusement park attraction in which a person pounds a platform with a mallet to knock a ball up to the top of the post where it hits a gong. "You're like that with your feelings," Miriam told her. "If you don't hit the gong, it doesn't count—you don't recognize it as a feeling. It's not that you're not feeling, but that the feelings are so small you don't find them worthy of notice. So your emotions end up seeming like they're all or nothing. Either the gong rings or you don't feel."

Your Ebb and Flow of Feelings

As you go through a day, occasionally remind yourself to notice what you're feeling right then. Take note not only of your strong feelings, but also of your moods and subtle shifts in feeling. Do you feel bright and alert? A little muddy and not quite here? Take a few moments to tune in and find out.

Notice how one feeling starts to fade away as you experience a new one taking form within you. This is like the "Awareness Continuum" of Chapter 6 but with a narrower focus, so that it's specifically an "Emotional Awareness Continuum."

Be aware of what you actually *do* feel rather than what you *think* you should feel. Notice when you think, "I shouldn't feel the way I feel." When are you annoyed or embarrassed, or surprised and delighted, that you feel as you do?

Accepting Responsibility for Our Emotions

Those who taught us to block off our awareness of certain emotions thought that they were doing what was best for us: "Don't cry. There's nothing to cry about. Come on now, be happy." Or, "Stop being angry with Mother and tell her that you love her."

When people said such things to me, I didn't stop feeling what I felt. But those feelings became the unspeakable, both to others and to me. Finally, I began to believe I didn't feel the way that was prohibited.

Likewise, when I tell you how to respond, unless you're strong enough to deter me I rob you of your opportunity to have your own feelings. I'm asking you to tell yourself you experience only what *I* say you do.

As I learn to recognize and accept my own feelings for what they are, I become less vulnerable to other people's ideas about how I "should" feel. As I come to live my own feelings more fully, I begin leaving others more room to have their own.

Our feelings are just as real when we don't know why we feel as we do. *One way I can invalidate your emotions is by demanding that you have a reason that makes sense to me for feeling as you do, or else!* I can invalidate my own emotions the same way.

Along with the right to have my own feelings goes the responsibility for feeling as I do. As long as I make you responsible for what I feel—"You make me mad," "You've crushed me," or "You've destroyed my afternoon," I don't have the right to feel as I wish. I'm at your mercy. I believe I respond as you want me to or unintentionally cause me to.

I can, however, start to move from responding to external stimuli—other people's pressures and demands—toward responding to internal stimuli—my own choices. I can work toward reducing my bondage to my automatic old emotional responses from the past.

Hitchhiking is taking someone else's trip by borrowing his or her way of feeling. You come in tense and I respond by going into my own tension. You come in laughing and relaxed and I relax and feel comfortable, too.

Having my thumb out doesn't mean I have to take any ride that comes along. When you feel bad with yourself, I can offer you comfort without having to feel all of what you're feeling. Likewise, I can say to you, "I'm hurting," without asking you to hurt, too. Often all I'm saying is, "Hold my hand—I'm afraid." As I develop my ability to feel my life for myself, I'm less likely to rely on you to carry me along emotionally.

Dominant Emotional Themes

In some groups and social settings, like families, only certain feelings are allowed. In *pseudomutual families*, for example, everyone is supposed to be happy and smiling all the time. To do otherwise brings instant disapproval from other family members. But members *do* feel hurt, angry, disappointed, afraid, etc. These feelings are more painful and distorted because there's no avenue to express them clearly. Paradoxically, there's also a sense of vulnerability that goes with everyone's being careful.

In *pseudohostile families*, by contrast, there is also a split between surface currents of emotion and the deeper currents, but what's on the surface is bickering, arguing, fighting, and apparent hostility, because that's the only way family members know how to say, "I care." What's hidden is affection and the desire to make contact in more loving ways (Wynne, Ryckoff, Day & Hirsch, 1958; Wynne, 1965).

A family or person dominated by one kind of emotion, or *dominant emotional theme*, as James Bugenthal (1980) calls it, is like a painting with just one color. A person's own dominant theme may differ from that of his or her family, or a person may display one dominant theme at home and another elsewhere. As an experimenting teenager, Denise was characteristically angry and argumentative at home, and sweetness and light with her teachers and friends at school.

Since the commitment to a dominant emotional theme results in limiting responses to a narrow range of feeling, reactions are sometimes inappropriate. Hank's dominant theme is to be a jokester. Everything's funny: "Oh, Eva died, eh? Well, she was a real boozer, wasn't she? Heh, heh, guess the old demon rum finally got to her." Another person finds everything sad and depressing, with endless sighs.

Think about your friends and your coworkers on your job. Which ways of feeling are "acceptable" and which are "unacceptable"? Are there feelings that they show and encourage you to show, and others that they seldom show and discourage you from showing? What are the "unspoken rules" about showing feelings?

COMBINATIONS AND COMPLEXES OF FEELING

Emotions often travel in groups. *Ambivalence* is a key word in our emotional vocabulary. We all have mixed feelings. Every child is sometimes very angry at his or her parents, however much he or she also loves them. I have many different feelings about every person who is important to me.

When you feel angry or rejecting toward me, I can hurt myself by imagining that's the only way you feel. I forget that you can get mad at me and still care about me, and that sometimes you're mad at me *because* you care about me. When I have some strong feeling, it may be the only one I'm aware of, but my other feelings are still there, and before long I'm likely to feel one of those other ways.

When Jeannie gets into an argument with her husband, instead of being angry, she starts crying. She was a "good girl" when she was a child. (Perls once commented, "Behind every 'good boy' or 'good girl' is a spiteful brat.") Jeannie is frightened of her anger. She doesn't take care of herself and she doesn't let her anger out, so she sits and whines, or breaks into tears. Her husband Dave does just the reverse. He expresses anger easily but has a hard time expressing sadness and hurt.

Discovering and recognizing our range of emotions is important work—so we can know all we're feeling, and can, when we choose, communicate it to others. Here's a way to explore combinations of feeling in yourself:

Levels of Feeling

Take a piece of paper. Think of a recent situation in which you experienced a strong emotion. Write down the emotion and a few words about it.

Now sit back and recall the situation vividly. See what other feeling underlies the first one. Write that down, with a few words about what it's saying.

Afterwards, write a dialogue between these two voices. Give each a name or initial and let them talk or argue with each other. Don't try to "decide" what you want them to say, but rather *find out what they spontaneously do say* by recording whatever emerges without stopping to censor or ponder it before you write. Continue until each feeling side of you seems to have "said its piece."

Then share what you've written, and the feelings about it that emerge in you now, with a classmate, fellow group member, or someone in your daily life who will listen receptively. Or if you prefer, take a few minutes by yourself to contemplate what you've written.

Jung called a cluster of stuck-together emotions, ideas, and behaviors a *complex*. Freud and Adler later applied the term to such now well-known patterns as the *Oedipus complex* and the *inferiority complex*. In the latter, a child receives messages that he or she is inept and not valued, but often masks the resulting feelings of inferiority with thoughts that "I have to be better than anybody else—I'll show them all!" This can emerge in attention-seeking behavior, impatience, arrogance, frequent fighting, or a tendency to depreciate other people—which in turn can contribute to creating inferiority complexes in them.

In complexes that developed in an environment where frequent harsh punishment was the rule, feelings of guilt, anger, fear, and a desire for revenge are often found together, along with depression and a diffuse anxiety that the world may cave in at any moment. Guilt about feeling angry and wanting revenge is heightened when some affection was mingled with the punishment. One way of handling such feelings is to deny them by glorifying the parents and their punitive attitude, while displacing our vengeful aggression toward them onto others who are smaller and weaker (Missildine, 1963).

Jung suggested that a complex can dominate a major portion of a person's life. He wrote, "Complexes . . . are not only long-enduring but are very powerful and closely interlinked. . . . [They] appear as the chief components of the psychological disposition in every psychic structure" (1974, p. 4).

An all-absorbing quest for security, possessions, sensations, power, prestige, or fame is almost certain to be rooted in an emotional complex in which we feel incomplete unless we attain that end. But such a quest also serves to distract us from perceiving the ways we feel incomplete, and whatever sadness and anger we feel about that. These "incomplete" feelings include feeling unworthy or inadequate—and insecure in my lack of worth or adequacy. Ironically, I'm afraid I'll lose my fragile self-esteem by confronting the very issues that, once resolved, would allow me to feel the deeply rooted self-confidence I need to feel genuinely secure.

When two different complexes that lead to contradictory feelings and actions are activated at the same time—for instance, one involving power and one involving guilt—I'm apt to feel terribly chaotic and confused—perhaps even "crazy."

To the degree that I can free myself from a complex, or weaken it, I become able to feel more richly, think more clearly, and act more freely. Such a freeing, awakening, and healing is the ultimate value sought when someone consults a psychologist or psychiatrist.

ALTERNATIVE WAYS OF HANDLING EMOTIONS

A Hebrew in ancient Egypt observed that the best Egyptian archers were the ones who knew how to hold the bowstring tight, when to pull back, and when to let go. His observation provides the key to a basic question about emotions: how to handle them effectively so that they work for us rather than against us.

That question has two aspects: how to deal with our responses to what's happening to us right now, and how to work with our emotional life in ways that will help us feel better in the future.

Forms of Holding Back Feelings

Even when we hold our feelings back, we express them—if to no one else, at least to ourselves. When we feel a flash of anger in a situation where revealing it will obviously do no one any good, we express it to ourselves before we unhook from it: "I'm mad; it's old stuff that doesn't fit this situation; I can let go of it." When we handle an emotion by suppression or repression, we express it in such forms as muscle tension.

The first two categories of holding back, repression and suppression, are attempts to *avoid experiencing the emotion.*

Repression is denying my awareness of my feeling—telling myself I *don't* feel that way and believing it. Only at a subliminal level do I know what I'm doing. Repression is tiring, because as psychoanalyst Otto Fenichel declared, "Repression is never performed once and for all, but requires a constant expenditure of energy to maintain [it]" (1945, p. 150). More about repression in Chapter 14.

Suppression involves consciously trying to push the feeling down and not experience or express it. "I don't want to feel that way now, and I'm going to put my energy into not feeling it." It can include telling myself I *shouldn't* feel that way. Suppression is easier to deal with than repression because I know what I'm doing. If I let up a little in my fear and judgment that a certain feeling is not okay, I have the option of finding other ways to handle it.

Tom, a carpenter, repressed some of his feelings and suppressed others. He complained that time and again he would think of something he "should have said" a couple of hours before. At work, for instance, his foreman said, "Tom, that window frame on the left side of the building should have been set in." Tom felt confused and embarrassed, mumbled something in reply, and went on with his work. Later he was eating his heart out because he just remembered that he couldn't set the frame in because the other workers didn't have the studs up.

Tom carried around a lot of anger that he didn't let himself feel. For him, anger was "wrong" and "bad." When he began to stop judging his feelings, he began to speak out when it was appropriate instead of bottling himself up.

Holding back but experiencing a feeling fully involves giving a feeling little or no external expression in words and actions, but allowing myself to explore internally my experience of it. This makes my "inside information" about myself more available to me than it would otherwise have been. Being open to this self-knowledge includes *wanting* to experience my feelings, at least briefly, even when I'm uncomfortable. That's not unthinkable: After all, we sometimes pay good money to be frightened or horrified at the movies—even "unpleasant" feelings can be exciting.

I'm more likely to be effective and satisfied when I act from a clear sense of what I'm feeling than when I'm confused about it. Often enough, simply acknowledging a feeling is all I need to do with it. Then I can let it go.

Holding back and substituting an incompatible action means that I act in a way incompatible with how I feel, hoping my feelings will change to fit my actions. If I feel depressed, I may do something exciting; if sad, I may visit a vivacious friend; if grumpy, I may meditate.

Forms of Revealing Feelings

Often the most satisfying thing I can do with a feeling is to express it in words or actions. Then, through the psychological alchemy of finishing an unfinished event, it begins to belong to my past rather than my present. This process of discharge through expression is the basis of Freud's theory of *catharsis*. He wrote,

> If . . . [a] discharge of feeling . . . occurs with sufficient intensity, a great part of the affect disappears; common speech bears witness to these facts of everyday observation in the expression "to cry oneself out." . . . If the reaction is suppressed the affect remains attached to the memory. (1959, Vol. 1, p. 30; Vol. 5, p. 109)

Describing the feeling is the mildest form of cathartic release. This is telling you how I feel, in a normal conversational voice. To have you hear me can help me feel better. When I'm on the ragged edge, your listening can be profoundly reassuring.

If my trust for you is still limited, to tell how I feel now may involve a level of self-disclosure that can feel threatening. It leaves me vulnerable to attack—especially if I've learned that there are certain ways I "shouldn't feel." When I'm willing to risk a little, describing my feelings can be a way of reaching out and making contact. It provides information and begins a dialogue that can help you and me deepen our relationship. "Talking my feelings out" can also help me become clearer about what I actually do feel.

Sometimes describing a feeling is not enough. When my feeling is overpowering, or when my description of it just doesn't seem to affect you, I can *show the feeling.* Showing feelings is presenting them in a manner and tone of voice that accurately reflects my level of emotional intensity at that moment.

Whether I incline toward describing or showing depends greatly on my personal history, and we need to respect each other's differences. A stoic Swede and a voluble Venetian will have little luck trying to change each other's preferred forms of expression. We get along best if we learn to express ourselves both in ways that feel good to us and ways that others can hear. We also do well to learn to hear others' feelings through the forms of expression that are comfortable to them.

Acting out the feeling, the most extreme form of revealing feelings, includes a whole range of behavior that may or may not be appropriate. *Within appropriate limits:* I behave in a way that corresponds to how I feel. If I feel loving, I may caress your cheek and hair. If angry, I may strike a cushion or go out and split wood. *Outside appropriate limits:* I might press myself on you when you don't feel receptive or break windows when I'm angry.

Acting out a feeling can be a satisfying way of giving it form—or it can get me in trouble. Acting out loving feelings can be delightful—if you're receptive. Acting out aggression is equally gratifying when deflected toward a harmless target—like the enterprising young man who towed a wrecked car to the edge of a college campus and, for a small sum, allowed students coming out of final exams to pound it with a sledgehammer.

Forms of Detaching

Detachment strategies are intended to change the way we feel by working directly with our emotional responses.

Unhooking is a strategy I can choose to use when one of my automatic emotional responses has been triggered: I may find that I have other responses available that fit this situation better and let go of my first response so that a more effective one can surface. Unhooking doesn't try to change our basic patterns of emotional responding, as do defusing and transcending (described later), but rather involves saying, in effect, "I don't have to—or want to—feel that way *in this situation.* I can let go of that feeling now."

When one of my emotional responses is "hooked," it may or may not be to my advantage. You cry, and I feel guilty. You come on angry, and I knuckle under. I'm apt to feel *caught,* so that nothing I do makes me or anyone else feel better.

When I unhook, I don't deny what I feel in response to your hook. If you come at me with anger, I may feel angry in return. Yet I have enough awareness of what's happening in me that I have other responses available, too. I might say, "You sound upset. What's eating you?" As I become less susceptible to getting hooked, I respond in a wider range of ways to a wider range of people.

Defusing involves decreasing the intensity of my emotional response to a given situation. Defusing is appropriate when I'm emotionally reacting now in a way that fits circumstances of my past but not those of my present, or when my emotional reaction is appropriate but excessive. Contemporary defusing procedures are presented in detail in Chapter 12.

Transcending a feeling means cultivating an alternative feeling state, such as inner peace or compassion, so that a disturbing feeling comes to be perceived as only a small part of a larger, more important perspective. Buddha described the basic principle 2,500 years ago: "Hatred does not cease by hatred at any time. Hatred ceases by love. This is an unalterable law."

For most of us, such transcendence is a tricky approach to working with feelings. I've seen numerous spiritual devotees convince themselves that they'd transcended feelings they were clearly repressing. A telltale clue to repression masquerading as transcendence is a "holier than thou" attitude. Genuine transcendence includes transcending taking oneself so seriously, and characteristic attitudes include flexibility, humor, and a willingness to let others be as they are.

DIRECTNESS, DISCRETION, AND SIGNALING

People are less often defensive when I tell them how I feel if I'm careful to express my feelings as my own feelings and not as "facts" about them. In Rogers's words:

> To say . . . "What you are doing is all wrong," is likely to lead only to debate. But to say "I feel very much annoyed by what you're doing," is to state one fact about the speaker's feelings, a fact which no one can deny. (1961, p. 319)

Before I give a feeling full expression, I want to *"look both ways."* In one direction is my feeling itself; in the other is my environment. Having the right to feel as I do need not mean expressing it in any way I please—I can look for the way to express myself that's least likely to hurt others or make them feel bad.

I can get along without breaking into a belly laugh in the middle of a funeral. I can get along without shouting my anger at a timid soul who has a hard time handling intense emotion: That's the point where expressing myself turns into punitive indulgence. *Rather than putting others on the defensive, I want to present my feelings in ways that they can acknowledge and respond to with their own feelings.* I can find a way to express myself that suits the situation where I am.

I'm more likely to hear your meaning, and you mine, when we care about each other. I can more easily read my supervisor's signals when he says, "What the hell did you do with that piece of work?" if I know that he's also willing to say, "What a beautiful piece of work you did!"

We can also learn our signals to ourselves. When Noel gets frustrated and angry on a job, he puts down what he's working on and walks out of the shop. He's learned that getting a cup of tea or talking to someone for three or four minutes cools him off. When he returns, he usually feels better, and his improved attitude is reflected in his work.

NOURISHMENT AND POISON

All of us sometimes "poison" ourselves and each other. In some ways each of my parents poisoned me, just as in some ways I unwittingly poison my children. At times my mother was poisonous toward me by refusing to acknowledge the good things I'd done and putting me down for not having done enough. When I did something good on Tuesday, it was: "How come you didn't do it on Sunday, too?" I introjected that attitude and sometimes still do that to myself. But more often now, when I start to put myself down, I'm aware enough of what I'm doing that I can stop.

I've also learned that every time a person's stinger flashes out to poison someone else, a little valve opens and the poison shoots through the person who does the stinging, too. Expressing malicious or injurious feelings, statements, and actions reinforces those habits of thought and feeling in myself.

Torture, Sabotage, and Assassination

Three common ways of poisoning ourselves might be dubbed torture, sabotage, and assassination. In *torture,* I refuse to let myself be as I am or let the world be as it is, even though I'm not willing to make any changes. I convince myself that whatever I do and experience is wrong. If I feel hurt, I think I shouldn't feel hurt. If I feel good, I think I shouldn't feel good. I find nothing good for me in what's happening but do nothing to change my situation.

In *sabotage,* I find some way to fail, to derail my projects and intentions. I may have a good program, but I don't let myself follow it. If I know how to get a good payoff in a situation, I do something else. Even when I *do* get where I'm going, I've made things hard for myself along the way. But after I've screwed up today, I'll probably find some energy to come back and screw up again tomorrow.

Through *assassination* I can immobilize myself completely. "Why even try? I know I'll fail." I immobilize myself. My assassin stops me cold. I feel there's no way I can do anything good for me or for you. Severe depression is an example of such self-assassination. Or I may only kill part of me, like my capacity to laugh and feel joy.

Ignoring someone is a potent form of poison directed toward others. I make you invisible by poisoning you with my ink eradicator. A sexist male can make a woman disappear by treating her as a generalization rather than an individual. A white racist can make a black person disappear by treating him or her as a nonperson.

Nourishing Me and You

The opposite of poisoning is nourishing myself and others. One day Fritz Perls was finishing a difficult film. When we got together afterward, he was bushed. I said, "Wow, nice day, blah-blah-blah," and he said, "Listen, I really don't have the energy for bullshit. Let's go somewhere and you can tell me what you want."

We found a place, sat down, and talked for a long time. As we parted, Fritz said, "I was so tired that I wanted to talk for fifteen minutes and go to sleep. We've talked for an hour and a half and I'm completely refreshed." He was able to use what was going on with us to revitalize himself.

One way I nourish you is to give you my aliveness. A way I can poison you is to give you my exhaustion and ennui. This is a frequent problem in marriages: You and I give all our best energy to our work, to housekeeping, and to taking care of the kids, and all we have left for each other is our exhaustion.

I don't always have to want to nourish you. Sometimes I hear you needing and I don't want to give. Nevertheless, when I hear you say again, "I know you don't want to give, but I still need," I may be willing to give even though it's not so easy for me then; and I'll feel good about it when I do. At other times I need to take some time just to take care of myself.

When I'm being nourishing, I experience a clarity about what I want for me and from you. My vitality flows from me to you, picks up your aliveness, and comes back to me.

12

Fear and Anxiety, Depression and Grief

We all experience death, injury, illness, separation from loved ones, and failure in our enterprises. At such times we need to find ways to handle our suffering without being destroyed by it or adding to it.

Lillian, who grew up in the South before desegregation, knew certain kinds of fear, anxiety, and attendant pain especially well. "My defense," she writes, "was separation and never getting involved; therefore I never had to risk not being accepted. In other words, I 'stayed in my place.' It was hard to continually walk past those poor white kids calling me 'nigger.' It hurt—inside where nobody could see. To avoid that hurt, I learned to suppress most of my real feelings. And I did not value myself very highly."

It *does* hurt when the need to be accepted and loved as we are goes unfulfilled. If that pain of unmet needs persists, I'm going to shut it out of my awareness. As I do, my needs that led to it may be shut out, too. Or they may be filled by substitutes, as in a desperate quest for things, power, or sensations.

Pain is an alarm signal. It tells me that something's wrong. I protect myself by avoiding and/or reducing the trauma. But if my finger is already burned and there's nothing I can do about it, I may try to decrease the pain.

Psychological pain is analogous but more complicated. At some time in my past, when painful events seemed inescapable and overwhelming, the anesthetic of drawing the curtains on painful memories and painting a kinder picture that's easier to live with was useful to me. It may be less useful now.

When I deaden my ability to feel, my payoff is that I feel less pain. However, I also feel less pleasure—though I may not realize that. And I create physical pain in the muscles of my body as I literally tighten up against the psychological pain. As a result, certain places in my body never get the rest and relaxation they need.

Beatrice, a college senior, recalls, "During a massage training session, as two masseuses worked on my chest, I began to laugh uncontrollably. The instructor immediately came over, placed his thumbs on two points on my chest, and encouraged me to breathe deeply. My laughter turned to wild crying. Later on I found out that my explosive crying covered great pain. When I had experienced that pain deeply, it gave way to love and joy."

FEAR

Fear and pain are close associates. I need and want some of my fears. They have survival value, helping me survive dangerous situations, avoid needless injuries, and escape unnecessary pain. A commitment to being "cool" can diminish our appropriate fears about such dangers as nuclear waste and the abuse of dangerous drugs, so we're willing to gamble when there is no winning. But too much fear can lead to mistakes in thinking and behavior and make it hard to concentrate or remember crucial information (Rachman, 1978).

Several problems are associated with learning based on fear.

First, it can be unusually difficult to change. The unlearning and relearning process is slow. As a result, some fears that once protected us now confine us. Since my fear impels me to avoid or escape from situations like those that were threatening in the past, at an emotional level I never fully recognize that the old dangers are gone or greatly diminished.

Second, fear can stop me from perceiving what actually exists and lead me to think I perceive things that aren't there. When this is extreme, it's paranoia. Of course, my fears may not be paranoid. During the 1950s, 1960s, and early 1970s, many people who were afraid the CIA and FBI were watching them were considered paranoid. Later, it turned out that they were right. So I need to keep my capacity to check the message I'm getting from my fears against other information.

Third, fear generalizes easily to other events that resemble the ones we're afraid of. An increasing area of our power and potential becomes "off limits"—not only the specifically punished fear-inducing act but also others associated with it. If I get my tang tongueld-up when I'm with an authority, for instance, I may be protecting myself against saying something that might get me in trouble—or that might have done so long ago, even though it wouldn't now.

Disguised Fears

We disguise some of our fears in ways that deceive us, our enemies, and even potential friends. With the right combination of fears I can convince myself that I'm so inadequate that the moment a new relationship starts, I'm ready to be rejected. To protect against that, I may come on as tough, indifferent, or "superior." In response, you back away—even though we may both be attracted to each other. Though I may want to make contact desperately, I use my fear, and my fear of my fear, to keep myself isolated and lonely.

When fear masquerades as anger (and vice versa), conflicts between individuals and nations become more than they were intended to be. It's hard to disengage from fear-based anger, with the frequent result that so much is invested in so little.

Fear can be disguised as strength. Strength that's based on inner security shows up not in domination of others but in "the kind of self-trust that makes it unnecessary for an individual to be forever proving his prowess" (Overstreet, 1971, p. 93).

When fear is disguised as "goodness," we can identify a "tendency to define virtue in terms of *refraining from . . .* of resisting temptation rather than affirming life" (Overstreet, 1971, p. 98). Such "goodness," with its many taboos and prohibitions, may self-righteously condemn those viewed as less "moral." Critics of Western religions condemn the fear-guilt-retribution triumvirate at the base of some churches' theologies. Within the churches themselves are movements actively seeking to reduce fear as the incentive for religious commitment and substitute a more loving basis for a relationship with God.

Fear can even be disguised as love. If I'm afraid you may become too independent and not need me as much as I want you to, I may be possessive, jealous, and excessively "helpful" as I try to keep you from developing the ability to take care of yourself. You can see this happen with spouses, lovers, and children.

One fear common to most of us involves being "found out." Our secrets are things we keep hidden because we're ashamed or embarrassed. You know they're so terrible that others would want nothing more to do with you if they knew about them. You might try this:

Secrets

This works best with ten to fifteen people, though it can be done with as few as seven or as many as twenty.

Identical pieces of paper are passed out to everyone. Each person thinks of something he or she has seldom or never revealed to anyone—some carefully guarded secret—and briefly describes it on the piece of paper, which is then folded and put in a hat. The pieces of paper are shuffled, and everyone draws one out. (People who draw their own return it to the hat and pick again.)

Each of you talks about the secret you've drawn *as if it were your own,* telling how you feel having a secret like that. Others can ask questions if they want.

No one ever finds out whose secret belongs to whom. *Do not in any way make fun of anyone else's secret.* The temptation to do this can be strong, especially if someone else's secret touches off your anxiety.

Terror

At times the word *fear* is not enough to describe the way I feel. Once when I was skin diving, from opposite sides of a coral reef an enormous shark and I swam face to face thirty feet apart. Instantly I was in a state of full-blown terror. He was toothy and cool!

Sometimes there are stages. I begin with just a vague sense of *discomfort.* I'm a little uneasy, a little jumpy.

Then I start getting *anxious*. The event I'm concerned about is getting larger. I'm reacting more. I'm not sure I have all the resources I need to handle it.

I begin to be *afraid*. The power of the event grows as it looms in my thinking. The feared aspects begin to get more focused, closer. I feel less and less adequate to deal with the situation.

The event grows even larger; I'm feeling more and more helpless, and that's when *terror* strikes. The situation has become more than I believed myself capable of dealing with. Inside, if not observably, I start to shake and tremble.

In my terror, as I'm frantically looking around for resources, I conclude that nothing I do or don't do will affect what happens. The event grows still larger and closer, and I *panic*.

One aspect of this process is the presence of anxiety throughout all its stages—my apprehension about what's *going to* happen. Another component is starting out thinking I have the resources to deal with whatever's coming up and using them fully—to no avail. That's the point, when I feel that I have no resources left, that I want a competent counsel available—one who won't respond by prescribing a tranquilizer and telling me not to worry.

Feeling terrified may or may not have a concrete, observable basis. Fears from my past may combine with my present circumstances in some unexpected, subjectively overwhelming way—my inner demons, if you will, start to rattle their chains, moan their moans—or do nothing but stand there staring at me.

Or my terror may be based on well-defined circumstances. In the paratroops in World War II, I was working in intelligence before a major jump. As information arrived, we were constructing the sand table—a three-dimensional map of the drop zone. As more and more data came in, the chilling realization took form that there appeared to be no way of living through the mission. I went through all the stages of fear just described as that conclusion became more and more inescapable, and I went emotionally dead with my feeling of being unable to do anything to change the circumstances. When we were about to take off, word came that Patton's tanks had just rolled through the drop zone. The combat veterans were very quiet; the new recruits whooped, joked—and some even protested.

We don't have to pretend we're not afraid when in fact we are. Children's fears are to be appreciated as their reality. Many children are afraid when they're alone in bed at night. In one study, 47 percent of two year olds were afraid of the dark (Rachman, 1978, p. 117). In that shadowy, silent time all a child's fears can surface, though the child may minimize them by saying they're caused by "bears," "robbers," or the noises and shadows of the night.

I wish we could all agree that *it's all right to be afraid* and not be ashamed of our fearfulness. In our own ways, we are all afraid.

ANXIETY

The line between anxiety and fear is sharp and clear at some points, while at others it blurs and disappears. We speak of *fear* when we think we know what we're afraid of and *anxiety* when we're unsure. Psychiatrist Clarence J. Rowe defines anxiety as "an unpleasant uneasiness, apprehension, uncertainty, agitation, or dread that stems from an unidentified anticipated danger" (1980, p. 44). Even the definition is scary!

Anxiety and worry are also related. A student whose anxiety is connected to writing difficulties reports,

> I've barely begun to write my term paper and already I'm worrying that it won't be good enough and I might not get the grade I want. Anxieties like these snowball: My grade point average won't be good, I might not get the other half of my scholarship. I won't be able to stay in school, and—I get immobilized, block the flow of my thoughts and feelings, and can't write.

But anxiety has its positive side. In an intriguing study, social psychologist Irving Janis (1971) interviewed patients facing surgery and divided them into three groups: "Nonanxious" patients were cheerful and optimistic about the surgery and slept well the night before. "Moderately anxious" patients reported some tension. They wanted reassurance and information about the surgeon's procedures. "Highly anxious" patients were jittery, couldn't sleep, and were extremely worried about complications and possible death.

How did these three groups respond to the surgery? The *moderately anxious* patients recovered fastest, handled the postoperative procedures best, and had the highest morale. In that situation, concluded Janis, moderate anxiety is healthy and desirable. The same is probably true for numerous other stressful situations.

Anxiety may be classified as *acute* or *chronic*. Acute anxiety comes quickly, is intense, and is soon over. It's a transitory response to a troubling situation. Chronic anxiety is less intense and lasts much longer . . . but for a lifetime?

Anxiety can develop in connection with our defenses against deeper fears, painful memories, or terrifying aspects of the world around us that we don't wish to recognize. The inevitable fragility of strategies of avoidance results in a pervasive vague anxiety that leaves us overwhelmed. This has been called *neurotic anxiety*. Many of us feel at least a little of it. When I notice that I'm tensing up physically, I can unclench my hands, loosen my stomach and shoulders, breathe deeply, and sometimes even unhook from my anxiety response. But if I'm anxious without realizing it, as many of us often are, I don't have that choice (Horney, 1950, p. 74).

Terrors of Tomorrow—Scary Scenarios

Part 1. Sit back, relax, and ask yourself, "What have I done today that feels good?" Remember those incidents vividly. Then turn your attention to your body and notice where and how you feel good in your body as you remember those pleasant events. Do that before you read on.

Part 2. Now think about how one of those things you did today that feels good could backfire on you tomorrow. Vividly imagine the possible negative outcome—plan it out in detail until you start to feel a little anxious about it. Then notice where and how you feel that anxiety in your body—check all the places you've begun to tighten up.

What common themes emerge? If you're doing this with others, you can discuss your experience.

Existential Anxiety

Psychoanalyst Karen Horney suggested that most children experience some measure of *basic anxiety*—a sense of being isolated and helpless in a potentially hostile world. This insecurity can be triggered by a wide range of events, such as domination, indifference, disparagement, or overprotection. This basic anxiety, Horney maintained, limits a child's ability to relate to others spontaneously. "He must deal with them in ways which do not arouse or increase, but rather allay, his basic anxiety" (1945, p. 41; 1950, p. 18). In an adult, she continues, that basic anxiety has either decreased or has become overlaid with other anxieties.

In many adults, it is replaced by existential anxiety. Pain, tragedy, separation, and death touch us all, as do such larger circumstances as the prospect of nuclear war and the poisoning of our earth. These are not small matters. We have a choice: One option is to confront our anxieties about those events, do what we can about the events themselves, and handle our anxieties in ways that keep them from impairing or destroying our ability to relax and enjoy ourselves. The other option is to block off our anxiety by restricting our awareness.

Rollo May (1976) maintains that as we mature, we can perceive and accept an increasingly "open world" with more possibilities for pain as well as pleasure. James Bugenthal (1976) adds that when we exercise our freedom and make a choice, we "administer death" to other alternatives; thus life always includes the existential anxiety that goes along with the large and small "deaths" of giving up other possibilities. Ernst Becker (1976) identifies our *ambivalence* about knowingly making such decisions as the crux of anxiety. To decide and act knowingly, he says, is to be visible and responsible—and alive. To avoid doing so is to be invisible, not accountable—and dead.

Anxiety surrounds each journey from the old and familiar through unknown territory into new ways and possibilities. Some of us try to invent a completely predictable existence and learn only grudgingly that life lived fully is always a balance between resting in the familiar and stretching for the unknown.

Uncertainty and Excitement

"Anxiety," declares Perls, *"is the tension between the now and the later"* (1969b). When I'm completely in the present, actively responding to what is happening in *this* situation, I have minimal room for anxiety about what's *going* to happen.

In Perls's model of anxiety, when I become interested in something I get excited. My mind and body differentiate this excitement into feeling—feelings of attraction, revulsion, anger, fear, joy, and so on. This emotional excitement, in turn, energizes my muscular system. "You can't imagine anger . . . ," he states, "or joy . . . without muscular movement. These muscles are used to move about, to . . . touch the world, to be in contact" (1969a, pp. 63–64).

When my excitement does not find its way into movement and activity, Perls suggests, I experience anxiety, which is *bottled up excitement*. The suppression of *any* excitement—not just fear—produces anxiety. So I become anxious when I want to respond, but hold back—out of my uncertainty about whether what I do will bring applause or rotten eggs. "To *realize* that [the rotten eggs are] not a catastrophe, but just an unpleasantness," comments Perls, "is . . . part of waking up" (1969a, pp. 3, 31).

A crucial element in anxiety is *restricting my breathing*. If I'm excited, I need more oxygen. When I breathe deeply, I move toward being alive with my excitement. When I hold my breath, I move toward being paralyzed in my fear. More about breathing in Chapter 15.

Even though I feel anxious and I can't do anything about what's going to happen, I can take care of myself by becoming aware of what I'm doing now. If I'm anxious about getting up and talking before a group in three minutes, I can notice how I experience that anxiety at this moment in my breathing, my heartbeat, and elsewhere in my body.

My existential choices are clear: I can move with my excitement into my aliveness, or freeze myself into immobility. There is anxiety in either direction. Now, what do I want?

DEFUSING FEARS AND ANXIETIES

As any demolition expert will tell you, defusing is delicate work where we take the destructive potential out of a possibly explosive event. It requires appropriate knowledge and careful, sometimes courageous handling of the situation. In emotional defusing, we work either with memories of early experience or with present life situations to reduce the power of whatever formerly triggered the anxiety.

Most strategies for defusing fears and anxieties, whatever specific form they take, involve two essential elements.

First, *repeated safe contact* with a situation that resembles the one in which my fear or anxiety was originally learned. Safe contact involves support, reassurance, and nonjudgmental confrontation in a situation that induces only a moderate level of fear or anxiety—a level I can handle—and in which, unlike the original situation, *nothing threatening happens*. Since in the past my fear or anxiety led me to avoid such situations and not confront or experience them, I never learned that they're no longer so threatening as they once were (Eysenck, 1968).

Second, I learn a new response that's incompatible with fear or anxiety to replace my old fearful response. I learn, for example, relaxation techniques and how to use them between confrontations with threatening material. Relaxation and fear are *psychologically and physically incompatible*. If I learn to relax in a situation I used to fear, I'll be less afraid.

In the basic desensitization process for getting rid of old fears and anxieties, as again and again I act in ways that resemble the way I'm afraid to act—or experience the situation that arouses my anxiety—and no harm comes to me, eventually my entire body learns that nothing bad will happen when I act that way, especially if I consciously relax whenever I feel my fear or anxiety emerging.

If my fear is strong, I don't want to start right off doing something that's very similar to what I'm afraid to do. Using the principle of *successive approximation* (see Chapter 22), I begin with situations that are only a little like the one I fear and gradually move to situations that are more like it.

Systematic Desensitization

This highly structured approach developed by Joseph Wolpe (1982) is ideal for fears and anxieties that are so powerful you completely shy away from events related to them. Systematic desensitization is useful not only for a fear so strong that you feel uncomfortable doing things even remotely related to it, but also for fears and anxieties about things that happen with no action on your part, like sudden loud noises. The effectiveness of this process depends on your ability to visualize and fantasize.

Begin by thinking about your fear or anxiety until you can describe a specific situation in which you'd expect to feel it at its maximum intensity. Write that down in precise detail.

Now jot down a variety of other situations also related to that "most feared event" that you can either create for yourself or put yourself into—some that are similar to the most feared event, and others that are only a little like it, and hence less frightening. Write each item on a separate strip of paper, so you can move them around easily.

A woman afraid of heights, for example, included "standing on a kitchen chair," "descending steep bleacher steps," and "moving in a high-rise elevator" among her mild items, and "being at the top of a Ferris wheel," "standing near the edge of a cliff," and "rockclimbing up a cliff" near the top.

When you have a list of at least ten situations, order them from the least to the most frightening. Check your ranking by having another person read off each situation as you sit or lie with your eyes closed. If they're ranked correctly, you'll feel just a little more fear with each successive situation you imagine. If you feel less fear with an item than with the previous one, reverse their order. If you notice a big jump in fear from one item to the next, think of one or two more items that will fit between these two *so that the increase in fear is small.*

These scenes have to be *specific,* so that when the description is read a particular scene comes immediately to mind. When you have your list, or *desensitization hierarchy,* sit back in a comfortable armchair—or better yet, lie down in a place where you feel secure—and take at least ten minutes to relax completely. Then allow a calm scene where you feel very good and happy to come into your mind—a beach, a spot on a river bank—perhaps a favorite place from your memories. Vividly imagine yourself there, feeling as relaxed and good as you can.

Next, switch to *vividly imagining* the least frightening item on your list. When you begin to feel afraid, remove your attention from the threatening item, go back to your pleasant scene, and relax your body again. When tension becomes minimal, again imagine being in the threatening situation. Continue this alternation until you remain relaxed and unafraid as you imagine the previously threatening situation.

Then continue to the next item on your list. Doing three or four items a day, in a session lasting an hour or so, is plenty. Sometimes you may even need to devote an entire session to a single item.

This procedure *works most effectively if you do it with a partner* who reads the scene from your list for you to imagine and gives you relaxation instructions whenever you hold up a finger indicating that you feel any fear or any tension in your body.

In Vivo Desensitization

In vivo here means "in the real life situation." In this approach you begin by making a list as described above and then *physically go through* each situation on your list, beginning with the easiest one and gradually moving to more frightening ones. You might want to go through a given kind of situation several times before moving to the next item on your list, or you might skip certain items.

In vivo desensitization and systematic desensitization can be combined. You can put your emphasis on working with fantasy scenes, incorporating real life events when feasible. Or you can emphasize going through real life situations, using fantasy as an adjunct when needed.

Modeling

Behavioral psychologist Albert Bandura has developed an approach to reducing fears and anxieties based on the fact that *imitation* is one of our basic ways of learning. He has emphasized the role of a *model*—who handles the threatening situation comfortably. Many people, for instance, are afraid of snakes. If I'm the fearful person, fearless Bandura's strategy would be to handle the snake in front of me. If my fear is strong enough, I might begin by watching through a window while he handles the snake in a neighboring room. Once I'm willing to enter the room with the snake, there's more modeling by others interacting comfortably with it. When I'm ready to touch it myself, I don't have to figure out how to do it. Since someone has just shown me, I need only *imitate what the model does*. Then I experience the reward of knowing that I've touched the snake successfully—and also the reward of approval by others present. After watching the model some more, I may progress to picking up the snake and holding it in my hand. Watching alone is not enough—I must also *participate*, by doing as the model did. Such sequences of modeling and imitation typically involve a graduated presentation of increasingly difficult tasks (Bandura, 1969, 1977; Ritter, 1969). Sometimes Bandura uses *response induction aids*—like a pair of heavy gloves for handling the snake until I'm comfortable without them.

The most powerful model, it turns out, is often not the practiced expert—a *mastery model*—but rather someone who is just a little beyond the point of successfully doing what the fearful person wants to do—a *coping model* (Bruch, 1975).

Repetition is also important. The decrease in fear or anxiety is more pronounced and more permanent, Bandura found, if a person practices doing what he or she was formerly afraid to do over and over again.

In daily life, when I'm trying to help someone else overcome a fear of something I'm not afraid of, I have the advantage of a built-in model—me. When my young daughter was taking "Tadpole I" swimming lessons, she faced a fear common to many of the children in her class: fear of putting her face under water. With that and related fears, the instructor first modeled the desired behavior and then used more advanced children in the class as a model for the others—being careful to *accept each child's present behavior and feelings at each moment.*

Once you've become less fearful about something, expose yourself to such situations on a regular basis if you have a chance to. That will help keep your old fears and anxieties from returning.

DEPRESSION

Going anywhere seems to go nowhere. Doing anything seems to mean nothing. I've got the blues.

The "blues" are a universal experience. We all feel happy and sad, elated and depressed. The trouble comes when we get depressed and can't seem to get out of it.

When I'm stuck in my depression, after a while I feel frustrated and bored with where I am and what I'm doing. Each new avenue I take seems dark and shrouded. Since no pathway I see looks promising, I may stop trying any of them.

The Experience and Meaning of Depression

Along with feeling down in the dumps, my depression may be seasoned with dashes of anxiety, irritability, or guilt. It's a statement of my unexpressed and unrecognized anger. It can involve social withdrawal and loss of interest in activities that used to be enjoyable. My deluxe depression may include self-blame, indecision, thinking that life is meaningless and futile, and a sense of worthlessness or helplessness. On good days I can mask depressed feelings with compulsive sex, drinking, overeating, or smoking.

B. F. Skinner (1953) speaks of depression as the loss of accustomed rewarding events. In response, I feel deprived, apathetic, and perhaps angry and helpless. The rewards may even have been only expected rather than experienced, for I may be just as depressed over unrequited love as over love lost.

Many young people get depressed when they move away from home and its host of environmental supports. That kind of depression tends to fade as a person makes the transition toward self-support.

Following up on the idea that depression is related to not getting enough enjoyment out of life, Peter Lewinsohn and his colleagues (Lewinsohn, 1982) found that depressed persons report a lower daily average of pleasant activities, lower rates of social activity, and more discomfort dealing with others—at least in groups and in situations that require assertiveness. They also discovered that depressed behavior is sometimes unwittingly encouraged and maintained by well-meaning sympathy and support. A certain amount of "Yeah, that's tough," is appropriate, but after that, "Forget it—you're just wallowing in it" may be kinder.

Martin Seligman and his colleagues identified *learned helplessness* as an aspect of depression. Many depressed people, they discovered, at some point spent considerable time in a situation where their actions had little effect on what happened to them. They learned to view events as uncontrollable—that life is based on "luck." If I believe that only lucky people succeed, and I don't seem to be lucky, I may feel apathetic and powerless. I can feel depressed even when good things happen to me, when they occur without regard to what I've done and I feel helpless to maintain that good fortune. My blue skies are always dark blue.

Seligman's group hypothesized that when depressed people fail at something, they lay the blame on themselves; but when successful, they place the credit elsewhere. Thus, *developing a sense of being able to affect what happens to me* can be important in moving out of depression (Seligman, 1975; Abramson, Seligman & Teasdale, 1978).

Exploring Depression

Mostly I want to get rid of my depression and feel better, but not always. At times I want to feel what I'm feeling—both to live the experience and because there may be some deepening of understanding that comes out of it for me.

Next time you feel depressed notice your thoughts, your feelings, your sensations. *Be interested in your own depression and use the tool of the awareness continuum* (Chapter 6) *to observe yourself there.* You can feel your depression as a vague, amorphous whole, and feel it in its nuances, changes, and details. You can become an expert on the subject of your own depression.

Sometimes people like to do routine tasks when they're depressed. That can be done with the mind and feelings spinning around out of touch with the here and now, or it can be done with presence and focus. When I'm right on the ragged edge, I find comfort in doing something very simple, like scrubbing floors or washing windows, my car, or me, slowly and with awareness of what I'm doing in each moment. Yes, I do windows.

Carrying out the process described in the following exercise, with the help of a caring friend or partner, can help you deepen your awareness of your depression or of other emotional states.

Exaggeration

Don't just be depressed, be *terribly* depressed. Go into the very center of your depression. Exaggerate it. Repeat the things you've been feeling, thinking, and saying to yourself in an exaggerated, overdramatic way. (Will someone please bring up the Oscar?) Let your body assume any movement or posture it feels like assuming—whether that's to huddle up like a fetus; to wail, moan, or yell and roll on the floor. Don't ask the other person to say or do anything but see, hear, and be with you.

To exaggerate, I have to do consciously what I've been doing unconsciously and automatically. Thereby I develop a greater measure of conscious control over those responses. And in the larger than life—even caricatured—exaggeration of the things that I've been doing, I become aware of new dimensions.

You can use exaggeration with sorrow, joy, or any other way of thinking or feeling you want to know more fully.

Searching for the function our depression serves is longer and more complicated. It takes us into examining our fantasies and dreams, pointing to our unfulfilled and dissatisfied aspects. It's apt to be trying to tell me I need to make some kind of important change, though I may not know what that is.

But when I'm depressed, I feel little energy for finding out how to give vitality to the parts of me that hold promise. I repeat my safe, ineffective ways and reinforce my illusions (and your view) of my helplessness. Alternatively, I can start moving out of my depression toward new ways to meet my needs and begin to follow through on my involvements and projects.

Sometimes the statement the depression is making comes out fairly easily, and sometimes not. Things become complicated when my helpless depression has evolved into my way of relating and controlling my relationship with you. You may support me as a way of being my strength and rescuer. Thanks?

Moving Out of Depression

Just as the sources of depression differ from one person to another, so do the processes for moving out of it. For some of us, strengthening underdeveloped social competencies helps—through assertion training, learning to communicate clearly, etc.

For others, learning to express feelings that have been held in is crucial. One kind of depression has been called *frozen rage*—it occurs in people who have learned no way to express their anger.

Howard, for example, came in for therapy because he had recurrent seizurelike tremors for which his doctor could find no physiological reason. He was extremely depressed and locked up his anger tightly. In a counseling session, as he began to express his anger toward his father he cut himself off abruptly and his whole body went into a violent spasmodic tremor—a muscular expression of his withholding of his intense feelings. Learning to describe and express his resentments and anger helped Howard deal with his depression and decreased his tremors.

According to psychiatrist Aaron Beck (1976), we become depressed when we view ourselves as deprived, deficient, or defeated. This "3-D" devil expresses itself in a paralysis of will and a lack of motivation. Anticipating failure, I'm unlikely to undertake much activity, and when I feel like a burden to others, I avoid socializing.

One dimension of feeling inadequate is feeling victimized. In this self-pitying state, I keep repeating to myself—and perhaps to others—statements about being overwhelmed, incompetent, and oppressed. Once I recognize this cycle of self-pity, I have the option of doing something else instead.

Psychiatrist A. John Rush (1978) suggests confronting thought processes that contribute to feeling worthless and inept by using the *triple-column technique*. Divide a piece of paper into three columns. Title the first column, "Specific events associated with unpleasant feelings," the second column, "Thought," and the third column, "Evidence for or against the thought." When an event you feel depressed about occurs, fill in the three columns. In Rush's example, a young woman wrote, "Attended football game and felt depressed and despondent" in the first column. The thought (cognition) that led to her feeling that way was, "I was a boring date." Her evidence for concluding that was, "My date concentrated on the game rather than me." But when she listed all the other evidence she had available, it included his explaining what was going on in the game to her, being very attentive to her when they went out to dinner afterward, and friends telling her that he was shy. Taken all together, the information contradicted the thoughts that led to her feeling depressed.

For additional approaches that can be used with depression and further information about the approaches just described, see the "Success and Failure" and "Reframing" sections of Chapter 17, the last section of Chapter 21, and Chapter 22.

GRIEF

"When you are sorrowful . . ." writes the Lebanese philosopher-poet Kahlil Gibran (1969, p. 29), "you are weeping for that which has been your delight."

Grief involves loss—of a friendship, job, possession, opportunity, stage in life, or a family member or intimate companion. The pain of grief involves wanting what *was* to continue, as we prepare to live with what *is*.

Josephine, a woman in her sixties, writes, "When my first counseling session began, I was surprised when suddenly I found myself weeping for my husband Cary, now dead four years. I had been fearful of going back into those terrible, engulfing moments when the irreversible truth that he was gone forever swept over me. It was a real fight to get back to trusting my emotions."

Feeling and Expressing Grief and Sadness

Kübler-Ross (1974, 1975) and others identify various stages in the grieving process. These stages can occur with smaller losses as well—like a child losing a favorite toy. The first stage is *shock or denial*. In my dazed disbelief, I can distort reality and move to recover the lost person or object. Then a stage of *resentment, anger,* or *rage* may occur—outraged, I storm at the universe for taking who or what I loved away. I may even feel resentment or anger at the departed person or other object of loss. This gives way to *despair* or *depression*, including mental anguish, feeling empty and helpless, and loss of hope. Then there is an *acceptance* and *recovery* stage in which I learn to live with the loss—it becomes part of me and my past—and I go on with life. A grieving person may fluctuate back and forth through those phases.

Mark took his young son on a group camping trip. Mark's son died on the trip. No one really knew what happened—one morning he just didn't wake up. Despite the exceptional anguish that the death of a child can bring, the well-meaning minister told the family not to grieve because the boy was with the angels. For six months the family members pretended they had no grief, and the tensions almost destroyed the family. When they finally acknowledged that they were bottling up their sorrow and gave themselves permission to mourn, they began to be able to talk to each other again.

When someone I love dies, I want to feel my grief fully, even if that means sitting back and howling. At such times, I don't need any restraint on the intensity of my feelings. If I go through the depths of my sorrow, I feel less need to hang onto it and I have a better chance to come out on the other side well and whole again.

In India there is a tradition that when someone dies, the person who was closest to the departed one repeats the story of the death to each new visitor, and the visitor often replies with a story of his or her own loss and grief. In retelling the event, the bereaved person gradually begins to live with the fact of the death and sometimes notices, "This woman I'm talking to who has tears in her eyes—it's her loss, too. I don't feel so alone in my grief." The awareness of death becomes a part of the process of life.

When someone I love dies or we part ways, I may lose more than that person: I also face losing part of myself that was called out by that person. So as I grieve, I want to offer that part of myself a chance to keep on living. Gordon Tappan (1974) describes a way to do this. Try it now:

Dialogues with Someone Who's Gone

Take a pen and paper, and give voice to the part or parts of yourself that came to life in the presence of someone who has passed out of your life. Then give that person a voice, allowing your thoughts and feelings to flow spontaneously onto the page and not worrying about whether that person would really say what you're putting in his or her mouth.

Pay special attention to any areas that were left unfinished between you and that person: anything that was left unsaid that needs to be said. Continue the dialogue until you've said all the things that seem important. Repeat it as you need to.

Some of us (men mostly) suppress the urge to cry when we feel it. I want, however, to respect myself in my ability to feel my sadness fully and put aside my inhibiting controls and fears. New lines of research suggest that healthy crying may have positive physiological effects, breaking down certain toxins in a person's system (Day, 1980, p. 46).

Many women in our culture have learned to use crying to cover other emotions. Just as anger can mask grief, for instance, crying can mask anger. Tears that nourish don't sting. When my crying leaves me feeling cleansed, refreshed, and awakened, it's nourishing. When my tears hide other feelings, my eyes burn and my tears have a salty sting. That kind of crying can also be a way I avoid contact with you or manipulate you.

It would be an error to make crying a "should." Some people have other ways to express their sadness, and simply don't cry or feel an urge to. Others cry only when happy. Whatever your manner of expressing it, when you are in sorrow, go ahead— *be* sorrowful. Being in that state contains the key to transformation. The feelings you have avoided are *still there* and will be until you live them through. If you're sorrowful but "can't bear the pain," unfortunately there's no way you can make it vanish from your life and your memories. In your living through it, you become better able to help yourself and others.

Terminal Illness

A terminally ill person is dealing with death, with feelings about losing his or her reason or control, and with concerns about burdening family members, about separation, and perhaps about not completing important tasks or other obligations.

The family mirrors many of these fears. Family members may be afraid they'll be unable to handle the stress of caregiving or the financial burden. They're afraid of what losing the ill person will mean to the family. They're afraid the death itself may be painful or ugly (Donovan, 1976, pp. 15–18).

Sometimes a "conspiracy of silence" is maintained in which the family knows the worst and keeps it from the ill member. In most cases, the person is fully aware of the severity of the illness and doesn't need "protection." A conspiracy of silence denies everybody the chance to deal directly with anxiety, share remaining pleasures, plan realistically for the future, and have the important intimate exchanges that they all need. It is tragic when after the death, for years or perhaps a lifetime, each person in the family carries a burden of unfinished "things I wish I'd said" (Feifel, 1977, pp. 222–230).

By contrast, several years ago when a cousin-in-law of mine who was the father of five died, everything was in the open. Despite the difficulties and demands on their energy, the family cared for John at home during his last months rather than sending him to the hospital. They had many long conversations and deep sharing. Things that had been left unsaid in the past were said along with present feelings. When I visited before his death, we had a long, moving conversation that's an important part of my memory of him now.

Avoiding Unnecessary Suffering

About a third of our suffering is inevitable, said Buddha, *but we ourselves create the rest of it.* We can learn to diminish that other two thirds. If I'm alive, I experience sadness as well as joy, pain as well as pleasure. I needlessly oppress myself if I think that my life "is not the way it should be." I don't need the extra suffering of thinking, "I *shouldn't* be suffering right now." As Hobart Thomas sums it up, *"I belong to this realm of tears and beauty, the earth."*

DEATH

The more directly I confront the inevitability of my death, the more fully I can be alive now.

"A human life is like that moment when a raindrop skates and bounces on the surface of the ocean before merging with the sea," says biologist Don Isaac. My life is brief, and when I die, the great stream of life itself goes on, reborn in new bodies and new forms, evolving onward from its ancient origin. "Our human life but dies down to its root," says Thoreau, "and still puts forth its green blade to eternity."

In our culture, we shy away from accepting death as part of our process. Funerals and everything associated with them are often mechanical and antiseptic. Death itself is an event that seldom comes up in our speech. By shying away from facing the prospect of my death, I avoid considering what it means in terms of the way I live my life.

Jeannie's father died slowly, and they spent several weeks together before he died. As he reviewed his life, he talked most about the opportunities he'd missed—the things he would have done but didn't. "I said no to life too many times, Jeannie," he said. "I hope you don't do the same."

His words helped Jeannie make some major changes. She changed jobs, developed new friends, became meaningfully involved in her community, and took a vacation she'd been talking about for years.

Elisabeth Kübler-Ross, a Chicago psychiatrist, interviewed several hundred people who were revived after they'd been declared medically dead. "We came to fantastic findings, terribly intriguing," she says. These people describe how they "float out of their body . . . they have a feeling of peace and wholeness, a tremendous feeling of 'stop all this attempt [to revive me], I'm all right.' . . . Not one of them has ever been afraid to die again" (1975).

Some of us let our individual identity die by identifying ourselves completely with some mass organism—i.e., "the company," "the corporation," or "the agency." Authors believe that books live beyond their lives. The pseudoimmortality we gain through such identification can lead to neglecting the sources of nourishment we need to keep ourselves alive as individuals.

While old age is seen as a prelude to dying, it is also a place to do another kind of living. "Take kindly the counsel of the years, gracefully surrendering the things of youth," says the *Desiderata*. As we surrender the things of youth, we can gradually enter into the things of maturity and age.

In proportion as we live fully in the now of each day and each time in our lives, we can love and laugh and play in all the seasons of our years.

13

Anger and Aggression

*M*y anger is typically a response to frustration or arousal. *Arousal* might result from an intense noise or from someone else's being angry or upset. *Frustration* occurs when I'm blocked from trying to do something, and my anger may be not only a statement of my frustration but also an attempt to remove the obstacle.

In most cases, anger serves a communicative function. In a study by experimental psychologist James Averill (1981), the consequences mentioned by people who experienced a friend or family member's anger included: "Realized your own faults" (79%); "Gained respect for the angry person" (44%); "Lost respect for the angry person" (29%); "Relationship with the angry person is strengthened" (48%); "Relationship with the angry person became more distant" (55%).

Clearly, anger cuts both ways, leading to a gain or loss of respect, to a closer or more distant relationship. The question of how to deal with our anger in ways that help us feel better and get what we want, rather than ways that lead to trouble and feeling bad, is an important one.

ANGER AND OTHER EMOTIONS

Anger seldom occurs by itself. It can occur together with many other emotional responses, but there are a few with which it is especially often paired. One of these is hurt. When I'm angry with another person, if I look beneath the anger, usually I find pain. My anger is a defensive, protective response. I can use it to discover where I feel hurt. At the same time, knowing that others' anger is often a response to pain as well as a means of self-protection can make it easier to accept anger from them.

Shame, Humiliation, and Guilt

Shame is the painful feeling that goes with thinking I've acted in an inadequate, improper, harmful, or disreputable way—and that others know about it. Like embarrassment, it has more to do with how I believe you see my "shameful event" than with how I assess the event independent of you.

When I am *humiliated*, I feel reduced to a lower position in my own or others' eyes. I feel disgraced and my self-respect suffers. Art, now in psychotherapy, recalls: "My childhood was a series of humiliations. Like being given a 'Mohawk' haircut against my will and being sent to school that way, being dressed in girl's clothes and then made fun of, and being made to wear soiled underwear over my head and face for wetting the bed. Needless to say, I was a confused, anxiety-ridden child."

Guilt, in a legal sense, involves breaking a law and being judged guilty. Psychological guilt is my feeling that I'm "bad" for doing what I'm doing, especially when my action is contrary to my image of how I'm expected to behave. I feel guilty when I violate others' standards, my own standards, or standards I've borrowed from others and accepted as my own. I may even plead guilty to an imagined offense and then feel inadequate or unworthy.

Guilt is a favorite manipulative tool—the "gift" that can last a lifetime. When I manipulate you with guilt, such as by reminding you that I've done so much for you that you can never possibly repay me, I don't have to make my demands explicit. I don't risk having you say "no." If I control you effectively, you can keep busy meeting my needs and at the same time feel you can never do enough for me. How can you blame me after all I've been through with you?

Resentment

When I suppress anger that I feel, I'm apt to convert it to resentment or even hate. Hate is deluxe resentment. In direct proportion to your contribution to my feeling guilty, ashamed, or humiliated, I'm likely to resent or hate you. If I'm sufficiently afraid of losing your love or am otherwise intimidated, I may stop myself from being aware of my hatred or resentment.

Perls spells out the relationship between guilt and resentment: "Behind every feeling of guilt is resentment. . . . It feels much nobler to feel guilty than resentful, and it takes more courage to express resentment than guilt. With expressing guilt you expect to pacify your opponent; with expressing resentment you might stir up hostility in him" (1969b).

When you feel guilty, Perls suggests, find out what you resent. He maintains that behind every resentment there are *demands,* and we stop being resentful only after we get them out in the open. For instance, a demand to my father might be, "I want you to appreciate me for who *I* am, not judge me based on your expectations." Here's a way to explore this:

Resentments and Demands

Write a letter to the person toward whom you feel resentful. If that person has died, write the letter as though he or she is still here.

Tell that person how you feel manipulated, and how you feel about that. Then ask yourself, "Beneath these resentments, what *demands* do I want to make?" Write down the demands.

When you've finished, put the letter away. After a week has passed, read your letter. Send it or not, as you wish. (You may write many letters that you don't send.)

Those who taught us by guilt, shame, and humiliation came through that same school themselves. Once I've cleared out my file of resentments against you, I can appreciate that you may have done the best you could. This process, *catharsis*, works when I have said the "unsayable" and I continue to exist, and exist in relationship to you. When I finish my unfinished business with you, I don't have to carry it around anymore. At the same time, I confront my fear of expressing feelings I've held in and develop my ability to express them.

Resentment and Hate

"My aunt invented the cold war," said Allen. "She was always throwing cold, twisting jabs at me and my uncle while pretending to be the nicest person in the world." When I hold back my anger out of my fear of what will happen if I express it, I feel resentful. When I feed this resentment enough, I can reap a harvest of hate. In most cases, both resentment and hate are anger plus fear, or anger plus loss and helplessness.

Fran had been brutally raped and beaten. When she entered counseling, she was understandably fearful and would not let herself express her strong sense of being violated. She worked hard to allow herself to scream, rage, and mourn the event. When at last she was able to do that, she recovered some sense of dignity and stopped projecting her hostility toward the man who had raped her onto other men.

Putdowns—a common form of hostility—often disguise anger. When I disguise my anger in a putdown—as in sarcasm, for instance—I'm hoping that you'll be wounded by my anger but not recognize it for what it is: I'll have said it to you and you'll know I've said it, but you won't be able to blame me for it. When I find myself being cold or cutting, I'd better look to see who or what the source of my anger is.

Anger is short-lived. It's an event. Resentment and hate are institutions. When I hang onto my resentful or hateful feeling toward you, I don't genuinely deal with its sources. Angry communication that clearly confronts genuine issues can lead to warmth in a relationship, but festering resentment is cold, muddy, and leads to separation, not communication. A comic once remarked, "What I love about hate is that it makes revenge such a pleasure."

There's another side of it, too: Separation and alienation can lead to mistrust and resentment. I mistrust what I don't know about.

Projection is often heavily involved in hate. I hate you when you say and do things that put me in touch with qualities I reject in myself. Ugh! We've all experienced this: I utterly detest someone, and then a friend who knows us both says casually, "You two sure are a lot alike." I could kill him!!

SUPPRESSING AND REPRESSING ANGER

Unexpressed ongoing anger is toxic waste in storage. Instead of being used to seek out more sources of aliveness, it just seeps, leaks, and erodes.

There are various flavors of bottled-up anger. One is anger drowned in tears. That's often a lady's choice, since it "isn't ladylike" to show anger openly. Women get angry just as often as men but are as "ladies" more likely to hold their anger in and cry (Averill, 1981). My client Patricia used her tears to distract herself from her anger until she learned to use them as a signal to herself that she *is* angry.

Another approach to bottling up anger results in burying feelings beneath a facade of superrationality. *Fortune* sums up the current management environment as "cool is in." Self-control is the ideal and anger is withheld for fear one won't be promoted. This "I am not mad" syndrome is often part of a larger "I don't feel anything" pattern. The suppressed anger is apt to go first toward oneself—physical ailments in the body and self-depreciation in the mind; and second, toward subordinates, the family, and the dog. Victims respond in various ways, including sneaky revenge (Kiechel, 1981, p. 205).

The process of *retroflection* is involved in the first case—I redirect anger meant for others back against myself. My anger produces a whole series of physical events. Nerves fire off messages faster, hormones are released, my heartbeat speeds up, my stomach stops digesting, and my skin becomes warmer. When my anger is intense and I allow it no expression, I convert it into such forms as headaches, hypertension, ulcers, fatigue, high blood pressure, or cardiac problems (Pelletier, 1977, pp. 63, 150–151). I don't like the exchange rate.

When I deaden my angry feelings, I freeze part of myself—including some of my spontaneity, sensitivity, and creativity. When I don't feel, it's more difficult for me to touch and do.

Focused and Distorted Anger

Focused anger fits the situation that provokes it. *Distorted anger is out of proportion to the situation.* It's usually a product of my hidden feelings, wishes, and an assorted collection of resentments. My rage at my young daughter's desire to take a couple of extra minutes to dress in the clothes *she* wanted instead of those closest at hand was anger distorted. When I explored that issue with another psychologist, I found myself drawn back to the age of two. My feeling of being frustrated and held in when I was ready to leave and my daughter was leisurely going through her clothes reminded me of my rage when I threw a temper tantrum and my grandmother shook me and then pinned me to the floor. My rage, so inappropriate to the present situation, *was* appropriate to the old one it belonged to.

When my anger is distorted, I want to discover what underlies it. Then I can deal with that. As long as I'm dealing with old ghosts or "hidden agendas," I'm not likely to handle present situations well.

Childhood Anger

As children, we had occasional temper tantrums. When we learned to inhibit them, someone forgot to tell us that it was okay to be angry, but that some ways of being angry are more effective *and* less offensive than others. As we found various ways to deny and disguise our true, honest anger, it emerged as "purified" anger and, in some cases, *self-righteous* anger. In that state it becomes the junk food of emotional nourishment.

We've learned both the stated and the unstated rules governing how to disguise our anger. In new relationships anger can emerge before we've had time to agree on rules for handling it. New couples and families, for instance, are often so overwhelmed when even their focused anger surfaces that they feel helpless and wrong.

According to Dreikurs and Grey (1968), there are several patterns of distorted anger that we've all been exposed to and all recognize.

1. *Demanding undue attention.* "Hey, look at me. Look! Look!" Some of this is natural. It can become excessive when a child feels bypassed or hampered by lack of self-assurance.
2. *Pulling a power play.* The child tries to control and manipulate, often out of a sense of powerlessness or "not counting for much."
3. *Being vengeful.* "I'll get you back for that." Underneath, the child feels hurt and, in his or her revenge, may be committed to being "bad" and "unlikable."
4. *Acting helpless.* "I can't do it. Don't ask, expect, or hope for anything from me." A discouraged "failure" is resentful of parents' expectations for "unreasonable" (any) success.

Passive-Aggressive Anger

If I have a hard time confronting you openly with my anger, I may send my message by retreating into cold silence or by going in the kitchen and banging the pots and pans around—and perhaps accidentally breaking your favorite glass. I don't tell you I'm angry, but through my tone of voice, my movements, and my other signals, you'll get the message. And there's nothing you can do to make things right until I've punished you to my satisfaction. This is called *passive-aggressive* behavior.

My friend Sarah writes, "When I'm on the receiving end of passive-aggressive anger, I want to totally close up. I tighten up and wait for the boom to fall. Part of my punishment is the slow torture of waiting. My mother got us conditioned to where if she raised her eyebrow, we knew we're going to 'get it,' but didn't know when. Her tactic was to wait until I was especially vulnerable, until I wanted to do something really badly—go out on a date, for instance—and then say, 'No, because of what you did last week,' which hadn't been mentioned in the meantime."

My unspoken but continuing anger (resentment) allows me to feel self-righteous and at the same time avoid being clear about my grievances and putting myself on the line to work things out with you. "I can't help being late," or "Can I help it if I'm forgetful?" are hard to argue with.

When I'm on the receiving end of passive-aggressive anger, I get angry in return. If I suppress this anger instead of confronting the other person, at that point I victimize myself and become 50 percent responsible for the continuation of the passive-aggressive process. I can break the spell by confronting the other person: "If you have something to say to me, I'd like to hear it. I'll listen to your anger, but I don't want your slow poison."

ANGER IN RELATIONSHIPS

Therapist and educator Carmen Lynch (1978) describes three techniques many of us use to support the belief that expressing anger is bad, destructive, and useless:

1. *The debt syndrome.* Getting angry would mean ingratitude, as though gratitude and anger can't coexist. "After everything she's (I've) done for me (you) . . ."
2. *I can convince myself of your "fragility" or "weakness."* The statement here is, "You can't handle my anger. Therefore I'd better not mention it." I'm so thoughtful in my projections.
3. *"The bomb gets dropped on Luxembourg"* or *"Stop me before I sneer again."* I'm afraid that the power of my wrath is so overwhelming that I'll go out of control and be sorry, so I dare not say anything at all.

But unspoken anger can keep us apart at least as effectively as anger that's displayed explosively or distorted into blame or judgment. By contrast, when we share our focused anger, we can become closer. Knowing that we care enough to listen and work problems through deepens our mutual trust.

When you do reveal your anger, I can hear you better when you tell me how you feel (risky business) than when you focus on how bad I am.

THE CATHARSIS VERSUS DETACHMENT CONTROVERSY

Shall I tell you politely what I'm mad about, scream and rage about it, or do my best to transcend it and forget it? This issue touches a long-standing controversy.

The question of how to best handle anger is more than a personal one: Whole cultures favor strategies that differ sharply from one another. In Italy, a common response to anger is yelling and gesticulating. In Thailand, gracious composure is the ideal and people seldom quarrel or shout. An American professor at the University of Chaing Mai said, "People here are less bothered by frustrations we can't do anything about and less easily upset by little things. On the other side, they don't cope adequately with confrontation."

Physiological studies, points out my colleague David Van Nuys (1975, pp. 14–15), show that *both* meditation (a key procedure in "transcending" anger) and catharsis can lead to lowered pulse rates and decreases in other stress indicators.

A study by social psychologist Jack Hokanson provides an intriguing lead. He had noticed that unlike men, who often get belligerent when insulted, the women he observed more often said something friendly to try to calm the insulting person down. Physiological data showed that acting friendly brought down their arousal level just as responding belligerently brought it down for men. Their friendly response appears to involve a type of transcendence: Unhooking from the angry response and substituting a different one. In a follow-up experiment, Hokanson found that rewarding women for acting aggressively brought about a change in their physiological response pattern so that aggressive responses began to lead to a catharsislike decrease in blood pressure, and rewarding the men for acting friendly led to decreased blood pressure following friendly behavior (in Tavris, 1983).

It appears that we *can* learn to let go of our anger instead of feeding it, and that in the meantime the most cathartic form of expression differs from one person to another and depends on our personal history.

Van Nuys offers his own criteria for distinguishing whether we've really transcended our anger or need to express it directly: "When your guts are churning; your breathing is short; your voice is getting clipped, or loud, or unusually soft; or you're getting obliquely sarcastic, but doing your damndest to suppress it; that is not detachment. That's denial. [Then] it is important to own your own anger and deal with it" (1975, pp. 14–15).

My guideline is this: When I suppress my anger—and then feel bad afterward—I need to work on stating it assertively. But if I roar out my anger on the smallest pretext, the task that faces me is either to change to a nonblaming, nonaggressive form of expression or to work on unhooking or defusing. In both instances, the required work involves doing what I find hardest.

A critical dimension of either approach is *learning the difference between assertion and aggression*—overtly toward others or inwardly toward ourselves.

The catharsis versus detachment controversy has been confused by the mistake of equating aggression with catharsis. "Catharsis is unwise," some critics insist. "A person who vents his or her feelings through aggressive acting out, and feels better as a result, is likely to keep on doing so." Turning back to Freud, we find that far from suggesting that we give our violent anger direct expression, he feared that the fragile veneer of civilized behavior could all too easily break down, as he saw happen toward the end of his life in Hitler's Germany. As Freud described it, catharsis involved acknowledging, experiencing, and appreciating our feelings, not acting them out. It involved giving credence to my tears and my angry storming so that I *would not need* to store them away or act aggressively.

But my own experience suggests that one form of acting out my feelings—even my anger—can have particular value. That's *acting them out in a way that causes no intrusion or assault on the rights of others.* Nathan Azrin (1967) found that when he shocked a monkey, it hit a ball in its cage as hard as it could. It even learned to pull a string that lowered the ball into its cage so it could hit it. When I hit my finger with a hammer, like Azrin's monkey with its ball, I feel much better if I smack a nearby two-by-four with the hammer. Some people don't need to do that. As for me—it helps. But I won't hit the two-by-four hard enough to damage it because I paid good money for it. I *learn to discriminate* between harmful and harmless ways of acting out aggression when holding it in completely isn't comfortable.

George Bach (1970, 1974) suggests a ritual called "The Haircut" for use when a backlog of unexpressed angry statements has piled up into a load of simmering resentments. The purpose is to clear the air without getting caught in a cycle of verbal aggression.

The Haircut

First I get your permission. This takes away the feeling of being ambushed. If this is a bad time for you, nothing I say is likely to lead to constructive change.

When the time for the haircut comes, we negotiate how long it can last, how far apart we stand or sit, and how high the person giving it stands in relation to the other. Standing higher than the other person usually makes the person giving it feel more powerful.

We take our agreed-upon positions. If there's a time limit of, say, three minutes, you have the watch. I let loose with everything I'm angry or upset about that I haven't been telling you. "I resent . . ." "I'm angry with you for . . ." and so on, saying it the way I feel it. (I may start out quietly and need a couple of minutes to get fully into my feelings.)

You don't reply until later—like the next day—in order to think over what was said. You can state in advance what is "below the belt"—too touchy or painful to be mentioned. But beware of "putting your belt line too high" so that you stop me from dealing with matters important to me.

After I've had my say, and you've had time to think it over and reply, I can make a request for change, and we can negotiate, as described in Chapter 27.

AGGRESSION

Perhaps it's the ultimate irony: Humankind's capacity for blatant aggression, which helped us to dominate every other species on the planet and to drive many species into extinction, now threatens our own survival and our peace of mind.

The capacity to murder and destroy and the capacity to act with great love and gentleness coexist in each of us. Once, when my own survival was at stake and I was both afraid and enraged, I murdered a man. (The Army later tried to give me a medal for it.) Without denying that this is part of me, I can choose to what extent, and in what ways, I want to let it be part of my life.

Four Patterns of Aggression

Aggression takes various forms.* If it's physical aggression, we call it violence. If it involves trying to make people feel bad or look bad to others, it's verbal aggression or emotional abuse. Evidence is overwhelming that most men are more physically aggressive than women, and apparently women tend to be more verbally aggressive than men (Feshbach, 1970, pp. 190–192). It emerges in at least four general patterns:

1. *Threat-based aggression.* This includes self-defense; aggression that grows out of fear, as with a cornered animal; defense of helpless other persons; and territorial defense.
2. *"Irritable aggression."* We may respond aggressively to pain or irritation. Pain often leads to lashing out. When two animals cooped up together in a small chamber are shocked, they're apt to fight each other. And the popular notion that a "long, hot summer" can mean trouble has been supported by studies of

*Although aggression is a behavior rather than an emotion, it is so closely linked with anger, in ways that will be described, that its inclusion in this chapter seems appropriate.

102 riots and other disturbances in U.S. cities from 1967 to 1982: The violence consistently occurred during heat waves. Even the irritating effect of cigarette smoke can predispose people to be more aggressive: A 1978 study showed that people are apt to be more punitive toward others in a smoke-filled room than in one filled with clean air (Berkowitz, 1980, pp. 341–343).

3. *Frustration-based aggression.* I may behave aggressively when something stops me from getting what I want. This is more than deprivation: It includes an *expectation* about what I intend to do or get. If I'm deprived of something but don't expect to get it or to be able to do it, I'm less likely to feel frustrated to a point of aggression (Dollard et al., 1939). In discussing frustration, Neal Miller (1941) and Robert R. Sears (1941) both noted that the way we react to it depends on our history of past learning.

4. *Instrumental aggression.* This gets me something I want, like a child who gets a toy by hitting another child or threatening to, or someone in authority who uses threats to obtain compliance (Feshbach, 1970, p. 161).

Aggression and Anger

Aggression is not a "simple" expression of anger. In studies of convicted murderers, for instance, a peculiar phenomenon appears: Many one-time murderers have never been charged with any other crime and have a life history of being quiet and mild mannered. The morning headline screams, SUBURBAN WOMAN STABS HUSBAND TO DEATH IN KITCHEN! and in a television interview later that day a neighbor says, "Why, I've never heard her say an angry word in all the time I've known her." So, my love, do me a favor and yell at me once in a while. I'll live longer.

We find two sources of anger-related aggression: In one case, anger is channeled directly into violence instead of into more constructive forms of expression. In the second instance, anger that is withheld turns into resentment, and emerges as direct or passive aggression at some future time.

Aggression based on *displacement* occurs when I am aggressive toward someone other than the person I'm actually angry at. I'm afraid to talk back to my boss, but I can be nasty to my mate.

Another form of aggression involves projection. Disowning my own angry and aggressive feelings, I project *the cause of my unhappiness and dissatisfaction outward onto others, then try to attack it and eradicate it there.*

THE SOCIAL CONTEXT OF AGGRESSION

Authorized aggression refers to the aggression of soldiers killing in a war, a member of the police jailing and torturing a member of the opposition, and the like. Some structure of authority has authorized the aggression, sanctioned it as socially acceptable, and probably pays and applauds the perpetrator who carries it out. And the authority may, as in El Salvador, protect the murderers when they're subjected to criticism.

Indirect aggression, unlike other forms, involves no direct act against a victim. Rather, it involves acting in ways that make it easier for others to be aggressive, such as a bystander who eggs an aggressor on or someone who creates more effective instruments of violence for others to use.

It's hard for me to acknowledge my acts of violence and oppression for what they are—statements of my own incompetence. Isaac Asimov's character Hardin in *Foundation* says, "The temptation was great to muster what force we could and put up a fight. It's the easiest way out, and the most satisfactory to self-respect, but nearly invariably, the stupidest. . . . Violence is the last refuge of the incompetent" (1970, pp. 84–85). Frequently it leads to results just the opposite of those it was intended to produce. Violence, like war, doesn't determine who's right, just who's left.

The Roots of Aggression

Some people are more aggressive than others, and childhood influences seem to have much to do with it. Feshbach (1970, pp. 216–217) found that aggressive children tend to receive less warmth and nurturance from their parents than nonaggressive children, and that the *fathers* of aggressive boys, in particular, are likely to be colder, more intolerant, and less interested in their sons than other fathers (1970, pp. 216–217)

Relating to others in assertive yet caring ways can take the place of aggressive patterns. This involves deliberately learning effective ways to solve problems, so that irritation and frustration are reduced (Feshbach, 1970, pp. 170–177, 216–218).

Aggressive children also tend to come from families where there's a good deal of physical punishment. Since *imitation* is one of the most powerful elements in human learning, the punishment that an adult thinks will deter a child's violence may instead be more powerful as a demonstration of how to be violent (Bandura & Walters, 1963). Getting punished may also be a way for a person to "pay the dues" for being aggressive, so that he or she feels free to aggress again.

We need both to *avoid rewarding aggression* and to *teach other ways to handle the situation*. A nonviolent form of punishment to lower the aggression level while more rational or more loving ways of handling the situation are being learned may be appropriate.

Another source of violence has broad implications for our society. Black writers like James Baldwin and Maya Angelou have pointed out that in the poverty underclass of our nation, and especially among minorities, violence is one of the few avenues open for people to feel a sense of power and effectiveness. Where there are few jobs or other avenues to self-respect and the respect of others, and people feel little power to affect their environment and their lives, violence a way to feel powerful. This is not a revolutionary act but a surrender to feeling hopeless and helpless.

Our society encourages violence in our games and recreation. In many games the more you kill and destroy, the higher your score. And Christmas morning, looking out my window, I see a street full of kids shooting at each other and launching model nuclear missiles against imaginary cities. That's a hell of a way to celebrate the birthday of the Prince of Peace.

In a dramatic demonstration of the *weapons effect*, social psychologist Leonard Berkowitz found that angry men attacked one another more often with electric shocks when a rifle and revolver were nearby than when badminton racquets were present. Another study showed that even photographs of guns can heighten the intensity of the attacks that men who had been insulted wanted to inflict on their tormenter (1980, pp. 348–349). I'm pleased to see that in recent years children's TV programs have become less violent—and more creative and interesting. I hope a similar change takes place in adult movies and prime-time TV.

Our sports "cheers," too, from junior high school to college, have to do with smashing, killing, hitting, and the like. The speeches of Presidents and other politicians, when dealing with matters that have no inherent connection with anything violent at all, are repeatedly cast in violent terms. "The *weapons* we will use in the coming *battles* to *combat* inflation . . ." and so on. We could speak instead of "the tools we will use to explore and solve these problems," or of "the hard work to find solutions."

We are a people of contradictions. We laud peace, yet the God many of us most revere is presented in a violent form, nailed to a piece of wood. Actually, the cross was not used as a symbol of Christianity until the Dark Ages. Before that, the symbol was a fish. Lenny Bruce commented that we're lucky Jesus was executed two thousand years ago instead of recently, because Christians would all be wearing necklaces with miniature electric chairs hanging from them.

Violence in the Family

Violence occurs more often in the family than anywhere else, declare researchers who studied more than 2,000 families over an eight-year period (in Morgenstern, 1980). In this strange drama where people terrorize those others whom they love the most, the commonest events are wife abuse and child abuse.

A four-and-one-half year follow-up of fifty abused children found that over half had chronic low self-esteem, few friends, and were generally unhappy (Martin & Beezley, 1976).

Violence against a wife or child severely damages the chances for a trusting, mutually giving relationship. The abused person feels trapped and constantly anxious about impending assault. And even when children are not themselves abused, they're sure to distrust and may hate the abusing father, and distrust the abused mother. A violent man suffers guilt and shame about his violence and also experiences the uneasiness of living in a house of psychological barbed-wire fences.

Once a cycle of abuse starts, it continues or gets worse unless the spouse does something to stop it. Any little irritation can serve as a pretext for violence. Hoping that things will change and wanting to believe the abuser's promises to reform, the victim may do nothing to break the cycle. A wife may be afraid that she and the children couldn't make it on their own, or that if she has her husband arrested, he'll lose his job. She may not mention the violence even to friends and relatives, out of intimidation or a fear that it marks her as a "failure" as a wife and mother.

Anne Ganley (1981), a leading authority on domestic violence, declares, "There's a myth in our culture that says, 'Any of us in this room, when we hit a certain breaking point, will become violent.' " In fact, we respond differently. Some of us laugh, some cry, some turn inward, and some have learned to be violent in the family. We can unlearn that and learn alternative responses.

"Violent individuals," Ganley continues, "minimize and deny the effects of what they do. She's in bed with a broken jaw and he's saying, 'We had a little argument.' Abusers won't change so long as they can keep on doing this. Someone has to confront them."

Ganley describes abusers as "externalizers," viewing themselves as controlled by events outside themselves. "I do it 'because of my wife,' or 'because of my work.' " In some ways we may be victims of circumstances, but our actions and reactions are always our own.

Abusers and victims of domestic violence are increasingly contacting their communities' social services departments and women's shelters and seeking professional help in handling the problem.

Institutional Violence

When carried out by the State, violence is within the boundaries of the law. When the State is being violent towards me, I lose many of my rights. Economic, ethnic, and racial factors typically influence the way a matter is treated by law enforcement authorities and the courts. When I was living in the ghetto, on various occasions policemen were unjustifiably violent with me or my friends. Such abuse of legitimate authority provide models that ultimately many of us imitate.

War is a socially approved form of authorized violence. We drill young men over and over to perform the act of killing automatically and choicelessly when the signal comes. When the war is over, nothing is done to extinguish this conditioned readiness to kill, so that under stress the ex-soldier may turn it towards his own society or himself. This complex tragedy is seen as part of what is now called *delayed stress syndrome.*

We don't solve complex, frustrating problems when our response is the oversimplified one of axe or A-bomb. Gandhi stated eloquently: "What difference does it make to the dead, the orphans, the homeless, whether the mad destruction is wrought under the name of totalitarianism or the holy name of liberty or democracy" (1965, p. 55)?

In its oppressive frustration, our government jails and exiles young men who refuse to become instruments of authorized violence. Here again we reward violence and punish nonviolence.

Nonviolence: Mahatma Gandhi and Martin Luther King, Jr.

One of history's most unusual political revolutions occurred when India ended Britain's colonial occupation through nonviolent resistance. The leader of the resistance movement, who inspired the nonviolent campaign of Martin Luther King, Jr., for civil rights several decades later, was Mahatma Gandhi. We lost a crucial opportunity to learn to solve problems nonviolently when we turned our backs and our guns on Gandhi and King.

The nonviolence they advocated, which Gandhi called *ahimsa,* was not just a tactic but a way of life, expressed on the job and with neighbors and family. It was not only a negation, a refraining from, but an affirmation of the spirit of love and an element in the quest for self-realization. In Gandhi's words: "Man as animal is violent but as spirit is non-violent. The moment he awakes to the spirit within he cannot remain violent. . . . Active *ahimsa* necessarily includes truth and fearlessness" (1965, p. 27; 1960, p. 126).

Nonviolence proved to be such a powerful force in India that when India had succeeded in its quest for self-determination, after Gandhi's death Nehru outlawed nonviolent demonstrations against the Indian government (Alinsky, 1972).

Some commentators have suggested that to be effective, nonviolence must evoke a violent response. Not necessarily. In the Diablo Canyon antinuclear sit-in in 1982, for example, which enjoyed great media attention, organizers took great care not only to enforce their own nonviolence, but also to discourage violence by state troopers by carefully photographing each arrest. In many conflict-of-interest situations, an excellent alternative to aggression is negotiation that seeks to accommodate the legitimate interests of everyone involved. For guidelines in such negotiation, turn to Chapter 27.

14

Defensive Processes—
And Beyond

My interest in events inside and outside me grows out of my awareness, and my wish to make contact grows out of that interest. In turn, contact leads to new areas of awareness.

By contrast, when aspects of my environment are uncomfortable, painful, or overwhelming, I may want to minimize my contact with them to allow the rest of my life to continue.

Ways of avoiding contact with ourselves and others, however, can become so habitual and generalized that they interfere with our ability to enjoy ourselves. For example, certain "inhibitions" do that. I'm "inhibited" when I don't do something I'd like to do because I'm afraid of someone's disapproval.

AVOIDANCE OF AWARENESS

We all defend ourselves—by escaping from a threat, acting vigorously to nullify it, or diverting it. By attending clearly, I can deal effectively with most threats. But I get into trouble when my method of defending is to deceive myself about what's happening.

When my awareness of an event becomes unpleasant, painful, and uncomfortable, my options include blocking out the experience and denying my discomfort. These tactics lead to distorting or denying reality. In an 1899 paper on the substitution of neutral memories for painful ones, Freud wrote: "Since the elements of the experience which aroused objection were precisely the important ones, the substituted memory will necessarily lack those important elements and will in consequence most probably strike us as trivial" (1959, Vol. 5, pp. 51–52).

Through such substitution, I can become *alienated from myself*—from those qualities that live on in my shadow side hidden and unseen by me—though they're often visible to others.

I can *resist* awareness by putting something else between me and the threatening thoughts and feelings. I look at the issue and see only the distraction I've put between me and it, or don't see anything there at all.

I can *avoid* awareness by looking away from the issue. I let myself be sidetracked by my world of distracting events.

Staff members of a local hospital spent most of a series of meetings talking about ways of dealing with patients. That was a real concern, but they were using it to avoid another important matter: their own feelings of satisfaction and dissatisfaction in their work. They thought they "should" be concerned only about the patients and that their personal satisfaction was not a legitimate issue. Finally they began to realize that their feelings about their work affected their effectiveness with patients.

One way I can distract myself from feeling uncomfortable is by *jumping from one thing to another.* When I feel embarrassed, I may scan for some event that can distract me. Then my attention jumps to that distraction, blocking out my thoughts and feelings about my embarrassment. All this happens in an instant. When some kind of apparently unconnected chatter or nonsense comes through my mind with great force, for example, I look for what's behind or underneath it.

Jumping from one thing to another can also help me avoid facing my problems with another person. You and I may need to deal seriously with matters important to us both. But as soon as we touch a sensitive topic, one of us brings up something else. If that in turn gets touchy, we find yet another new issue to distract us: Perhaps I suddenly have to go to the toilet.

Distraction works especially well in groups, since each person brings in sources of distraction. I've attended meetings in which we had important things to do but got almost nothing done. We consistently moved on to something else before finishing the previous matter. After such meetings, I've found myself thinking, "We spent two hours in there and we didn't finish *anything.* " For this to happen, we all have to agree tacitly to let ourselves be distracted. Such cooperation!

This can also occur in counseling: When a person says, "Let's move on," it's wise to doublecheck: "Do you feel finished with that—ready to close the books on it?" Almost invariably the response is, "I guess not."

Hiding one feeling behind another is another form of distraction. I might, for instance, joke about something that's frightening to me. In the paratroops, I was the funniest guy you ever heard. I'd look around and see some of the men on my plane trembling with terror. I knew that same terror. My way of handling it was to get so funny that by the time we had to jump we were laughing so hard our eyes were watering— another way to cry. I'm sure some people resented my avoidance. I'd rather not have to be funny when I'm afraid.

I can also avoid something by getting irritated or angry about it. Often my irritation or anger is a straightforward response to the present situation. But when I'm angry about past history—my own or in general, like rehashing the Civil War—I'm probably using my anger to resist being in touch with something that's going on in me or in you right now. The same is true when I'm angry about some possible future event like "What will happen if . . . ?" My irritation or anger about an event in some other time and place is likely to provoke anger from you in return. The fight or tense exchange that follows blocks out all awareness of the current event that I wanted to avoid. You're so helpful.

THE DEFENSE MECHANISMS

Freud called some of our defensive processes *mechanisms*. Ordinarily they operate in an apparently adaptive, "mechanical" way that lies outside our ordinary consciousness. Most of the defense mechanisms are exaggerations of normal processes. They are a source of problems when they distort our real world in our attempts to respond to its stresses.

A Minicatalogue of Defense Mechanisms

No doubt you've always wanted a convenient catalogue of the principal defense mechanisms. Here it is.

Compensation. I try to compensate for a real or imagined lack in one area by doing well in another. A physically handicapped person may become an outstanding artist or scholar. A parent may make up for personal disappointments by bullying the children to achieve.

Deflection. The aim is deflected, off target, or out of focus. "I hate to sit in a room with smokers," instead of, "Jean, please smoke in the hall." Or the complaint deals with a detail instead of the main point. Can be useful in maintaining contact by saying something softly, like the Chinese, "We will consider it for discussion," instead of "No."

Denial of reality (often shortened to *Denial*). I behave as though unpleasant thoughts, facts, wishes, actions, or situations do not exist or are not so, and believe an alternative, more satisfying image of how things are. "He couldn't possibly have taken a bribe. The jury must have made a mistake."

Idealization. I construct a glorified image of a person or object, support it with inner speech and imagery, and show it in attitudes and actions. All politicians want precinct workers who are prone to such overestimation. It helps to enlist other mechanisms such as *rationalization* and *denial* in its support.

Identification. Adopting another's values, attitudes, and behavior (in reality or fantasy), I think of myself as similar to that person. *Normal*: Children identify with parents in learning conscience, values, and the like; a movie audience identifies with E.T. *Pathological*: A psychotic identifies with Napoleon or other powerful figure in history.

Introjection. I uncritically "swallow whole" some way of being. Unless I evaluate what's acceptable and unacceptable to me, I can end up suppressing my personal self. Like identification, introjection is important in early socialization.

Isolation. I compartmentalize and isolate events or ideas that may, if recognized as similar, lead to questioning my beliefs or feelings.

Obsessions and compulsions. Being unable to keep all-insistent thoughts out of my mind, or rigidly carrying out repetitive tasks that keep my thoughts and energy distracted.

Projection. By assigning my unacknowledged and "unacceptable" desires, feelings, impulses, shortcomings, and disliked qualities to others, I'm less vulnerable or subject to criticism. My con artist self thinks everyone is dishonest; my sexually repressed male self sees all women as out to seduce me. This mechanism is an essential element in paranoia and war.

Rationalization. I substitute acceptable, worthwhile motives and logic for unacceptable acts or feelings. This protects my self-image. I unconsciously attribute admirable motives to my behavior when it is actually animated by greed, selfishness, revenge, or other reprehensible motives. *Sour grapes:* "A close relationship would intrude on my community responsibilities." *Sweet lemon:* "My firing him is a valuable lesson." *Exploitation:* "Business is business."

Reaction formation. I do just the opposite of a strong unconscious urge, believing I don't have that "reprehensible" desire and am repelled by it. The feeling, attitude, or behavior may be fanatical, rigid, or grossly over-done. I become overly protective when my hostility is too much; my "super nice guy" could probably kill you. My extensive sex life, scorecard and all, comes out of scared and inadequate feelings that I won't acknowledge.

Regression. I retreat from present threats and conflicts by returning to less mature behavior. An older child may show increases in bed-wetting, tantrums, and crying when the new baby arrives. That's normal. In other circumstances, however, regression may be a deficient process reflecting a loss of mature function.

Retroflection. Doing to myself what I would like to do to others. Angry at you, I strangle myself with my throat and chest muscles. Instead of directing effort toward my environment to satisfy my needs, I make myself the target of my own behavior, dividing myself into doer and done-to. May show up in statements like: "I must control myself"; "I have to force myself to do this."

Sublimation. I direct sexual or aggressive energy into creative or other socially approved channels: sports, dancing, art, and so on. I can have my strong emotions and, through socialization, can express them with full intensity in productive ways.

Undoing. "Undoing what has been done" is my attempt to cancel out the consequences of some unacceptable behavior. I can thus seem to make it nonexistent, sometimes by magically or symbolically repeating it in a different way. For instance, I repeat again and again "what I should have said."

Wish fulfillment. In my fantasy, I imagine satisfactions that seldom occur in real life. As a frail boy, I dream of myself as Superman. This practice becomes harmful when the daydreams interfere with taking real steps to get what I want.

Withdrawal. Withdrawing from a disturbing situation is sometimes adaptive, but may hamper constructive attempts to cope. May be accompanied by apathy and hopelessness. Often cloaked in reserve, formality, and apparent self-sufficiency. Or the person may become submissive, shy, and retiring.

Now that you have a convenient shopping list of more defensive processes than you ever wanted to hear about—what do you do with it? The point, said psychoanalyst Karen Horney, is to start to *notice the ones you use*, listen to yourself using them, and think back over which others you've used in the past.

Each of us uses defense mechanisms according to our needs and disposition. Freud speculated in a 1937 paper that such mechanisms are necessary at certain points in our development but later become counterproductive. When we cling to them, he suggests, they "produce an ever-growing alienation from the external world and a permanent enfeeblement. . . . The expenditure of energy necessary to maintain them proves a heavy burden" (1959, Vol. 5, p. 340).

Psychoanalyst Wilhelm Reich added the idea of *character armor*—apparently superficial traits or habits that cover deeper anxieties. Someone apprehensive about intimacy, for instance, might adopt formal speech, dress, and/or physical mannerisms that discourage others from making overtures toward close contact. Horney suggested that a person may weave together many such traits in a *protective organization* that pervades all aspects of his or her life (1945). Someone anxious about intimacy could take a job involving little contact with others, live in an impersonal apartment building, and avoid marriage or marry someone who similarly stays away from closeness (White, 1972, p. 227).

The Special Case of Repression

Repression fits in the catalogue of defensive maneuvers as an all-inclusive process: Unacceptable ideas or feelings are express-mailed to my unconscious bearing the label "Forget it." Repression occurs in conjunction with many defense mechanisms described earlier and is present to some degree in most of our lives. Anna Freud saw it as a particular hazard:

> It is capable of mastering powerful instinctual impulses in the face of which the other defensive measures are quite ineffective. . . . It is also the most dangerous mechanism. The . . . withdrawal of consciousness from whole tracts of instinctual and affective life may destroy the integrity of the personality for good. (1937, pp. 52–55)

Freud himself saw repression not as a single event but as an ongoing process that is continually maintained and monitored. The repression can be maintained by one defense mechanism today and a different one tomorrow, just as political repression can be maintained by a police crackdown today and a clever propaganda campaign tomorrow.

"DEXTIFYING"—THE INNER WORLD OF DEFENDING, EXPLAINING, AND JUSTIFYING

I rationalize when I think everything about me has to "make sense" in terms of ideas I already hold. Like Spock in *Star Trek*, I don't allow myself to be illogical and unreasonable or to act in ways that don't fit my self-image or my old "shoulds." I've forgotten that *it's all right for contradictions to exist in me.*

The term *dextifying* is a contraction of the terms *defending, explaining,* and *justifying.* Dextifying usually combines rationalization with some of the other defensive processes described earlier. It is a useful word because defending, explaining, and justifying are often used hand in hand for similar purposes.

This incident illustrates the process of justifying: One morning I stopped at Jerry's Friendly Service to clean my windshield. I gave the windshield a squirt or two from the bottle of water on the gas pump.

Jerry came barreling out of the station. "Don't you ever ask a person before you use his things?" he screamed.

"Sorry," I said, "I was only cleaning my windshield."

He got even angrier and started to lecture me as if he were virtue itself. In an uptight voice as nasty as his own, I told him off and *peeled* out of his station. (Inadvertently, I kept his bottle.)

I felt good, getting the last word.

Driving down the road, I thought about how stupid and selfish he was, how much he deserved to be told off, and how glad I was I had told him off. That's called *justifying.* I was convincing myself that what I did was "right."

When I justify, I make my actions fit my self-image of being "in the right." I reduce my chance to see if I acted as wisely as I could. I also close myself to experiencing what Jerry's world is like for him. I justify when I feel that I have to have a reason or an explanation for everything I say or do in case someone (me, for instance) questions me.

When defending, explaining, and justifying help me avoid some real unwanted outcome, they're useful. If I get stopped by a traffic officer, by the time he gets to my car I want to have the best dextification going.

When my dextifying doesn't serve some deliberate purpose, I view it suspiciously. To the degree that I'm justifying, explaining, and defending what I did, I'm less present and less aware now. But I can learn to let go of my dextifying—at least sometimes. The Sufi Sheikh Saadi of Shiraz told this story: "A lout abused a man who patiently said: 'O you of bright prospects: I am worse even than you say. I know all my faults, while you do not know them' " (in Shah, 1970, p. 87).

My dextifying distorts what happened. I can seldom truly say "why" I do the things I do. As children we don't know *why* we got angry, or took something, or hit little brother. If I did know, and told the truth, I'd "get it." I could say something about the where, when, or what. But since Mama or Papa demands an explanation or justification rather than a description, I think one up. Eventually we start believing our own dextifications. With people of all ages, "Why did you do . . .?" questions are almost always communication breakers that invite the other person into dextifying.

Try this: For an entire day, instead of asking why you or anyone else did something, ask "*What* did you do?" "*How* did you do it?" Ask "what" without implying "why," and without implying any judgment or accusation. What difference do you notice in the kind of communication that occurs?

Here's a useful exercise:

Feedback and Defending

This is an exercise in which each of us is a "listener" who gets "feedback" from as many as will give it to us about anything they want to say to us. Feedback can include feelings and observations about past or present events involving the listener.

In a group of five to twenty-five people with a leader or instructor, let that person be the first listener. The "timekeeper" sits to the left of the listener and allows five minutes for feedback—no more. Feedback is directed *to* the person. After five minutes, the listener selects a new listener and gives the watch to the person on his or her left, who becomes the new timekeeper.

The feedback consists of direct, concise, specific statements to the listener. As listener, you are allowed any *two-word* acknowledgment of each person's feedback—or you can say nothing. You have to "sit on" all your dextifications—no defending, explaining, or justifying out loud permitted. Becoming aware of your dextifying process—which you'll hear inside your head—is as important a goal of this exercise as getting and giving feedback.

When everyone has had a chance to be listener, describe what you experienced . . . without dextifying.

If you don't have a group to do this exercise with, take a day or a week to pay attention, on a moment-by-moment basis, to your process of defending, justifying, and explaining yourself.

Three social psychologists compared the way people responded to excuses, justifications, and apologies (Hupka, Jung & Porteus, 1981). By their definition, in an *excuse*, I admit the harm in what I did, but deny or minimize my responsibility for doing it. In a *justification*, I accept responsibility for doing it but maintain that it needed doing and deny that it was a negative act. In an *apology*, I accept responsibility for the act, recognize its harmful effects, and ask your pardon.

Hupka and colleagues asked people to imagine that their partners had either flirted or had intercourse with someone else, and then asked how they felt about the partner's excuse, justification, or apology. Excuses included, "I was drunk" and "I don't know what came over me." Justifications included, "I wanted to experience her"; "She made me feel loved"; "I have a right to do what I want"; and "You're never around." Apologies were variations of, "I have no excuse. I was wrong."

Partners most preferred apologies. If they wanted to continue the relationship with their original partner, excuses came next, and justifications were least liked. These results suggest that justifying sets up the partner as an adversary in the issue at hand.

You don't have to justify any way that you are. Just be, and know how you're being. You don't have to justify your existence. You're here.

REOPENING CLOSED FEELINGS

I may do something a thousand times and still be unwilling to perceive it, if my incentive for keeping it out of my awareness is strong enough. During counseling, one child wailed, "You always say, 'Just a minute,' *and then you forget about me.*" Her father replied indignantly, "I don't do that!" Until he's willing to confront his resistance to recognizing how little importance he gives his daughter's demands, the situation will continue.

When I resist awareness, the main thing is not to force myself to stop resisting—which is impossible—but to *get to know the processes* I use to stay out of touch with thoughts and feelings I find frightening or painful. My resistance itself becomes the focus of my awareness. As I discover how I dim my awareness, I can choose how and when I want to keep doing that, and how and when I don't. When I park one of my defensive processes on the shelf, I don't lose it, but I can choose when and where I want to use it.

Reopening closed feelings is a different process than the *cognitive* learning that most of us are used to. In this *affective* or emotional learning, change comes more through responding to situations with our feelings than through grasping them with just our intellect. Hopefully, previously blocked-off feelings entering my awareness may seem less frightening, less overpowering now. I become more able to say what I feel when I feel it, and I don't build up a backlog of unexpressed feelings that I inappropriately dump on whoever's available when I've reached "the last straw" and blow my lid (that is, my cover).

I can start opening up to my feelings in areas where I feel fairly safe. I don't have to terrorize myself with, "If I touch the lever, the sluice gates will open and I'll drown."

I can get a better grasp of how I'm feeling when I use my body to help me. Here's how:

The Message of Movement

Right now, stand up and walk around. Feel how you move, in your torso, your arms, your legs.

When you have a clear sense of how you're moving, *exaggerate* that movement as much as you can, whether it's a brisk, energetic movement, or a draggy, heavy one. *Notice how you feel as you move,* and allow a statement—not more than a few words—that fits the way you feel to come into mind. Or if no words come, find a sound. Continue to move in an exaggerated way and repeat the phrase or sound that has surfaced again and again for several minutes. When you've finished, ask yourself: "What's the message for me in what I've done?"

MEETING AND MOVING THROUGH AN IMPASSE

As I let long-hidden feelings emerge into the light, I sometimes find myself stuck. I no longer want to act in my old ways, but I'm not sure what to do instead. Even when I'm just living my daily life, I sometimes get similarly stuck—like when I've wanted to make contact with another person but have stopped myself. The point where I stop myself, out of my uncertainty and fear, is an impasse.

Perls states:

> The impasse occurs originally when a child cannot get the support from the environment, but cannot yet provide its own support. At that moment of

impasse, the child starts to mobilize the environment by playing phony roles, playing stupid, playing helpless, playing weak, flattering, and all the roles that we use in order to manipulate our environment. (1969a, p. 36)

In my impasse, I have one leg in my past and one leg in the future. I'm refusing to act in my old way, but I can't act easily in my new way yet. I'm stopped, immobilized, confused.

Confusion is an excellent distractor. When I'm confused, I don't see anything clearly—especially not what I want to avoid seeing. When I explore my confusion, I often find that I want two different things but can't have both. The situation is like that of a person wanting two lovers. "Which one shall I choose?" may be an issue. Kurt Lewin, the father of modern social psychology, called this an *approach-approach conflict*.

On the other hand, I may feel attracted to a certain person but also afraid of him. This is an *approach-avoidance conflict*.

Or I may have two lovers and strongly like and strongly dislike certain things about each. This is a *double approach-avoidance* conflict (Lewin, 1935).

An impasse may be a double approach-avoidance conflict. I dislike my old way, but it's easy. I'm attracted by the new way, but it's scary and uncertain. An impasse is a crucial point in growth. At this point, actively or by default, I choose whether to be alive, to move forward into unfamiliar challenge and uncertainty, or to retreat to my well-worn ways and, in a sense, to die. I face an *existential crisis*.

Moving Through an Impasse

I can move out of an impasse by focusing on what I'm doing right now. How am I keeping myself stuck and dead? What can I do to find my aliveness? The *dialogue* can be a useful tool to help me explore what I want to do:

Dialogue at the Impasse

Many people find that they can do this exercise most easily with pen and paper.

First, identify yourself completely with one of your two opposing forces—the pushing-forward force or the holding-back force. Become totally that point of view in your mind and feelings and *write to* the opposing force, noting everything you can about how you feel and what you think right then. (For example, as your pushing-forward force, you might write, "I have no peace as long as I stay where I am. I want the freedom to . . . ," and so on. As your holding-back force, you might write, "I get many things I want very easily here, such as. . . .")

Then switch. Become the opposing force. Give yourself time to sink into this other thinking-feeling place.

Now write a reply to the you who just spoke. Describe what's happening with you at the present instant.

Continue the written conversation, switching back and forth between the opposing voices whenever you feel ready to. Stay with short statements in your exchange—no more than a few lines. Sometimes one-line statements are the most valuable. Avoid rambling monologues that take you away from the confrontation between the opposing forces.

If you don't like to write, you can do the same thing talking out loud. Arrange two chairs facing each other. Identify each chair as one side of the dialogue. Make your statements out loud, switching back and forth between the two chairs. Usually it helps to assume the physical posture and tone of voice that go with each side.

(If you live with other people, you can warn them in advance about what you're going to do, so they won't think you're going nuts as you talk back and forth. You can even show them these instructions: "Look— it says right here in the book to do this.")

Or you can close your eyes and do your dialogue inside your head.

A sometimes frightening aspect of working through an impasse is that when I give up my old way before I have a clear sense of my new way, I may spend some time in limbo.

In the days when I was heavily committed to my "showman self," I was sometimes so busy acting that I didn't tune in to important events in other people and in myself. I didn't know what my alternative would be, so I felt anxious when I stopped "performing." When I stop worrying about the impression I want to create and start paying attention to my present experience, my anxiety can diminish rapidly . . . and I can still enjoy performing.

Sometimes when I've moved through an impasse and into a new way of behaving, I go back to check out the old behavior before leaving it completely, just to make sure it's still there and available. This is normal—not something to despair about. First, it reassures me that I can still use my old ways when I want them—I haven't "burned my bridges behind me." Second, it's a means of testing my new-found strength. I feel stronger when I know I can cross the bridge again and continue on my new road.

Layers of Energy

Moving through an impasse often requires getting in touch with deeper levels of myself. Perls views the personality as consisting of several layers. At the surface is the *cliché layer*. Reverend James Walker describes it well: "The cliché layer consists of the tokens of relationship that we take for granted, such as saying, 'good morning,' shaking hands, and various other forms of limited relationship. . . . These tokens *can* be leads or openings into more meaningful contact. . . . Or they can be ways of setting limits to our relationships" (1971, pp. 94–95).

Beneath the cliché layer lies the *roles and games layer*. I pretend so I can get what I want. I get into trouble when I forget that my role is a role, that my game is a game. My mask sticks to my face, I can't breathe well, and I forget who I am beneath it.

When I break through my role but have just begun to sense my underlying personal self, at first I may feel as though I'm in a void, with no ground beneath my feet. This is what Perls calls the *death layer*.

This death layer, or *implosion layer*, is where I deaden my senses and put my brakes on. I turn my energy in on itself and *implode* (opposite of explode). I've dropped my social front but am not yet in full contact with my inner excitement. I may feel bored, lonely, or flat and desolate—like an emotional wasteland.

There's one place I can always find this energy I keep locked up: in my body. When I am tight and tense, I can be sure I have some imploded energy. When I focus my awareness on how I constrict my muscles, deaden my body, and make myself heavy as I move, thoughts and feelings connected with these sensations start to come alive.

When I contact these feelings inside me, I may *explode* out of my death layer into a wild display of my grief or anger or joy—or even orgasm if I've inhibited my sexual energy.

This newly unleashed life force demands expression. At this crucial point, some people make the error of saying, "I'm finished with my phony social self!" and throw their whole social living situation overboard—family, home, job, everything. For some people, this can be right. For others, it's not. Being for me involves me in caring for you. Caring for you is part of my being for me.*

HAPPINESS

Happiness is a goal we seek or a by-product of our involvement in activities we enjoy or deem worthwhile. From either perspective, we can identify some of the principal obstacles to happiness and assess how best to deal with them.

Obstacles to Happiness

Drawing from the thinking of Abe Arkoff (1980), we find that the obstacles to happiness include:

1. *Feeling worthless—that you're of no value or a "bad person" and your life is no good.* Congratulations, you're poisoning yourself with introjected evaluations borrowed from others.
2. *Not allowing yourself enough pleasure.* This is the glory of the workaholic, who's always running and pushing to get the next thing done: "I have so many crucial things I have to do!" To counter this, evaluate how many of these "crucial things" will realistically result in your life falling apart if left undone. Do those, make a list of all others, and start replacing them with relaxing pleasures. Allow yourself enough "hedonic units" in the form of relaxation and pleasure, remembering that these can contribute to "achieving" as well as to happiness.
3. *Feeling a deficit of excitement or fulfillment.* You've locked yourself into daily routines. Find where you can make room for fun, excitement, or creative activities.

*At some point in your growth process, you may find consultation with a professionally trained counselor helpful. To find a good counselor, ask around among friends who have used such services, call the mental health facility or growth center in your community, check with the psychology or psychiatry department of your local educational institution, or ask your community worker or clergyman. In choosing such an advisor, *trust your feelings* about anyone you consider seeing. The most competent person in the world won't be worth much to you if you don't trust him or her.

4. *Feeling a deficit of warmth and caring, touching and holding.* You might try saying, "I really need a hug right now" to someone likely to be receptive. This may involve developing your assertiveness. A second approach is to let others contact you—to hear their needs and respond to them. Once you respond to others' needs, they're more apt to respond to yours. A third approach is to change some of your environment to provide what you need, like taking a massage or dance class.

Desire and Happiness

When I want, I have options. When I need, I'm more demanding. When I'm hungry, I can wait to eat, but when I'm starving, I can't. My needs may be physical or psychological.

When I'm concerned only with my survival, I have less room to think about you. When I'm dealing with my desires, I have room to think about who you are, what we have available for each other, and what we don't. As I begin to recognize the difference between what I need to survive and what I want in order to feel fulfilled, I can look more clearly at how my ways of getting what I want affect my existence.

Experimental psychologist John Houston talks about two aspects of desire. One is that we want things we can't have; the other is that we may not want what we have. The latter point is especially intriguing: For us to get maximum pleasure from satisfying a desire, he says, we have to feel at least a little bit deprived. "Eating a banana cream pie after just having consumed a banana cream pie is not as satisfying" (1981, p. 4).

Houston suggests that we're happier when we're meeting and overcoming obstacles, and then enjoying the rewards, than when all our needs are automatically and continuously satisfied. He suggests the intriguing strategy of *intentional deprivation.* My friend Judy describes an excellent example: "When I lived in Italy with my husband, who worked for the Army, he could get anything he wanted at the PX. Since the finest liquors, tax free, were unbelievably cheap, every night we drank the finest. The edge quickly went off our enjoyment of the rare and wonderful liquors. Finally, I began to scour the countryside for local wines available at reasonable prices to everyone in the area. We discovered that they, too, added to our enjoyment of a meal, and when we occasionally had the 'very best,' it felt like a special occasion."

As I desire, so I live, say the *Upanishads* (1957). With possessions, relationships, achievements, or any other area of my life, I may not realize that some of my "wants" are really introjected scripts—someone else's "should wants." I can examine each of my desires. Will fulfilling it help me feel better with myself and my life?

There's still, however, that other troublesome side of desire: wanting what we can't have. One of the keys to liberation is learning to let go of our attachments to what we desire—to say to myself, and feel at a deep level, "So be it; that's all right," when I come up against something I can't have.

For most of us, this runs counter to our usual habits, as mirrored by the Asian monkey trap:

> A coconut is hollowed out and attached by a rope to a tree. . . . At the bottom of the coconut a small slit is made and some sweet food is placed inside. The

hole . . . is just big enough for the monkey to slide in his open hand, but does not allow a closed fist to pass out. The monkey smells the sweets, reaches in with his hand to grasp the food and is then unable to withdraw it. The clenched fist won't pass through the opening. When the hunters come, the monkey becomes frantic, but can't get away. There is no one keeping that monkey captive, except the force of his own attachment. All he has to do is open his hand. But it is a rare monkey which can let go. (Goldstein, 1976)

Ken Keyes uses the term *addictions* for attachments that are so strong that we refuse to be happy unless they're satisfied. "An addiction," he writes, "is any desire that makes you upset or unhappy if it is not satisfied. Even if an addiction brings you pleasure, it is usually short-lived" (1975, pp. 12–13). When I'm intent on satisfying an addiction, I relinquish most of my consideration for anybody else.

When I'm willing to accept a somewhat different experience instead of what I wanted, says Keyes, my addiction is transformed into a *preference*. I don't *have* to have it. I can accept what *is*, detach from that desire, and enjoy myself another way. I don't know any other way to become a rare monkey.

I don't have to feel bad about the desires I do have. Some time ago, for example, my car was stuck in the mud. At last we got it out; then, as I backed down the long road, I got stuck again. I was in a hurry, feeling hassled and uptight. The second time was the last straw. Believe me, I strongly desired not to be stuck. I got out of my car, jumped up and down, beat the ground with my shovel, and screamed and shook my fists at the sky. My emotional age at that point was about two—counting the time *in utero*.

At the same time, I could appreciate the exquisite absurdity of what I was doing. I could see the comedy of that moment in my life for what it was, laughing with myself while I was tearing my hair out. I'm glad I didn't put myself down by telling myself I "shouldn't" feel upset.

As Zen master Jakusho Kwong points out, if I'm the fourth horse on the team, instead of trying to be first horse I can be the best fourth horse I can. Then I *am* the first horse. I don't have to sit waiting to be something I'm not, instead of living now.

Laughter, Joy, and Joie de Vivre

Laughter is so widely accepted that the restraints against it are more apt to be from the inside than from the outside. Feeling good is allowing my energy to move, to flow and be free. If I stop myself from showing my good feelings, I stop the flow of my life force and I *actually don't feel as good*. I don't hurt anyone by enjoying myself.

Your Space for Feeling Good

In the course of your day, check out when and where you feel free to laugh, sing, dance, clap, and crack jokes, and when and where you don't. Are there places where some people wouldn't expect you to feel good, but where you feel good nonetheless?

Many times I come through painful places in my life by finding moments when I can smile at my situation and find some lightness in it.

I can't do this by going around my pain and pretending it's not here—I have to go through the pain to get to the other side. When I can laugh at myself in my difficult situations, I'm more open to new ideas and new approaches.

The other day I really got angry, picked up the dining room table, and bounced it like a checkerboard. Suddenly I realized what I was doing and saw how impressed my family was with my great rage as I jumped up and down as though I were going to move the universe. Then we all broke up laughing. That added something important that said, "I am my anger as I am my laughter and my love."

If my life were *only* absurd, it wouldn't be worth it. When it's so exquisitely absurd that I can stand here breaking up with laughter at myself, its very absurdity is nourishing.

15

Embodied Being

Returning from the islands of French Polynesia, where most people walked and moved in a way that seemed harmonious and integrated, I stepped out of the airport bus terminal onto a busy San Francisco street. As I watched people move along the sidewalk, many looked as though a rigid but invisible barrier separated their heads from their bodies. Heads, filled with busy mental energy, were planning, worrying, or reading the paper—perched atop seemingly disconnected bodies that trudged mechanically along.

Until recently, the body has largely been left out of Western psychology. We've tended to view the mind as the total person and everything else as peripheral. Complex social attitudes about "bad" bodies show up in taboos that we've only recently left behind: We can see them, for example, in the ways people once dressed—how little of the body was visible, even in bathing suits.

Eastern cultures made the body a more integral part of their systems of personal development. The Indian word *yoga* means "union," and a crucial union was that of mind and body. In China and Japan, the martial arts combine physical movement with a carefully focused development of attitude and awareness. As these disciplines become more popular in the West, interest in how our bodies relate to our minds increases. This chapter explores that side of our nature.

TOUCH

Most of us need more hugging, touching, and cuddling than we give and get. Infants in institutions who don't get touched enough in caring ways sometimes actually die; and when I don't get touched enough, I wither a little.

We need to hold each other. We need to feel a pat on the back for a job well done, need to feel someone cradle our head from time to time. Ashley Montagu says touching completes the nervous system. Stanley Keleman adds, "The surface of our body teaches our brain about the world. The . . . experience and feeling that results from touch or not touch . . . paints for us a picture of a friendly or unfriendly world" (1975, p. 46). Perhaps we so often touch with fists and weapons because we're afraid to touch with open hands and hearts.

Interesting studies of touching have been conducted. There are two groups, for example, in a public library. With half the library users, a librarian touched their hands slightly while checking out books—a glancing touch—apparently by accident. With the control group, there was no physical contact. In a follow-up survey, those touched had more positive attitudes toward the library than those who had not been touched.

When I asked students about their family experiences with touch, the replies included these:

Jack: My family rarely touched each other after babyhood. At present I like to touch others I'm close to, but feel nervous and tense when they touch me.

Norrie: My father was overtly affectionate until I reached puberty. Suddenly I was in another category of female and he became cool. I wondered whether I'd done something terrible.

Olivia: Physical affection was always plentiful at home. I enjoy touching very much now. I often find myself wanting to hug and touch.

Tony: When I was in high school, when my friends walked into my kitchen they'd find my parents giggling, hugging, and kissing—nothing but pure, honest affection. In our friends' families, by contrast, touch came only in the form of a slap or swat.

Tracy: I'm so afraid to touch, yet it can mean so much. Now I'm taking risks and listening to that little voice that says, 'I think I need a hug,' and I'm trying each day to 'touch' a little bit—and even to give people hugs when I'm brave enough.

How we respond to touch depends not only on our family customs and our own choices, but also on our culture. In some cultures, people touch each other many times in the course of a five-minute conversation; in others, they might talk at length and not touch once. In some, lovers walk arm in arm together; in others, even holding hands is taboo.

Touch can be affectionate, patronizing, intimidating, urgent, imploring, or ingratiating. To send my intended message clearly and effectively, I must choose the right moment, the right context, and the right kind of touch. Touching you in the wrong way, or at the wrong moment, can provoke your irritation, defensiveness, or anger. In my bioenergetic training, one workshop leader alienated me with every touch while another leader touched in such a way that I was willing to let myself risk and learn.

Here's a way to contact your own feelings about touching and being touched:

Touch Contact

This is a group exercise. Everyone (except, if you wish, a caretaker member or the leader) puts on blindfolds. From where you're sitting or standing, reach out and contact the space around you through your sense of touch.

When you feel ready, you can move slowly around the room. As you touch objects, notice their form, their texture, their scent and temperature. When you meet another person, make contact through your own and that person's touches. (Do your best to stay away from the "Who is this?" game—it takes you away from your sensing into your mind.) Notice how the other person responds to your touch: Be sensitive to messages about how he or she does and doesn't like being touched. If you don't like some way the other person is touching you, communicate that nonverbally. Notice how you contact people.

Afterward, take some time for each of you to discuss what you did and how you felt.

We never lose our need to touch. Therapist Bruno Geba tells how one of his associates, visiting a retirement home, went over to an old lady who always sat silently in a corner:

> I . . . asked how things were going. She responded with an empty and forlorn look. . . . Her fingernails and cuticles were in very bad condition and a lot of rough skin on her fingers was starting to break open. . . . After I had finished [cutting her nails] I took some cream out of my handbag and began massaging her hands. . . . I recognized the strange mixture of upcoming tears and a certain delight in her eyes. She said that I had been the first person in a long time to touch her in this way, by massaging her hands. She had forgotten how good it felt.

Geba concludes, "It always amazes us after working a couple of weeks in a convalescent home to see how hugging can become a part of everyday living. Through this direct body contact the human bond is vitally strengthened and a new degree of intimacy and trust is established" (1974, pp. 46–48).

HEARING OUR MIND-BODY LANGUAGE

By the way I move and hold my body, I can tell you much about who I am and how I feel. With one movement, one gesture, one position of my body, I can convey my anger or my love, my authority or my submission, my gentleness or my pain, my comfort or my discomfort. "Even when I don't think I feel like telling my husband when something is wrong," says Emily, "he notices my nonverbal messages. I'm becoming aware of how my body language can say so much when verbally I say so little."

Julius Fast (1971) declares, "We all, in one way or another, send our little messages out to the world. We say, 'Help me, I'm lonely. Take me, I'm available. Leave me alone, I'm depressed.' "

This *paralanguage* of nonverbal communication, which includes touch, movement, gesture, eye contact, and the sound of the voice, can tell us much about what's going on with ourselves and others, in the context of the situation.

Just as the meaning of a word depends on its sentence, the meaning of a look, gesture, or posture depends on its context. Crossed legs might mean "Go away—I want to be alone now," "I'm afraid—please reassure me," or "I got tired of sitting in another posture and this one's comfortable."

In many cases a nonverbal statement is an aspect of what I'm doing in a larger sense with all of me. Mind-body therapist Stanley Keleman asks,

> What attitude are you meeting the world with right now? . . . Cautious and distancing? Depressed and withdrawn? Bombastic and outgoing? Identify the attitude with which you greet the world, and locate it somewhere in your body. Is it in the back of your neck? Is it in your eyes? Is it in your stomach or in your shoulders or in your knees? Wherever you locate it . . . notice how it shapes your thoughts and actions, your self and your responses. (1976, p. 172)

Here's an exercise to help you sharpen your sensitivity to nonverbal communication.

Audio and Video

Get together with three other people you do not know well to make a group of four. Two of you will be talkers and two will be observers. The talkers sit directly facing each other, and each observer sits to the side, out of the way but in a position to easily see the face and the entire body of one talker. Each of you observe only one talker—don't concern yourself about the other person.

The two talkers have a conversation with each other.

Meanwhile, the two observers are to *consciously not listen to* the explicit content of the conversation. This is an experience in paying attention to nonverbal communication.

So imagine that you're a TV camera and can turn the picture and the sound on and off independently. In your mind, "turn off the audio" or put your hand over your ears and direct all your attention to the other's posture, gestures, movements, and facial expressions.

Then "turn off the picture"—close your eyes and attend totally to the other's tone and voice, how he or she comes into and moves out of the conversation. You might imagine music playing in the background that goes along with the person's way of talking. What is it—hard rock, chamber music, blues?

After about ten minutes, stop the conversation. The observers now have five minutes to give the talkers feedback about what they heard and saw. Then the talkers and observers switch roles and repeat the process.

Some nonverbal messages depend on a cultural background for their meaning. Among middle-class white people in the United States, for example, looking directly at someone indicates honesty and sincerity—even while saying, "I am not a crook." But among Puerto Ricans, a woman who looks directly at a man is communicating defiance or a sexual come-on. By contrast, many Puerto Rican women walk in a way that in the United States might easily be mistaken as a sexual invitation (Fast, 1971).

In your daily contact with people, you can become more attuned to the meanings their nonverbal statements hold. You can do this not only in your own encounters, but also by watching strangers at a distance—at a nearby table in a café, for instance, guessing what stories their postures and gestures tell.

Van Dusen describes trying to feel what it's like to be another person "from the inside":

> As a boy in San Francisco, I traveled everywhere on streetcars. . . . I designed a game that later proved useful. For example, an old lady gets on the streetcar and sits down. . . . I become her for a little while. I study everything about her, and reconstruct my world as this old woman.
>
> My tattered cloth shopping bag is precious; it contains food for a week. I put it down between my legs to hold onto it. I have to hang on—these cars jerk so— . . . one slip and I would fall, breaking my bones. So noisy. So confusing. . . .
>
> Sometimes I would even try the person's movements—try the tremor of an aged hand that has so little power to grasp things.
>
> As an adult, this game was very useful to me in dull administrative meetings. (1972, pp. 23–24)

Here's a way to experience another person's rhythm and flow:

Mirroring

Do this exercise without speaking. Sit behind another person. Both of you close your eyes and start rocking. Explore different rhythms of rocking and find one that feels right for you.

Now open your eyes and pick up the movement of the person in front of you. Mirror that person's movement and body posture as closely as you can.

After several minutes, close your eyes again and go into your own rhythm. Feel the difference between your rhythm and the other person's.

Now, both of you turn around. You go into your own rhythm, and the person behind you will do everything you just did.

After a few minutes of this, stop and face each other. Now mirror each other face to face. Decide nonverbally who will begin to move and who will mirror, and when to shift back and forth. Try a mundane event, a magical event, a playful event.

If you have a little more time available, now move to a new partner and again do face-to-face mirroring for five minutes. Feel how moving with this partner is different from moving with the previous one. Then go on to a third partner for a final five minutes. After that, return to your first partner and discuss your experiences.

Fast reports that a friend of his threw a nonverbal cocktail party. " 'Touch, smell, stare and taste,' his invitation read, 'but don't speak'. . . . We all stood and milled around, danced, gestured, mimed, and went through elaborate charades, all without talking. We knew only one other couple, and all our introductions were self-made. . . . Amazingly enough we ended the evening with a clear and deep knowledge of our new friends" (1971, p. 75). And when a family in which the two children had fought incessantly for years tried being nonverbal for just an hour, before long the son sat down on his older sister's lap and she started acting very "motherly" in an affectionate way. They all shared the realization that her constant admonitions, which her brother had interpreted as hostile, came from a caring concern about him.

LIVING WITHIN OUR BODIES

If you do not find it within yourself, where will you go to get it?
—Zen saying

How I move and hold myself and how I've formed my body says something about how I perceive, inhabit, and deal with my world. Popular language recognizes this in such expressions as "openhanded," "stiff-necked," "standing firm," and a "push-over." Therapists Ron Kurtz and Hector Prestera write, "Attitudes and fixed muscular patterns reflect, enhance, and sustain one another. It is as if the body sees what the mind believes and the heart feels, and adjusts itself accordingly" (1976, pp. 1, 3).

Stanley Keleman describes in detail how one person's body mirrors her life:

> Roberta . . . complained that she never got what she wanted, which was to be loved but also to be independent and free. . . . She . . . claimed that men treated her as a sex object, and yet she dressed and acted provocatively. Roberta was about five feet five, dark haired and trim. . . . She tended to be stoop-shouldered, with contractions in her chest and throat, and had a permanent pout. . . . The pout was testimony to her self-indulgence, while her constrictedness indicated her diminished willingness to love and to be loved. She presented a quality of hardness in everything she did. (1976, p. 99)

Like many of us, Roberta was alienated from her body, accustomed to the idea that you're supposed to have a body to look at but not to live in. Even most of our clothes are for show instead of movement and comfort. A body is something we *use*. We do things to it instead of being in it.

Among some traditional American Indian peoples, this mind-body separation does not exist. The old languages have no separate word for mind—anything you call body is the total being. That implies a different kind of relationship to ourselves. When I'm doing something physical, I don't "command" or "will" my body to act. Rather, I act in a more unified way from within myself.

My colleague Stashu Geurtsen (personal communication, 1982) says, "For decades I treated my body as 'my' servant. So in sports I would push myself in ways that caused fantastic injuries and keep right on playing. But now when my body is working I'm continuously scanning it from the inside, finding where the tension is. I feel much better, and I seldom get injuries."

Walking and Grounding

"When we walk," continues Geurtsen, "we can pay attention to the kinds of compensations we normally make—ways we favor and protect particular areas of our bodies. Through my awareness I find other ways of minimizing whatever pains and tightnesses I have, so that as I walk I'm relaxing and aligning my body and moving it as efficiently as possible."

Some counselors speak of *grounding*. They ask, "What is the nature of this person's connection with the earth? What kind of support do the feet and legs provide the upper body? Does this person seem to be 'walking on eggshells,' or rather to 'know where he stands' "?

The way I walk may change to fit the way I feel. When I feel overburdened, for instance, I'm apt to stoop forward as I stand and walk. When I have a solid sense of myself and feel good about what's happening, I'm likely to "have my feet on the ground"—and, if I happen to notice, to literally feel the ground solidly beneath me. And when I'm euphoric, I may "feel like I'm walking on air."

Here's an exercise that lets you try out different ways of standing. With each, you can sense the nature of your relationship to gravity and feel how grounded you are.

Three Stances

Stand with your knees locked, your chest stuck out and inflated, your butt jutting out backward, your shoulders pulled high, and your chin thrust defiantly upward and forward. Do all this to an exaggerated degree. Then start to move your arms and head and to walk around in this position. Feel how you breathe. Then look at yourself in the mirror, or, if you're in a group, notice how others look in this position. Notice whether anything about this way of standing feels familiar.

Then relax and shake out your arms and legs. Now assume a new stance in which your knees are again locked but this time your legs are together, your shoulders are rolled forward with your hands held in front of your body, and your head is hunched down between your shoulders. Again move, look, and feel.

Shake yourself out again. This third time your feet are parallel a shoulder's width apart. Flex your knees and position your pelvis above your feet—neither thrust forward nor thrust back. Drop your shoulders, let your jaw drop, and hold the upper part of your body straight but not rigid and let it "settle down into" your knees. Let your feet and legs and buttocks become heavy and feel the earth underneath them. Without moving your feet, swivel your hips, then move the rest of your body, feel your breathing, and finally move around the room as you did before. This is called "Horse Stance" in Tai Chi and the martial arts.

Health and Pleasure

The central insight of Freud's student Wilhelm Reich was that the mental energies, processes, and defense systems that Freud so carefully observed and articulated are not just events in the mind—they shape and affect the entire body.

A healthy person, Reich maintained, displays a graceful, rhythmic flow of movement, an easy graceful alternation of tension and relaxation in response to the conditions of the moment, as we see in children who have not yet formed many inhibitions and repressions (1949, p. 348).

Alexander Lowen, a neo-Reichian who developed a therapy he calls *bioenergetics*, emphasizes the importance of pleasure in our existence. "Pleasure promotes the life and well-being of the organism," he writes (1976). He maintains not only that it's easier to be warm and loving when we feel pleasure, but that the very movement of reaching out for what we want is itself pleasurable.

Blocking and Armoring

When our reaching out leads to punishment and pain, we retract, draw in. That's healthy. The trouble comes when reaching out to do, explore, and express ourselves in our world *consistently* leads to punishment and pain. Then, anxiously anticipating punishment whenever we feel an impulse to reach out, we learn to contract our muscles as soon as we feel that impulse. Our inhibition becomes locked into our body. The ebb and flow of expansion and contraction is interrupted and we find ourselves chronically contracted, holding on tightly to avoid "unacceptable" expressions of our aliveness.

When I hold back my self-expression, I'm in conflict between my impulse and my fear. Every complex involves such a conflict. Complexes are often called *hangups*. As examples of how we can be hung up, Lowen mentions a man who dislikes his job but stays because of the security, and a person who's strongly attracted to another but is afraid of being rejected and left feeling hurt if he or she discloses the attraction. In both cases, conflicting feelings prevent effective action.

When such hangups don't get resolved, says Lowen, the hangups actually hang up the body. He calls one common pattern the coat-hanger hangup: "The shoulders are raised and somewhat squared off, head and neck incline forward. . . . I call this the coat hanger because it looks as if the body were held up by an invisible hanger" (1976, p. 186).

When the holding back of a given kind of excitement is chronic, we begin to lose our awareness that the tension is there. The emotion that underlies the impulse becomes transformed into a fixed muscular attitude. Reich declared, "It is as if the affective personality put on an armor . . . on which the knocks from the outer world as well as the inner demands rebound. This armor makes the individual less sensitive to unpleasure but it also reduces his . . . capacity for pleasure and achievement" (1949, p. 342).

Such *character armor* can be deceptive, for rigidity can give the illusion of strength, as in locked knees that produce the illusion of stability. And the armoring doesn't always feel like armor. It may not take the form of hardness. Keleman says deprivation during the first two or three years of life often leads to underdeveloped muscles and weak skin tone—the flaccidity of apathy rather than the hardness of suppression.

Rather than admit that I've blocked off my connections with my deeper self, cut myself off from important pleasure, and limited my perceptions of what's possible, I may make a virtue of my narrowed options and conclude that the experiences I don't allow myself are bad. I live out my available patterns with self-righteous zeal—for instance, "Touching and being held aren't manly. Dancing is disguised sexuality. . . ."

But despite those conclusions (or because of them), I feel anxious and depressed, withdrawn and alienated, or develop stress-related illnesses. Fortunately, all this can be reversed.

STRESS

Many people have only recently realized the connection between stress and disease, but most of us heard about psychosomatic illness decades ago.

Psychosomatics

For many of us, the term *psychosomatic* still means malingering: "It's all in your mind." But recently a different view has emerged: "Too rigid a distinction between mind and body," writes Nikolas Tinbergen, a Nobel laureate in physiology and medicine, "is of only limited use to medical science, (1974, pp. 14–15). And Kenneth Pelletier of Langley-Porter Neuropsychiatric Institute now uses the term . . . "to convey the concept of a fundamental interaction between mind and body which is involved in all diseases and all processes affecting health maintenance" (1977).

In this view, almost all illness is psychosomatic. Though I may have no observable disorder, if I *feel* unwell, in some way I as an organism *am* unwell. And as Hans Selye, who pioneered the study of stress, asks: "If a microbe is in or around us all the time, and yet causes no disease until we are exposed to stress, what is the 'cause' of our illness, the microbe or the stress" (1974)?

This *holistic* view is at the heart of a revolution in health care. In Southern California, for instance, Don Isbell and Sally J. Nelson developed a stress reduction program for nursing personnel in the Kaiser-Permanente medical organization. "Cost-effectiveness of this type of program," they write, "[is] in terms of decreased incidence of illness, greater job satisfaction, and improved performance due to increased self-awareness and self-care among program participants" (1980).

The central element of a holistic approach is the view that one is an active, responsible participant in the process of healing oneself and staying well, rather than a "passive victim of a disease or a passive recipient of a cure" (Pelletier, 1977, p. 33).

Thus we each choose how to react to stress. Recognizing that we have such choices opens new doors. Perry (1962) and Laing (1969) have pointed out that a mental breakdown can be a breakthrough, paving the way for a reassessment and restructuring of the life elements that provoked the breakdown.

Let's look now at the nature of stress itself.

What Stress Is—And Isn't

Imagine yourself walking along a dark street. Suddenly a hooded figure appears forty feet away. All the alarm systems in your body go off at once: As adrenalin shoots through your bloodstream, your breath quickens, your muscles tense, and your thoughts race toward a decision about how to respond. Your entire organism is ready either to challenge the menace or flee for your life. This is the *fight or flight response*—a full-scale stress reaction that helps you meet the dangerous situation. After you've fought or fled, there's that moment of heaving a sigh of relief and collapsing in relaxed exhaustion—the *relaxation rebound*—to get back your energy before you return to normal functioning.

Although "facing the menace" is a classical example of the stress response, stress occurs in countless different situations—not just threatening ones, but pleasant ones as well. When the Oscar awards are announced, the stress is as great for the winner as it is for the other nominees.

Stress is both desirable and necessary. All living organisms, from plants to people, have stress alarm systems that help them cope with their environments. If things get dull, we actively seek out experiences that will cause a little stress.

According to Selye, stress is an organismic state, a psychophysiological response. The situation that provokes it is a *stressor*. Selye defined stress in two slightly different ways: as "the rate of wear and tear on the body," and as the state produced by the *General Adaptation Syndrome*, or GAS, which Selye identified in 1976. The general adaptation syndrome's three stages are:

> *Stage 1: Alarm:* A biochemical "call to arms" to all the body's emergency readiness systems occurs. Responsibility for dealing with the stressor is delegated to the appropriate organ or system.
>
> *Stage 2: Resistance:* The appropriate system of defense goes into action, "keeping the stressors at bay." This might mean enraged aggression against a threatening person, finding a nonaggressive way to neutralize the threat, or sending white blood cells against invading bacteria. The organism tries to handle the situation adequately and return to equilibrium. Isbell and Nelson (1980) point out that "resistance" often includes two substages: The initial defensive or aggressive stance can move into a second, more sophisticated problem-solving process.
>
> *Stage 3: Exhaustion:* Under prolonged and continuing stress, the organ or process handling the stressor may wear out or break down. Another alarm reaction is triggered and the body tries to find another way to cope. Choices include physically withdrawing or psychologically disengaging from dealing with the issue. This stage may end in "giving up the struggle"—by retreating into neurosis, psychosis, disease, or death.

Appropriate stress responses help us handle the events of life. For example, if in my exhaustion phase I push myself too hard and too long and get sick, my body is telling me I have to put all my Important Business aside and rest. My total organism is wiser than my conscious mind, which sometimes keeps pushing even when I need to take it easy.

Effects of Excess Stress

Ongoing stress can cause me to feel troubled, hopeless, or always tired. These effects all diminish the joy and happiness in events that otherwise might bring delight, and leave me anxious, depressed, or both.

Stress can cause me to compound my problems, in such forms as heavy smoking; alcohol or drug abuse; excessive worrying; lowered feelings of competence and self-esteem; making more mistakes than usual; forgetting; having accidents; and conflict with other people. Stress can trigger excess anger and hostility in situations that don't call for such intense reactions.

The long-term effects of stress have been amply documented. From hemorrhoids to heart attacks, the body objects to chronic tension. I regard hemorrhoids as a "truth button," a message to myself: "I'm getting too tight-assed about things. I need to pay attention to keeping my sphincter muscles—and the rest of me— relaxed."

Other effects of prolonged stress are even more threatening. Cardiovascular disease is the best known, including high blood pressure, arteriosclerosis, strokes, heart attacks, and coronary thrombosis. Headaches, ulcers, diabetes, cancer, and other diseases have also been linked to excess stress.

Stress-related problems are not, as was once thought, just an older person's malady. Teenagers and even children sometimes get ulcers, for example. Pelletier writes, "Stress affects both sexes and all ages. . . . Some people are vaguely aware that their personal stress is taking a heavy toll. Others are sure it is, and they have the medical bills to prove it" (1977, p. 4).

If my stress response occurs too often, it can lead to the condition Curtis and Detert (1981) call *stress gone bad*: The autonomic nervous system and the endocrine pathways are retrained so that they no longer maintain homeostasis—the body no longer returns to a relaxed, normal state between stressful events.

We can distinguish between acute and chronic stress. *Acute stress* is the momentary fight or flight response in which the body prepares to handle an emergency. *Chronic stress* is stress gone bad: a state of low-level but ongoing mobilization involving chronic tension and ongoing secretion of corticosteroids in the body.

Chronic stress is a common response to the kinds of stressors many of us face daily in modern society, many of them ambiguous or complex: The boss says something that may mean trouble, the car won't start, someone whose goodwill you need is rude or insulting . . . *ad infinitum*. Neither fighting nor fleeing is appropriate, but biochemically you're prepared for just that (Goldberg, 1978, p. 27).

Stressors: Events That Trigger Stress

"For most of us," write Curtis and Detert, "the stressor that is most readily perceived is usually the one that initiates the stress response" (1981, p. 19). We are also affected by other stressors that we don't even recognize.

A *primary stressor* sets off the stress response. Other events resulting from the primary stressor that keep the stress response activated are called *secondary stressors*. Getting fired might be a primary stressor, for instance, and then worrying about how to pay the bills becomes a secondary stressor.

Although "too much to do and not enough time to do it in," together with the tense, breathless rushing around that's usually a consequence, is a stressor, having too little to do can also be stressful if your disposition is to be active. In a study of 1,540 bank officers, those with too few job-connected stressors had as many stress-related physical disorders as those with too many. Rigidly monotonous routine work has similar effects (Goldberg, 1978, p. 29).

To name a few other important stressors: One is intense *responsibility*—especially when it affects others' lives or welfare, as in the work of pilots and air traffic controllers. Another is feeling a *lack of control* over events in your life. In an Institute of Life Insurance poll, between 1968 and 1976 the percentage of the population that felt they had personal control over key areas of their lives dropped from 58 percent to 39 percent (Goldberg, 1978, p. 9). A related stressor is *unpredictability* of events in your life. *Decision stress* is the press of weighing many alternatives in a short amount of time. *Suppressing anger* in response to putdowns and extreme frustration has been shown to be stressful (Funkenstein, King & Drolette, 1957), and so have such environmental conditions as air pollution, crowding, and noise.

In a study comparing piecework to fixed-salary work, when piecework production rose substantially, so did workers' reports of discomfort, pain, fatigue, and exhaustion. It appeared likely that in the long run the cost to workers in health and morale, and to the company in sick leave and turnover, more than offset the increased production (Levi, 1968).

Another stressor is *change*. Any change in a person's life requires some adjustment, and when too many must be made too quickly, a high level of stress results—and illness and/or accidents often follow.

Thomas Holmes and Richard Rahe at the University of Washington School of Medicine studied people of diverse backgrounds using the Social Readjustment Rating Scale. They found that someone who accumulated 300 or more points on the scale within twelve months had an 80 percent chance of becoming ill, injured, or severely depressed within the following six months. Between 150 and 299 points, the chances were 51 percent; below 150 points, 37 percent. You might want to take a few minutes now to study their scale, reproduced on page 186.

An adaptation of this index for college students includes, "Entered college; Held a job while attending school; Change in major field of study; Change or conflict of values; in use of drugs or alcohol; in amount of independence and responsibility or in dating habits; Engaged to be married; Broke or had broken a marital engagement or steady relationship; Trouble with school administration; and Major change in self-concept or self-awareness" (Marx, Garrity & Bowers, 1975).

Life Stress Units

Life Event	Numerical Value
1. Death of a spouse	100
2. Divorce	73
3. Marital separation	65
4. Jail term	63
5. Death of a close family member	63
6. Personal injury or illness	53
7. Marriage	50
8. Fired at work	47
9. Marital reconciliation	45
10. Retirement	45
11. Change in health of family member	44
12. Pregnancy	40
13. Sexual difficulties	39
14. Gain of a new family member	39
15. Business readjustment	39
16. Change in financial state	38
17. Death of a close friend	37
18. Change to different line of work	36
19. Change in number of arguments with spouse	35
20. Mortgage over $10,000	31
21. Foreclosure of mortgage or loan	30
22. Change in responsibilities at work	29
23. Son or daughter leaving home	29
24. Trouble with in-laws	29
25. Outstanding personal achievement	28
26. Spouse begins or stops work	26
27. Beginning or ending school	26
28. Change in living conditions	25
29. Revision of personal habits	24
30. Trouble with boss	23
31. Change in work hours or conditions	20
32. Change in residence	20
33. Change in schools	20
34. Change in recreation	19
35. Change in church activities	19
36. Change in social activities	18
37. Mortgage or loan less than $10,000	17
38. Change in sleeping habits	16
39. Change in number of family get-togethers	15
40. Change in eating habits	13
41. Vacation	13
42. Christmas	12
43. Minor violations of the law	11
Total Points	____

Source: "The Social Readjustment Rating Scale" by T. H. Holmes and R. H. Rahe, 1967, *Journal of Psychosomatic Research, 11*, p. 213.

The "Type A" Behavior Pattern

When cardiologists Meyer Friedman and Ray Rosenman decided to have the chairs in their reception room reupholstered, the upholsterer commented, "It's so peculiar that only the front edges of your chair seats are worn out" (1974, p. 71). The worn front edges turned out to be one sign of what Friedman and Rosenman later called the *Type A behavior pattern*—one in which some people *place themselves under avoidable stress* that other people don't. This pattern, which is highly correlated with heart disease, involves an *aggressive, chronic struggle to achieve more and more in less and less time.* In this "hurry sickness," observe Friedman and Rosenman, a person subjects himself or herself to continuous time pressure.

Other elements often found in the Type A pattern are

> An intense desire to compete with and defeat others
> Aggressiveness, turning into a "free-floating but well-rationalized" hostility
> Counting (rather than enjoying) the units one has, whether measured by dollars, achievements, or status
> Stereotyped thinking and action

Type A behavior includes two important elements: (1) The predispositions of an individual's personality must be set off by (2) an environmental challenge. Without both elements, Type A behavior doesn't appear.

Friedman and Rosenman also identified what they term the *Type B* pattern. These people felt much less pressured by time and were less likely to measure their achievements by the number of things done, items possessed, or events experienced. Their ambition and drive was no less than that of the Type As, but it seemed to steady them and to provide confidence and security. There was no correlation of Type A or Type B behavior with occupational position, power, or success.

What to Do about Excess Stress

The message underlying excess stress can vary according to the person or circumstances. It may point, for instance, to a need for more recreation, or for changing jobs or environments. More generally, it can mean learning to do things in a more relaxed, less frantic way.

We can manage our stress level through self-monitoring: paying more attention, at the moment-by-moment level, to our breathing, the tension in our bodies, and our attitudes toward what we do.

In addition, it's helpful to *consciously monitor our energy level.* An activity can be much more stressful when I'm tired than at other times. I need to learn when my energy is equal to the demands I want to place on it. Too often, my body is ready for a rest but my mind goads me onward.

Nelson and Isbell (1978) ask people in their stress management workshops to undertake a *self-care month:*

> You [can] measure the stress you feel, rating it on a scale from 1 to 4: 1 equals No stress; 2 equals Minor stress; 3 equals Moderate stress; 4 equals Severe stress. . . . [and] begin to sort out your most difficult types of situations. . . . In a

small pocket notebook which you carry with you . . . note situations as they occur and write them down briefly with a stress level rating. Example:

Kept waiting for an appointment—2

Fight with spouse—3

"Had" to stay late at work again—3.

This notebook can help you assess when stress is mounting and you need to do something to reduce it. It can also be useful to make a *graph* in which you chart your stress level day by day over a period of time. (Just don't get uptight about it.)

Another way to reduce stress is to *be more assertive about what we do and don't want.* It's extremely stressful to agree—out of guilt, timidity, or feelings of obligation—to do something I really don't want to. I'm likely to be fighting myself the whole time I'm doing it—and perhaps hating myself (and you) for it. It's also stressful when I don't assert myself by going after something I care deeply about.

Management consultant Ann Murphy Springer, in an article called "Taking the Stress out of Christmas" (1981, December 20), doesn't rule out any options. "Why is it too late to cancel?" she asks. "You probably made those arrangements a month and a half ago, and they're probably saying, 'Gee, I wish we hadn't accepted the Boyntons' invitation' at the same time you're saying, 'Gosh, I wish we hadn't invited the Springers.' So call them and say, 'Look, let's give each other the gift of a quiet evening at home. Come to dinner on Twelfth-night.' . . . There should be room in an adult relationship for this kind of flexibility."

Every now and then, I find myself so scattered and distracted that I jump out of my skin at small disturbances and see things all out of proportion to their real importance. This is a warning signal that holds an important message: that I need to drop everything and be with myself—now! I need some time to be quiet—to center myself, and relax. When I disregard this warning and plunge ahead with what I've been doing, I'm highly susceptible to illness or injury. My body itself is apt to put the brakes on and *force* me to stop for a while.

Many of us have times in our lives when we "go crazy"—some of us in an extreme enough way that we need some time in our local mental health center to get ourselves together again, others in less extreme ways that we handle on our own. Crazy times are important. They're strong messages, with red lights flashing and bells ringing, that we need to make certain changes in the way we live.

In daily life we often handle symptoms of minor craziness by suppressing them with tranquilizers or other drugs. This may be the worst thing to do. When *I have such a symptom, I want to experience myself fully and pay attention to what I'm telling me.* I can find out how I'm violating my own inner nature, stop doing that, and start giving myself what I need that I'm not getting. At such times of "feeling crazy," it's also a wise move to avoid all possible actions and decisions until I'm clearer and more composed. I have begun to realize that no one is so important to me that I'm willing to push myself to high blood pressure and ulcers for the sake of someone else.

I once found this anonymous prayer engraved on a plaque:

Slow me down, Lord.
Ease the pounding of my heart by the quieting of my mind.
Steady my hurried pace with a vision of the eternal reach of time.

Give me, amid the confusion of the day, the calmness of the everlasting hills. . . .

Teach me the art of taking minute vacations—of slowing down to look at a flower, to chat with a friend, to pat a dog, to read a few lines from a good book . . . and inspire me to send my roots into the soil of life's enduring values.

WORKING WITH OUR BODIES

We can work with our bodies through such means as breathing, relaxation, and exercise.

Breathing

When I breathe deeply, I move toward being alive. When I hold my breath, I move toward being paralyzed in my deadness, fear, or anxiety. At times when I'm bored, excited, or afraid, I try to remember to *breathe fully.*

You can make a point of paying attention to your breathing during the day whenever you remember to. Let your other concerns drift away for a few minutes and just feel yourself breathe. Notice whether your breath is shallow or deep, jerky or regular. If you find yourself spontaneously starting to change as you pay attention, allow that to happen.

There are entire yoga systems called *pranayama* built around the breath, in part because breathing is a function that stands at the gateway between the voluntary and involuntary functions of the body. Working with breath is a way to affect what ordinarily happens "automatically."

Two kinds of breathing that most people can easily learn to distinguish are belly breathing and chest breathing. To feel the difference between these, lie on your back with one hand on your stomach and one hand on your chest. Continue to breathe normally and notice which hand rises and falls. Probably it will be the hand on your chest.

Next, close your eyes for several minutes, as if you were going to drop off to sleep. Then again notice your hands. At this point, you may find that the hand on your chest is almost motionless and the hand on your stomach is rising and falling. Most of our breathing when we're asleep is belly breathing.

If you want to try a special breathing pattern that you can use at other times to help you become more centered and relaxed, continue on to the "Figure 8 Breathing" exercise. This pattern is called "the circulation of the light" in the ancient Chinese text *The Secret of the Golden Flower* (Wilhelm, 1956, pp. 30–45). You can do this in a sitting or standing position after you've learned it, but you can learn it most easily lying on the floor (a bed is too comfortable).

Figure-8 Breathing

Lying on your back on the floor with your arms by your sides, imagine that you're inside a large number "8." The middle of the 8 is at your waist. Your head and torso are inside the top loop, and your legs and feet are inside the bottom one.

Do not try to adjust your breathing in any special way. Just *imagine* the pattern of breathing described here and allow your breathing to match itself gradually to this pattern.

Imagine that your breath enters your body through your navel, filling your stomach with air, as in belly breathing. Then it passes from your navel to your spine and moves upward along your back until it reaches the very top of the 8 somewhere at a point far out above your head. At this point your lungs are totally inflated, and for a moment you feel motionless.

Then as you exhale, imagine your breath moving down along your face and chest and stomach to complete the top loop of the 8, going into your body at your waist again, emerging through your anus, and going down along the back of your legs to reach another point of motionlessness far beyond your feet, at which point you've completely exhaled. Then your breath returns up along the front of your legs and enters your navel again, and so on.

Once you've mastered the figure-8 pattern, return to straight up-and-down breathing, then go back to figure-8 breathing. Notice how they feel different.

Relaxation

Relaxation, like breathing, can help us keep ourselves well, *preventing* physical and mental illness rather than treating it. Two effective ways to achieve deeper relaxation than we normally do are presented here (see Chapter 20 for others). The breathing techniques just described can also lead to deep relaxation.

Progressive Relaxation. In 1929, physiologist and physician Edmund Jacobson recommended the use of a technique called *progressive relaxation* to supplement medical treatment for a wide variety of disorders (1938). In conjunction with figure-8 breathing, it's useful anytime you want to relax deeply. For the deepest relaxation, it's ideal to have three quarters of an hour available for this, but as little as fifteen minutes can be useful.

A Basic Progressive Relaxation Exercise

Loosen your clothing and lie down or slump comfortably in your chair. Feel your contact with the ground, bed, couch, or chair. Make relaxed, full contact with this surface that's supporting you. Imagine your body becoming very heavy, not trying to hold itself up at all. If you're uncomfortable in any way, move so that that part of you becomes comfortable. Let yourself breathe deeply enough to get plenty of air. Don't try to hurry this process—take the time you need.

Now begin to tighten the muscles in your left foot. Tense them for about ten seconds and notice your sensations as you do.

Then let go. Let all that tension flow away. Imagine your feet becoming very heavy and comfortable as that happens. Keep your attention focused in your physical sensations.

If you have ample time, repeat the process described in the last two paragraphs twice more, allowing the relaxation, heaviness, and feelings of well-being that begin to flood your feet to become deeper each time. If you have only fifteen minutes, continue with the exercise, recognizing that even deeper levels of relaxation can be achieved when you take time to do it fully.

Now, go through the same process with your left and lower leg, tensing and then relaxing, taking all the time you need. Then your left upper leg. Then, in turn, your right foot, lower leg, and upper leg. In the same manner, tense and relax each part of your body: your buttocks, pelvis, stomach, back, and chest; each hand, lower arms, and upper arms; your neck, jaw, eyes, and forehead.

When you're finished, take ample time to just sit or lie there, experiencing and enjoying.

Eventually you may be able to eliminate the initial tensing.

Massage.   Massage can soothe and relax our tensions and ease the hard knots where we keep our muscles constricted. In some cultures, it's part of daily life for many people. In California, it's becoming widespread, but a friend from New England recently told me: "On the East Coast and in the Midwest few people would go get a massage when their body is tense and tired—there's still a suspicion that massage is synonymous with illicit sex."

We hope that attitude is changing. Contemporary body therapies such as *structural integration* involve separating areas of muscle and cartilage that have become stuck together; massage practices such as *shiatsu* and *polarity massage* actively push the tension out of bunched, knotted muscles; and Swedish and Esalen massage are deeply soothing and replenishing. Even self-massage has become popular: You can grab each of your shoulders with the opposite hand and work them around, push the tension out of the hard cords of muscle that run along your spinal cord with your knuckles, and reach most other areas of your body with both hands. Feel where your body is tense and manipulate that area in ways that feel good.

Massage is a gift we can give each other. The areas where most people accumulate the greatest tension are their shoulders, their muscles running from the top to bottom of the back along either side of the spine, and the calves. The techniques described in the next exercise provide ways to work on these three areas. Then you'll have beginning skills to exchange massages with friends or loved ones, and you can continue to develop your skills by asking them to show you the massage strokes they know.

Basic Massage

The shoulders. (1) With the person being massaged sitting up as you stand behind him or her, place your hands on one shoulder with fingers in front and thumbs behind. Work the muscles around, kneading and pushing gently at first, then with more pressure as the muscles begin to loosen up. Then do the same for the other shoulder. (2) Place one thumb next to the neck on one shoulder, then press with moderate force as you rock it forward and then back. Repeat this motion as you move outward toward the shoulder and then back toward the neck. (3) Grasp the shoulder near the neck between thumb and two fingers and give it a brief rapid shake. Again continue out to the shoulder and back with this same motion.

The back. With the person lying on his or her stomach, kneel above the legs and place your thumbs one on each side of the spine, between the spine and the cord of muscle beside it. Then, first on one side and then on the other, with moderate pressure push your thumb across that cord of muscle toward the outer edge of the body. *Never push across these muscles from the outside toward the center.* Move all the way up and down the spine with this motion. At some point the person is likely to say, "Ow, that hurts there," or "That feels wonderful." Stay on that sore spot for several minutes, working from a couple of inches above it to a couple of inches below it, adjusting your pressure by the person's feedback—"Too hard!" or "A little more pressure, please."

The calves. (1) With both hands on the calf, knead and push as with the first shoulder stroke. (2) With the person lying on his or her back with knees bent up and feet flat on the ground, kneel in front of the feet, place your forearm behind the calf, and press it against the calf as you move it in a clockwise circular motion. (3) With both of you in the same positions as in (2), place your thumbs in the depressions along either side of the shinbone and reach around either side with your hands so your fingertips press inward on the center of the calf. Exerting pressure with both thumbs and fingertips, move up and down the calf.

In massage, two things are especially important. First, place your awareness in your hands. Focus on sensing instead of thinking. Closing your eyes may help. Enjoy yourself while you're giving as well as getting a massage: If you're getting tired, do it more slowly and restfully. Second, when receiving a massage, tell the masseur or masseuse what feels good and what doesn't, what you especially want work on, and when you want more work on a given spot. When you're giving the massage, actively solicit this feedback.

Exercise and Sports

One morning over tea I was talking with Stashu Geurtsen, who is a marathon runner, a tennis pro, and a psychologist. He was using tennis as a vehicle for describing a unique approach that can be applied to any kind of sport or exercise.

"In conventional tennis," he was saying, "you're on top of the court and in command of the racquet and the ball. In what I call 'Zen tennis,' by contrast, before you pick up a racquet, I want you to calm yourself, feel your breath and body, move slowly and sense yourself as you move, and get used to the idea that at any moment you can stop and shake out whatever tensions and anxieties you're expressing in your body. From there, you give the racquet freedom to do what it needs to do. If it sends the ball in a direction you don't want, that's okay. Soon your body says, 'Oh, that's not what I want.' You get a total kinesthetic sense of what you're doing. The important thing is staying *inside* your movement, tossing the ball with all of you, hitting it with all of you, being aware of the court with all of you. Once you begin to build that awareness from inside the body, all the technique stuff just falls into place. This process sets up a different kind of relationship between you and the game."

"What about breath and balance?"

"If my breathing becomes shallow and high, I know I'm playing with my shoulders, my ego, and my tensions. In that position, I'm not connected to my lower body, so it has to begin compensating. Every move becomes a compensation for everything else, rather than my body moving as a unit. Many people, when they get into a game, use a battlefield metaphor, trying to smash the ball and 'defeat and enemy'—with no grace, no giving, and no caring about the other person. The way I play, you put the ball at the limits of their ability to return it, rather than where they can't touch it, with an appreciation for the other person's shot, as if it's yours. Your intention is to extend the other person and extend yourself."

Part Four

KNOWING OUR MINDS

16

Thinking

*P*ablo Picasso used to watch children form meanings from the concepts available to them, and let them enter his studio and rearrange work in progress. They could think and respond without issues of prestige or their hidden agendas determining their processes.

To know what to think about, and how, we have to perceive and interact with our environment—an environment filled as much with illusions as with realities. Psychologist Sheldon Kopp (1980) points out that illusions start early in childhood. We learn a deceptively comforting fairytale vision in which frogs become princes and goose girls become queens. Growing up means modifying illusions: accepting princes who owe mortgages and queens who assert feminist rights. But as we grow up, we buy into adult illusions. These include mistaken ideas about what we're like and how we have to live our lives, and distorted concepts of the way our world "is," or "has to be." The illusions of both childhood and adulthood include not only our conceptions of the world as we've been told it is, but also of the world as we experience it and then tell ourselves it is.

What we "tell ourselves it is" can come out of an intuitive intelligence that goes beyond the limits of ordinary rationality. Albert Einstein's relativity theory, Max Planck's quantum mechanics, and Niels Bohr's insights into subatomic matter and energy went beyond the rational to pave the way for some of the technological leaps of the past quarter century. And Heisenberg stated with his *uncertainty principle* that we can't observe or participate in events without influencing their nature and outcomes. Another physicist, Fritjof Capra, points out that some of the statements of modern physics echo those of Buddhists who studied consciousness two thousand years ago. "The external world and [a person's] inner world," wrote Lama Anagarika Govinda, "are . . . of the same fabric in which the threads of all forces . . . are woven into an inseparable net of endless, mutually conditioned relations" (in Capra, 1977). Today we can see how a commitment to conventional modes of reasoning about the nature of reality can limit us, just as it would have greatly slowed scientific development.

Carlos Castaneda's teacher addressed that issue. "Yesterday you *stopped the world*," he told Carlos. "What stopped inside you . . . was what people have been telling you the world is like" (1972, pp. 253–254). We maintain our conception of the world with our internal talk, and as we talk to ourselves we also choose our paths, perhaps repeating the same choices endlessly. Cognitively oriented psychologists like Albert Ellis (1975) have said the same thing. "I want you," Don Juan said to Carlos, "to learn how to get to the crack between the worlds and how to enter the other world. There is a . . . place where the two worlds overlap. The crack is there. It opens and closes like a door in the wind" (Castaneda, 1972, p. 195).

Though the "other world" Don Juan was speaking of was a radically altered state of consciousness, anyone who is not totally trapped in a given pattern of perceiving can find smaller "cracks" in our ways of structuring our words and thoughts and see through them to other ways of understanding. This chapter and the next one open a way to seeing through these small cracks.

CONCEPT AND REALITY

According to phenomenologist Merleau-Ponty (1964), beneath a thought there lies a "first opening" on things without which there could be no productive thought. This "first opening" is our contact with the thing or event itself, unencumbered by ideas about it. As Zen Master Mumon put it:

> In spring, hundreds of flowers; in
> autumn, a harvest moon;
> In summer, a refreshing breeze; in winter,
> snow will accompany you.
> If useless things do not hang in your
> mind, any season is a good season for you.
> (Reps, 1957, p. 106)

To help us break through our limiting concepts to a direct yet multidimensional experience of our world as it is, Zen sayings remind us that no statement or concept is identical to what it tells us about, as noted in Soseki's haiku, "Butterfly, these words from my brush are not flowers, only their shadows" (Miura and Sasaki, 1965, pp. 98, 104).

Our concepts are almost always in some measure arbitrary, depending as they do on the way we group events to suit our purposes. We can learn to tailor our concepts to fit reality instead of trying to stuff reality into our concepts.

The Meaning of Truth

"Truth calls to us, drawn by the innocent laughter of a child, or the kiss of a loved one," wrote Kahlil Gibran. When I see, touch, and smell a rose, I experience it directly and know it as it is. This is my personal truth. I'm unlikely ever to know the *whole* truth of it. Someone else may experience the event differently and know other sides of it. Consider the very expression "to see something in another light." A landscape looks different in the soft, warm light of sunset than at high noon. Truth exists in each of these experiences.

I consider a statement or concept true *to the degree that it helps me clearly experience and respond to the thing or event it represents:* a rose, a pancake, a landscape, this statement.

I'm clear with myself to the degree that what I tell myself coincides with what I know and feel at deeper levels of my awareness. I'm clear with you to the degree that I tell you what I think and feel, rather than pretending to think and feel otherwise. I speak my personal truth to the extent that what I say corresponds to the event as I experience it.

We all have areas where what we tell ourselves is not consistent with what we know at deeper levels. Take Augie's mother. As Augie made his mark in the world—in the record business, he said—he began coming by to pick up his mother in a big, expensive car. Some people whispered that Augie was "in the rackets," but his mother would believe none of it. Yet she would constantly wring her hands as she sat smiling in Augie's limousine. She was always proud of how well her son had done—until the day Augie was killed by the mob.

When I realize that I've confused or deceived myself in some way, I don't have to justify my self-deception. I did what I did. That's who I was then. Now I can find new ways to be.

Another dimension of personal truth lies in considering how, when, and where I find truth *in what I do,* and how, when, and where I don't. To have the deepest influence, says the *I Ching,* I must live my truth as well as speak it (Wilhelm & Baynes, 1967, pp. 144–145).

When I make decisions, I want to avoid letting my wishes, beliefs, or ideology blind me to important realities. I want to listen to my heart as well as to my head, and to the "truth buttons" that keep me honest with myself. In many cases right and wrong are not clear-cut. The choices are never easy when I know that either I or someone else will suffer in some way no matter what I do. When I insist that everything I do is "right" and "good," I avoid the poisonous or destructive elements in what I do. When I insist that everything I do is "wrong" or "bad," I overlook the helpful, caring qualities I do have.

Truth Buttons

Since the body is usually more truthful than the thinking mind, something that happens in your body can tell you what you're doing below the surface of your awareness.

Physical tension is a "truth button" that everyone can use. When you feel your face, hands, stomach, or sphincter getting tight, check out what's happening with you. Something may be going on that you haven't recognized.

Characteristic physical or verbal mannerisms are also sometimes truth buttons. (Several years ago I realized that anytime I began a question, "Just out of curiosity . . . ," it meant that I was about to ask someone an important question. And a helpless shrug of my shoulders meant I was not exploring the options open to me as I faced a problem.)

Concrete and Abstract

Alfred Korzybski (1958), a Polish-American scientist, linguist, and philosopher, noted that defects in language, which are handed on from generation to generation along with useful information, can lead to grave errors in thinking and communication—in part because our meanings can differ radically even when we use the same words, as the following demonstrates:

The Word and the Thing

Sit comfortably, notice any tight spots in your body, and relax them. One at a time, read the words listed below, the left column first, then the next column, and so on. After each word or phrase, close your eyes for fifteen to twenty seconds and allow all the images and associations it triggers to come into your mind. Then read the next word or phrase and repeat the process. Cover up all the words except the one you're going to read to help you focus on just one word at a time. (Ideally, do this in a group, with one person reading the words aloud at appropriate intervals while others keep their eyes closed.)

tree	democracy	property	black and white Hol-
cloud	Ted Kennedy	farm property	stein milk cow
lake	Ronald Reagan	living being	Farmer Jones's faithful
flame	communism	animal	old Holstein
city	Joseph Stalin	farm animal	"Bessie"
love	Fidel Castro	cow	

Finished? If you did this in a group or with another person, take a few minutes to share some of the responses and meanings some of these words evoked in you. If not, imagine the variety of responses you would get to each word from different people.

What did you visualize with *animals?* That sequence demonstrates Korzybski's *abstraction ladder.* Farmer Jones's cow Bessie is on the bottom rung of the ladder. She's the concrete event and if you've met Bessie, when I mention her you know exactly what I mean. Each previous word on the list—Holstein, cow, farm animal, and so on—is another step up the ladder. Also, notice that there are two different abstraction ladders. From *farm animal,* one leads to *animal* and *living being* while the other leads to *farm property* and *property.* We form different abstractions for different purposes.

When you and I think and talk, the higher we go on the ladder the more likely we are to be thinking and talking about *different things.* We get into trouble when we forget that we're dealing with abstractions and act as though they were concrete things and events. For instance, two men may argue about whether it's women's nature to stay home and care for children or to want to go out and have a career *without realizing that the question has no answer.* When we move from *women* as an abstraction to individuals, we find that it's Sharon Adams's nature to want to stay home with the kids and Maria Beltran's to want a career.

When you and I disagree, we may have stated our disagreement in an abstract, general way. We can clarify what we're talking about if I give you a concrete instance of what I said abstractly and ask you for the same: "I'm not sure just what you mean—will you give me an example?"

Governments have manipulated people's thinking by creating abstractions, as in Vietnam, asking us to think of entire nations as the abstraction *enemies* and disregard our concrete awareness of the people in them as individuals. Politicians are frequently skillful at taking a question they don't want to answer, raising it to the next level of abstraction, and talking about that instead of about the issue at hand. For example, "homeless thousands in the cities" becomes "the threat of socialism and the welfare state."

I can also use my abstractions to avoid personal events. For instance, you tell me about something that made you feel terribly lonely. I reply, "Yes, I read an article about loneliness the other day. . . ." I've moved from your specific event to the abstraction of *loneliness.* We miss the contact we make when I respond to *your event.*

Our words and concepts—the maps in our minds—can even come to have a structure all their own that falsifies the real events they represent. Korzybski (1958) reminds us that no matter how good a map we make, the map is not the land that it depicts. His classic statement, *"the map is not the territory, the word is not the thing,"* is a basic principle of clear thinking.

Listen now as Perls skillfully guides a woman from her abstract statement to her concrete events:

> *F [Perls]:* . . . So let's have the dream.
> *M:* . . . I'm with my sister, and—and we have a lot of fun together.
> *P:* In the dream? [*M:* Yeah.] What kind of fun?
> *M:* We talk together, we do things together, we—
> *P:* What do you do together? You see, I can't understand abstract language. I must have something real to work with.
> *M:* We—we escape together, we—
> *P:* You escape together.
> *M:* We escape from people, and—
> *P:* I don't understand the world "people." From whom do you escape?
> *M:* From my parents. (1969a, pp. 132–133)

The ability to think and converse on an abstract level is important. Without it we would have, as semanticist Wendell Johnson says (1946, pp. 276–282), a basketful of information but nowhere to go with it. Through abstraction, we connect our facts and consider their implications with our imagination, fantasy, and sometimes illusion.

Johnson notes that "dull" writers and speakers often remain locked into just one level of abstraction. Either they stay so abstract that we never quite find out what they're talking about or they stay at the level of detailed description without tying their facts together and considering their implications, causing us to ask, "So what?" Interesting writers and speakers, suggests Johnson, play up and down the levels of abstraction as a harpist moves up and down the strings.

Cognitive and Emotive Meaning

Words have not only *cognitive* but also *emotive* meaning—they evoke feelings as well as trains of thought. In Buddhist psychology this is called *vedana:* Every mental event and every sensory experience has a positive, negative, or neutral feeling tone, sometimes subtle, sometimes powerful (Anderson, 1980, p. 49).

The emotive side of our language can misdirect us in two important ways: First, emotive meaning can mask cognitive meaning, whipping up emotions so that logic gets lost. Conversely, neutral terms can be substituted for heavily loaded ones to dull the force of a statement and make mundane something that would otherwise be provocative.

Philosopher Howard Kahane (1976, p. 98) points out that the second approach was used during the Vietnam war. Euphemisms were developed: Concentration camps became *pacification centers,* precision bombing became *surgical strikes,* sampans became *waterborne logistic craft,* and napalm became *selective ordnance.* More recently, tax increases have given way to *revenue enhancers,* huge multiwarhead ICBMs are termed *peacekeepers,* and death has become *negative patient-care outcome.* David A. Wiessler (1984, p. 95) writes in *U.S. News and World Report,* "As Benjamin Franklin would say in 1984, nothing is certain except *negative patient-care outcome* and *revenue enhancement.*" When thinking fosters painful or threatening feelings, we defend against it.

LOGIC AND ILLOGIC*

When I listen to myself, I can be alert for the ways faulty logic leaves me inept and feeling bad. When I listen to you, others, or the media, I want to distinguish between the actual information I get and what the source wants me to believe and to do with it. Almost every source of information has a viewpoint and an "I want" statement built in.

Logic is a set of rules designed to make our statements consistent with each other. Illogic often points to untruth, but something that's logical may not be true. Philosophically, an argument is *valid* if it follows the rules of logic. Otherwise it's *invalid.* A

*We are indebted to Kahane's *Logic and Contemporary Rhetoric* (1976).

conclusion is *sound* only if valid and based on true assumptions. We look now at several common logical errors, some of them neon arrows that tell us that someone's trying to mislead us.

Invalid Reasoning

Here the information and assumptions presented may or may not be accurate, but there's no valid connection between them and the conclusion. For example:

Ad hominem argument (literally, "argument [directed toward] the man") attacks the person. "You're too inexperienced (or weird, or old, etc.) to know anything about that." *Ad hominem* arguments often involve ridicule. On August 26, 1970, U.S. Senator Jennings Randolph, speaking to the Senate, dismissed women's liberationists, and thus their arguments, as "a small band of bra-less bubbleheads." An *ad hominem* argument *has nothing to do with the evidence or the issue at hand.*

Appeal to authority uses someone's prestige as a substitute for information: "Daddy always did it that way, so it must be right." When we hear from authorities, we do better to listen to their evidence and reasoning, which can help us make up our own minds, than to their opinions and conclusions.

Appeal to popularity, a variation on *appeal to authority.* "Everyone thinks so." Or "Rosenquist can't be guilty—twenty-seven respected local citizens and his mother vouched for his character." Another variation is *traditional wisdom:* "It's never been done, so it shouldn't be done."

False analogy. One thing is likened to another when in fact there's an important difference between the two events. For example: "Cops are a bunch of little Hitlers!" In fact, police are elaborately bound by regulations, and most do their best to uphold the laws. Hitler considered himself above the law.

False classification, or *false labeling.* An unemployed person might be labeled "lazy" despite many genuine attempts to find work. And there are politicians who use the term *communist dupe* for anyone who opposes their programs or policies.

Jumping to a conclusion, or *insufficient evidence.* Here there's relevant evidence, but not enough to warrant the conclusion that's drawn. "I didn't get the job. I guess I'm just a loser." Responding to just one aspect of the situation, the conclusion jumper ends up in the mudhole.

Non sequitur (literally, "it does not follow"), sometimes called the *irrelevant reason.* The reason given for accepting or not accepting a conclusion is irrelevant to it. One congressman went on and on about the need for more housing for citizens of this great country when the issue was not that at all, but whether the bill before the House was the right one to provide it (Kahane, 1976, p. 14).

Red herring. An irrelevant, usually emotionally loaded matter is brought up to distract attention from the real issue. The name comes from an alleged practice of dragging a herring—a strong-smelling fish—across a trail to throw off a pursuing dog.

Slippery slope. Without supporting evidence, an action is presumed to lead inevitably to an unwanted event, which will lead in turn to another unwanted event, and so on. "Let you stay out till 9:30? If I do, next week you'll be drinking and petting in the back seat of someone's car, soon you'll be dragging in at 3 a.m. and before long I'll have an unwed mother for a daughter!"

Two wrongs make a right. This says that if you do something harmful, it's okay for me to do the same.

Reasoning That's Unsound Even If Valid

In this case, even when the arguments are logical, the assumptions or information on which they're based are false or unknowable.

Begging the question means endorsing without proof some form of the very question at issue. "We have to go to the reception because we decided that's what we were going to do this evening."

Loaded labeling mixes up facts and value judgments, making it hard to tell which is which. Sometimes this is done intentionally to deceive, and sometimes even the speaker or writer doesn't know the difference.

Questionable assumption means making an assumption that's inadequately supported. "Since our kids don't care enough to get top grades in high school, I'm sure not going to lay out money for college." Perhaps they do care, but can't hold down their part-time jobs and get top grades too.

Straw person means distorting someone's views or actions and then attacking the person on the basis of the misrepresentation. For instance, advertisements attacked a candidate who voted against a bill for "voluntary school prayer" when actually the bill made school prayer *compulsory.*

Suppressed information. Even data that's accurate may be biased if only the information that supports one side is given. What's *not* said can be as important as what *is* said.

Whether the task at hand is to clarify the issues in a family spat or to measure the integrity or intelligence of candidates for public office, listening for these forms of faulty reasoning can be helpful.

FURTHER PATHS TO CLEARER THINKING

Two other tricky rhetorical devices deserve mention here. One is the use of words like *clearly* and *obviously,* with the implication that any reasonable person will certainly agree. We can ask, "*To whom* is it obvious?" What seems obvious to you may not be obvious at all—or even believable—to me. I want to be able to challenge you when it's not.

Similarly, in *incomplete comparisons,* compared *to what,* or *to whom,* is often left unsaid. "Better or worse than what, or whom? Best or worst for what?" (cf. Bandler & Grinder, 1975)

Now let's shift from the details of cloudy thinking to some larger issues.

Subjectivity and Objectivity

"Let's be objective about this" is a statement that assumes a mantle of instant respect. By *objectivity*, we usually imply indifference to the outcome. This attitude requires being "emotionally neutral" about a matter. It assumes gathering as much evidence and information as we can, taking into account all the differing viewpoints available.

In reality, I seldom feel completely neutral about anything important to me. To be "totally objective," I'd have to become someone who doesn't participate in life but only observes. Even a physicist in a laboratory is using instruments that are technological extensions of the physicist's own way of seeing the world.

All I know for certain is, "This is what I am experiencing." Actually, *I'm most objective when I describe what I am experiencing as my experience and no more than that.*

Wearing a mask of "objectivity" is a handy way to avoid acknowledging my biases, feelings, and world view—I may say, "I'm just being logical," when actually I'm heavily emotionally involved in what I'm saying.

To be open to the facts, I have to be willing to see my biases and what they mean to me. Then sometimes I can see past them. This "subjective" stance helps me be as "objective" as I can.

Dualism and Polarities

Most of us are accustomed to thinking in *either/or* terms: things are either "this" or "that." "Is the water hot or cold?" "Is she tall or short?" "This is true and that's false." "We're good and they're bad." This way of thinking is called *dualism*. Such a dualistic, either/or thought pattern can cause us to think that ideas that seem to be contradictory cannot all be valid. For example, I cannot both love you and hate you. I must love *or* hate.

Most things and events fall along a continuum of similarity to each other, like degrees on a thermometer. Yet once I've accepted the either/or assumption, I see the matter only in that way.

Many questions cannot be answered in the terms in which they're put, especially when they require an either/or answer.

Similarly, *if you and I want to work out some trouble we have in our relationship, we'll both have to give up the idea that one of us is right and the other wrong.*

New possibilities can open up when we start to think in terms of *polarities* instead of dualisms. According to an ancient Chinese saying, "Things that oppose each other also complement each other." In each side of a polarity, there is some value and some drawback. Mao Tse-Tung (1967) writes eloquently on this subject in *On Contradiction.* I can carefully consider the validity as well as the limitations in the side of the polarity I reject, and the shortcomings as well as the advantages in the side I accept.

Then I move out of the stuck place I'm in when I cling to one end of the polarity and negate other options.

For instance, my friend Lillian was unhappy with her tendency to become "mother" in all her relationships with people. With time, she also came to know the "little girl who needs to be taken care of" inside her. At first she disliked both. Eventually she found that the mothering she could give her "little girl" could be nourishing; and her "little girl's" aliveness helped her "mother" creatively.

In *paradoxical logic* (Suzuki, Fromm & DeMartino, 1960), ideas that appear to be or are contradictory may also be true. Paradoxical logic works because our ideas leave out many aspects of the real events that underlie them. The omitted parts of the real events may all be valid, even though the ideas we use to talk about those events may seem to contradict each other.

Buddha learned something about who he was from his extremes of being a wealthy prince and a penniless wandering ascetic. Out of these experiences he forged a *middle way* that suited him (Kelen, 1969). Remember that there may be not just one but several different kinds of "opposites" to a given idea or action.

Linear and Lateral Thinking

The left hemisphere of the brain, which controls the right side of the face and body, regulates the kinds of thinking that most intelligence tests measure: logical reasoning and the ability to manipulate verbal and numerical concepts.

The right hemisphere, which controls the left side of the face and body, regulates spatial, artistic, creative, and intuitive mental tasks. This side of our brain can grasp a situation in its entirety, without grappling and figuring (Ornstein, 1977).

Innovative thinking can occur through bringing together two or more different frames of reference. That's how Archimedes found a way to measure the volume of an irregular shape. Needing to know whether a crown that had been given to the king of Syracuse was pure gold, he struggled for days to think of a way to measure the crown. Then one day when he took a bath, he saw the water rise in the tub as he lowered his body and the solution came to him: The crown would displace a volume of water, which was easily measured, equal to its own volume. The answer came from putting together the "measuring the crown" frame of reference with the "taking a bath" frame of reference. Only when he was relaxed and off guard, bathing instead of working, did the needed new frame of reference enter his consciousness (Koestler, 1964; Hampden-Turner, 1981).

Such *divergent* or *lateral* thinking (De Bono, 1971) is essential to creativity, which requires both it and *convergent* or *linear* thinking alike. Frank Barron (1968) found that on clinical tests, creative people score high on both flexibility and intellectual ordering. And Calvin Taylor found creativity to be "a reconciliation of 'opposite' endowments, as . . . remote things were associated, richness was pruned to parsimony, and an insatiability for intellectual ordering rose phoenix-like from seeming chaos" (in Hampden-Turner, 1981).

George Prince (1970) presents a method for opening our minds to lateral thinking and avoiding the trap of dualism that has been widely applied in corporate and government settings:

Brainstorming and Action Planning

Get a group together and pick out some problem you'd like to solve. Divide your meeting into two parts. In the first part, criticism of any idea is forbidden. Everyone is free to toss in any ideas, no matter how crazy, wild, and impractical some of them may seem. People can also offer spin-offs from others' ideas, elaborating on or adding to the original ideas in any way they wish. During this process, if anyone criticizes an idea, others gently remind them that criticism is reserved for later. One person writes down all the ideas.

Then, after the flow of ideas has stopped, the group moves into evaluation. Now, as you each bring out the faults in the ideas that have been suggested, avoid being strictly negative and try to find ways to make each idea work, regardless of who suggested it. Then you may find yourselves with several good ideas to choose from.

We can most easily step outside the old worn grooves and think creatively when we *both* separate our illusions from our realities *and* find ways to integrate our fantasies in our processes.

17

Beliefs and Attitudes

*O*ur beliefs, attitudes, and values are closely connected. This chapter examines each of these three components of our character.

BELIEF AND EXPERIENCE

I believe that the sun will come up again tomorrow. I believe that if I take a certain road, I'll get to town. These *beliefs* are expectations that grow out of my direct experience in knowing my world.

Some things I believe because other people tell me they're so. An astronomer tells me that a planet we call Pluto revolves around the sun. I've never seen it, but I believe that it exists because I trust the methods of astronomers.

We can call these *rational beliefs*. Rational belief is *belief supported by available evidence*. We can also distinguish *blind belief*, which is *belief in the absence of evidence*, and *irrational belief*, which is *belief contrary to available evidence*.

Dogmatism includes both blind belief and irrational belief. Dogmatically held beliefs are data based on limited personal experience or hearsay. I may end up distorting my experience to fit my beliefs.

In *The Open and Closed Mind*, social psychologist Milton Rokeach (1960) has shown that we usually know much more about what we believe than about what we don't believe, and that this tendency is stronger the more tightly we hold to our beliefs. By staying ignorant about anything I don't agree with, I can avoid changing. On the other hand, by finding out more about those things I don't believe in, I can open up to growth and learning. Open scrutiny of what *is* leads to innovation and renewal.

My colleague David Peri, who is both a Miwok Indian and an anthropologist, was trained as a shaman, a healer. "The shaman's path of learning," he once told me, "includes strict training to believe nothing, to accept only what we have experienced for ourselves. I was taught that the most important thing of all is to know what I do not know."

Mary, who was listening, asked, "Then do you hold nothing sacred?"

"On the contrary, I hold *everything* sacred. I hold my knowing of the world so sacred that I take every chance to make it more accurate. Refusal to question some contradiction in my understanding of reality means that I do not respect my view of things *enough*. A view that I have questioned mercilessly merits far more reverence than one that I have never challenged."

IMAGES: BELIEFS ABOUT OURSELVES AND OUR WORLD

My imagination is helpful when I want to keep some distance from what's happening in me and around me. I can use my ability to fantasize to avoid being overwhelmed by my pain or my fear. In the ghetto where I grew up, when we kids were singing and dancing in the street our fantasy became our reality, and we lost sight of the garbage lying all around us.

If I'm here and now in my fantasy, rather than distracted by it, it can be a rich place for me. The important thing is that I know I'm in my imagination and that I can move in and out of it, as befits the occasion.

Yet images can also work against us. I used to buy records thinking that there were certain kinds of records I "should" have. I had an image of a "proper" record collection. Finally I realized how limiting that was and began to buy only music that I really like to listen to.

Relating to an image of another person, rather than to the other as he or she is, distorts relationships. In this process of *idealization,* each person finds ways to avoid seeing how the other doesn't fit the image in his or her mind. When the image finally fades and the two stand naked to each other's gaze, they find—sometimes too late—that who they wanted isn't who they've got.

The Self-Image

My *self-image* is a picture of myself that I carry in my mind. If I grow up among people who accept me as I am, the self-image I develop is apt to be flexible. As I change, I reweave my image of myself. When you try to deal with me as I once was, I can say, "I'm not the same as when you knew me before. Here's how I am now."

The shakier my definition of who I am, the more easily I'm threatened by anything that challenges that definition. So I turn my finest angle to the camera. What I can't admire, I don't see.

My image of myself affects what I make available for you to perceive. For example, if I see myself as "important," I'm asking you to respond to me as "important."

In my daydreams and my daily life, I can lose time and energy trying to make myself "look good." I plaster my life with pictures of a temple so no one will know I'm really a used-car lot.

One day my friend Sally and I were talking and I made some guesses about what she meant. She replied, "No, not any of those things. I was just talking to hear myself talk." How refreshing! She didn't have to keep up the image of always being sensible and intelligent.

Another dimension of self-image is that most of us have ideas about what we can and can't do. I can't do some things only because I've never put time and effort into learning them. But my self-image tells me I "can't do those things," so I live within the narrow limits of the self-fulfilling prophecy I've created for myself.

Psychologist Prescott Lecky studied a group of students who spelled badly. These people had no lack of ability—they spelled foreign words as well as anyone. But in their own minds, they were "poor spellers." When they tried to spell in English, their every act conspired to uphold that self-concept. Lecky found that the poor speller "expects his defect to be condoned and treated sympathetically." So he was clever enough to find an image that was more important to the students than that of being poor spellers. That was an image of themselves as self-reliant and independent. When Lecky showed his students how those two pictures of themselves clashed head on, many of the "poor spellers" started spelling better (1973, pp. 178–180).

Idealized Images

My image of how I want to be can be a starting point for learning. At first glance, the process seems straightforward. I often behave in some way I'd rather not. I see another way of acting I like more. So I try to act that way. (This is a useful and sometimes even necessary process.)

The danger, however, is that if I become obsessed with my image of who I want to be, I can lose sight of who I am.

I may set my perfectionist ideals so high that I have little chance of reaching them. I protect myself against being criticized for not having high ideals, or against ever having to make a realistic effort to meet my ideals, since I've set them so high that they're impossible to attain—and therefore I needn't really try. And I also condemn myself to unending self-torture for never meeting them. Idealizing another person can lead to just as much anxiety about being inadequate as idealizing myself can cause—as I defend myself against recognizing how I really am.

On the other hand, I can imitate a special quality I find in another person and move in the direction of behaving in a way I admire without having to act just like that person. That leaves me free to find my own expression of my new way.

Feelings of Inferiority and Striving for Superiority

Alfred Adler, one of the pioneers of modern psychology, wrote at length about feelings of inferiority and superiority (1964). In many of his patients he observed a process he called "striving for superiority" that originates in a feeling of *inferiority*. As a child, I *am* inferior in many ways compared to the adults around me. Yet if those adults help me to do so, I can feel delight with myself as I am now—I don't have to compare myself to anyone. But if adults and other children think they have to make me feel small so that they can feel big, they will tell and show me in many ways that they're superior.

As I grow in size and strength, I begin to imitate their ways. I step on others and make them feel small so that I can feel superior by comparison. (Even after those who made me feel inferior are in the grave, I may still be trying to compensate for the feelings of inferiority they induced in me by making others feel small so I can feel big.) Thus I keep the vicious circle going.

Feelings of caring and satisfaction are outside the hard-core dualistic game of superior and inferior. When I start appreciating myself as I am, I don't have to feel superior.

Finding Your Talents for Success

Risk. Explore your strengths: What do you like to do? What do you actually spend your time doing?

SUCCESS AND FAILURE

For most of us, success and failure are important parts of our self-images.

When I've failed consistently, I may conclude that I can't succeed at *anything*. If so, a central fact is that I'm *very successful at failing*.

If I'm successful at failing, I know one thing for sure: I get some kind of satisfaction—some *secondary gain*—out of failure. "I actually fail" is the central event. But there are secondary gains, such as your sympathy—"Aw, what a shame. Well, you tried, and you're a good fella. Keep trying. Keep plugging." If, when I fail, I get support and warmth from you that I don't get at other times, I may learn to fail in order to get those goodies.

When I consistently fail, I get something else, too: predictability. I know what to do to fail, what circumstances to do it in, and how I'll respond to my failure. I face little uncertainty. If I'm a school dropout who is saying, "I know how to fail—I can do that well," I'm apt to be afraid that if I change I'll be faced with doing something I won't do as well (something I'll be just average at, or even worse than average). So I carefully guard my image of myself as a "failure."

As I listen to you tell me how you're failing, I may notice that you speak well and easily. You tell me you like to shoot the breeze with people. Okay, let's see how you can get paid for that. A good talker might do well in public relations, or promotional work, or sales. Or as a radio announcer or social worker. Or a teacher. If you work in a factory, check out the union. You might become shop steward. Even if you see nowhere to go right now, you've done something by getting your energy together to explore. Sometimes it takes time to find your way. What counts is that *you're moving in the direction you want to move in.*

Appreciating Your Competence

Find some everyday activity you do easily. Like pouring yourself a cup of tea, or unlocking and opening a door. Pay attention as you do it, and do it with special ease and style.

Then congratulate yourself on how well you did it. "Good! I really did that well!"

Take a few moments right now for some everyday activities. Put down this book, tie your shoelaces—do several things like that. Give yourself plenty of appreciation for doing those things so well and so successfully.

Throughout the rest of today, notice the many things in your daily life you do well.

Maybe you exchange a few pleasant words with the clerk at the store as you make a purchase. As you turn away—"I did that well." *Find where you are typically successful,* and give yourself lots of *immediate, moment-by-moment* appreciation for doing those little things so well.

Next, begin watching for things you sometimes succeed and sometimes fail at. For instance, perhaps you don't often do or say little things to help other people feel good. Give yourself *extra* appreciation when you do succeed at these things.

Pay special attention when you get into failure-talk inside your head. Notice the body position you go into when you feel like a failure. Exaggerate it. Do it to the point where you feel ridiculous (to get fully in touch with what you do). Then talk your failure-talk out loud to yourself, exaggerating that, too. Take as long as you need to hear clearly what you're doing to yourself.

Now you can do something else. From here on out, whenever you notice that you're in your "failure posture," move into a posture that lets you feel good in your body. When you notice failure-talk inside your head, you can cancel the rest of it and direct your attention into ways of thinking that involve encouraging or rewarding yourself.

Belittling and putdowns from others make it easier to feel like a failure. Statements of confidence and support from others, by contrast, can help me feel competent. The more willing I am to use the statements of support I get and avoid people who belittle me, the more easily I can move toward feeling capable of standing on my own two feet.

Many people spend so much time generalizing their problems that they don't get down to working on specific things. "My problem is self-confidence. I can't do anything different now, because self-confidence takes time to get." If you pick out something you *can* do, and do it, already you're successful. Tomorrow, if you wish, you can do a little more.

Success and Failure on Our Own Terms

Suppose I have a job that fits everyone's image of success. "Look at what a great job he has," they say. But I don't like what I'm doing. There's something else I'd rather do. I may face pressure from people who think I'm crazy to give up that "great job" to do something that pays less or has less prestige. But if I'm in touch with what I want from life, I can withstand that pressure. I can start to define "success" in *my own way* instead of someone else's. I can make decisions that will help me lead the life I want to lead, instead of those that will make me *look* successful—unless looking successful is something that I value very highly. I don't have to poison myself by trying to live a life that is not my own, in order to fit someone else's image—or my own obsolete image—of me. I can find a way to be successful *in my own terms.*

ATTITUDES

Every attitude has both an *affective*, or feeling, component and a *cognitive* component: beliefs about the person, thing, or event involved in the attitude. This includes beliefs about how that person, thing, or event will help or hinder the achievement of our personal goals. Each attitude also has a *behavioral* component: how we behave, and feel we ought to behave, toward the object of our attitude. We develop attitudes both through our conscious choices and through a lifetime of conditioning.

Horowitz (1966) demonstrated that behavior change can lead to attitude change, and points out that we infer our attitudes from our behavior. Based on what we perceive ourselves doing, we attribute certain attitudes to ourselves. When I ask a woman her attitude toward brown bread, she may reply, "I must like it, I'm always eating it" (Bem, 1965, 1967, 1972).

But that's only half the story, points out Herbert Kelman (1974). Though she may infer a positive attitude toward brown bread from her actions, that attitude will in turn affect her behavior as she looks for brown bread in the market. Our attitudes are influenced by what we do and they in turn contribute to our behavior.

Cognitive Consistency and Balance

Social psychologist Fritz Heider (1946, 1958) studied how attitudes do and don't fit together, and why they change. People feel impelled, he argued, to keep *consistent* relationships among their beliefs, opinions, and attitudes. If these don't fit, they feel distressed and want to change their attitudes or actions.

To be perceived as inconsistent, cognitions must come into conscious confrontation with each other. For example, many residents of the Eastern Nevada and Southern Utah fallout belt supported nuclear testing until their neighbors and relatives started coming down with cancer. A positive attitude toward nuclear testing began to seem inconsistent with a positive attitude toward good health and long life.

Heider held that we try to keep our attitudes in a *balanced state:* one in which our various attitudes fit together harmoniously (1958, p. 201). When new facts upset the balance, we look for a way to change an attitude that will restore it. So if I like and respect you, I may feel uncomfortable when we feel differently about important events or ideas. I expect you to feel as I do about important matters, yet we disagree on this one. That discomfort may provoke us to search for some way to agree. "People tend," writes Hollander (1981), "to share the attitudes of those they like and to like those who share their attitudes."

The same options are available when the attitudes in question are toward another person. If I like you and our attitudes about Rebecca differ, I may begin to *change my attitude toward her* so that it's more consistent with yours. ("Actually Rebecca doesn't seem so bad.") Or I may *change my attitude toward you* ("How could I like someone who thinks the way you do?") Or I may try to *persuade you to agree with me* so that our attitudes will be similar. These dynamics are often involved in pressures toward conformity.

If I like you, I may see your views as more like mine than they actually are. If I dislike you, I may see them as more different than they are. I may *distract myself* from being aware of something that's inconsistent with a strong attitude. Kurt Lewin called this *leaving the field.* I may physically get up and go, or psychologically depart by daydreaming or picking up a magazine. If I want consistency more than I want clarity, my clarity may suffer.

I may also minimize the relevance or importance of the issue, or differentiate what's involved in our disparate views. Suppose you and I feel differently about a certain senator. As we talk, we find that you favor his proposals for the economy, while I dislike his views on defense. As you explain his economic program, it sounds all right to me, and you discover that you don't like his views on defense any more than I do. Our attitudes are really about *different things.* In this case, focusing on specifics allows us to achieve consistency and also learn something.

Cognitive Dissonance

Leon Festinger (1957) broadened the meaning of cognitive consistency when he suggested that people seek consonance not just between attitudes, but also between attitudes and actions that are related to them. He used the term *cognitive dissonance* rather than *imbalance* for the tension we feel when our attitudes and actions seem inconsistent. He found that most people want to think they've done the best thing and will go to great lengths to avoid thinking they've done something wrong or stupid. Thus if I act in a way that harms another person, I may make myself dislike that person in order to justify my action in my own eyes. For instance, an employer may exploit his workers, then rationalize his action by viewing them as "ignorant, shiftless, and good for nothing."

Festinger suggests three ways to reduce dissonance: changing our behavior, changing the way we look at events that cause dissonance, and seeking out new cognitions that help reduce the dissonance. A smoker who's worried about her health, for instance, may stop smoking, deny that it's really very dangerous, or think, "It's relaxing and I smoke a low-tar brand."

Research on dissonance has stressed two kinds of situations. The first is a situation requiring decision making: Whenever we freely decide between two or more alternatives and commit ourselves to one of them, dissonance occurs, because there is always *something* desirable about the option forgone and *something* negative about the choice we made. The urge to reduce that dissonance can lead to a reappraisal in which we feel even more positive toward our chosen alternative and more negative toward the other one than before we decided.

For example, Knox and Inkster (1968) found that after placing their bets, bettors at a racetrack are more confident that their horse will win than just before they placed them. And Brehm and Cohen (1962) found that after children chose one of two toys they had rated as equally attractive, their liking for the toy they selected went up and their liking for the other one went down.

One way we can reduce postdecision dissonance is through *selective exposure to information.* The man who just put his last five bucks on "Dragging Tail" rereads the parts of the racing form that inspired him to make that bet and pays less attention to the rest.

Cognitive dissonance studies have described situations where we do something inconsistent with our beliefs or self-image *with minimal justification.* In many cases, people given just barely enough incentive to get them to do something—in one study the "something" was eating grasshoppers—develop more positive attitudes toward what they did than those who were given much larger incentives. "Eating grasshoppers must be okay," the underlying reasoning seems to run, "because I chose to eat them." By contrast, if the payoff for eating them was big, I figure I just did it for the money.

In a second kind of situation that doesn't meet the requirements of importance and perceived free choice, a different prediction often holds: Our attitudes become more positive toward the things we're significantly reinforced for doing (Goldstein, 1981).

Prejudice

Prejudice is a judgmental attitude, coupled with blind or irrational beliefs, that I hold strongly and resist changing.

One kind of prejudice we all share is prejudice about ourselves. "I can't do this"; "I don't know how to do that"; "Intellectuals like me aren't supposed to be able to fix cars, or fix washing machines," and the like.

Prejudice is a *way* of thinking, feeling, and acting. The more prejudiced I am toward people and events "out there" in my world, the more prejudiced I'm likely to be about myself.

My prejudice may take the form of feeling hostile toward an entire group of people. When I do that, I respond to any member of that group as a "group member" rather than as a unique individual (Allport, 1958). I may prejudge a member of the group without ever having met that person. When I'm prejudiced *in favor of* a person or group, I may refuse to perceive, believe, or do anything unfavorable about that person or group, and act in ways that give them special considerations. People's attitudes about the Reverend Jim Jones led them to their deaths in Jonestown, Guyana.

Prejudice can be both a result and a cause of lack of information about others. Knowing very little about some group I distrust, I may also prejudice myself against wanting to learn anything about them and keep myself ignorant through the mechanism of *selective inattention.* Social psychologist Edward E. Sampson writes of an experience with his own prejudice:

> [When] I had the opportunity to spend a year in [Southern California's Orange County], I began house hunting with a noticeable chip on my shoulder. I just knew that when "they" heard I was from Berkeley, they would cringe and color me Moscow red.
>
> I finally found a house I wanted to rent. . . . The owner and I chatted amicably. In the yard next door a man was watering his lawn. My new landlord looked at him, looked at me, and said with a little laugh in his voice, "He's a Bircher." . . . My luck. The house I pick to live in for a year has as its neighbor a member of the ultraconservative John Birch Society. . . .

I treated this neighbor rather coldly. . . . My house had a swimming pool; he and his wife had none. Would I invite them to use mine? Hell, no!

Even I mellow eventually. About three months before I was to leave Southern California my neighbor and I got into a friendly conversation. He happened to mention at one point that he was a butcher. I nodded. About five minutes later it hit me. *Butcher* . . . Bircher. What a fool I was! . . . Who would ever have expected to hear "butcher" down there in Bircher country? (1971, pp. 150–151)

Sampson's story is not unusual. Each of us has one like it. We are all prejudiced. The less prejudiced I am, the more likely I am to be willing to look into myself and discover the prejudices I do have.

Some prejudices are tied in with *scapegoating*. Scapegoating is dumping the blame for my troubles on someone who has had little or no part in creating them.

As I come to know my prejudices, I can stop short of translating them into discrimination.

COGNITIVE RESTRUCTURING, OR REFRAMING

During one of the many nineteenth-century riots in Paris the commander of an army detachment received orders to clear a city square by firing at the *canaille* (rabble). He commanded his soldiers to take up firing positions, their rifles levelled at the crowd, and as a ghastly silence descended he drew his sword and shouted at the top of his lungs: "Mesdames, m'sieurs, I have orders to fire at the *canaille*. But as I see a great number of honest, respectable citizens before me, I request that they leave so that I can safely shoot the *canaille*." The square was empty in a few minutes. (Watzlawick, Weakland & Fisch, 1974, p. 81)

Each of us often uses the principle of *reframing*. When I say something that you "take the wrong way," I reply, "You misunderstood—I meant something quite different . . ." and then go on to establish a framework of meaning different from the one that you'd inferred.

What Reframing Is

To reframe something, declare communication theorists Paul Watzlawick, John Weakland and Richard Fisch of the Mental Research Institute in Palo Alto, is "to place it in another frame which fits the 'facts' of the same concrete situation equally well or even better, and thereby changes its entire meaning. . . . The situation itself may remain quite unchanged and, indeed, even unchangeable. What [changes] is the meaning attributed to the situation, and therefore its consequences" (1974, p. 95).

Reframing involves getting people to observe, "How else can I think about this situation and what I'm doing in it?" Instead of telling ourselves the same story day in and day out, we think of a new one that not only cast things in a different light, but may even be more plausible than our old one.

Variations of this process have evolved under several names. Albert Ellis (1975) has developed his well-known *Rational Emotive Therapy* (RET). Behavioral psychologist Arnold Lazarus (1971) coined the term *cognitive restructuring*, which is used here as a general term for RET and all the cognitive behavioral methods.

All these approaches aspire to teach us how to expand the way we feel and act by extending what we think. For instance, "I made a mistake on that job. How terrible!" A "mistake," which may not be so awful—we all make plenty of mistakes—is thus transformed into a "disaster" *because I classify it as such*. Then I may feel and act as I would in a disastrous situation: Disaster *becomes* my reality. When many of us believe the same thing and talk about it to each other, what we believe is *reified*—regarded as a "real thing" in its own right.

Symptoms at Work

"One thing that people rarely understand," state Bandler and Grinder (1979), "is that people's symptoms *work*." Often we neither appreciate the positive purpose underlying a troubling pattern nor recognize how the pattern accomplishes that purpose, because the entire process is largely unconscious.

Reframing is most effective when it's based on the *theory of positive intent* described in Chapter 2. Reframing that includes this additional element will henceforth be called *positive reframing*. Bandler and Grinder, for instance, mention an overweight woman who had several times lost 45 pounds and gained it back. It turned out that her underlying positive intent in staying overweight was to protect her marriage: She was afraid that if she were slender and attractive, she'd be propositioned and might accept.

Salvador Minuchin (1969) practices reframing with families. He calls it "enlarging the focal theme." Family members will mention some terrible problem and he'll say, "It's great that you're talking about that." And it *is*. It means they want to make some kind of positive change, and they've had the strength to bring it out and deal with it instead of hiding it. Troublesome old themes are transformed into new forms that open up possibilities.

From this perspective it makes sense to regard any self-destructive or self-limiting pattern as a message from some part of me. Recurrent headaches, for instance, may be a signal that I need to work less and play more.

Restructuring Faulty Thinking Patterns

Albert Ellis and Aaron Beck have both emphasized the process of replacing irrational ideas about ourselves and our lives with rational ones. Among the irrational beliefs that Ellis identifies as extremely common are these:

> That you ... *must* have sincere love and approval almost all the time from all the people you find significant. . . .

That . . . because something once strongly influenced your life, it has to keep determining your feelings and behavior today.

That people and things should turn out better than they do; and that you have to view it as awful and horrible if you do not quickly find good solutions to life's hassles.

That you must have a high degree of order or certainty to feel comfortable. (Ellis & Grieger, 1977, p. 10)

Most of these irrational beliefs involve the idea that we "must" behave in certain ways, or that events "should" happen in some prescribed fashion. All lead to negative judgments about ourselves and our existence. Ellis calls this process "musturbation."

He suggests that we also be alert for *awfulizing*—telling ourselves that certain things are awful or terrible, such as "It's *awful* when my date cancels." A variation is *catastrophizing*—"It would be a disaster." We can likewise listen for self-talk about things we "can't bear," as in "I can't *stand* it when my boss ignores my suggestions."

Beck (1972, 1976) points out that our self-defeating beliefs and attitudes are not completely irrational but overstatements: too extreme, too broad, or too arbitrary. Once a self-defeating idea is identified, both Beck and Ellis proceed to test the limits of its rationality. The "Logic and Illogic" section of Chapter 16 provides a guide to doing that.

Beck points out several ways we're especially likely to distort our ideas about ourselves. We've already met *dualistic thinking*, like interpreting a mild rebuff as total rejection; *jumping to conclusions* without evidence to back them up; and *overgeneralization*, such as concluding from one mistake that I'll never be able to do anything right. Beck also mentions *errors of omission*, like emphasizing a detail while ignoring its larger context, and *personalizing*—incorrectly referring an outside event to oneself: "She's terribly angry—it must be something I did."

When we're stuck in self-defeating attitudes, another person can be helpful. Bandler and Grinder describe how therapist Carl Whittaker reframes his clients' complaints:

> The husband complains "And for the last ten years nobody has ever taken care of me. I've had to do everything for myself. . . ." Carl Whittaker says "Thank God you learned to stand on your own two feet. I really appreciate a man who can do that. . . ." (1979, p. 172)

Here's something you can try:

Positive Reframing

Choose a partner you trust and sit near each other. One of you begin by revealing a negative attitude you hold about yourself—some unfavorable evaluation of who you are or how you handle some aspect of your life.

The other person is your reframer. The reframer will guess at the positive intent underlying your behavior, or will look for anything else positive in it he or she can find, and will articulate that for you.

For instance, you say, "I could kick myself for getting angry at my husband and children so much." Your reframer might reply, "Your husband and children are very important to you." You respond by saying either, "No, that doesn't strike home," or "Yes, that's right." If your response was "No," your reframer tries again. If it was "Yes," you reveal another negative attitude for your partner to reframe.

After five minutes, change roles. For the next five minutes, you reframe your partner's negative attitudes.

Reframing may involve actions as well as attitudes. Ellis, for example, frequently gives his clients "homework" that involves *in vivo* desensitization as described in Chapter 12. A shy client may simultaneously learn to be more assertive as she learns that it isn't a disaster when her assertion doesn't get her all that she wants.

VALUING

Values are central, enduring appraisals of what's important to us in ourselves, our lives, and our larger world. Some values we choose consciously; others we introject—incorporate uncritically and unconsciously.

Infants have a natural sense of what helps them live, grow, and feel good, and what does not. They positively value food and negatively value hunger. But when full, they negatively value food. The infant, writes Rogers, "values the holding and caressing . . . values new experience . . . and is endlessly curious and forever exploring. . . . Unlike many of us, he *knows* what he likes and dislikes. . . . He is not at this point influenced by what his parents think he should prefer, or by the opinion of the latest 'expert' in the field, or by the persuasive talents of an advertising firm" (1961, pp. 6–8).

As the infant grows, those around him command him to accept their fixed values in place of his own organic valuing process:

"But I don't like canned string beans, Daddy."

"Don't be silly. These string beans are delicious." Daddy *negates (disconfirms) the child's experience of the world, then defines the world for the child.*

The *values clarification* approach made popular by Sidney Simon and his colleagues includes comparing our own valuings with those of others. One way to make such a comparison, suggest Simon, Howe and Kirshenbaum (1972), is to imagine that you're emigrating to another country and can take only one suitcase. Make a list of what's so important to you that you want it in that suitcase. Besides physical items, you can include a few ways of thinking and behaving that you want to retain in the face of whatever you might meet. Then discuss your lists with others who have made their own. (To provide some guidance, one person can briefly describe the place you're emigrating to.)

There are gradations in our level of commitment to anything we value, from thinking about it quietly to ourselves, to making public statements, to actively doing something about it, to doing something about it and trying to arouse others to do so, too. I *actively value* something to the degree that I'm willing to *put my energy into doing something about it.* My valuing process shows itself in my interests, preferences, decisions, and actions. I see most clearly what I value when I look at how I spend my time, money, and energy.

Marty says he values peace and social justice, but so long as I've known him, I've never seen him put any energy or resources into those directions. He spends most of his spare time sitting home reading mystery novels, and appears to me to value that activity more highly than peace and social justice.

On the other hand, Marty does at least *say* that he values peace and justice. We can call these *cognitive values*. When he begins to do something about them, they become *active values*. Here's a way to examine your own values:

Cognitive and Active Valuing

Fold a blank sheet of paper down the middle. At the top of the left-hand side, write "Cognitive Values." List, in the order that they come to you, the dozen or so things that you consider your most important values. Then rank the items, putting a "1" by the one you consider most important, a "2" by the next most important, and so on. Do this before you read on.

Turn the paper over and write "Active Values" at the top. Jot down, as specifically as possible, how you spend most of your time, money, and energy. Then rank these items according to how much you put into each. Be honest with yourself.

Compare your active values and your cognitive values. What do you discover? The more your cognitive values and active values go in the same direction, the more at peace with yourself you're likely to be.

Now draw a circle below your list of active values. Divide it like slices of a pie, with your highest-ranked active value the largest, and the size of each slice reflecting the amount of time and energy you put into it. Then contemplate your pie.

18

Anticipation, Uncertainty, and the Present Moment

*A*t no time are we beyond time. The past influences who we are today, and our anticipations and uncertainties about the future shape our behavior in the present. Yet the present moment—this time and this place—is where our life occurs.

ANTICIPATIONS AND EXPECTATIONS

An *anticipation* is a prediction that I think will probably come true. Anticipations rest on history. I've watched water boil and I have solid information about its boiling point. If I go up 10,000 feet, however, the water-boiling process changes, and so do my anticipations about it.

My anticipations also change when I go inside myself 10,000 feet. The deeper I go, the less my actions will be as they were before I started my journey.

There is a subjective difference in the ways many of us respond to the words *anticipate* and *expect*. When I *anticipate*, I'm looking forward to a probable event. When I *expect*, I go a step beyond that. I feel more strongly about having it happen or not happen. I make an underlying or overt *demand* that you act as I expect you to, and I'm apt to respond less flexibly when things don't go as I think they should.

I create trouble for myself not only when I expect something from you that you haven't agreed to, but also when I leave too little room to move to alternatives with shifts in circumstances. In a rigid expectation, I don't allow for the possibility that the event might not occur as planned. I set myself up to feel helpless and victimized, while the other(s) involved are bad and at fault. In a tentative expectation, I can foresee a possibility of the event's not occurring as planned and can be ready to work out alternatives.

The same holds true for my expectations of myself. Suppose I'm dieting and expect to lose a certain number of pounds this week. I don't and thus feel terribly disappointed, even though I may actually have lost some weight. Out of my disappointment, I get anxious about not meeting my expectations. Out of my anxiety, I eat.

This kind of cycle occurs in any area where my goals are too high and/or I have no alternative responses available. The more I belittle myself for not living up to my expectations, the less likely those expectations are to be fruitful for me. *As long as I've moved in the direction I wanted to move in, even if only a little bit, that's progress.*

I live in a fuller and richer world when I'm willing to enjoy the experiences that come, even when they differ from what I was anticipating. A *parallel experience* is something like the one I wanted, but not quite the same. A *counter experience* is very different from what I anticipated. I can even seek out and create parallel and counter experiences instead of always doing the same kind of thing. In so doing, I avoid the deadliness of the same scenario of plans and expectations year after year and avail myself of many possibilities.

Commitments and Choices

People do some things as I think they will. The grocer will surely sell me a loaf of bread, unless he's run out. As he gives me the bread and I pay him, we fulfill each other's expectations.

In other cases, I might have a hope, but not an expectation. A friend might tell me, "Maybe I'll have time to drop by this afternoon and maybe not."

But if she tells me, "I'll be there around five," I have an expectation. If she doesn't come, I may feel upset—with reason. Had I known she wasn't going to come, I might have done something else I can't do now.

When I want to be able to count on you for something, it's a good idea to make clear, explicit statements. As I've discovered since, my payoff for not making clear requests is that I don't have to confront you about meeting them. But when I don't make my wishes clear, I seldom get what I want.

If I meet a person I find interesting who says, "Let's get together sometime," I'm likely to reply, "When?" If the person is noncommittal and says, "Well, sometime," or something else that suggests only lukewarm interest, I back off. But if the person says something like, "Let's look at the calendar," I'm willing to go ahead.

My life is simpler when I make few promises and keep the promises I make. It's especially important to keep promises to children. It's hard to appeal to reason when I've broken a zoo date with a child.

"But you promised . . ."

I can make up for my broken promise by going to the zoo next week. But if I often break my promises and don't make up for them, I can affect a child's aliveness. Why expect anything if it doesn't happen? When I break a promise to a child, I teach him or her not to trust me and not to trust the world.

Both you and I live with some unmet expectations. When my disappointment is deep, I don't want to deny my feelings and say, "I'm not really disappointed." I can feel as I do, and then go on from there.

Catastrophic Expectations

When something is important to you or me and we don't know what will happen, fearful fantasies about it may intrude. At such times I touch the world only through the screen of worry that I weave around me, brooding on my morbid thoughts like a stewing hen on rotten eggs. Perls calls this a *catastrophic expectation*.

I remember times when I did little more than sit around waiting tensely for a letter or for the telephone to ring. That guaranteed that I stayed miserable. My catastrophic expectation was a way I stopped myself from moving. Instead, I can find ways to be alive. Even when I'm waiting for a call, I can be where I can answer the phone and still do something I enjoy.

Expecting the worst can bring on the outcomes we fear. If a fantasied catastrophe dominates my mind, I have less attention for what's going on right now, so probably I'll be less alert and less effective.

And since people tend to act toward you in the way that you expect them to, show a person you expect the worst and you just may get it. (Show people you expect the best from them and you may get that, too.)

The person who goes in for a job interview with a strong sense of his or her competence is apt to communicate that. He or she is more likely to get the job than someone with identical skills who doesn't expect to get it.

Bertrand Russell writes,

> Both happiness and efficiency can be increased by . . . [thinking] about a matter adequately at the right time rather than inadequately at all times. When a difficult . . . decision has to be reached . . . give the matter your best thought and make your decision; having made the decision, do not revise it unless some new fact comes to your knowledge. (1930, p. 72)

Sometimes, even those catastrophes that do occur open new possibilities and new directions. With the Sufi Attar, we can remember this tale:

> A powerful king . . . one day felt himself confused and called the sages to him. He said:
> ". . . Something impels me to look for a certain ring, one that will enable me to stabilize my state.
> ". . . And this ring must be one which, when I am unhappy, will make me joyful. At the same time, if I am happy and look upon it, I must be made sad."
> The wise men consulted one another . . . and finally devised [a ring] upon which was inscribed the legend: THIS, TOO, WILL PASS. (in Shah, 1970b, p. 74)

Wishful Thinking

> "Maybe if I just ignore it, the problem will go away."
> "I can fake it through."
> "Tomorrow the money will come in the mail."

When I think this way, I neglect the work I need to do to affect reality. I don't make adequate preparations or take reasonable precautions. I'm taken by surprise when events don't happen as I expect them to. That kind of thinking gets in the way of coping with my reality—and at times, of paying the rent!

On the other hand, sometimes I move from wishful thinking into feeling and using my creative, productive magic by being willing to *do something* to turn my wishes into realities. Then I contact my power and find my faith in my ability to create and do.

Your Expectations and Mine

One of Fritz Perls's best-known statements is, "I am not in this world to live up to your expectations, and you are not in this world to live up to mine" (1969a, p. 4).

It's easy to remember the first half of that comment and forget the second half. When misread this way, it goes, "I don't want you to expect anything from me, but I'm going to keep on expecting something from you."

A couple comes for counseling. The woman, who is extremely ambitious, expects her husband to live up to her endless goals for him. But the man is changing. He says, "I'm not here to live up to your expectations," and walks out. He expects her to go into a less striving way of life but doesn't tell her that. If he told her, they might negotiate their differences. Without that communication, the husband's "I'm not here to live up to your expectations" becomes a stopper—he forgets that she's not here to live up to his either.

It's important that the expectations in a relationship be explicit and mutually acknowledged. If both you and I are talking only about "What *I* want," we're stopped cold. If we want a continuing relationship, we've got to talk about the expectations we both have and how each of us is willing or unwilling to respond to the other's expectations.

I Can Give You; I Want from You

In a group, with everyone standing, each person seeks out each other person in the group for a brief interchange of not more than a couple of minutes. The two of you look silently at each other for a moment, and then each of you says to the other, "I can give you . . . " and "I want from you . . . " Then you each find another person to do the same thing with.

When all the pairing off is completed, each of you discuss with the rest of the group the kinds of expectations you found you were placing on yourself and on other people, those that others most typically placed on you, and what you do that encourages such expectations.

I value being able to be who I am with another person—confused and vulnerable, decisive and strong, or whatever. Sometimes I seem inconsistent as I express different sides of who I am. The more we allow each other that inconsistency, without insisting that the other only behave in predictable ways, the more room we have to change and grow, and the more deeply we can understand each other.

YESTERDAY, TODAY, AND TOMORROW

Our anticipations and expectations grow out of our yesterdays, affect our tomorrows, and actually exist in the present moment.

The Past

My present includes my memories. These are my roots. I draw on them for the lessons they hold and the good feelings I can find there.

But I can also use the past to steal the life out of my present. One way we do this is by naming. Once named, a thing need not be looked at anymore. It's got its category and that's that. "By trying to understand everything in terms of memory, the past, and words, we have . . . had our noses in the guidebook for most of our lives, and have never looked at the view," declared Alan Watts (1968, pp. 99–100).

Sometimes names, labels, and categories are useful. Other times we do better to forget the category and allow ourselves to experience the present object or event as fully as we can.

William Glasser (1965) notes that in schools, mental hospitals, jails, and juvenile homes, we imprison people in their pasts. Everyone who works with a given person expects that person to act as the case history describes him or her. Caught in those expectations, the person is indeed likely to act that way. So Glasser refuses to read case histories, working instead in those areas where the person shows strength and promise. He avoids the contagion and contamination of expectations. My own experience is that most of the information that has been compiled about a person tells me little about his or her present capacity to learn. I'm glad I'm not imprisoned in people's conceptions of me as I was ten years ago. There *are* specific incidents in my past that influenced my life in important ways. But no one who has been collecting data about me knows which personal events and subjective experiences are my crucial ones.

Unfinished Situations

When my mind returns again and again to some past situation, I may need to do something I haven't yet done, or finish dealing with my own thoughts and feelings about past events. Perls used the term *unfinished business* for these unresolved situations. When I finish something or resolve a problem in my life, I feel good. Thoughts about unfinished business don't distract me while I'm doing other things. When I leave something unfinished that I could finish, like a problem concerning someone that clouds my vision every time I see that person, I feel at least a little uncomfortable.

Kay and Warren have been divorced for three years. When Kay and I talk casually, she almost always mentions her past life with Warren. "He used to do this, he didn't do that," and so on. She distracts herself from and interferes with what's going on now by constantly referring to the past. She has a lot of unfinished business she's putting her energy into, and is not paying enough attention to what she could be doing for herself now. Nothing she does today will change yesterday.

Some people spend years obsessed with things they did long ago. Their past mistakes dominate their present lives. When I find myself dwelling (not just casually reminiscing) on a past event, I wonder what unfinished thoughts and feelings I pushed out of my awareness at the time and what potentially valuable messages they contain, waiting for me to hear.

We all act in some ways that turn out badly. Mistakes result from bad information, faulty decision making, or chance. We did what made sense at the time, given what we knew and how we felt then. The trouble comes when I feel that I'm "bad" and "wrong" and punish myself for that mistake. An equally self-defeating response is to convince myself that mistakes I've made weren't mistakes at all. That leaves me with poorer information to base present and future actions on.

Much of our unfinished business comes from situations we've never confronted adequately with friends, mates, siblings, parents, former lovers, or others. I may want to tie up my loose ends with you, but if I'm anxious about how you'll respond, I may stop myself.

Or even if I've told you how I felt, I may refuse to let the past event be past. Keeping you feeling guilty about what happened back then gives me a tool to control you. Out of your guilt, you say, "Okay. I'll do what you say." But if you're alive and well, you'll resent me at this point.

If you've done something that I still have strong feelings about, I need to tell you how I feel without attacking you, and we need to deal with that and with your feelings about the matter.

When you don't follow through on a commitment you've made to me, there's a piece of unfinished business in my mind. If the matter is unimportant, I throw it in the garbage can with all those other unfinished events that could clutter up my life if I let them. The garbage can is another way to finish them.

We live with unfinished business. Life is a continuous flow between opening up new situations and closing old ones. I become hungry and I eat. I begin a project and I carry it through. I don't understand what someone says and I ask that person to explain. The trouble comes when I don't eat, or when I stop the project though I should complete it, or when I don't ask what the other person means and go away wondering, interpreting, and worrying. This can be a source of chronic fatigue.

We need to learn to close our accounts. To complete a situation before we leave it instead of putting it off until "one of these days." To be sensitive to when we don't have closure on a situation, and to care enough to tell others when we need closure on something between us. We also need to know when we've done all we can:

> A monk told Joshu, "Please teach me."
> Joshu asked, "Have you eaten . . .?"
> The monk replied: "I have eaten."
> Joshu said: "Then you had better wash your bowl."
> At that moment the monk was enlightened. (Reps, 1957, p. 96)

The Future

"No day comes back again. One inch of time is worth a foot of jade," wrote Zen Master Takuan. Yet how many people spend almost their whole lives getting ready to put on their performances, instead of living now! Even when I have to prepare for a performance, I can find ways to be here—and to enjoy my rehearsal.

(If you think you'll be happy only when you achieve this or that, you may well wait forever.) People who only look forward to the future hardly ever catch up with it. Every tomorrow becomes today. I'm most likely to live the way I want to live tomorrow if I start to live that way today.

When I feel anxious and I can't do anything about what's going to happen, I can take care of myself by noticing what I'm doing *now*. If I'm anxious about getting up and talking before a group in three minutes, I can pay attention to how I experience that anxiety now in my breathing, my heartbeat, my stomach, my hands, my jaw, my sphincters, and my shoulders. As I become interested in those events, I'm likely to become less anxious. It's a way of grounding myself.

Another way to start being here in each moment of my life is by developing a clear awareness of how my mind wanders from the here and now. When, moment by moment, I'm fully aware of what I'm doing that keeps me from being here, I'm here.

My present fantasies about my future may not fit who I am when the future comes. For example, George grew up in a Navy family and was going to be a Navy pilot. His history gave him his fantasy of his future. He entered the Naval Academy and began his training. About halfway through, as he experienced his dream coming true, he found that it didn't fit who he had become and had a breakdown. He ultimately left the Navy and is still working out his guilt about doing that.

If my future is to nourish me, it has to grow out of my present rather than just out of old expectations from my past.

This Time, This Place

> Tanzan and Ekido were once traveling together down a muddy road. . . .
>
> Coming around a bend, they met a lovely girl in a silk kimono and sash, unable to cross the intersection.
>
> "Come on, girl," said Tanzan at once [and] carried her over the mud.
>
> Ekido did not speak again until that night. . . . Then he no longer could restrain himself. "We monks don't go near females," he told Tanzan. . . . "Why did you do that?"
>
> "I left the girl there," said Tanzan. "Are you still carrying her?" (Reps, 1957, p. 18)

Only this moment exists. The future and the past are dreams. Memory is a collection of old phonograph records and photographs. The smell of a street I walked along five years ago, the taste and texture of a taco at a vendor's stand—these things are vivid in my mind as I remember them, but they're not like the smells and tastes and touches I experience now.

When I lose myself in yesterdays and tomorrows, my todays drift into a ghostly realm in which much of my aliveness disappears. If I'm lost in dreams of what might be or might have been, I never feel quite satisfied. The food is never *quite* good enough, or filling enough. I can glut myself on every sensual gratification and every kind of entertainment and still keep wanting *more*.

There is, of course, no way I can ignore my past and future. When I insist on being *only* in the now, I'm not using what I learned in my past, or taking stock of what I'm doing today in relation to where I want to be tomorrow. Planning for tomorrow goes hand in hand with appraising what I need to do for myself now.

My present moment is the *pivotal point* of past and future. It's the expression of all that has happened, and the place where I must apply my energy to affect what will be.

At the same time, I want to be careful to avoid confusing my present event with yesterdays that are in some way similar to it. When my wife and I first got married, we had some trouble in communication. She took many of my statements to mean what her former husband would have meant by them. With some hard work, we realized that this was what was happening. She was still carrying her former husband, much as Ekido carried the girl all day.

A man who had worked hard to become an attorney decided to run for city council. Among family and friends, his wife began calling him "Mr. Mayor," although he hadn't yet even been elected to the city council. When he objected, she replied, "Well, I expect you to be." He wasn't.

She never said, "Now is okay. What you're doing now is enough." And she *didn't recognize* that she had the present and future mixed up. Their relationship ended in divorce.

When we don't realize that we're not in the present, we *may not have our present experience available to us*. Gil was having trouble with his colleagues in a training program. Over and over he tried to assume roles of authority that fit his past but not this situation. He acted like the boss and expected the others to act like subordinates, even though they were all equal in authority.

When forced to recognize what he was doing, he immediately looked forward to doing something in the *future*. He was *going to* stop being ambitious. He *would not focus on* his *present* behavior—on what he was doing with himself and his peers right then in that training program. That left most of his present unavailable to his awareness.

With another person, I can pay attention to whether the effect of what I'm saying or doing brings the two of us more fully into what's happening with us now, or away from it. If it takes us into there and then, is that all right with me in this situation?

When I feel a yearning to "move on," I first check to see whether there's something uncomfortable happening here that "moving on" will help me avoid.

If I'm hurrying to get *there* with my mind filled with where I'm going, my hurried state exists not only in my mind, but in my body. So when I get where I'm going, I'll still feel hurried, and I probably won't function at my best.

Synchronizing your breathing with your walking provides a way to center yourself while carrying out your daily affairs. *Even while you're getting there, you can be here.*

Walking and Breathing

When you notice that you're hurrying, stop. Close your eyes and take one full breath—one slow complete cycle of inhaling and exhaling. Then begin to walk again, according to one of the following patterns. (A *full step* is a step with the left foot and a step with the right foot, so that in four full steps each foot touches the ground four times. We could call this eight half-steps.)

For walking at moderate speed: Take four full steps with each incoming breath, and four full steps with each outgoing breath. Pay careful attention to staying with this pattern.

For meandering along: Take two full steps with each incoming breath, and two with each outgoing breath. This will slow you down.

For getting somewhere fast: Take three full steps with each incoming breath, and five full steps with each outgoing breath, regulating the amount of air you breathe in and out to fit this rhythm. This Balinese walk is a vigorous rhythm that will let you cover a lot of territory fast while staying in touch with yourself and your surroundings.

As you do each of these walks, the main thing is to keep your walking and breathing synchronized. Each time you notice that they're not together anymore, stop completely and start off again with them together. Focus your attention in sensing your breathing, the movements in your body, and what's around you.

A variation on any of these walks: After inhaling and counting as described here, relax your jaw and shoulders and hold your breath as you walk; count for the same number of steps as during the inhalation, and then exhale for the same count.

Time Planning

Time management consultant Alan Lakein (1974) suggests that a little judicious planning now can make future nows more rewarding. He suggests that about 80 percent of our satisfaction and enjoyment comes from only 20 percent of our activities, but points out that much of our time goes into routine tasks that "have to be done," leaving less than we'd like for that 20 percent we really care about.

Timing Your Interests

To try Lakein's approach, turn a sheet of paper sideways and make three columns. Label the first "A," the second "B," and the third "C." Then list all the activities you spend time on during a week. If an activity is a source of major satisfaction, list it in the "A" column. If it's intermediate in value and importance to you, or very important but not terribly rewarding, put it in the "B" column. Finally, list the remaining items, including all routine tasks, in the "C" column.

Next, number the items in each column according to value and importance. "A-1" will be your most highly valued item, and so on.

Items can, of course, change their position within a column and shift from one column to another. Paying the utility bill may be a C-12 when it first arrives, but when the electricity is going to be shut off if it isn't paid today, it ranks much higher. But an item usually works its way up the list gradually—not overnight.

Set up situations where you let yourself go ahead and do the desirable, rewarding "A-1s" and "A-2s" instead of following your old habit of waiting until the apparently necessary Bs and Cs are out of the way: "Well, I'll play piano as soon as I've vacuumed the bedroom and taken the garbage out and. . . ."

You can view your list as a ranking of priorities. Reserve specific blocks of time in your weekly schedule for your As, give as much time as you must to the Bs, and let the Cs fight for what's left.

But Lakein counsels against trying to plan and schedule our time too tightly, so that we leave ourselves no room to flow spontaneously with our moods and impulses. We can remember Thoreau's comment: "A broad margin of leisure is as beautiful in a man's life as in a book. . . . Nature never makes haste; her systems revolve at an even pace" (1960).

Times when I'm completely here are beautiful to me. At such moments, there's nothing in my mind about what I've left undone—about what I expect to get done to be on top of things. At those times I'm not "on top of things"—neither am I "behind things." I'm just *with* things, however they are.

UNCERTAINTY

*Everything comes of itself at the appointed time. This is the
meaning of heaven and earth.*
—I Ching

If I knew that everything would go the way I wanted, I would have no future. The future is the dimension of possibilities. Without uncertainty, tomorrow would be no more than yesterdays already written, waiting to pass by.

In almost any situation, after I've done what I can, forces I do not control—and may not even know about—have their play. That's the wheel of fortune, the cosmic game of chance, the Hand of God. We can curse and fear the working of these unseen forces, or accept, work with, and learn from the situations they create, painful as that may sometimes be.

In my life I've comforted myself with *external security* through accumulated possessions, many relationships, and anticipations of tomorrows that promised what I thought I craved. But no matter *how* much external security I have, I never feel secure if it's my only form of security. I'm always fearful of losing it.

"You possess only whatever will not be lost in a shipwreck," said the Sufi El-Ghazali (in Shah, 1970b, p. 57). As I increase my ability to depend on myself, I develop *internal security*.

When I take a risk, I may be behaving either assertively or foolishly. When I don't act on what's important to me, I may be behaving either timidly or prudently.

Gambling on something that's important to me is acting assertively. Putting myself into jeopardy for values *you* say are important that *I* don't care deeply about is acting foolishly. When I act foolishly or timidly, my life and world seem hollow. When I act assertively, my life is sometimes joyful, sometimes painful, but always full.

Crossroads

Sit back, relax, and allow important choice-points in your life to come into your mind. As they do, jot down a word or two to help you remember each one.

When you've recorded about ten of these "crossroads," stop and look back over them. Is there any consistent pattern in the kinds of choices you made? How many were high-risk ones? How many were safer, low-risk ones?

In fantasy, at each crossroad take the alternative path or paths that you didn't take at that time. As you do, listen for any messages each of these "roads not taken" holds for the way you're living your life now.

Then choose one crossroad that you feel drawn toward exploring more deeply and conduct a written dialogue with your unchosen path(s)—and, if you wish, also with the path you chose. Switch back and forth between yourself and that path, rapidly and spontaneously writing out statements of only a line or a few lines each, as long as your energy for doing that lasts. Then, if you're doing this in a group, some of you may want to share what you learned from your dialogues. (Adapted from Progoff, 1975)

Spontaneity

When I'm spontaneous, my words, actions, and all that I am respond uniquely to *this* moment, *this* situation. I don't need to think of what to do or how to do it—I just *do* it. Spontaneity is letting-happen rather than premeditated action.

Discovering how I allow myself to act spontaneously is especially helpful if I tend to inhibit my acts and censor my words. I can do so in casual situations more readily than in the stress of crisis. Many of us have convinced ourselves that studied, careful ways of acting are the only safe ways available, not letting ourselves take the risk of experiencing the good feelings of allowing our words and actions to flow together freely. But as a friend commented, "Usually it's better to be off the wall than up against it."

"Learning to be spontaneous" may sound like a contradiction. Think of it, then, as unlearning our ways of being contrived and manipulative. Spontaneity is not the opposite of self-discipline; it is the opposite of inhibition. True spontaneity can go hand in hand with self-disciplined learning. In one sense, spontaneity takes the utmost discipline—that of tuning in to what I genuinely feel like doing, learning how to do it, and doing it, despite my fears. We admire speakers, comics, actors, and actresses who have disciplined themselves in their art and bring their spontaneity into delivering their material, in part by attending to themselves and their listeners from moment to moment.

But spontaneity does not mean doing anything I please, regardless of the consequences to me or others. The word can be used to lend respectability to self-indulgence. It can serve to justify lack of consideration, or stepping on other people. Then spontaneity becomes an excuse through which I evade responsibility for "accidentally" harming others. In that case I'm not being spontaneous—I'm being carelessly needy and egotistically greedy.

Natural Cycles

> To every thing there is a season, and a time to every purpose under the heaven:
>> A time to be born, and a time to die; a time to plant, and a time to pluck up that which is planted; . . .
>> A time to weep, and a time to laugh; a time to mourn, and a time to dance; . . .
>> A time to get, and a time to lose; a time to keep, and a time to cast away.
>> (Ecclesiastes 3:1–6, King James translation)

In one sense, my life is a journey from one point to others, some points near, some points far, and all different. In another sense, my life is a series of cycles, of returning again to events that are like events I've known before but that I experience in a different way each time.

When I'm aware of where I am in the cycles of my own life, I can act more wisely. I don't set forth on something new when I need to finish here and draw in my energies. I don't keep working on the same old thing long beyond my time for new beginnings.

When I'm trying to do something and keep running into obstacles and having things go wrong, it may be a message that this isn't the right time, or that I shouldn't be doing it at all. I may need to reassess my goals, wait for a more auspicious moment, or make my moves with greater thoughtfulness, subtlety, and patience.

No Tomorrow

One thing I know for sure: I'll never get out of this life alive.

An ancient formula for living is to live each day as though it were the last day of your life, which in fact it might be:

> Death is our eternal companion. . . . It has always been watching you. It always will until the day it taps you. . . . Death is [a] wise advisor. . . . Whenever you feel . . . that everything is going wrong . . . , turn to your death and ask if it is so. Your death will tell you that you're wrong; that . . . "I haven't touched you yet." . . . Whatever you're doing now may be your last act on earth. . . . There is no power which could guarantee that you are going to live one more minute. (Castaneda, 1972, pp. 54–55, 109)

I was once in a wartime situation where I felt that there was indeed no tomorrow. Suddenly everything seemed different. Each smell, each item my fingers touched, each thing that came to my eyes, was absolutely pure, fresh, and beautiful.

I had a great sadness about no tomorrow for myself. If my life was to end already, I had missed a lot. I wanted more, though I had given myself many good things.

Similarly, singer Joan Baez writes that as a teenage girl she fought constantly with her sister. Her friend Ira Sandperl suggested that each time they started fighting, she pretend that it was the last hour of her sister's life. Within several months the fighting ended, and the two girls grew to love each other deeply (1969, p. 71).

19

Dreams

On the Malay Peninsula, the Senoi have reportedly created a way of living that centers on their dreams. Upon awakening, members of the tribe consult their dreams for messages. If a person dreams of feeling angry toward someone, or of hurting or killing that person, he or she shares the dream with the person, and then the two resolve the tensions between them. Members of a family share their dreams upon awakening and then work on problems the dream reveals. Each day in the village council they discuss the new understandings and ideas that grow out of their dreams, and important tribal projects and decisions are based on dreams. When someone reports an especially interesting dream, other members of the tribe might say, "Go back into your dream tonight and see if you can bring back a new dance, or a new teaching, for us" (Stewart, 1954).*

This chapter is about how to understand and work with your dreams. "As you regard your dreams as important," writes Patricia Garfield, a contemporary authority on dreams, "They will become more relevant for your waking life. . . . [You] will receive and remember helpful dreams" (1976, pp. 60, 66).

Several steps can help you remember your dreams. First, a *dream log* is a great help. Keep a large notebook and a pen by your bed. In the morning, *as soon as* you're awake enough to write, record your dream from beginning to end, with as many specific details as you can remember. If you recall only a tiny fragment of a dream, write down that fragment. It's often enough to work with. But record the dream *immediately*—in a few minutes it will probably be gone. Waking with an alarm can help.

---

*There is some question about the degree to which the Senoi use their dreams in the manner described. Whatever the case, the ideas are provocative.

Record the details of your dream, while still lying down if possible, in the order you remember them. For maximum recall, occasionally stop and close your eyes while writing. If a dream contains a unique verbal expression—a name, poem, or song—record that first, before it drifts away. When you feel resistant to writing down a dream—"It's too much trouble, I'd rather just lie here"—make a special effort. The dreams I'm most reluctant to write down are sometimes the most important ones.

When you wake up at an exciting place in your dream, try *continuing to dream* in your half-awake state of consciousness instead of stopping the dream by waking up fully.

In your dream log, *give each dream a brief title* that captures some unique element of it, to make remembering it and referring back to it easier.

A friend of mine described having a dream, waking up, writing it on a pad beside his bed, and going back to sleep. Upon awakening, he couldn't remember the dream. Gleefully he turned to his pad, only to discover that it was totally blank. He had dreamed the whole sequence!

FUNCTIONS AND CHARACTERISTICS OF DREAMS

Available evidence shows that each of us has several dreams each night, whether we remember them or not, and that our dreams serve an important function: People who are repeatedly awakened during *rapid eye movement* (REM) sleep, when most dreaming occurs, become irritable, anxious, and fatigued. People awakened equally often during non-REM sleep periods do not (Dement, 1976). Anticipating such findings, Samuel Lowy (1942) suggested that dreams serve to regulate our emotional life as we sleep.

But though dreams may not exist to serve our waking consciousness, they can be of value to it. Freud, who called dreams "the royal road to the unconscious," drew attention to the richness, power, and depth of meaning in dream imagery. He used dreams as therapeutic tools to deal with unresolved past conflicts that affect our present lives. Jung, who maintained that dreams point to unsuspected depths of wisdom in everyone, emphasized their connection to present life situations. Dreams, he said, compensate for things missed in our conscious lives, expressing parts of us that we allow no other outlet for. Perls spoke of dreams as the "royal road to *integration*," pointing as they often do to forgotten parts of our personalities that can, when reclaimed, help us be more whole. He viewed a dream as an *existential message*, a statement about something unfinished or emergent in a person's life. He declared, "I believe that any single dream contains the essential message about our existence."

The Existential Message

Make a one-sentence summary of a dream you've had. Now take a look: What does that one-sentence label mean to you? Does it say anything about how you're living or not living your life at this moment? If so, that's the existential message of your fantasy or dream.

Getting lost in too many words can destroy the essence of the existential statement. That's the value of the one-sentence summary.

Evidence suggests that dreams serve to reveal us to ourselves in ways that consciously we may not wish to see. Agreeing with Jung that the dream describes, night by night, the present state of the dreamer's inner life, pioneering dream researcher Calvin Hall (1966) concluded that dreaming is a natural picture language in which thoughts are translated into images with no intent to mislead or deceive the dreamer. Hall also found that people seldom dream about events in the world at large, except as symbols for personal concerns. Rather, we dream about our own conflicts, anxieties, and relationships. "A dream," he wrote, ". . . is not a newspaper story or a magazine article. . . . It is a personal document, a letter to oneself."

In my dreams, I find a voice that speaks of who I am and what I want, rather than who I think I am and what I think I want. In one study, Garfield (1976, pp. 73, 188) reports that as people became more accepting of their dreams, they became more accepting of themselves. (She suggests that proper use of dreams can increase self-reliance and independence.) As I learn to listen to my inner voice, my dreams can be my inner guide. And sometimes they're also rehearsals for my performance in the theater of life.

I can also give myself *healing dreams,* in which I handle a painful situation from my past in a more effective way than I originally did, or find a nourishing element in a situation that seemed only toxic. As this healing process occurs, my old situation loses some of its painfulness and becomes a resource I can draw upon (Rossi, 1972, p. 166).

But consulting our dreams isn't always easy or pleasant. It's sometimes beautiful, sometimes terrifying. To work with our dreams is to witness all this, and learn from it.

THREE WAYS DREAMS CAN HELP US

When Sally was thinking about going to Europe for the summer, she couldn't quite decide whether to or not. One night in a dream, she saw a giant theater marquee brilliantly lit up with the words "DO NOT GO TO EUROPE." In such ways my dreams can tell me about a decision that I've already made at a deeper level, while with my conscious mind I think I'm still struggling over it.

Ann Faraday, author of *Dream Power* (1981) speaks of the "three faces of dreaming." A dream, she points out, can provide information about facts or events in the outside world. It can mirror the dreamer's inner feelings and conflicts. And it can guide our growth by bringing us into contact with submerged potentialities.

Dreams Can Tell Us about Our World

Among the most dramatic dreams are *clairvoyant dreams* that tell us about something that is occurring somewhere else and *precognitive dreams* predicting events that later come true. Sometimes such dreams are accurate in their details, and sometimes they're a little off the mark, like getting the characters wrong though an event itself turns out as dreamed.

Faraday concludes that all the cases of such dreams she studied were instances in which the dreaming mind was a better "detective" than the waking mind. Concerned with other things, the awake person doesn't use available clues, but the dreaming mind does. In some cases, a precognitive dream is a "warning dream" that comes true before the person acts to avert the event it warns about.

Warning dreams alert us to attend to something we've been neglecting, to keep events like the one we dreamed about from happening. They point to things we know but have pushed to the back of our minds. My message in a dream about someone tripping and falling down the stairs may be "Fix the broken step—now!" In other warning dreams, people have dreamed that they were getting ill and ought to see a doctor before they had any conscious hint of it.

Warning dreams can also signal problems in relationships—like a loss of interest or an underlying conflict that needs to be resolved. A warning dream doesn't mean we *have to* deal with what it brings out, but is dramatizes what we may be up against if we don't.

Dreams that involve *seeing through people* are a special kind of warning dream. Faraday writes,

> My husband dreamed that a new business colleague . . . served vegetables that were full of worms. My husband felt this was the dream's way of saying that his colleague was untrustworthy, so he checked his suspicion and found it correct. . . . This [shows] the necessity of checking on the accuracy of the dream perception before taking action, as the whole thing could have been pure fantasy on my husband's part. (1981, p. 173)

Reminder dreams are also a kind of warning dream. I dream that I left the car lights on and need to get up to turn them off. Or of an upcoming event that consciously I'd forgotten about. Reminder dreams are not a substitute for an appointment book, but they can point to something I forgot to record in it, or forgot to notice when I was looking through it. In a larger sense, our warning dreams are reminder dreams in which we tell ourselves to take care of something that we've been neglecting.

Faraday makes a check for possible factual information her first step with any dream that refers to real people, things, relationships, or life situations. She doesn't, however, recommend trying to find a factual message in a dream unless it's fairly obvious. My losses at the race track attest to the soundness of this caveat.

Dreams Can Mirror Our Lives

Long ago the *Tibetan Book of the Dead* declared that everything in our dreams comes from our own minds: "O nobly-born, whatever fearful and terrifying visions thou mayst see, recognize them to be thine own thought-forms" (Evans-Wentz, 1960). Except as just described, dreams don't tell me how things outside me actually are, but they say a great deal about my reality *as I experience it*.

When our dreams change or distort waking realities, as they usually do, the changes and distortions can tell us much about ourselves and our circumstances. A woman who dreamed that her husband was resuming a recent affair, for instance, checked and verified that he was not. Her dream was saying that the affair was not over for *her*—that it was still an emotionally unfinished situation that she had to find a way to bring to closure.

Here's a way to get a sense of how your dreams mirror your existence. It's also a starting point for some of the other ways of working with dreams that will be described.

This Is My Existence

Tell your dream to another person in the first-person present tense, as if you were having the dream right now: "As I enter the rundown room, several people are talking to each other. No one looks at me. I feel invisible, and queasy in my stomach." You may want to close your eyes as you describe the dream so that you can reexperience it as vividly as possible. *Be sure to mention how you feel* at each point in the dream: "I feel invisible, and queasy in my stomach." These statements of feeling, often overlooked, are crucially important in working with dreams.

After each brief statement about the dream, add the words, *"This is my existence."* "As I enter the rundown room, several people are talking to each other. No one looks at me. *This is my existence.* I feel invisible, and queasy in my stomach. *This is my existence."* And so on.

When you've finished, discuss your thoughts and feelings about the dream with the other person.

If you're alone, you can do the exercise out loud to yourself.

As you relive the dream, stay alert for any sensations like tensing your muscles or feeling your heart race or your breathing quicken. The places in the dream where you feel some excitement are likely to connect with issues in your life.

To fully understand a dream, said Freud, we need to look at the waking events preceding it—especially experiences we rejected or suppressed during the day, and those that are unfinished. Knowing the context helps us discern the meaning.

Dreams Can Guide Our Growth

Our dreams can point to personal resources we've overlooked, to changes in who we are, and to ways we neglect important needs. They can also clarify our actions, intentions, and life situations. A dream that confronts some self-deception or punctures a myth can be a healing experience, for it makes me more whole than I was before.

Nightmares, and frightening parts of dreams that aren't nightmares, often contain dramatic messages about something I'm not dealing with effectively. Many people, when troubled by nightmares, understandably want to get rid of them—but that's ripping out a warning light when it flashes. The frightening forces that nightmares represent are sometimes nothing more than my anger with myself when I've tried to tell myself something over and over, but haven't paid attention: "If you won't listen to me, I'll *scare* you into listening." There are ways to get rid of nightmares, soon to be described, but it's unwise to do that until we've heard what we have to say in them.

A *series* of dreams with similar themes points to a message that's struggling to be heard. The scenario that runs through the series deals with something that's important in your life right now. For example, for several months I dreamed of doing something wrong and having to go back to fix it: I turned onto the wrong road, repaired a machine incorrectly, gave a message to the wrong person. This series of dreams told me that I needed to slow down and pay more attention to what I was doing. Even more dramatic is the *repetitive* or *recurrent dream*. If a dream occurs again and again, says Perls, some matter that you haven't dealt with is asking for your attention. Sometimes these repetitive dreams are nightmares that show you how you frustrate yourself.

The following ways of working with our dreams can both illuminate our inner situation and guide our evolution toward greater knowledge and appreciation of ourselves.

FINDING MEANING IN DREAM SYMBOLS

My dream reflects a network of ideas and experiences in my life, and there is value in exploring it as a whole. On the other hand, particular events in dreams that may hold special messages are worth exploring in extra depth. Treating important dream events as *symbols* is one way to do this, especially when a dream makes no sense at first.

Since the inner logic of a dream differs from the kind of logic our waking minds are used to, our dream messages may seem contradictory and confusing until we learn how to work with them. But that's not always so: Sometimes a dream pictures our circumstances, dilemmas, or opportunities so clearly that the meanings are obvious. Dreams of cramped spaces, for example, usually suggest that a dreamer feels closed in. Sometimes a single dream image can convey a message that words would be hard put to equal. A dream may describe how we've been viewing ourselves in some life situation without recognizing it. Faraday (1981) mentions a woman who dreamed of a man in chain mail and knew immediately that the dream was portraying her husband as a "chained male."

Dream images are more unpredictable and revealing than waking thoughts, says Calvin Hall (1966), partly because we can more easily censor the latter to fit our self-images. "The meaning of a dream," he writes, "will not be found in some theory about dreams: it is right there in the dream itself." Psychiatrist Montague Ullman and his coauthor Nan Zimmerman add, "When we allow them to, dream metaphors help us to objectify our unacceptable emotions so that they can be talked about and even laughed about" (1979, p. 171).

The language of dream symbols is largely individual. Anyone who claims to tell you what a certain symbol in your dream "means" is probably mistaken. Jung stressed that we need to be willing to abandon preconceptions and suggested that we translate our dreams in any way that makes sense to us.

Archetypes and the Collective Unconscious

Certain dream symbols that arise out of experiences common to everyone have *related but not identical* meanings for many in whose dreams they appear. Jungian analyst Ira Progoff suggest that we are like wells, each of us unique, but at the source tapping a common stream that connects us all. We are all loving, bitchy, bawdy, sorrowful, afraid, and all the other things that every man and woman has been. Jung gave the name *archetypes* to widely shared symbols that denote these universal qualities. He found that many of his clients expressed such themes in epic dreams of dying, divine heroes, and slaying monsters.

An archetype's content is learned through our individual experience and takes on the unique personal forms that we allow to emerge out of the common human heritage that Jung called the *collective unconscious*. Thus my dreams are both my own creation and expressions of themes important to people in all times and places. You and I may both dream of a child. The *child archetype* usually suggests some kind of unrealized potential within the dreamer. As we explore what that symbol evokes in us, I may get in touch with how I make myself dependent on others and refuse to take responsibility for my own life, while you discover ways to open yourself to a more spontaneous, less programmed way of living.

Some Common Meanings of Dream Symbols

In addition to appreciating the uniqueness of symbolic meanings, familiarity with some of the more frequently reported symbolic meanings may also prove useful. Color, for example, often conveys feelings, though these, too, are individual: Your red may mean love while I use it for anger. The quality of the color can also be significant: Bright yellow may convey a sense of aliveness, while a muddy yellow may imply stagnation. The specific meaning of a color is often related to the context of the dream and what it has meant in our experience.

In some dreams I'm an observer, while in others I'm an active participant. In still others I'm both. Being both a participant and an observer may mean I'm breaking through old understandings to a deeper level of awareness. Rossi (1972) reports a dream in which a woman experienced herself as a building and also as an observer watching as the building, which represented part of her old self, fell over.

Houses and buildings, or parts of them such as rooms, doors, halls, and stairways, have important meanings. But when the action takes place *in* the house or room, as we re-view the dream events, we may overlook the setting. "In my experience," writes Faraday, "the dream house . . . [symbolizes] our relationships, life-situation, and psychic space. . . . Dreams in which a house is undergoing alterations or having extensions built . . . usually indicate a personality change in the direction of expanded consciousness, often accompanied by improved bodily health" (1981, p. 216).

Our *suitcases, boxes, basements, dungeons*, or *jail cells* suggest that we keep important parts of ourselves locked up and don't allow them expression. These might be parts that we conceal from others or from ourselves. Frequently, what we are confining contains some important kind of vitality. You might try closing your eyes, opening the box or door, and watching to see what and/or whom you let out.

People in our dreams can have many meanings. First, they may represent themselves: A dream about my father may be about my father. Or they may stand for others: A friend, colleague, public figure, or stranger I met in passing yesterday may stand for a person from my past with whom I have something unresolved. Or a dream character may represent something I'm beginning to sense or feel about myself, or someone close to me. Perls maintained that *everyone and everything* in a dream represents some aspect of myself, in addition to whatever other meaning it might have.

Some dreams contain *transformations.* A block of ice melts into a puddle. An airplane changes into a bird. An old man turns into a young woman. Rossi (1972, pp. 149–150) suggests that transformations that seem sensible and familiar can reflect evolutionary changes in a person's life or personality. Slow tranformations, like the growth of a plant or the coming of dawn, tend to reflect long-term trends of personality growth. Transformations that seem absurd or that are sudden or abrupt may mean that the person faces a crucial situation that he or she needs to deal with immediately. Ugly, harmful, or otherwise unpleasant transformations may signal a blockage of the growth process that the dreamer needs to pay attention to, whereas those that seem pleasant or beautiful are more apt to represent constructive, desirable changes in a person's way of living and being.

Time and space in dreams reflect our feelings and our inner psycho-logic. A momentary dream event can represent a three-month process in waking life. Size, distance, and spatial relation all can change to compose the picture message of a dream (Ullman & Zimmerman, 1979, pp. 132–133).

Some dreams contain strong positive images: people, animals, trees, or objects that represent positive aspects of yourself. When they take the form of living beings, the Senoi call them "dream friends."

The symbolic meanings just described are only suggestive. Many of your meanings will be unique to you. With any dream symbol, suggests Faraday, the general principle is always to ask yourself why you've chosen this particular symbol rather than another (1981, p. 198). You may also find it useful, adds Garfield, to develop a *personal dream glossary* by discovering what kinds of real events are consistently connected with what kinds of imagery (1976, p. 185)

Your Associations with Dream Symbols

Here's a way to work with your own dream symbols:

Symbolic Equivalents

Imagine a movie screen. Take an important event or symbol from your dream and project it on the screen.

Then clear the screen and allow another scene or symbol that for you is somehow equivalent to the one from your dream to flash onto the screen. Allow whatever it is to come spontaneously—don't try to force yourself to come up with a scene that "makes sense" to you as an equivalent to your dream, for this would hinder the free flow of your fantasy process.

Then, rapidly, one after another, flash other "symbolic equivalents" of your dream on the screen. If you're doing this with another person or a group, report the scenes in your mind aloud as you experience them, so the other person(s) can imagine them along with you.

What does this process tell you about the existential message of your dream?

This technique can be applied to other events in your life besides dreams.

When Garfield interprets the symbols of her dreams, she writes down the associations. Then, also in writing, she reconstructs the dream based on her associations to the symbols. She states:

> Suppose my record reads: "I am with my daughter in a living room. I want her to help me put out a fire that has started. . . . She is unbelievably stubborn and annoying." The "translations," . . . using my associations, might read: "There is a small problem that needs attention. The childish part of me resists cooperating. I feel angry at myself." I proceed through a dream record sentence by sentence "translating" in this fashion. It is important to incorporate associations of current feelings. (1976, p. 186)

A dream symbol may mean I'm in touch with the potential it represents, or it may mean I'm not in touch with it and would do well to contact it. In working with symbols I want to *open myself to everything within me that's connected with that symbol* and see what comes. The moment a symbol attracts my attention, it holds some promise for me.

Polarities are important in working with dream symbols as they occur in dream dialogues. Jungian psychologist Gordon Tappan (1974) comments,

> When I dream of being an eagle, my first feeling may be one of flying, soaring, feeling at one with the air around me. To experience what's *in contrast with* that, I open myself to the shadow side of my eagle nature, to see what's the reverse of my first impression. I find myself diving from the sky, clawing and screaming as I strike and carry off my helpless prey.
>
> Then I explore the polarity within each side of this main polarity. My flying and soaring can also have to do with being flighty, being inflated, having no real substance, being out of touch with the ground. My clawing and striking can also be strength, expressing my confidence in my ability to take care of myself without *having* to claw and strike.

Experiencing both the positive and negative sides of a dream helps me find my potential and power.

DIALOGUES WITH DREAMS

Everything in my dream, maintains Perls, expresses a part of who I am. Different parts of me come through as different characters or objects in my dream. A policeman, a thief, the bridge they're running across, and the river flowing beneath the bridge are all aspects of me. When I work with my dreams to *reown* the fragmented, projected parts of myself and *reown* the hidden power and potential my dreams reveal, I move toward an *integration* of parts of myself that I've separated from one another.

If someone toward whom I have conflicting feelings, or with whom I need to work something through, appears in my dreams, this tells me that I may need to deal with that real-life situation. But from Perls's point of view, that person also represents a dimension of myself. Once I've dealt with the specific issue that centers on that person, I can continue onward to explore the side of me that person represents. In so doing, often I find that the crucial battle is with myself rather than with the other person.

Extending Jung's advice to engage dream characters in dialogue and let them "speak for themselves," Perls developed a dramatic method for working with dreams. To use a dream, he recommended, don't cut it to pieces and interpret, but bring it to life and relive it. In dream dialogues we connect with the "aliens" in our psyche by talking to them and then reversing roles and *becoming* them. Thereby we *experience how we feel and how we are* as these alienated parts of ourselves, instead of just intellectualizing. That green monster scowling through a window in my dream gives me a chance to dialogue (and identify) with my own "monster energy."

Dialogues depend on identifying an important polarity and letting the two sides engage each other. The first step in learning to dialogue with your dream-beings is to learn the technique of *identification*. Remember the "Projection onto an Object" exercise in Chapter 8? You might take a couple of minutes to do that now with two different but related objects, alternating back and forth. In a similar way you can bring a dream back to life. In this next dream, we see how the identification process helps one of Perls's clients move toward greater gentleness with herself and a deeper contact with her life energies.

> *F:* Will you please play the license plate.
> *L:* I am an old license plate, thrown in the bottom of a lake. . . .
> *F:* Well, how do you feel about this?
> *L:* . . . I don't like being a license plate—useless. . . .
> *F:* Okeh, now play the lake.
> *L:* I'm a lake . . . I'm drying up, and disappearing, soaking into the earth . . . (with a touch of surprise) *dying.* . . . But when I soak into the earth, I become part of the earth—so maybe I water the surrounding area, so . . . even in my bed, flowers can grow. . . .
> *F:* You get the existential message?
> *L:* Yes. . . . I can paint . . . I can create beauty. I can no longer reproduce . . . but I . . . I water the earth, and give life. . . .
> *F:* You see the contrast: On the surface, you find . . . the license plate, the artificial you—then when you go deeper, you find the apparent death of the lake is actually fertility. (1969a, pp. 81–82)

The next step after identification is to let two elements in a dream talk directly *to* each other. To undertake a dream dialogue, first make a list of *all* the details in the dream you want to explore. "Get every person, every thing, every mood," says Perls,

> and then work on these to *become* each one of them. Ham it up, and really transform yourself into each of the different items. . . . Have a dialogue

between the two opposing parts and you will find—especially if you get the correct opposites—that they always start out fighting each other . . . until we come to an . . . appreciation of differences . . . a oneness and integration of the two opposing forces. Then the civil war is finished, and your energies are ready for your struggles with the world. (1969a, p. 69)

Your dialogues may be in your imagination, on paper, or out loud using the double-chair technique (see p. 169).

A dream character or image that seems like no more than a minor detail can sometimes hold the most important message. These minor elements can represent parts of us that we disown, or at least avoid attending to. When you have trouble playing some part of your dream, declared Perls, you're almost certain to be dealing with an alienated part of your personality.

Notice what's missing in a dream as well as what's present. In a dark and somber dream, warmth and color are missing. When I see my face in a mirror, my body is missing. In some dreams, what's missing is obvious; in other cases it's more subtle: In an emotion-provoking situation, I may have no feeling, or inappropriate ones. What's missing may indicate something important about what's missing in my life now, or about a "hole in my personality" where I need to develop some aspect of myself.

The destructive power in my dreams is most apparent when I feel most powerless. As I contact my energy and vitality, the violence in my dreams dies down.

LIVING WITH THE DREAM

"I know that if we meditate on a dream sufficiently long and thoroughly," wrote Jung, "—if we take it about with us and turn it over and over—something almost always comes of it" (in Faraday, 1981, p. 125). This is an elemental way of working with a dream—to contemplate it throughout the day—or the week, if need be, returning to it again and again in different states of mind, examining the meanings and perspectives coming from it.

20

States of Consciousness

Gene Roddenberry, creator of *Star Trek,* once commented: "Infinity extends not only outward, but also inward, in all directions. The cosmos outside us and the cosmos inside us are one and the same." The journey into inner space includes exploring our own states of consciousness and learning to move beyond some of the limitations we've grown used to.

USUAL STATES

Each of us experiences several states of consciousness each day, though we may or may not recognize them as such. Sometimes my mind is sharp and alert, and I think and speak clearly and well. Other times I feel dreamy, hazy, tense, or agitated. All this is a normal flow. Sometimes I can selectively tune myself to a given state; other times my mind drifts from one to another.

Traditionally, states of consciousness have been defined in terms of mental events: dreams, hallucinations, verbal problem solving, prereflective awareness (the direct sensing of something that precedes our thoughts about it), and so on. More recently, Western psychology has recognized that the type and level of physical and emotional arousal also play a role: Verbal problem solving in a crisis, for example, is different from verbal problem solving in which I'm peaceful (Ornstein, 1977; Pelletier, 1978). In different states, the body has different chemical and muscular responses. The technique of *biofeedback* is based on that fact: It uses ongoing measurement of such physical responses as skin temperature and brain waves to help us identify and guide what we're doing with our minds and bodies.

Recognizing and Entering Different States

At times my state of consciousness is not appropriate to my activity, or I seem to be "imprisoned" in a state that hinders my effectiveness, health, or peace of mind. In a study of normal persons living in Hawaii, psychologists Martin Katz and Ken Sanborn (1981) found that almost half reported feeling "as if they cannot get certain thoughts out of their minds." Katz and Sanborn remark, "This is a little shocking. We fool ourselves into thinking we have control over our minds. We don't."

In different states of mind, the very same street can seem friendly or threatening. A large part of what the world "is like" depends on how we view it, as this Sufi tale shows:

> A father said to his double-seeing son, "Son, you see two instead of one."
> "How can that be?" the boy replied. "If I were, there would seem to be four moons up there in place of two." (in Shah, 1972, p. 172)

On the other hand, we're aware of some of the changes our minds go through and the way certain kinds of events affect us. The sound of noisy machinery or the wind through the trees moves our consciousness in different directions.

How can we use our recognition that even in daily life we move in and out of different states of consciousness? There are at least three ways.

First, we can develop the habit of noticing, at any given moment, the state of consciousness we're in. Sometimes that leads to spontaneous adjustments: I notice that I'm angry and agitated in a situation where that does no one any good, and I stop producing thoughts that feed that way of being and substitute more relaxed, compassionate ones in their place.

Second, we can regulate our activities to fit our patterns of consciousness. When we were building my house, the head carpenter did all possible thinking and calculating in the morning. In the afternoon we finished work that we'd started before lunch, just sawing and nailing. "I make fewer mistakes," he said, "if I figure things out early in the day when my mind is alert. And after four o'clock, when I'm most fatigued and inattentive, anything dangerous or difficult is off limits." Similarly, we've all experienced looking for something we've lost and being so hurried and harried we look right at the object and don't see it. Later, when calmer, we're more apt to find it.

Third, we can alter our states of consciousness to fit the situation. We may do this with food or drink. Or we can express a feeling we've been withholding or change what we tell ourselves about a situation. Meditation, described later in this chapter, is a powerful method for producing such alterations.

We're likely to be more effective and enjoy ourselves more when we use the various states available. I don't want to spend all my time sitting in quiet contemplation: When I need to be assertive, solve an equation, or saw up logs, I need to move into mental dispositions that fit those activities. Physiological evidence confirms this: When I meditate, for instance, my brain produces mostly alpha waves, indicating relaxed passive alertness, with a scattering of theta waves, which is characteristic of deep sleep. When I start working a math problem, it switches into beta waves, which reflect a state of actively manipulating concepts.

Alternate Realities

We have available not only alternative states of consciousness but also *alternative realities* to which we can respond. Remember Korzybski's admonition that the map is not the territory? Now we take that one step farther. Imagine, says psychologist Laurence LeShan, two maps of the New York area. One shows roads, buildings, bridges, and other familiar features. The other, a map used by airline pilots, shows only radio beacons. These equally accurate, useful maps of the same area have no symbols in common. Each is a valid picture of the same reality, but neither is *the* valid picture. In our concepts of the way things are, sometimes we get caught in just that trap. We assume that our ideas about things—our maps—are the *only* correct ones. That causes problems, LeShan points out, because *no one world picture works completely*. A world view is not a map of reality but of one way of conceiving of it (1977, pp. 34–35). We can draw upon many perspectives and at the same time seek to understand the patterns that connect them.

This doesn't mean that all ideas about the nature of things are equally valid. We're likely to operate more effectively if we have various "maps of reality" to serve different purposes. Then we have options.

Certain elements in a world view sharply restrict our available states of consciousness. These elements are: (1) a conviction that our way is the only "right" way to construe events; and (2) a self-righteous attitude accompanying this conviction. These viewpoints have roots in an underlying feeling of personal inadequacy: At some level I feel unloved, unfulfilled, or powerless. My dogmatic attitude anesthetizes these uncomfortable feelings. Unfortunately, it also stops me from doing much about them. To maintain my limited picture of reality, I stop myself from entertaining perspectives or states of consciousness that might modify it. Thus, rigid ideas about the nature of reality interfere with our flexibility and the full use of our consciousness.

Walt Anderson (1980, p. 79) describes the simple exercise of adding the phrase *up to now* to any statement about what kind of person you are, what you believe, what you like or dislike, and what you can't do.

Distraction and Centering

In response to the stressors of modern living, it's all too common to be hurried and distracted. Charlene, a psychology intern under my supervision, used every moment to learn as much as possible. She worked six days a week and studied on the seventh. As she collected so much from outside her, I could see her losing touch with herself. She began feeling as though bits and pieces of her were flung all over the map. Finally I said, "You need to slow down and connect with yourself, so that when you're with someone, you're there."

When I take time to center myself before entering a situation or starting to talk with someone, I'm more in touch with myself and more in touch with the person or the task. To find my own center, sometimes I need time by myself to find out what I feel and think, and what I want for myself now. At other times, I need a way to center myself amid my activities. Here's one method:

Physical Centering

Stand with your feet pointed forward and shoulder width apart. Unlock your knees so that your legs are flexed. Be sure your head is erect and your shoulders are loose. Close your eyes, and from your feet—not from your waist—begin to move as far in a clockwise direction as you can without falling over. Move slowly, with one full inhalation and exhalation each time you go around in a circle, exhaling as you go through the front half of your circle and inhaling as you go through the back half.

When you've fully tuned into the rhythm of your circular movement, gradually make your circle smaller, continuing to coordinate your breathing and movement, until your circle becomes very tiny.

Now stop at the center of your circle, where you are perfectly centered in relation to gravity: as if there were a rod coming from outer space and going right through your body toward the center of the earth. Check to be sure you're at this perfectly centered point by moving slightly forward, then back, then to the right and left, then back to the place of perfect balance, your knees still slightly flexed. Then take three deep, slow breaths. As you do, let any tension that's left in your mind and body flow out with your outgoing breath, and let a sense of complete well-being flow in with your incoming breath.

Once you can center yourself in this way, there's a shortcut you can use when you need to. Close your eyes and go directly to where you think your physical center is. Check your centeredness by moving slightly in each direction and then take your deep, slow breaths.

You can also center while you're sitting. If you're on a chair, sit well forward so that you don't touch the back when you're at the rear of your circle. If you're on the floor, double a pillow or cushion and sit on the forward edge of it (not in the middle) so that your knees are tilted slightly downward and you can keep your spine erect easily. Otherwise you'll probably have to lean forward uncomfortably to stay upright.

One form of centering can be called *quiet time meditation*. Robert was struggling with whether to get a divorce. He appeared constantly upset and unsettled, saying, "I can't seem to get any perspective on it."

"How much time do you give yourself to sit with your thoughts and feelings, free of distraction?" I asked.

"None," he replied. "As soon as I get home I turn on the TV, and it's on until I go to bed. Whenever I'm not watching it or doing something else, I read a paper or magazine."

"Try sitting quietly with yourself for half an hour each day with no TV, no radio, no magazines, no distraction of any kind," I suggested. Giving himself that time made a big difference.

Such times when we're with ourselves without *doing* anything are an essential part of being centered. I don't go into those quiet, empty times with a program: "I must deal with this thing"; or "I must solve this stuff." I may *have* things I need to deal with; I always have unfinished business I've neglected. If they come up, I deal with them. If not, I just experience myself as I am right now. This is my time to be with myself, with no distractions, and to *get out* of the programmed character of so much of my daily life. I can focus on the feeling, the "texture," the "color" of my experience at this instant.

If I always have a lot to deal with when I sit down, it means I'm not giving myself enough quiet time to keep current with my life.

In its simplest form, meditation is simply a calming of the mind. With the pressure of outer tasks and distractions set aside, our inner clamor can die down and we can truly listen—both to ourselves and to our surroundings. The first time I experienced my silence, I was shocked by the lack of chatter in my head.

"TRANSPERSONAL" AND OTHER ALTERED STATES OF CONSCIOUSNESS

The last two decades have witnessed great interest in altered states of consciousness: those produced by drugs, those that occur spontaneously, and those induced through meditative disciplines.

People under the influence of LSD, psilocybin, peyote, strong marijuana, and other drugs report experiences of minutes stretching into hours, distances expanding and contracting, intensifications of sensation, hallucinations, and experiences described as total oneness with humankind and the universe. Such experiences can be either extremely beautiful events or incredible nightmares from which there seems no escape.

Other drugs, like the various kinds of "downers" available by prescription and illegally on the street, cause a lowering of arousal level, a pleasant mellowness, and sometimes loss of muscular coordination. Still others, like cocaine and amphetamines, cause heightened alertness and a speeding up of the metabolism without great alterations in the content of consciousness. And narcotics like heroin and opium lead to hallucinatory dreams, severe and often lifelong addiction, and loss of interest in almost everything except the narcotic. Many other drugs can also be addictive, including such socially acceptable ones as alcohol, tobacco, and caffeine.

"Transcendent" experiences that occur spontaneously have been labeled *peak experiences* by Abraham Maslow (1976). These are times of feeling "at-one with everyone and everything" that occur unexpectedly and that sometimes profoundly affect our subsequent lives. Tibetan writings, which refer to such states as a "higher alertness," describe them with terms like "stillness," "openness," "clarity," "peace," and "freshness" (Anderson, 1980, p. 173).

Such experiences are often part of what have come to be called "transpersonal" states of consciousness. Transpersonal states include an element of transcending our usual perceptions and definitions of reality as well as an identification with the welfare of other people and beings rather than being limited by our own cravings and strivings. Psychologist Sam Shapiro writes, "A transpersonal perspective . . . rejects any fixed upper limit . . . of self-actualization . . . and also discourages the suggestion of comparison and achievement. Transpersonal realization is not a state to desire or achieve in any traditional sense. . . . [It] is a form of grace in which a person's preexisting transpersonal essence is revealed" (1982).

Transpersonal consciousness does not consist only of ecstatic events. To pursue peak experiences can create an intrusive division between them and ordinary daily living. Transpersonal consciousness and peak experiences, Shapiro points out, are not the same: Though transpersonal consciousness can lead to peak experiences, obsessively seeking peak experiences can interfere with transpersonal consciousness. I lose the identification with something larger than myself and end up back on square 2: sensation seeking.

But when I welcome transcendent experiences in whatever form they take, whether dramatic and overpowering or quiet and almost ordinary, another side emerges: I find a quality of awe and wonder in everyday events—like picking up a warm, newly laid egg. In this state I just *am*—hanging out with myself, you, the children, the cosmos, and I know it's all right. Psychiatrist Gerald May calls this a "pilgrimage home." He writes,

> [A] pilgrimage . . . starts from a certain familiar territory where . . . there are few surprises. Then one begins a journey into lands that are not so familiar. . . . Many things seem special. . . . Then, when the journey is finished, one goes home again. . . . Nothing has happened to change the world, and on the outside one may not appear to be too much different for having taken the trip. But inside, there is a difference. (1980, p. 29)

A few lucky souls develop the capacity to experience such states naturally and easily. The rest of us have to work for them. Meditation is a practical method for doing that. It doesn't guarantee to take us into such a state but creates a readiness in us in which it's more likely.

MEDITATION

Formal and informal meditation techniques are tools to alter our states of consciousness. To many people in the West, the word *meditation* has a mystical and vaguely suspect feeling about it, but actually it's a practical, clear, simple process that anyone can use.

What Meditation Does

Meditation helps us experience directly what we're doing in our minds and bodies. It helps us strengthen our ability to focus our attention where we wish and to minimize distraction. It augments our ability to reduce mental clutter, think clearly, and deal with problems effectively. We may be able to do less and accomplish more as a result of accurately perceiving what we do and don't need, or need to do.

Usually we can't do as yogis sometimes do, spending days in meditation, but as little as five minutes of formal meditation can significantly contribute to changing your mental, emotional, and physical state—including blood pressure, heartbeat, breathing, and muscle tension. Certain informal techniques require no extra time at all because they involve doing what you would do anyway, but in a somewhat different way. You've already encountered some of these exercises in Chapters 6 and 18.

Gerald May writes,

> Blink your eyes, take a breath, and see. And stay with that seeing until you begin to add something to it. Then blink your eyes, take a breath, and see again. . . . This is the way things are, before any thought about it, before any fear or desire. . . . In meditation, you have the opportunity of easing your grip on all your preconceptions, . . . and finding out that you are still there. . . . You realize that . . . hassles . . . are merely figments of an overzealous mind. (1980, p. 33)

The Zen tradition advocates developing a *mirror mind.* Fujimoto Roshi (1961) says, "The function of the mirror is to reflect what is before it. . . . It remains quiet in spite of the activity of the reflections."

Many people, when they first begin to meditate, complain about distractions. Barking dogs, vehicle noises, people entering the room—all these seem distracting. The concept of the mirror mind teaches us to *be aware of these events as they are*—they're not just distractions, they're things we notice as part of our meditation. "So this is what's happening now!"

Nondirective meditation turns such noticing inward. In this *practice* you sit in a formal meditating position (described later in this chapter) and try to be aware of each thought and feeling that arises in you, noting your experience without judging it.

Most meditative techniques involve *concentration:* consciously directing attention toward a specific object. A common misunderstanding is the idea that concentration means pushing things you don't want to think about out of your mind. Actually, that's impossible, because if you're trying to "not think about" something, you're still thinking about it. Rather, concentration involves focusing on what you *do* want to pay attention to. If your attention wanders elsewhere, that's okay. Just bring it back.

So suppose I'm meditating on a candle, observing it carefully. A thought arises in my mind: I notice it and let it go. Another arises and drops away. Then another and . . . suddenly I notice that I'm watching mind movies of somewhere else and the candle has been forgotten. So I let the mind movies drop away and return my attention to the candle. That's concentration.

Each different approach to meditation has its merits. You can learn to trust your intuitive sense of what you need for you at any given time. The best way for one person may be the hardest for someone else. You may want to try several different methods for a week or two each before adopting one. Eventually you may find that you use different methods for different situations.

In general, the more distracted I feel, the more demanding the meditative technique I need to slow and center myself. When I'm fairly centered to begin with, I can use a very simple meditation.

Some people have their own equivalents of meditation. For example, when my friend Mike goes fishing, he gets completely absorbed in each moment of what he does. As the fly hits the water, that moment is all that exists for him. Mike is centered in each instant *of his experience of fishing*.

Posturing Our Minds

Sit on the forward edge of a chair or cushion as described in the exercise "Physical Centering." If you're sitting on the floor, or outdoors on the ground, lay the sole of your right foot along your left thigh, and then your left leg on top of your right, so that your left sole touches your right thigh. (Or you may find the reverse more comfortable: left leg below, right leg on top.) This is called the *half lotus* position. If this is hard for you—and some people's knees just aren't built to lie down flat—you can sit in a simple cross-legged position or sit upright on a chair without touching the back of the chair. If your legs are unusually flexible, you can lay each foot over the top of the opposite thigh in the *full lotus* posture.

Now center yourself in relation to gravity. Then pull your shoulder blades back and your head backward in relation to your body so that your ears are approximately in line with your shoulders and your gaze slightly downward. Then drop your shoulders into a relaxed position.

You can lay your hands in your lap or on your legs. One position is to place your left hand, palm up, on your right hand, so that your left fingertips touch the spot where your right fingers and palm connect. Then touch your thumbtips so that your thumbs and first fingers form an oval. This is called a *mudra*.

Alternatively, lay your hands palms up on your knees. Then slide them up toward your waist until you find a place that feels comfortable. Now start with them by your waist and slide them down toward your knees until you feel comfortable. Finally, find the place somewhere between the two you just found that feels best. Touch the thumb and first finger of each hand together.

Holding this posture is not so easy. Your back may get tired. Your legs may hurt. Your body is likely to slump as your mind drifts, so that you have to bring yourself back into the proper posture. But this straight-spine position not only allows the deepest breathing but also stimulates the nervous system in a way that helps you stay alert. Zen Master S. Suzuki writes, "To take this posture itself is the purpose of our practice. When you have this posture, you have the right state of mind, so there is no need to try to attain some special state. . . . If you slump . . . your mind will be wandering . . . you will not be in your body" (1970, pp. 26–27).

When you find yourself slumping, you can pay attention to how you feel in the position you've moved into. Sit that way for as long as you want to, continuing to be aware of the sensations in your body. Then when you're ready to, sit in the centered posture again. This position is appropriate for most meditative practices.

Methods for Meditating

Most of the techniques described here include holding an erect posture and keeping a focus on your breathing, for breathing stands at the gateway between voluntary and involuntary functions. Working at that interface can help increase our conscious control over the autonomic nervous system.

Mantra Meditation. The meditative approach best known in the West is probably Maharishi Mahesh Yogi's *Transcendental Meditation,* or TM (1975; Bloomfield, 1975). This variety of mantra meditation involves repeating the *mantra*—an especially chosen word or phrase—silently to yourself over and over again. TM teachers conduct an "initiation ceremony" in which they give each person a mantra. For some people this is very helpful. Others, like Ram Dass (1971), report excellent results with mantras that people choose for themselves. Actually you can use any word or phrase that feels right to you as a mantra, including one of personal importance to you or one from your own religious tradition.

Some people like the TM approach because it involves sitting in a comfortable chair rather than sitting up with an erect spine. In fact, any comfortable position will do. When I feel too tired for my usual meditation but want to calm and center myself, I do mantra meditation—sometimes while relaxing in a bathtub. If you fall asleep while doing this form of meditation, that's all right. As in other meditations, notice each thought as it begins to arise, and when you notice that your mind has drifted, return your attention to your mantra. Many people find it most effective to intone their mantra in correlation with the rhythm of their breathing. Here are some mantras, with their meanings and phonetic spellings.*

satya (sŭhtya). Truth
maha (mŭhŭh). Balance
shanti (shawntee). Peace
lung (luhnnnggg). Security
varuna (vawroonuh). Compassion
shunyata (shoonyawtuh). Emptiness
gandharva (gawndharvuh). Harmony
om (öhm or ahhum). Cosmic sound of all being

metta (mehtuh). Loving kindness
parmath (pahrmath). Selfless service
suvidya (sooveedyuh). Acting with awareness
ahimsa (ahheemsuh). Harmlessness and nonviolence
tapah (tahpah). Purification and austerity
sudharma (soodhawrmuh). Being true to your own nature

If you like, you can join the "mantra of the month club": Each month of the year, choose a different mantra for your meditation.

Following Your Breath. Sit in the centered posture. Focus your awareness in your chest, feel the movement of your breath from inside, and let your breathing be your consciousness.

Notice how shallow or deep your breath is, how tense or relaxed your chest, and whether you're breathing with your stomach, your chest, or both. When your breath is halting and irregular, or when you momentarily stop breathing entirely, notice that. When you remember to, check to see what you were thinking of a moment before that might have provoked the tinge of anxiety that caused you to stop breathing regularly. If you don't try to control or direct your breath but stay aware of it, eventually it will regulate itself.

Each time you notice an idea beginning to form, you have the choice of thinking about it or of keeping your attention on your breathing.

*Some of these have traditional classical Sanskrit meanings; others are usages from Tibet and Southeast Asia.

When you first begin "breath following," your mind is likely to be much more centered toward the end of your meditation period than toward the beginning. When you set aside a matter with a promise to yourself to think about it then, however, it's important to keep that promise: You have to know you really will think about the matter later.

Once you're adept at following your breath while breathing naturally, you might want to try meditating with the figure-8 breathing pattern described in Chapter 15. Take at least ten seconds for each inhalation, ten for each exhalation, and three to five seconds each for the still points at the top and bottom of the figure 8.

Counting Meditation. As you follow your breath, silently count one number on each inhalation, leaving your exhalation empty to experience yourself and your surroundings. Count "one" on your first inhalation, "two" on your second, and so on up to "ten." Take one complete breath just sensing your present experience, then begin counting at "one" again. When you notice that you've lost count and drifted off, return to the last number you remember. If you've lost track of where you drifted away, start over again.

You may want to close your eyes, visualize each number, and hear it in your head as you count. If you have a hard time seeing the number in your mind, try seeing just the top edge of it at first and gradually you're likely to be able to see more and more of it. Let each number remind you to feel your breath.

Once you're successfully doing the counting meditation described here, one small addition may help you to focus your attention. On your outgoing breath, silently count "one" each time, as you count from one to ten on your incoming breath. If you have your eyes closed, you might visualize this extra number as a subscript down in the right-hand corner of your visual field. After you've taken an empty breath and are ready to start counting from one to ten again, count "two" on every exhalation, indicating that you're on your second series of ten, and so on. Continue for ten series.

Contemplation, or Reflective Meditation. During meditation is a good time to contemplate difficult issues in your life and personal qualities you'd like to develop more fully. The latter part of a meditation period is usually the best time to do this.

Place an awareness of your subject for contemplation in the background of your mind. Don't "force yourself" to think about it—just let anything relevant that wants to come into your mind come in. If you want to let go of your object of concentration to follow a line of thought about the problem, go ahead.

If you're doing a long sitting meditation, you might want to break it up with a walking meditation—or you can do a walking meditation by itself. Try this:

Walking Meditation

Walking meditation involves coordinating your walking and your breath as described in the "Walking and Breathing" exercise (Chapter 18), but the walk is extremely slow and requires careful balancing.

Hold your hands in a mudra (see "Posturing Our Minds") in front of your stomach and then move forward with *one half step* (moving either foot from behind the other to in front of it) for each full cycle of breath.

Try to keep your legs in constant slow motion rather than using jerky start-and-stop movements. In a group, you can do this walking slowly in a line.

When your attention drifts away, bring it back.

Points in the Process*

As long as you're taking time to sit quietly with yourself, *everything you do is right.* Staying aware of what you're doing, whatever that may be, is the important thing.

When I first began to meditate using a breath-counting process, I went through several months feeling uncomfortable as I meditated. (Some people get through that period more quickly.) Over and over I was bombarded by strong urges to get up, to walk around—to do anything except keep sitting there.

What was happening? In everyday life, when I feel uncomfortable in my body, I move in a way that gives me relief. When I feel anxious, often I do something that distracts me. But when I sit in meditation, my response to each urge is the same: continue to sit and feel whatever I feel. Soon I begin to have available the new response of "continuing to sit and do nothing." I can choose to act in this new way of doing nothing, whereas before I had available only my old automatic response. Through my discipline, I gain freedom.

When my discomfort is physical, such as pain in my legs or back as I keep sitting, I can work with my awareness of my pain. Exactly where do I feel it? What is its character and size and shape? Does it change and move, or stay the same? I can do this with an itch, a tingle, or a soreness in a muscle at any time and any place, answering *these questions through direct awareness rather than with words.* I can experiment with moving my attention back and forth from my pain to my object of concentration. As I do this, I alternately make one my *figure* and the other one a more distant *background.*

Twenty minutes each morning and evening is a recommended TM meditation period. I prefer at least half an hour once a day. If your meditation is uncomfortable enough that you think you might not continue, shorten your meditation period. Or switch to an easier method that gives you immediate good feelings, like mantra meditation in a relaxed posture.

To help yourself stay in the present rather than drifting into fantasy, you can touch the thumb and first or middle finger of each hand together as you exhale and separate them a fraction of an inch as you inhale.

I have a small ceremony for bridging the transition back to ordinary consciousness when I finish meditating. With each of my final ten breaths, I focus on a different visual object or sound, and during that cycle of breath I study it carefully without letting my attention waver.

When you finish meditating, grasp your right wrist behind your back with your left hand, and slowly bend forward as far as you can or until your head touches the

---

*At some point during your experience with the meditative process, you may want to consult a qualified teacher of meditation. For a referral, contact your local recreation department, Asian institute, Zen center, or the activities office of a junior college, college, or university.

floor. Let any tightness in your body go so you can drop forward a little farther, but don't try to push forward using your muscles.

This bow is a sign of respect to everything around you that has shared your meditation time. If you're sitting in a lotus or cross-legged position as you do this, it's called the *Yogic Seal*.

If your feet are asleep after you've finished meditating, you can massage and shake them before you try to stand. Once standing, you may want to stretch to limber up your body.

A final word: Stories of people meditating are full of accounts of individuals breaking up in laughter. The right attitude toward meditation helps develop a lightheartedness, an ability to smile at ourselves when we notice ourselves being too serious. Meditation includes living fully in my joy and my delight—a cosmic, comic me.

Part Five

GUIDING OUR BEHAVIOR

21

Habits and Changes

*T*he adults who cared for us during childhood conditioned us to act in certain ways and not in others, though it's unlikely that they thought of it as conditioning. Many of these habits contribute to our convenience and our safety, our survival and our growth. When my learned automatic responses take care of routine matters, I can be alert to other things.

But efficient habits in routine matters can lead me to ignore my responsibility for making choices in important ones. I may inadvertently let my habits govern contacts with people about whom I care deeply, or govern my actions in situations where I need to be creative and original.

In school, some teachers helped us develop a sense of competence and love of learning and others taught us fear and failure. While some helped us find our own directions and make our own discoveries, others taught us to "line up" in mind and body and not ask provocative questions.

To the degree that I've been conditioned in ways that block my natural processes, I act like a robot reacting to programmed instructions in my memory banks. To become a robot has one real reward: It's *easier* to be a robot than to be responsible, since a robot simply responds as its program tells it to.

Perls, Hefferline and Goodman offer an interesting suggestion:

> Notice some of your habits—the way you dress, the way you brush your teeth, the way you open or close a door. . . . If . . . some alternative seems just as good . . . try to change. . . . Do you take pleasure in learning the new way? Or do you encounter strong resistances? . . . What happens if you watch someone perform a task similar to one of your own? Do you get annoyed, irritated, indignant at small variations from your own procedure? (1965, pp. 120–121)

Taking Inventory of Your Habits

Take an inventory of your habits. See which ones are useful and which ones you want to change. Do this with a pencil and paper.

What do you do habitually? Rapidly jot down as many of your habits as you can think of. Take about five minutes for this right now.

. . .

Finished? Now see how you feel about each of those habits. Next to each put a plus, a zero, or a minus, depending on whether your first feeling toward each habit is positive, neutral, or negative.

How many pluses did you mark down? Minuses? Zeros? Do you tend to see your habits in a positive or negative light?

Which minuses are harmful, and in what ways? Which minuses do you dislike even though they cause you no harm? Are the helpful habits as consistent as you'd like?

If you're with another person, discuss these questions after you've both done the inventory.

CHANGE

Change plays an important role in Christian and Jewish scriptures through the concept of repentance. There is a commonly held view in some religious circles that if I've been acting in ways that bring others pain or harm, all I need to do is recognize the right path and change my views and attitude. The Latin root of the word *repentance* means to *change one's behavior.* Saying, "I'm sorry," won't do it. *Acting differently will.*

Even with those aspects of ourselves that are difficult to change, we can learn *how to use* who we are in more nourishing and creative ways. Doing that is the content of the rest of this chapter and the two that follow.

Change and Power

Each of us wants to feel our own power, and we resent attempts by others to control us. Similarly, efforts to get others to do what we want them to can turn into "power struggles." Dolores observes, "Dad had an obsession about me not being around boys which drove me to be more interested in boys."

A common parental pattern, states Missildine (1963), involves constantly directing, with a steady stream of commands and reminders. This *overcoercive* pattern, as Missildine calls it, reflects the parents' anxiety about the child and about their adequacy as parents. It can lead to docile obedience without questioning or resistance; to compulsive procrastination and chronic fatigue; or to active resistance, with a chip on the shoulder toward anyone in authority.

In dealing with my own behavior, power is an issue only when one part of me resists what another part wants to do. What I need is clear internal communication about what each side wants and about possible choices.

In affecting someone else's actions, the supreme art is to do it in a way that allows the person to be and feel empowered and respected rather than manipulated.

Calibration and Homeostasis

Our environment can help or hinder our attempts to alter our behaviors. I may want to change, but face peer or family pressure to keep things just as they are. The people I live with and the institutions that affect me may be suspicious of change, encouraging me to continue to act in ways that they're accustomed to.

I can't always predict how you'll respond to my attempts to change. I can easily frighten myself about what you might do and spend a lot of time trying to guess where you'll accept my risk taking and where you'll reject it, instead of trying my new ways that feel good to me and then dealing with what you do in response.

In a sense, every person and every social group functions like a thermostat. When the room gets too cold, the thermostat turns on the heater to warm it up. When it gets too hot, the thermostat turns the heater off. Between these two settings, there's a band of acceptable temperature. This band, and its top and bottom settings, are the *calibration* of the thermostat. When I leave the room and you walk in, it may feel chilly to you, so you change the setting on the thermostat to make the room a little warmer. You *recalibrate* it.

Similarly, say communication theorists Watzlawick, Beavin and Jackson (1967), each of us has a defined range of allowable behavior for ourselves, and every family or other social group has a range of allowable behavior for its members. The range of acceptable behavior is relatively broad for some people and families, and relatively narrow for others, but whenever a person steps outside it, that person or his or her social group sends messages to move the person back into the acceptable range.

This practice provides a measure of stability. In one couple, for instance, the husband, Don, needs reassurance that he's a good person and provider, and his wife, Cecilia, wants to be dependent, so they play "Daddy" and "little girl" to each other. When he starts expecting her to do too much, she pouts. When she starts acting too independently, he frets. Then the other person moves back toward what's acceptable within their system. They maintain a *homeostasis*—a rough balance maintained by feedback from each other.

Every now and then a person or group has to recalibrate to fit changed circumstances: Don may say, "Cecilia, I don't need you to be just my little girl anymore. I'd like more of your adult woman and I want us to contribute more equally." In relationships where people's needs are openly discussed and resolved, such recalibration is an invigorating event. In a family, such a process is essential if the members are to develop their own independent identities.

But sometimes the adjustment switch on our interpersonal thermostat sticks, and it takes a crisis to break it loose enough for readjustment to occur—a mate having an affair, a son getting escorted home in a police car, or employees threatening to quit or strike. These are the kinds of situation that often bring a person or a family in for counseling or provoke a company to hire an outside consultant. The outsider's role is to help recalibrate the range of appropriate behaviors with all participants.

Jourard (1975) went so far as to suggest that we can have several different relationships with the same person by letting go of dead patterns and giving ourselves, and each other, room to be alive in new ways. Divorce, Jourard notes, often means that one partner or both feel a need to live in a different way than before. As an alternative to divorce, he is suggesting a way for people to radically redefine their way of living with each other while maintaining their relationship. I suspect that such redefinition occurs most often at points of major developmental change—such as when a child is born or leaves.

Limits

Once I'm aware of how I'm limiting myself, I have the option of moving beyond those boundaries. At the same time, I want to stay attuned to the ultimate limits of your nature and mine, and to those of the situation, so that I don't try to push beyond what's reasonable or possible.

Moving past my limits may mean taking a risk. Taking a risk does not mean acting stupidly. If I'm on the fourteenth floor, I won't test the limits of gravity by walking out the window. That's not a risk—it's stupid. In that situation, I *know* what the limits are. When I don't know what they are, I can look for ways to test them that won't harm me or other people.

One important limit is the fear that you "won't like what I do," or "won't like me." So I bend over backward not to offend you. I do things I don't want to do in order to please or impress you.

I can extend my limits by moving closer to the edge of my fears and discomforts instead of staying far back in the "safe" zone. At the same time, I want to live comfortably with those limits that feel right to me. Problems emerge when I forget that I set these limits and then think that the options I see are the only ones available.

Discipline is a valuable kind of limit. Letting my energy go in all directions is a way I can avoid going far in any direction. When chaotic families come in for counseling, the task is to help them develop discipline and limits that allow them to focus energies and get something done.

CHANGE AND AWARENESS

Change may involve learning new habits to take the place of old ones. First I try out my new way; then I practice it until it becomes familiar.

Change also involves developing more awareness of what's happening in me and around me. I start to act less automatically and more in tune with the unique aspects of what's going on.

For example, when people get angry with me, it's not necessarily because of me but because of what's happening in them. Not long ago I was on campus late at night and I needed a key that was kept in the boiler plant. The boiler plant supervisor's first response to my asking for a key was hostile. My first impulse was to reply with anger. Then I saw the fatigue in his face and commented that he looked tired. His whole manner changed. He relaxed. After a few words about his troubles in the shop, he was glad to be easier on both of us.

Self-Monitoring

Years ago, when I began helping people use positive reinforcement and extinction to change their behavior, I noticed an interesting phenomenon. The first step in such change programs is to "take a baseline"—to record the present frequency of the behavior we want to change. About a third of the people who were taking such baselines came in after several weeks and reported in amazement, "I've stopped doing what I wanted to change. We don't need a change program!" I learned about the power of systematically focused awareness in changing behavior—a procedure later labeled *self-monitoring* in the psychological literature.

I've carried out numerous self-monitoring experiments on myself. I used to have a habit, for example, that I called "persuasive talking." I would try to persuade my listener to agree with me. I talked *at* instead of *with* him or her. I wanted to stop talking that way. I tried paying attention to it and asked people to tell me when they noticed me doing it, but with no success.

Then I got a wrist counter. I started counting instances of persuasive talking and noted them on a graph. In five weeks I was down from many instances a day to just a few.

The wrist counter can be used to reduce the frequency of almost any behavior that isn't maintained by strong reinforcers as well as to take a baseline. Define as clearly as you can what you want to stop doing. Click your counter once each time you do it. Keep a graph, and every day draw a line equal in length to the number of times you clicked the counter.

Self-monitoring works like this: When I start counting some way I act, I experience intentionally as fully as I can how I feel acting that way, even if it's unpleasant. However, I may not know until later that I've acted that way. But before too long, that realization comes shortly afterward instead of a day or even a week later. "Ha! I just . . ." My attention is more focused on and accepting of that way of acting, so I don't work so hard to stop myself from recognizing it.

Eventually I'm aware of the act *as I'm performing it*. Then I can interrupt the old routine right in the middle. Ultimately I anticipate its onset and can stop myself even before I start to do it.

The basic principles are: Define the behavior clearly, count every instance of it you notice, and keep a daily graph.

Self-monitoring is most effective when you feel better acting in the new way. Even if I know that in the long run I would prefer acting differently, I'll probably keep acting in the old way if it brings me greater immediate satisfaction than acting in the new way would.

This is the principle of *immediate reinforcement: An immediate result affects a person's behavior more than a delayed result.* A small immediate reward or punishment can affect the way a person acts more than a large one later on.

There's also the fear of losing even those old satisfactions that no longer fit who I'm becoming. Psychologist Virginia Horowitz has noted people's resistance to change. They are saying in effect, "I'm afraid to change. If I do change, I may not get what I used to think I wanted."

Another approach is to *consciously do* what I want to *stop* doing. Yates (1958) had people with nervous tics deliberately practice the tic in front of a mirror. This was very effective in reducing or getting rid of tics.

Imitation

Zen Master Dogen once instructed: "According to an old Master: 'If you develop a close relationship with a good man, it is like walking in the fog or dew. Although you do not actively wet your garment, it gradually becomes damp' " (Dogen, 1971, pp. 62–63).

Take a look at the people you associate with. In time, you're going to become more like them. If that doesn't please you, find new associates. Who you spend your time with is a big part of who you are.

In his statement, "Do unto others as you would have them do unto you," Jesus was saying in part that imitation is a basic principle of learning.

My acts say more than my words about who I am and what I want. When parents tell their children, "Do what I say and not what I do," they're fighting one of the main ways people learn. When my words and actions give you different messages, the odds are good that you'll take me at my actions.

A father once said to me: "I just don't know what to do about my son. He tortures the cat, beats up his playmates, and nothing I do seems to help. Time and again I whip the living daylights out of him, but it does no good at all." Right!

Bandura and Walters (1959) found that aggressive boys were punished more by their fathers than were nonaggressive boys, and many studies have shown that after children watch someone in a movie act aggressively, they act more aggressively in their own play.

Lidz (1963) declares, *"The child unconsciously imitates what the parents are, rather than what they pretend to be."* And that's true whether we like it or not.

Edith, recently divorced, points to how a *lack* of needed modeling can cause difficulty: "When I was a child, all important decisions and disagreements occurred behind closed doors, and we children were excluded. If I'd seen my parents work out disagreements, I'd have had a better idea of how to deal with conflict and negative emotions in my own marriage."

As adults we tend to reflect the emotional tone we pick up from others. If you're warm and caring toward me, I'm more likely to feel that way toward you. And the same with hostility.

An apparent exception is ways of acting that call out *complementary roles*. If you come on like a parent, for instance, I may respond like a child. Yet even with complementary roles, the emotional tone of both persons tends to be similar.

As we've seen in Chapters 10 and 12, modeling has been widely used to overcome fears and develop assertiveness. But it's useful in making other kinds of changes, too.

Bandura (1969, 1977) has pointed out that effective modeling demands four elements: The learner must *pay attention* to the modeled behavior; *remember what was learned* from that observation; *have the capacity* to reproduce the desired behavior; and *feel motivated* to reproduce it. At five feet six, I will not play center for the Celtics no matter how much I watch Wilt Chamberlain!

I'm more likely to pay attention to a model's actions and to imitate them if I like or respect that person, and less likely to do so if I dislike him or her. I'm also more apt to imitate *coping models*, who model a task successfully but with some rough edges, than *mastery models*, who carry out polished performances (Bruch, 1975). For instance, students who get Bs and Cs often make better tutors for failing students than A students do. The A student is too different, too hard to imitate. B and C students have an easier time being in touch with the failing student and behave in a way the failing student can more readily match. So what do many schools do? They let only A students tutor.

Step by step, increasingly difficult behavior can be modeled and imitated. Such a systematic modeling sequence is called *graduated modeling*.

In much of our *observational learning*, observation is followed by trying out the new behavior. My preschool daughter tries on my swim fins and mask, picks up the broom to sweep after I've put it down, and, if I look the other way, drinks my beer.

Especially in young children, but to a degree in all of us, much of our imitation needs no outside reward to occur. The very act of doing something that we've never done before may be intrinsically rewarding enough.

Nonetheless, observational learning usually is most effective when the new behavior is followed by a reward. Little Roxanne hears big sister ask for apple juice, and imitates her: "Joots! Joots!"

"Isn't that cute," says the mother. "She's asking for juice." Mother's social approval rewards Roxanne's verbal behavior.

Roxanne tastes the juice, and its good taste is an additional reward. Roxanne becomes more likely to ask for "joots" in the future: A person who gets rewarded for doing as someone else has done is more likely to act that way again. In addition, our observations of the rewards and punishments that others get as a result of what they do affects the likelihood that we'll behave that way. This is called *vicarious reinforcement*.

Role Playing

One approach to redirecting behavior involves *role playing*. In this process I try out some modification of how I behave without having to make a lifetime commitment to it. In a low-risk setting, I choose a role that's mildly different from my usual one and then act it out. Chapter 10 described doing this in connection with assertiveness. Here we expand the possibilities. Within rather wide limits, you can be anyone you can imagine being, doing anything you can imagine doing. The great Russian director Stanislavsky used this principle to teach acting. His actors learned to *feel from the inside* what it was like to be the characters they were portraying.

The Magic Theater

For half an hour, all members of the group will stay within a particular room or other area.

As the session begins, go inside yourself and find an aspect of yourself that you'd like to try giving expression to. This may be an imitation of a way of being you've seen in someone else, or it may be some way of being you seldom express that is uniquely your own.

When you've found this, whatever it is, stand up, walk around the room, and interact with other people, *being this person*. Give yourself your full range of possibilities—gentle and caring, hard and angry, and so on. The only prohibition is that you don't hurt yourself or anyone else.

If you think of some way of behaving that you feel embarrassed or uncomfortable about and want to avoid, that might be a good one to try on.

An easy way out: "Usually I talk a lot, so I'll sit quietly in the corner." That can be real or it can be a ploy.

A way to stop yourself from getting involved: "I feel silly doing it, so I won't do it." You can get past that by giving yourself permission to be silly. You don't have to define being silly as not okay.

Now look at what you did during the last half hour. What doors opened up to you? What did you allow yourself to do that you seldom do? What ways of expressing yourself were closed to you in your role?

One way I use the theater is to explore my polarities. I've tried out many different roles and each time it's shed new light for me on some dimension of who I am.

When I consciously act out a role in my everyday life, my performance can be entirely to please myself, or it can be in some kind of relationship with you. I can become involved in my performance to such an extent that I lose touch with you or I can stay in contact with you. I can invite you into my drama, and if you're willing to join me there, we can make contact inside it, or I can step into your drama and contact you there. Trying out roles explicitly can sensitize us to the habitual and often unconscious role playing we do every day.

During my first year of teaching, I discovered that I was doing my job in ways that dulled me and kept me from growing. Much of the time I didn't enjoy my work. Then I discovered that when I wasn't having a good time, my students weren't either. I had to play my role differently to stay alive in the classroom. Now I lecture less. I am as much a guide as a teacher. I feel more alive, my students feel more alive, and we all seem to learn more.

CURIOSITY, COMPETENCE, AND THE SENSE OF EFFECTIVENESS

The ability to deal effectively with our environment affects our self-esteem, confidence, persistence, and involvement. Data about what increases our effectiveness comes from studies of curiosity and competence, of the "sense of effectiveness," and of "learned helplessness."

Curiosity

Taboos learned early from an adult's "Don't do this, don't do that, stop that!" even when we were doing nothing harmful may have stifled our curiosity. As children we learned to fear that many of our actions might be wrong or hazardous.

Many children who have reading problems have grown up with such taboos. Their parents endlessly warn them, "Don't look here, don't look there, don't open the drawers, don't open the closets, don't be curious, don't stare. . . ." The children learn how not to look, and then generalize, applying this habit of not looking to the reading process.

If I'm told—or tell myself—"Don't say anything about . . ." or even, "Don't look at . . . ," I hold back energy I would use for talking or looking. But if that energy is already aroused, it has to go somewhere—so perhaps my fingers start to fidget.

Now someone says, "Stop fidgeting. Don't jiggle." More holding back. I'm uncomfortable. Instead of expressing my discomfort of wanting to move but stopping myself, I make myself less and less aware, deadening my sense of my own possibilities.

As Harry Harlow's (1953) studies show, even monkeys have an innate drive to explore and discover. His monkeys learned to perform a complex task just for the reward of being allowed to look out the window of a box in which they were confined.

Competence

Exploration includes experimentation. We're curious not only about what's out there, but about what we can do with it. When a small boy grabs the spoon from his parent and tries to feed himself, the primary goal is not, as we can see by the debris beneath his chair, to eat more efficiently. The point is to *do it himself.* The encouragement from succeeding gradually leads to increasing competence in the tasks.

But sometimes we can and do interrupt that process. Have you ever watched a parent or older sibling get angry with a child who's trying to do something? If I say to my daughter, "How many times do I have to tell you? You're all thumbs," it shakes her confidence in her own ability. It interferes with her development of a sense of competence in dealing with her world.

Without realizing it, I may have a psychological commitment to her being all thumbs. If she becomes competent, I can't feel so superior any more. The same is often true of a supervisor and his or her workers. If the workers get really good at their jobs, the supervisor's status might have less impact.

Were I your mate, I could keep you dependent on me by keeping you from learning skills you need for you to make it on your own. Were I your parent, I could keep you dependent on me to nurture you, so that you don't nurture yourself—and continue to need me.

"Anything worth doing is worth doing badly," someone once said. Whatever her present level of mastery, instead of criticizing my daughter I can give her some appreciation for what she's done so far. "Good. You've done well with that one. Now—here's a little thing you can do to improve your next one." My comment can add to the reinforcement that being successful provides and can substitute for the natural feedback of success when it takes a while to change.

When I set *short-term* goals and give a lot of moment-to-moment support, reassurance, and appreciation, she learns that she *can* do things. She *learns to appreciate herself.* She starts talking to herself the way I've talked to her.

Bandura (1982) found that success at short-term subgoals can build intrinsic interest in a task where little or none existed before. Among children learning mathematics, those who had set attainable subgoals moved rapidly into self-directed learning. They mastered mathematical skills and developed interest and persistence in activities that previously didn't interest them.

The Sense of Effectiveness

My feelings of competence may be higher or lower than my real abilities. An accurate appraisal of my competence can keep me out of trouble. Nonetheless, we tend to develop a general attitude about our ability or inability to do things that sometimes distorts our appraisals of our specific competencies. Social learning theorists call this *self-efficacy*. It's a little easier on the tongue to speak of our *sense of effectiveness*.

Bandura (1982) finds that even in the face of obstacles, the stronger a person's sense of effectiveness, the more vigorous and persistent his or her efforts will be. Our sense of effectiveness increases, Bandura concludes, when new experiences contradict our old beliefs about our fears and inadequacies and lead to new skills that help us manage difficult or threatening activities.

Learned Helplessness

The other side of the sense of effectiveness, which could be called a "sense of ineffectiveness," is referred to as *learned helplessness*, which we encountered in Chapter 12 in relation to depression. It is the feeling and subjective observation that I cannot initiate or maintain necessary changes in myself or my life. Learned helplessness develops, according to Martin Seligman and his colleagues, when events are not connected to our actions, so that events that affect us seem uncontrollable—even when they're not. For instance, someone who's broke and unemployed may feel helpless and anxious in the face of very real demands from bill collectors and the landlord. If he also believes looking for a job would be futile, he's less likely to look or to seek out ways to be more employable.

Feeling helpless further lowers his self-esteem, which in turn leads to less effective thinking and decreased motivation (Abramson, Seligman & Teasdale, 1978).

One way to move toward feeling—and being—effective in changing rather than helpless is, as we've seen, to be successful in smaller changes. Another is to explore new ways to talk to ourselves about our success and failure experiences. People with a learned sense of helplessness, points out Lamson (1982), often make external attributions for success ("It was just luck") and internal attributions for failure ("I guess I'm just incompetent"). People with a sense of effectiveness are more likely to make external attributions for failure ("Conditions weren't right") and internal ones for success ("I have the ability to do it"). But a "sense of effectiveness" is not identical to actual effectiveness. I suspect that we are actually most effective when we accurately assess what we contribute to both our failures and our successes.

22

Contingency Management

I influence your behavior and you influence mine. The more you respond to my presence, however, the more careful I want to be that I don't intrude on your right to your own ways. Each of us can know what we're asking and giving, and avoid the kind of manipulation in which I trick you into giving something you don't want to give. Then we learn to trust each other.

The approach presented here involves studying cause-and-effect sequences and rearranging them in ways likely to lead to the changes we want. Such cause-and-effect sequences, or *contingencies,* are relationships between one event and another in which the occurrence of one makes the other more likely or less likely to occur.

TYPES OF CONTINGENCIES

The *results* of what I do usually determine how likely I am to do it again. Here's an example:

Father is in his easy chair watching TV. In comes little Freddie.

"Daddy, I want some orange juice."

"Later." Daddy's eyes remain glued to the screen. "Later" is a vague response.

Freddie stands there. Then, whining a little: "Daddy, *I want some orange juice.*"

"I told you *later,*" Daddy replies, his voice a little sharper. "Wait till the commercial. Can't you see I'm watching this program?" Has Freddie learned to trust Daddy's promise to attend to him during the commercial?

A minute passes. Freddie's voice is now a whine: "Daddy, I'm *really thirsty.* I want some orange juice *right now.*"

Daddy, very irritated now, glares at Freddie. "Didn't you hear me? I told you I'll get it as soon as the commercial comes on. Now don't bother me!" If Freddie doesn't trust Daddy's promise, he won't accept the "commercial" limit.

Now, Freddie's voice breaks into a loud screech—half whine, half cry. "But I'm really thirsty and I really want some orange juice and I can't get it and all I want is—"

"Oh, good grief! All right. I'll get it for you. I've told you not to whine like that!" With that, exasperated Daddy stalks into the kitchen.

The next day, Freddie's mother says to his father: "Henry, I'm at my wits' end. All Freddie does is whine and wail."

"I'm going to give him a real talking-to," replies Henry. "And if that doesn't do it, maybe a whipping will."

As matters now stand, when Freddie comes up and asks quietly, he gets no orange juice. No payoff. No reinforcement. When he whines, he gets what he wants. Daddy is *teaching him to whine* by rewarding him when he does and failing to reward him when he asks acceptably. He's selectively reinforcing whining.

Giving Freddie a talking-to won't help, nor will a whipping. It will help to set responsible limits ("Later" is not one of them), giving him satisfaction when he asks quietly instead of when he whines, and letting him know that's what's going on. In response to a whiny shriek, Daddy might commit himself to fulfill the conditions of the limits set: "If you ask softly, I'll get your juice at the next commercial"—and do so.

Freddie (quieter but still whining):   Orange juice, please.
Daddy: That's a little better. Try once more, like this (models a calm, courteous voice): "Orange juice, please."
Freddie (in a normal voice):   Some orange juice, please.
Daddy: Okay, I'll get it for you.

Whining and shrieking won't disappear completely. The sound an overtired or upset child makes is very likely to be a cross between talking and crying. At such times I want to drop my shoulders, breathe, be compassionate, and not get upset.

Rewarding and Punishing Events

Reward includes both *getting a positive reinforcer, or "goodie,"* and *avoiding or escaping from a negative reinforcer, or "baddie."* Roughly, a *positive reinforcer* is something we like to have happen. It is defined more precisely by psychologist B. F. Skinner, who discovered many laws of behavior and pioneered the practical application of behavioral psychology. He described a positive reinforcer as *any event that increases the probability of a response* (1953). A *negative reinforcer* is an event that decreases the probability of a response. *Punishment* may involve either getting hit with a negative reinforcer or losing a positive reinforcer.

Once we understand how rewards and punishments operate, events that have puzzled us start making sense. Here are the basic principles we've all experienced:

1. Any act that brings a reward tends to occur more often.
2. Any act that no longer brings the rewards it used to bring tends to occur less often. Eventually it may not occur at all or it occurs very seldom. This result is called *extinction.*

3. Any act that is punished tends to be suppressed, often temporarily, *but the potential to act in the punished way is still there.* Right? To whatever degree the behavior still occurs, its character is pretty much the same.
4. Both rewards and punishments are more effective the more immediately they follow the event, given that they're strong enough to make a difference.

When something I do gets rid of a negative reinforcer or allows me to avoid it or escape from it, I tend to do that more often. Thus, if my first contact with a situation is frightening enough, I may be so afraid of it from then on that I avoid it. So if at some future time the situation stops being frightening, I'll never find out about it. I act like a rat that's been shocked in a certain place and is afraid ever to go near it again, even if the shock button has been disconnected. That's much like what happens with someone who feels "burned by love" and is afraid to love again. In the experimental lab it's called *avoidance conditioning.* As the song goes, "I'll never love again—I've been avoidance conditioned."

There's also *escape conditioning,* in which someone repeatedly gets into a situation that was punishing in the past, or one like it, and always leaves so fast that he or she never discovers that the situation is no longer dangerous. When Jane, the oldest of five children, was only ten years old, her father died and her mother went to work full time. Jane took over the household and child-care responsibilities. At age seventeen she sought escape through marriage. Her husband, twenty years her senior, was abusive and adolescent. After her second hospitalization due to his violence, she divorced him. Now, ten years later, while she wants a family of her own and a relationship with a man, she allows herself to get into relationships only until physical intimacy is imminent—and then panics and flees.

Primary and Secondary Reinforcement

Escape and avoidance conditioning occur because of *secondary reinforcement:* Situations that once were neutral now *have themselves become punishing,* through their association with past pain. We may or may not consciously remember when and how this happened: "I don't know why, but I just feel uncomfortable around here," or "There's something about it I like, but I can't put my finger on it."

Primary reinforcers are innate and common to everyone—like food, drink, sex, and the opportunity to satisfy our curiosity. *Secondary reinforcers* are people, things, or situations that have been connected with primary reinforcers in the past. Through a process of association and conditioning, we now respond to them much as we once responded to the primary reinforcers with which they were paired. Thus an event that originally was neither pleasant nor unpleasant can, after it's been connected with a reward enough times, itself begin to be rewarding. The good feelings that go with something nice happening "rub off" on the person or the situation in which it happens. In his novel *Island,* Aldous Huxley writes,

> Dr. Andrew picked up the idea . . . in northern New Guinea. . . . Stroke the baby while you're feeding him; it doubles his pleasure. Then, while he's . . . being caressed, introduce him to the animal or person you want him to love. . . . Let there be a warm physical contact between child and love object.

At the same time repeat some word like "good." At first he'll understand only your tone of voice. Later on, when he learns to speak, he'll get the full meaning. . . .

Pure Pavlov. (1962, p. 221)

Bribery and Spoiling

Some people strongly object to the use of positive reinforcement, especially with children. "Why, that's just paying them off for behaving. That's bribery!"

Is it? Let's see. Here's a typical situation involving what we'd call actual bribery: A woman and her little boy are in a store. He's crying. "Listen," she says, "if you'll behave yourself for fifteen minutes, I'll get you an ice-cream cone."

What happens? For fifteen minutes he behaves, pouting and resentful. Then he gets his ice-cream cone, and soon he's back to crying. He has learned to do what mother says for fifteen minutes. He's probably also learning that misbehavior can pay off. (The sugar dosage isn't helping any, either.) His obnoxious behavior has been reinforced by attention and a bribe for temporary good behavior. Since the obnoxious behavior is positively reinforced, it becomes more frequent.

Compare this common reinforcement of irritating behavior to reinforcement of desired behavior. In the same store, when a mother who's consciously using positive reinforcement likes the way her son is acting, she'll tell him *right then*. She knows that immediate rewards work better than delayed rewards, so she doesn't wait till they get out of the store. By rewarding desired acts immediately, she's rewarding a *specific behavior*, rather than all the behavior that occurred while they were in the store. The boy knows exactly what he's being rewarded for.

Some parents "spoil" (read "confuse") their children. Spoiled children are used to getting what they want. We spoil children by *giving them rewards regardless of what they do*. Such children grow up feeling that the world owes them a living. That's just one symptom of a graver problem: Since these children don't face the consequences of what they do, they blame others and otherwise avoid taking responsibility for the results of their actions. This has been identified as an issue in teenage suicide.

Some people, even when they understand how positive reinforcement differs from bribery and spoiling, still don't like it. A typical protest is: "It just doesn't seem right to me to pay someone off for doing something that he ought to do anyway."

". . . that he ought to do anyway." That usually means ". . . that I think he should be doing now." Overlooked is the obvious fact that he *hasn't learned to do it yet*. That puts him in quite a bind. It's like giving a new worker a task he or she can't perform to your standards of perfection, and then getting angry because your standards weren't met.

I have found that *people who are most opposed to rewarding others for desired behavior are nearly always strong advocates of punishment*. Many of us were brought up on punishment-oriented discipline and we tend to repeat the same pattern.

Behavioral psychologists Roland Tharp and Ralph Wetzel (1969) found that some clients found ways to punish their children even when this was contrary to the behavioral change plan. They wanted to punish more than they wanted to bring about the changes they sought. Perhaps punishing was a way they could feel their power. It was also a way of displacing aggression that was related to other frustrations in their lives.

Discriminative Stimuli

We respond to many *signals* that something is about to happen, or that we should act a certain way—like the "Restaurant" sign that tells me I can eat there. In technical language, the sign is a *discriminative stimulus:* It's a signal that lets hungry me discriminate between that place where I can eat and others where I can't—like "Hardware." It's also a trigger—or stimulus—for the response of stopping at that place. Sometimes we can make desired changes just by rearranging such signals in our environment or by changing our ways of using them, as we will see later in this chapter.

POSITIVE REINFORCEMENT

Positive reinforcement is usually, but not always, "pleasant." As a schoolteacher complained: "Johnny constantly disturbs everyone. I tell him, 'Johnny, please be quieter.' Every time I do, he obeys, but three minutes later, he's doing it again. Even expressing my anger does no good."

Attention, even punitive attention, is a powerful positive reinforcer for Johnny. Any kind of attention is better than none at all. So paying attention to him every time he makes a ruckus increases the odds that he'll continue.

By ignoring him when he acts up and giving him attention when he's involved in constructive learning, he can be helped to change his behavior. "Johnny, I appreciate the way you've been working together with the other children for the past few minutes."

When I asked some teachers to actually keep count, they found that their communication with the children was *primarily* negative communication. They were amazed and appalled to find out that they were much less likely to talk to a child when something good was happening. Like most adults in our culture, many teachers criticize and punish far more than they appreciate and reward.

That sort of thing happens with hypochondriacs. Look how much attention they get when they're sick! Due to these *secondary gains,* their illnesses take center stage. There's the story about the hypochondriac who finally died: On his tombstone was the inscription "See!"

Some friends of mine taught their daughter to read using positive reinforcement. They began by giving her a raisin for every word she read. After a while, she was reading words fairly well. Then she had to start reading a whole sentence to get a raisin, so the task wouldn't seem too easy. Once she was doing well on sentences, they switched to a raisin for every page.

One Sunday morning the parents were awakened by their daughter's voice downstairs in the kitchen. Curious, they tiptoed down and peeked in. There sat their daughter at the table, a pile of raisins in front of her, reading aloud out of her book and taking a raisin after she finished each page!

Token systems involve using some kind of tokens which, like money, can be exchanged for various different items. Gold stars on a chart are tokens if a specified number of them can be converted into goods, privileges, or services the individual wants. My preschool daughter gets poker chips for picking up her clothes and toys, doing simple reading and writing assignments, and sometimes even looking after her younger sister. When we go to stores with her, my wife and I convert them into money for buying items she wants. Token systems that cover many activities and reinforcers, called *token economies,* are widely used in mental hospitals (Allyon & Azrin, 1968). Prison systems have initiated token economies, where they have sometimes worked and sometimes not. The distinction seems to be whether the institution uses the process for manipulation or education.

We can use reinforcement to change our own behavior by making something we'd like to have or do contingent on doing something else that we want to do but otherwise might not. Ernest Hemingway, for instance, used to set himself a daily writing quota. If he produced the required number of pages, he went fishing the next day; if not, he didn't. So at times he burned the midnight oil to earn that fishing trip.

A student whose writing habits are much weaker than Hemingway's might reinforce himself or herself with more immediate rewards—perhaps a cup of tea or a treat from the snack bag after an hour of writing, or half an hour if need be.

Appreciation

Along with affection and attention, appreciation is one of the most powerful and widespread social reinforcers. I enjoy letting my wife know I appreciate both the day-to-day things and the special things she does. This kind of reinforcement helps her value herself and do things with more satisfaction.

In couples counseling, it's not uncommon for one of the partners in a long-term relationship to say to the other, "I didn't know you enjoyed that." The other then replies, "Well, I *expected* you to know." That translates as, "I want you to do good things for me, but I won't tell you how or when." By cluing you in instead of expecting you to know, and giving you my appreciation when you do things I like, I'm telling you what you need to know to be good to me.

Some of us avoid giving each other appreciation because we know how to relate by arguing and being hard, and can pretty well predict how the other person will respond.

Whenever I'm helping a family "straighten things out," I listen for what any of the members *don't* want to straighten out. If there is longstanding discontent, each of the affected individuals must be gaining something from it or else it wouldn't last.

When we want to be warm and loving with each other, we can reward each other directly. I tell you what I want from you and when; I let you know when I'm feeling good about what you're doing; and I show my appreciation by doing things for you that you like.

Counselors sometimes fall into the trap of getting sucked in by the problems in a relationship. The couple or family comes in and says, "We're having trouble with . . ." The counselor focuses on the trouble and forgets to find the good places they have together that they can work from.

Identifying Appropriate Reinforcers

What's rewarding to me may not be rewarding to you. One person may like a lot of attention, while another may feel smothered by it. *Don't assume that because something is a reinforcer for you, it is a reinforcer for someone else too.*

One way to identify an effective reinforcer is to ask the person what he or she likes. Another is to *observe what that person values doing.*

What someone wants may depend not only on that person's general preferences, but also on what's happened to him or her lately. When I've just eaten, food is not much of a reinforcer for me. When I haven't had much loving for a while, a big hug and a warm smile are worth a lot. My levels of *deprivation* and *satiation* affect what's rewarding or punishing to me and what isn't.

Sometimes it's appropriate to identify just one or two important rewards. In other circumstances a "menu" of reinforcers may be more appropriate, so that the person whose actions are to be affected can actively choose from a variety of items or activities.

The Premack Principle

According to experimental psychologist David Premack (1965), the chance to do something that you often choose to do can be used to reinforce something that you seldom choose to do. This is known as the *Premack Principle.*

Behaviors we want to strengthen are almost always things we don't do as often as we'd like—*low-probability behaviors.* All of us have some *high-probability behaviors* we could use as reinforcers. Interestingly enough, these are not always "pleasant." One woman, for instance, liked to paint in oils, but seldom took the time to do it. She didn't like housework, but felt that she "should" clean thoroughly each day, so she did. After cleaning, she was usually too tired to paint. Housework was a likely behavior, even though she found it unpleasant. Painting was an unlikely behavior, even though she liked to paint. So, taking time to paint could be reinforced by doing her housework afterward. She changed things around so that she painted first, and then did the housework. Soon she was painting regularly. The low-probability behavior was reinforced by performing the high-probability behavior afterward.

Since the consequence (opportunity to do housework) must follow the behavior to be affected (taking time to paint), the other way around wouldn't work.

The Premack Principle has another important implication: Almost any behavior can either be reinforced or be a reinforcer. The very act of eating, which can often serve to reinforce doing other things, is sometimes affected by other reinforcers. For instance:

"How pleased I am that you're eating well and enjoying your food," Mother says as her daughter finishes her dinner.

Before, dawdling over food was reinforced by the parent's attention: "Don't play with your food." Of course the child ate more slowly than anyone else. Now, if she dawdles, her mother ignores it.

Positive Reinforcement and Society

One of the most important contributions of B. F. Skinner has been his consistent emphasis on moving away from learning methods based on punishment, pain, and fear toward those based on positive reinforcement. This is more than "permissiveness," or "leaving a person free to learn." A person raised "permissively" is free of many of the complexes that haunt those raised punitively, but carried to an extreme, permissiveness means that each person has to reinvent the wheel. Beyond permissiveness is a caring guidance that respects and fosters the other person's independence.

PRINCIPLES OF BEHAVIOR CHANGE

Sometimes knowing how reinforcement operates is not enough. Strongly entrenched behaviors may need a systematic program of behavior change, using additional principles described here.

Think Small and Be Precise

We do best when we set out to change no more than we need to. The more modest our ambitions, the greater our chances for success. Conversely, broader changes invite more to go wrong. The "small is beautiful" ethic applies here.

It's important to *be precise*. That means defining the change so specifically that we agree on observable criteria. For instance, a "positive attitude" can be defined more precisely as "doing mutually agreed-upon tasks without complaint." Doing a chore or not, and complaining or not, can be clear cut, though some tasks might need more care in definition. "Cleaning the kitchen," for instance, can be further defined as "clearing and wiping the table and washing the dishes."

Such a redefinition of a "positive attitude" has two advantages: It's smaller and more manageable, and the frequency of the behaviors in question can be counted.

Defining Behavior Precisely

With another person, one of you asks the other to change his or her behavior in a vague way, such as, "I'd like you to take better care of yourself."

The other replies, "Tell me what you want more specifically." The dialogue continues in this form until the request is specific enough that both agree that they know precisely what's being asked, that it's do-able and observable.

Then reverse roles and repeat.

Gather Data and Analyze the Contingencies

A behavioral approach to change includes counting how often an action occurs. For a week or two, *record every occurrence* of the behavior and tally the total for each day. Make a graph with "Days" across the bottom and "Number of Occurrences" up the side. This is your *baseline*. Unless we have a baseline, we may not realize when change has occurred, and may be critical of "lack of progress" when we should be appreciative. A teacher, for instance, sets out to decrease a student's specified disruptive behavior and increase the time spent working on assignments. The student's daily average during baseline is twenty-three specified disruptive incidents a day. Two weeks after the start of the change program, he may seem as disruptive as ever, causing the teacher to think, "This isn't working at all." Upon checking the record, she discovers that he's averaged only thirteen incidents per day that week. Because the disturbances that still occurred were more salient than the decrease, it was easy to overlook the progress. Because of the baseline, however, they knew they were making headway. The accompanying figure shows what his graph looked like.

We do more during a baseline period than just count frequency. We carefully observe the behavior we hope to change, the situation it occurred in, what happened just before it occurred, and what happened just afterward. We can sum this up as, *"Who is doing what (to whom), under what circumstances, with what effects."* These observations provide important information that can help us formulate a change program.

Number of Specified Disruptive Incidents per Day and Time Spent Doing Assignments

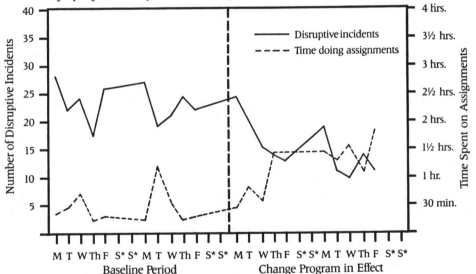

*No school on weekends means no data for Saturdays and Sundays.

One Step at a Time

When we are trying to learn something that's hard to do expertly right away, it helps to receive rewards for close approximations to the goal. This teaching process is called *shaping,* or *successive approximation.* At any point the learner only needs to do what he or she is capable of doing now. A guitar teacher praises a new student just for forming a chord correctly. Later, much more will be required to earn approval.

For ourselves or for others, short-term goals are important. Such goals let us experience successes regularly as we go along—or if we consistently don't meet them, they let us know we might be wise to try another approach. It's important to make these goals reasonable and achievable, and to reward ourselves—or the other person—when a goal is reached.

There are some things a person can't learn until certain prior developmental steps have been taken. For example, there's no way I can toilet train a child before he has developed some control over his sphincter muscle.

Behaviordelia (a Michigan collective of behaviorally oriented psychologists and their friends) has a rule for this: *"Start where the . . . behavior is at.* Not where you think it should be. And the best way to find out is to . . . look and see. . . . [Often your] assumptions about what the behaver can already do . . . are wrong" (1973, pp. 9.11, 12.1).

At the point where a person gets good at a simple task, we can change the criteria. We give appreciation now for something a little more difficult. It is important not to give appreciation for something too easily done. But *a good way to get nothing is to ask for everything.*

The Timing and Scheduling of Reinforcement

Reinforcement works best when it's in proportion to the difficulty or importance of the act: not too much and not too little. Whether the reinforcement comes every time or only every now and then, it must always *follow* the behavior, and the sooner the better. If it comes beforehand, it probably won't work—as some people have discovered after paying for work before it's done.

How often reinforcement comes is also important. *Intermittent reinforcement* is when we reinforce a behavior *only sometimes* instead of every time it happens.

Behavior that's been rewarded intermittently is hard to extinguish—especially if we don't know just when the rewards are coming.

At work I may have one supervisor who's almost always really there and tuned in. When she brushes me aside, I know she's in a bad place. With her I'm used to a constant schedule of positive reinforcement, so one nonreinforcement is enough. I'll wait until she's feeling better.

With a temperamental supervisor who sometimes responds, I've learned to expect my reinforcements on an intermittent schedule, so I might try communicating with him several times before I give up. If I've been getting a reward only occasionally, and I get nothing for a while, things may be as usual.

When I'm first teaching myself or someone else to perform a new behavior, I want to reinforce the action I'm looking for *every time it occurs.* Then gradually I want to make the schedule a little *leaner* and more irregular, so that the behavior will persist even when outside reinforcement is not immediately forthcoming.

Establishing Functional Behavior

Change usually endures only when a new way of acting *works in dealing with the world,* and continues to bring rewards. So in deciding to develop a particular behavior, it's important to think about whether there are outside rewards that will maintain it once it's been established—or sometimes "inside rewards" like those described later.

Our prisons, for example, are consistently ineffective when they fail to teach the inmates new skills and ways of acting that will help them once they get out.

ARRANGING THE ENVIRONMENT: STIMULUS CONTROL

An essential task in managing behavior is to rearrange the stimuli that trigger our actions. When I'm dressed up in my best suit of clothes, my bearing and language are likely to be a little different than when I wear jeans and a T-shirt. Formal clothes serve as a discriminative stimulus for myself and others for more formal behavior. This is called *stimulus control,* an approach that's especially appropriate when we want an already existing behavior to occur more often or less often.

Narrowing

Narrowing is a form of stimulus control in which we reduce the number of different cues that trigger our behavior. With a man who spent hours brooding and sulking, for example, behavioral psychologist Israel Goldiamond advised him to sulk to his heart's content, but in a special place: on a "sulking stool" in his garage where he might sulk and mutter for as long as he wished (1965). The approach to overeating described in the next chapter follows this same principle.

Strengthening Controlling Cues

This involves strengthening the signals that evoke a given behavior *(controlling cues)* or making them more distinctive. I feel more like doing yoga, for instance, when I put on a tape of Indian ragas, and meditation teachers recommend setting aside a special corner to meditate.

Goldiamond advised a young woman who had trouble studying to replace her dim lamp with a good one, turn her desk away from her bed, and use it *only for studying.* If she wanted to write a letter, read comics, or daydream, she was to do so in another room—not at her desk. She replied, "I'm not going to let any piece of wood run my life."

Goldiamond said, "On the contrary, you *want* that desk to run you. It is you who decides when to put yourself under the control of your desk" (1965, p. 854).

After a week the student reported that she'd spent only ten minutes at her desk but had studied during that time. Goldiamond congratulated her and suggested that she double the time the next week. By the semester's end, she was spending three hours a day studying at her desk.

Eliminating Alternative or Competing Responses

The foregoing example also illustrates the principle of keeping yourself—or the other person whose behavior is being changed—from engaging in extraneous activities while you are trying to control a given kind of behavior. The student was told *not to do anything except study* at her desk.

Fading

The stimulus that triggers a response can be changed through *fading*, like a dog owner who starts by shouting a loud "Sit!" while pushing his dog down on its haunches and, as the dog learns the response, gradually reduces the signal to a much quieter command.

One approach to teaching someone to write begins with tracing the letters, then fading the tracing lines to dots, and gradually fading out the dots entirely (Martin & Pear, 1983). The difference between fading and shaping is that *shaping involves the gradual change of a response while the stimulus stays about the same; fading involves the gradual change of a stimulus while the response stays about the same.*

There are two other points to remember in using stimulus control. First, it may take a while for a new discrimination to become strong enough to overrule old habits. Second, even the cleverest applications of stimulus control are likely to be short-lived unless the new behavior sequence is followed by positive reinforcement.

The Behavioral Consultation Group

In a group of five to twenty people who have read Chapters 21, 22, and 23 of this book, one person at a time takes a turn describing the behavior he or she wishes to change, and what the baseline data reveals. Others in the group act as consultants, suggesting elements that might be used in the change program. The person who described the behavior takes notes and later draws from the group's suggestions to formulate a change program.

Then another person presents a problem to the "consultants," and so on.

As follow-up, each person reports to the group on the progress or conclusion of his or her change program.

INTRINSIC MOTIVATION

A criticism sometimes leveled at the use of reinforcement is, "Won't the person become dependent on the reward and never learn to like the activity itself?" Where the goal is to get people to like learning for its own sake, that's a real issue.

As we all know, certain tasks *are* intrinsically motivating as others are not. It's rewarding to follow our curiosity and find answers. Incentives like grades and threats stimulate artificial interest in tasks that may or may not be intrinsically interesting.

Social psychologist John Condry (1981), reviewing numerous studies on intrinsic motivation, concludes that the short-term and long-term effects of rewards often are directly contradictory: A large reward is more likely to get someone to act as desired immediately, but it is less likely to generate continuing interest in behaving that way. A smaller reward, by contrast, is less likely to cause immediate change, but if it does, it's more likely to lead to long-term *intrinsic* interest in that way of acting. For instance, verbal praise as a reward (presumably weaker) often enhances intrinsic motivation under the same conditions that material rewards (presumably stronger) undermine it. We infer either, "I must have done it because of the payoff," or, "The incentive was so small that I must have done it because I wanted to." Our resulting dilemma: Should we use a larger reinforcement to get immediate change, or a smaller one to maximize feelings of intrinsic interest, running the danger that it might not be enough to bring about the desired change at all?

When we need to keep on motivating an action rather than doing so just once, diminishing the initial every-time reinforcement into an intermittent and then a very occasional schedule provides a solution. I might tell myself, "Since I get an external reward for doing this only every now and then, I must be doing it the rest of the time because I want to."

When intrinsic interest in something becomes strong enough that doing it becomes its own reward, extrinsic reinforcement can be dropped.

23

Handling Unwanted Behavior

*F*reud observed some of his patients repeating behaviors that were destructive to their social relationships, their work, and their hopes for happiness. Some observers called this the *neurotic paradox*. Actually there is no paradox. Once a way of acting has been learned, it needs a reward only now and then to keep it going. A behavior can be maintained by small immediate rewards even though larger punishments follow later on. A problem drinker, for example, may drink to dull the anxiety that's hitting now, even though this behavior leads to larger troubles later.

Communication theorists Watzlawick, Beavin and Jackson (1967) provide the intriguing observation that while positive feedback in response to acceptable new behaviors ("Yes, keep doing that") usually supports the change, negative feedback in response to unacceptable actions ("No, don't do that") tends to be effective only when unwanted behavior is a momentary disturbance that we want to stop. But negative feedback—which at its extreme shades into punishment—is not much help in making enduring changes. For that, positive feedback is more useful. This chapter addresses both kinds of changes.

USING STIMULUS CONTROL TO STOP UNWANTED ACTIONS

Stimulus control, as described in Chapter 22, is especially useful for decreasing or ending unwanted behavior. Basically, we avoid exposing ourselves to the events that trigger the unwanted actions. Veronica, who wanted to stop smoking, did 90 percent of her smoking at the kitchen table while studying, so she started studying in her bedroom and at the library, where she didn't smoke.

Grace, an obese eighteen year old, used several forms of stimulus control in her weight reduction program. First, she changed her food environment. When she opened the refrigerator, instead of ice cream, she found celery. Second, to reduce snacking, she carried a small plastic plate and utensils in her purse, and when she bought any snack—even a candy bar—sat down to eat it as if it were a regular meal. Bringing her snacking under the control of the dish and utensils greatly reduced it. Third, when she took seconds, she was asked to divide the portion in half and put half of it back. If she returned for thirds, she was to take only half of the half left from her seconds, and so on. (Ultimately, on her own, she began to do that with her first portion, so that even having seconds amounted to only three-fourths of a single helping.) Fourth, when others were present, she was to move away and eat alone. (Someone who eats more when alone might be asked to eat only with others.) She also started counting the number of times she chewed each bite to help herself attend to the taste and texture of the food.

In many cases there's not just one antecedent to an unwanted behavior, but a *chain* of them. In general, *it's easier to interrupt a chain of actions that lead to an unwanted outcome earlier in the chain than later in it.* When Ed, who's trying to stop drinking, has stopped at the bar after work to talk to his drinking pals, he has a tough time not drinking. It's a little easier for him to decide not to stop at the bar as he's driving by. But it's easier yet to choose a different route home that doesn't take him past the bar at all. He's interrupting the chain of actions at an earlier point.

THE PROBLEMS WITH PUNISHMENT

Punishment is a dramatic way to stop unwanted actions. It's popular for two reasons: Often it gets the other person to quit *immediately*, and it gives you the powerful feeling that comes with control. As a result, the punisher is reinforced and is likely to continue to punish. Nevertheless, there are important problems of effectiveness and long-term results associated with its use.

Practical Problems

Punishment acts by *suppressing* behavior, as Skinner's associate William K. Estes showed in 1944. The suppression is often only temporary. At some level the wish to act in the punished way is *still there*, but the person is afraid. When the threat of punishment decreases, the behavior returns. An extremely strong punishment may eliminate a behavior permanently, but as we will see, it's likely to have unwanted side effects.

Punishment tells a person less about what to do than reward. A person who gets rewarded for something learns *what to do* to get a reward. A person who gets punished learns only *one thing he or she shouldn't do* to avoid punishment, and not necessarily *what's acceptable.*

Since behavior that's maintained by the threat of punishment seldom becomes completely voluntary, someone has to keep checking on whether there's any misbehavior. Continuing surveillance is needed. This means that punishment-based control tends to be tiresome, expensive, and difficult to maintain.

In contrast, a person whose behavior is influenced through positive reinforcement will offer evidence of successful change. I'll never forget when my father was toilet training one of my little sisters by giving her lots of appreciation every time she pooped in the pot. One evening when we had company, my sister suddenly toddled into the middle of the room with the removable potty bowl in her arms and proudly showed us all what she had produced. She got the appreciation she wanted and deserved.

How Punishment Affects Us: Effects and Side Effects

What don't you do because you are afraid to? How much diffuse apprehension do you carry in your body in the form of muscular tenseness? Such present problems are the legacy of past punishments.

If as a child I was punished when I disagreed with my parents, I learned that I must not "talk back." To some degree I generalized this to all authority. Now I may be afraid to speak up or contribute to discussions with my boss or other authorities, even when I really need to.

A mother or father, angry at a child's crying, sometimes abuses the child and then feels guilty and cuddles or holds the youngster. Pleasure and pain become linked in the child's experience: Loving is good only when it hurts. In the sex-violence linkage that is so popular in pornographic literature, movies, and TV shows, we see the sadistic and masochistic behaviors that result from our punitively oriented society. The linkage is so common that in its milder forms people think of it as "normal."

To the degree that I've introjected punishment, every time I even *think* of acting in the punished way, I actually punish myself right then by tensing my body and talking harshly to myself.

Fear *generalizes* easily from one act or situation to another. If I punish someone for a particular act, I don't know for sure what I'm teaching. In her thinking, she may not separate the act from the situation she was punished in and may continue to be at least a little afraid of *situations that resemble* that one, and of the people involved—including me.

No one knows how to fully control, measure, and direct the effects of punishment. With positive reinforcement, my predictions about what will happen have a higher probability of being right. With punishment, I can only guess and hope.

Your Ways of Punishing and Feeling Punished

If you're in a group setting, go around to each person and make two brief one-sentence statements: "I can punish you by . . ." and "You can punish me by . . . " Don't try to think up what you're going to say in advance.

Stop in front of the person, look at him or her, and say the first things that come to mind. Then discuss with the group your style of punishing and the kinds of events that cause you to feel punished. Other group members can also do this. If you have no group available, do this by yourself.

The Punisher and the Person Punished

The relationship between the punisher and the person punished is potentially toxic. A child who feels punished, for example, may internalize the punishment I give, may learn how to conceal himself or herself—or both. He or she also learns how to punish in return, picking up my ways of punishing and using them to punish me. In this way, he or she can feel some power. This accounts for some of the painful confrontations of teenage years.

McIntire writes about the mother of a teenager who was picked up by the police for vandalism:

> When asked where her daughter usually went on her nights out, she answered, "Oh, I don't know. She never talks to me." "When was the last time she told you about school or activities with her friends?" she was asked. "I can't even remember," she said. "Oh, yes . . . she told me what one of those bad boys said about her figure—just as if she were proud of having boys think of her that way!" When asked what her reaction was, the mother answered with some pride, "*Well*, I told her that if I *ever* saw her with that boy again, I'd give her the whipping of her life!"
>
> What do you suppose the daughter learned from this little exchange with her mother? To leave some boys alone and not talk to them? Or to leave her mother alone and not talk to her? (1970, pp. 81–82)

Perhaps I've been afraid of warmth and loving feelings, but now I want to contact you in a more tender, affectionate way. If I've closed you out, I'm going to have a tough time redefining what I want with you. It'll be hard for you to hear me, to believe me if you hear me, and to do anything about it if you hear me and believe me.

Out of enlightened self-interest, if I want a relationship of sharing and caring with you, I'll move toward open communication and reward-oriented discipline and away from punishment-oriented discipline.

WHEN AND HOW TO USE PUNISHMENT

A good rule of thumb is: Resort to punishment only when you can't think of anything else that might work. Instead of using it casually, like aspirin, we'd do better to treat it as a dangerous prescription drug laden with side effects.

This is not so easy for those of us who grew up on punishment-oriented discipline. I feel sad at the way I sometimes—before I'm even aware of what I'm doing—lash out when it does no good. Unlearning old habits can be a long, slow process.

As we saw in Chapter 22, what we think is punishment may sometimes act as a reward. Temper tantrums are a classic example. Any attention given to a tantrum usually reinforces it. Let the person have the tantrum. Don't pay any special attention during or immediately after it. The tantrums will probably become less frequent and less intense.

Suppressing One Behavior While Strengthening Another

Punishment may be needed to help stop an unwanted behavior, as, for instance, when someone is getting hurt or may get hurt. If little Becky runs out in the street in front of cars, I may punish her for it while I teach her to feel good about staying on the curb. *This last step, to give positive reinforcement for staying on the curb, is vitally important.* When Becky goes out tomorrow afternoon and doesn't run into the street, I'll give her plenty of appreciation for staying on the curb. Of course, I'll also take plenty of time to explain why it's important to stay out of the street. Thus punishment can serve to suppress one way of acting while a new way is learned.

Loss of a Positive Reinforcer

One kind of punishment that's often effective and that can even have constructive side effects, *if it's used in a loving way,* is *withdrawal of a positive reinforcer.*

I learn from the consequences of my actions. Children face this situation when the toys they've left lying around are put into a locked box for a week or so.

Time Out

Time out is similar but not identical to the old practice of sending someone to sit in the corner. Basically it's a form of withdrawing positive reinforcement: The child is banished to a place where there is nothing interesting to do. Since kids like continuous activity or stimulation, as little as two minutes can be an effective general-purpose punishment. Time out has two great advantages: It doesn't involve doing anything that might harm the child or cause lasting resentment, and it cools down the situation rather than heating it up if it's used as described here, without fuss or humiliation. The important thing is a clear, immediate response.

Remember that the time out itself is the punishment—though this doesn't preclude talking about the matter after everyone has cooled down. If a child refuses to go into time out and you end up carrying him or her, be firm *and gentle.* Such refusals are apt to be rare when your response is to look at your watch and say, "That's thirty seconds more. Will you go in now, or shall I add another half minute?" And remember: Someone who's in time out is incommunicado.

When you announce that time out is over, it's over. Carrying grudges is unfair. The length of the time out is proportionate to the offense and the age of the child. With young children, a minute is sometimes enough and five minutes is a uselessly long time.

Self-Defeating Punishment

The forms of punishment with the most unpredictable and unwanted side effects are physical aggression, psychological abuse, and withdrawal of love.

Regarding *physical aggression,* the Balinese have a saying: "Hitting a child damages its tender soul." We saw in Chapter 13 how violent behavior is passed on in the family from generation to generation.

Psychological abuse, or "hitting a person with words or attitudes," involves saying or implying that there is something sick, bad, or defective, about the person. A diet of this results in low self-esteem.

Withdrawal of love was once widely recommended as a method of punishment. We now know that it can contribute to insecurity—in the relationship, the personality, or both.

Consistency and Warnings

Effective punishment is governed by the rule that a specific unwanted behavior will bring an unwanted consequence. *Consistency* is critical. Children and adults alike can get along pretty well if they know explicitly which actions will bring punishment and which will be rewarded.

Lisa, by contrast, gets chastised for actions she didn't know would lead to punishment. When she does things she's been punished for before, sometimes she's punished and sometimes not. As a result, she's thoroughly confused.

There's always a hazard that the underlying reason for punishment is not to change behavior but to even the score. When used, punishment is appropriately directed *toward particular behaviors*. This means punishing you *when you act in a certain way*—not whenever I feel angry.

When I'm not in a state of mind to follow that principle, I can tell you, "I'm very upset. Please stop what you're doing and give me some space, or I may get nasty."

If I want you to respect such signals, I have to be willing to reciprocate—whether you're a child or an adult. Demanding more than I'm willing to give breeds resentment.

Wendy and Jeff developed a nonverbal signaling system that worked well for them. Wendy never used to let Jeff finish what he was saying. This was a source of constant irritation and they were both unhappy about it. They developed a signal: When Jeff put his left hand over his ear, Wendy was to stop talking and listen to him. If she didn't, he was to turn and walk out. It worked.

A BETTER WAY: EXTINCTION

Unwanted ways of acting persist because they continue to be reinforced. Eliminate the reinforcement and these ways of acting cease, or at least decrease in frequency. *Extinction is a preferred method for getting rid of unwanted behavior.* Behavioral psychologists David Watson and Roland Tharp write:

> In punishment some unpleasant consequence is added or some pleasant event is taken away following your behavior. In extinction nothing happens. If [a] woman said, "Don't call me any more. I don't want to talk to you," that would punish the act of calling. If she simply didn't return calls—that is, she did nothing—that would extinguish the act of calling. (1981, p. 91)

Things aren't, of course, always that simple. Watson and Tharp point out that if we withhold the usual reinforcement for an unwanted way of acting, other reinforcers may rush in to fill the gap. They mention a student who was cutting class to shoot pool and play video games in a nearby arcade. He decided to withdraw those reinforcers by going home immediately if he cut class. But when he got home, he listened to his stereo, which he also enjoyed, and kept on cutting class. He needed to find ways to reinforce himself for going to class.

Punishment can prevent extinction. Conditions may change so that one of my old behaviors no longer brings rewards. If that way of acting has been suppressed by punishment, I have no chance to learn that I no longer get reinforced for it, so I keep on wanting to act that way.

In many cases extinction can be substituted for punishment. It tends to take a little longer, but once accomplished it's usually more lasting. When a well-practiced behavior doesn't bring its usual response, the person may get upset and even *intensify* it. But that's likely to occur only a few times, and then the unwanted response should begin to drop out—unless it's also bringing some other reinforcement.

Sometimes the reinforcement for an unwanted way of acting is attached to the behavior itself, like the taste sensations that go with eating. Or you may be unable to control others' responses, and hence the reinforcement they provide, such as my wife's conciliatory, solicitous response when I stalk out of the house in anger— something I'd prefer to stop doing. When you want to reduce a behavior but can't eliminate the reinforcement, *imagined extinction* may be useful. The entire process takes place in your mind. Ascher and Cautela (1974), for example, counseled an obese man who wanted to give up eating an especially tasty and fattening food first to imagine looking forward to eating it with great anticipation, then to imagine eating it, and finally to imagine feeling very disappointed at the taste and flavor. He did this about fifteen times each day and successfully eliminated that item from his diet. Similarly, I might imagine my wife responding with cool disinterest when I stalk out of the house.

Spontaneous Recovery

After extinction has occurred, a person may eventually try out the old behavior again, to see if it will work now. This reappearance of old behavior is called *spontaneous recovery*. The old way may pop up again several times before the person gives it up for good.

Sometimes, even when I think a behavior has been totally extinguished, there's one last return to it. I don't need to think that all is lost. This is not a "hello again," but a goodbye.

Developing Alternatives

Extinction works best when, as one way of acting is being extinguished, an alternative way is being strengthened. Eventually the event that used to trigger the old way of acting triggers the new, alternative response instead. Otherwise the extinction process may not work—or if it does, some other unwanted behavior may replace the old one.

This strengthening of new behavior works best when the person can't do the old thing while doing the new one. For example, the muscular and glandular activities that go with relaxation and those that go with fear *can't occur at the same time*. This procedure is called *substituting an incompatible behavior* for the old one.

Since the new behavior is weak, it should be reinforced *every time* it occurs and strengthened rapidly while the old behavior is being extinguished.

A colleague had a grandmother who constantly complained to all the family about everything. One of the woman's few pleasures was spending time with her family. But since she was so unpleasant to be around, most of her relatives avoided her. Our friend tried an experiment. First, for a time he recorded how much of her conversation was critical. Then he began ignoring her critical comments and paying a lot of attention to her other remarks. Whenever she started complaining, he looked out the window, cleaned his fingernails, and showed his boredom. But when she talked more pleasantly, he was interested, showing that what she was saying was important to him. In time, the griping lessened and the time they spent together was more satisfying.

But the rest of her relatives noticed no change. With them she continued to complain. So he let them in on what he was doing and asked them to do the same. As she became more pleasant to be around, they spent more time with her. They had decreased her critical, complaining behavior and strengthened more enjoyable behavior to take its place.

Contracts for Change

I can make the process just described explicit by telling you what I like and don't like, and how I intend to respond to what you do. A contract for change is a useful way to get this kind of explicitness.

When I want to change some way you or I act, I can say, "I want you to change in this way, and I'm willing to help you by . . . " or "I want to change in this way, and you can help me by. . . ."

Then you reply, accepting, rejecting, or modifying any part of my statement, and we negotiate until we reach an agreement.

The first item we negotiate is: "Do you want to do things differently?" If you say, "No, I really don't want to," then I make a personal reevaluation: How important is it for me? Perhaps it's more important at some times than at others. I may be able to tolerate your fingers in the peanut butter if we're just hanging around but really want you to keep them out if we're having company.

Our contract also specifies what I give you in return for your changing: a smile, a touch, a word . . . or maybe that doesn't matter much to you, and there's something else you want from me. So we each get something we care about—for instance, you stop wearing my underwear and I stop eating your dog food.

Part Six

LIVING IN RELATIONSHIP

24

Intimacy and Love

*M*y life is most enriching when I have your being and heart to experience my existence with me. I want you to see my canvas, hear my music, and feel my touch in all the ways that we are. This is such an intense need that despite sobering statistics and personal failures we continue marrying or forming relationships that we hope will endure and nourish us. Even the guru meditating in a cave perks up when his disciples come around.

Our quest for intimacy, to know another and be known, soul to soul, is propelled by our passion to be loved, cared about, and appreciated. Through these three elements of intimacy, we are affirmed as valued beings. Anything less is second best. Nonetheless, we often settle for familiarity, friendship, fame, power, or even popularity. We learn to accept and enjoy these compromises while we keep searching for an intimate relationship.

Intimacy evolves as we become involved in each other's lives and are willing to risk being transparent to each other. Transparent doesn't mean "seeing through" you. It means thoroughly looking in and seeing who you are for yourself and for me. You don't have to show me every miniscule aspect of yourself, but I do want to see and hear and feel what you make available to me. To the extent that I can, I want to question without condemnation and applaud without deification.

Intimacy is often confused with or limited to sexual contact. We cherish intimacy and go through our daily rituals with one another while remaining strangers to each other's richest thoughts and feelings, hopes and fears.

Karen states, "Four kids and fifteen years later, the sense of intimacy in our marriage is near zero. I feel trapped—like I have to play the part of someone I'm not. But we smile our phony little smiles and act like everything's all right."

Karen recognizes that she contributes to their situation: "I have trouble feeling close to others and get anxious when they try to be close to me. I have friends, but no one with whom I feel intimate."

An intimate relationship is hard to find. We may feel it as something missing—a deficit of close contact. Or we may hide behind a "tough" stance of total self-reliance. Either way, the obstacles to deeper contact usually are fears of risking and vulnerability that can be unlearned. Almost always the fears and dread in my head (and yours) are far worse than the reality when finally experienced.

Close Encounters

This exercise allows you to experience how different senses can contribute to a feeling of intimacy.

Sit facing another person. Begin by telling the other person where you'd like to look at him or her. "I'd like to look at your . . . Is that all right?" The person says either "Yes" or "No." If "Yes," then look at him or her there, in the way that you wish, for as long as you want to. If you want to look at any other part of the person, you can make those requests, too. Your partner may also say, "I want you to look at my . . . " and if you wish, you can oblige. Then reverse roles and repeat the process.

Next, do the same thing with hearing: "What I'd like to hear from you is . . . " Then your partner can say, "I'd like you to listen to . . . " When you've heard as much as the two of you want to, again reverse roles and repeat.

Now do the same with touch. I'd like to touch your . . . " and "I'd like you to touch my . . . "

With each sensory modality, either person is free to refuse any request. If there's something you dislike about the way the person is looking, hearing, or touching, or the response doesn't satisfy you, say so: "I felt rushed when you touched my hand. I'd like you to take more time."

As an option, if you and your partner wish, you can do the same thing with smell. Be aware of and respect your own and your partner's limits.

ASPECTS OF INTIMACY

Intimacy comes in various forms. *Physical intimacy* involves our touching, caressing, hugging, holding, and sexual expression. *Emotional intimacy* involves talking and listening to each other, exposing verbally *and* non-verbally our love, anger, grief, happiness, fear, jealousy, or other feelings. *Cognitive intimacy* is sharing ideas, and our feelings about those ideas. Writing this book involved some exciting, intimate explorations of ideas by the authors—but such rich exchanges of ideas are not part of all intimate relationships (Dahms, 1972).

Seldom does one element of intimacy occur completely alone. Indeed, difficulty in identifying the difference between what we think about an event and how we feel about it leads to many double messages.

Victoria, for instance, with the best of intentions kept telling her daughter, "It's important that you tell me how you *feel,* dear." When Carrie did just that, Victoria invariably replied with a thought or an idea. She was saying she wanted one thing, but her behavior was sending the message, "I have a hard time dealing with feelings." This came out clearly when Victoria and her husband were splitting up and Victoria was getting ready to go, leaving the kids with their father.

Victoria: I know this must be painful, Carrie, and I want you to tell me everything you feel.
Carrie (crying): I don't want you to go! I think it stinks!
Victoria (working hard to keep herself composed): I think it's very important for us to be able to talk to each other this way.
Carrie (raising her voice through her tears): I think you're being selfish. You're not being grown-up. You're walking out on us! I think you're a real creep for leaving the family.
Victoria: I'm glad you're able to say these things to me.

Victoria had done a good job of learning that her children were entitled to their own feelings, and she had worked hard and successfully to learn to encourage them to express those feelings. But she didn't let Carrie hear her own confused feelings—her pain, anger, conflict, and guilt. Victoria's and her husband's reluctance to express disagreements, frustrations, and resentments to each other played an important role in the breakup of their marriage.

When I believe I'm sharing my feelings and what you're getting are my ideas, we're both confused. I don't know how you can be so insensitive to my feelings, and you don't know what I'm talking about.

Communicating about emotions is an essential aspect of intimacy. It is the starting point from which we move toward *communion* of emotions. In communication we have exchange; in communion we have integration. Almost any event that occurs in an intimate relationship has some emotional component, whether it's the excitement of lovemaking, the passionate disagreement of an argument, or the quiet joy of a transcendent experience.

Vulnerability

We need somewhere in our lives to be able to let down our defenses and reveal our weaknesses. In an intimate relationship I can expose my soft underbelly and feel secure that you're not going to attack or exploit me. I can reveal the depth and breadth of my feeling and trust that you won't use it against me.

In being intimate, above all I don't want to hurt you—I feel bad when you feel injured. Without a clear, mutual commitment that neither of us will knowingly cause the other pain, we limit what we reveal and give. Even with that clear contract, there's risk enough.

Straight Messages about Feelings

There is a basic principle of intimacy that Kelley describes as *an ongoing sensitivity and considerateness toward the other person—a willingness to go out of my way for him or her, and even to 'put up with a lot' sometimes* (1979, p. 4).

Kelley's principle does not mean we have to maintain the deceit of appearing to be always accepting and understanding. Gene Alexander, a family therapist in San Francisco, mentions a woman—Melissa—who was telling her husband Cal that she was beginning to feel a little better with a part of herself that she'd been struggling with. Cal, who had related to her for years in a fatherly, therapist-like way, sat there saying, "I understand; I'm glad to see you're getting past some of those difficulties."

Gene turned to Cal and said, "Do you ever tell her to shut up? That you're sick of hearing that crap all the time, and she should save it for the therapist?" As he said that, Melissa's eyes widened and she involuntarily started nodding vigorously in agreement. She was perfectly capable of operating as an adult. By always "understanding and accepting," Cal was continuing to define her as a child. He, in turn, was tired of the "therapist-father" role and wasn't saying so, based upon his preconceptions of how a "good husband" was supposed to be.

Cal and Melissa were learning to replace that pretense with straight messages about their feelings. That's an important quality of an intimate relationship: You're entitled to a clear message about how I feel in response to what you do. Then you don't need to guess or be afraid of what's going on in me. And I'm entitled to tell you how I truly feel. That's part of the *freedom to comment* that keeps a relationship alive.

Learning to Be Intimate

Emily says, "My mother didn't want me. I was an 'accident.' When I was two years old, she left me in a foster home." As Emily talks, her eyes fill with tears. "I kept waiting for her to please come back, because she was the only person I loved or knew. After the foster home I went to an orphanage, where I grew up." She cries loudly, then becomes quiet and says, "Even now I hold myself back. I want people but I don't reach out. I'm afraid of any kind of closeness—especially with women—I'm afraid they'll leave just like my mother did."

Our basic training in being intimate with other people comes through close, caring relationships in early childhood. Harry Harlow's studies of infant monkeys reinforce this point. He compared monkeys reared by their mothers with monkeys reared alone and with others who had "wire surrogate mothers" or "cloth surrogate mothers" to provide solace and comfort. These were figures about the size of a mother monkey, made out of wire mesh, or wire mesh covered with soft terrycloth, topped by a crude "face." They were constructed so that the baby monkeys could cling to them and lie against them for hours. Some cloth and wire mothers had lactating "breasts," others did not. Monkeys reared with cloth mothers developed into adults who were much more secure and adventurous than those reared alone or with only a wire mother.

In another intriguing experiment, four surrogate "monster mothers" were created. One rocked violently. Another blew blasts of compressed air. A third had an embedded frame that would sometimes fling forward and knock the infant off the mother's body. The fourth could push out brass spikes from the area where the infant clung. But all had comfort-giving cloth surfaces. The results surprised Harlow. He comments, "The infant monkeys did not even leave the bodies of the air-blast and rocking mothers, since the mother is an infant's only source of solace or succor, and the only response of an infant in distress is to cling more tightly to the mother." With the throwing-frame mother and the brass-spiked mother, when they were thrown off they waited, crying and complaining, until they could return and then climbed right back up onto the monster mothers. Later followup showed that the effect of these early experiences lasted for a lifetime. "No experiment," writes Harlow, "could have better demonstrated the power of any contact-comfort giving mother to provide solace and security to her infant" (1973, pp. 17–29, 60–62). Analogously, battered children often try to protect and get love from their parents even while the latter are being abusive.

If I'm not sure someone will be there for emotional communion, my constant companion might be a pet or an object—the TV, my transistor radio, or a book or diary. These offer me involvement and control with minimal risk. Depending on how I use it, a relationship with a pet or object can serve to deafen me to my inner voices and images, or it can deepen my contact with them.

THE POLITICS OF INTIMACY

The *politics of intimacy* is the process of reconciling what we want from each other with what we want for ourselves. It involves processes for resolving our issues and be in a caring, valuing, loving relationship even when we're angry, hurt, or disengaged. That isn't easy. It requires paying attention to the internal and external environments in which events occur, to hidden agendas, to metamessages, and to our unfinished business.

Honoring Each Other's Boundaries

In a sense, each of us has boundary lines around what feels central to who we are. These boundaries help us define ourselves. We can ask each other to change ways of acting and feeling that are outside them, but asking for change in what's inside them is risky. Elise, for example, wants Rod to shift from being easygoing and nonassertive to being tough, aggressive, and competitive. The prognosis for that kind of change—and for the relationship when that kind of demand is urgent and continuing—is poor.

When you want more time alone and I seek more time for us together, I can feel unloved even when that's not the case at all. If our needs at a given moment differ, we can tell each other what they are and how strong they are and, if need be, negotiate. By being sensitive to these messages from each other, we can develop a flow of contact and withdrawal that respects what the other person wants right now, instead of hanging on or backing off.

The "Myth of Normality"

The *myth of normality* is the idea that there's an absolute "right" way for a couple or family to be—some standard of correctness that they're supposed to meet. Partners deny who they are and go so far as to act in ways that *neither one much likes* in order to do what they think is the "right" thing—to be a "normal" couple. With your respective backgrounds, you and your partner are a unique couple. Your ways of handling things won't be quite like those that fit *any* other couple best. The same goes for families with children. What's appropriate is what nourishes *your* relationship— or *your* family.

Sharing a Child's World

Parents and children of all ages miss out when a parent gets locked into "wearing the parental cloak" and doesn't look for an opening to grasp something of how things are from the perspective of the child.

Satir suggests a powerful exercise to experience vividly one crucial element of how a child's world is. Try this:

Seeing like a Child

1. Get a partner. Anyone you know who can spare five or ten minutes will do.

First, your partner stands looking down and you sit on the floor directly in front of him or her, first looking around, then looking up at the person standing, for about two minutes.

You both silently experience how you feel. Notice your bodies. Experience the sensations in your back, neck, and shoulders, and in your eyes and head.

Then talk about how you feel in these positions. How does the other person appear when you're looking up? How does he or she and the room appear when you're looking around and straight ahead?

2. Again have one person sit and one stand. Now hold hands for about thirty seconds. Then reverse positions. After that, again talk about what you experienced. (Adapted from Satir, 1972, p. 42–45)

When you're both on the same eye level, even the words "I love you" sound very different. When there's a Very Important Conversation, or when I want the most intimate contact I can make, I can get down where the kids are or sit them up where I am.

LOVE

Love is patient, love is kind. It does not envy, it does not boast, it is not proud. It is not rude, it is not self-

seeking, it is not easily angered, it keeps no record of
wrongs. Love does not delight in evil but rejoices with
the truth. It always protects, always trusts, always
hopes, always perseveres. Love never fails.
                              —I Corinthians 13:4–8

How's one going to get through it all? How can you
live if you can't love, and how can you live if you do?
                              —James Baldwin

We all somehow, magically, touch each other deeply. Our experiences of love transform both our way of being with ourselves and our way of being with each other. Through loving, I come closer to myself, I risk sharing who I am with you, and I open the way for you to share yourself with me. Times of loving can be personal celebrations in which you and I honor our relationship and in which we contact each othe1 deeply and carry something of each other with us when we part.

In the film *Heartland*, Grandma, a neighbor from some distance, visits Ellie, whose infant son died shortly after birth. Grandma is looking uncomfortably around the cabin and Ellie says, "You can look at me, Grandma—it's all right and we can talk about it." Their embrace of shared love, intimacy, and pain is startlingly beautiful and painful. In loving we can create the freedom to be visible and vulnerable that comes when we feel secure in another's caring and appreciation.

To love one another was Jesus's central teaching. Yet even he was only reminding us of a truth as old as humankind. Long before, travelers sometimes came to the tent of Abraham, who talked to God. Whatever the reason the stranger was there, Abraham stopped talking to God to give the person food and water. It was more important that he took time for this act of loving kindness than that he talk to God.

Give yourself some time now to go back as far as you like to recall your own experiences of the magic of loving. How do you contact those feelings in your life today?

In mature, enduring love relationships of whatever kind, people go through developmental phases. Early contacts with another person involve fantasies about not-yet-known aspects of that person and what the relationship may hold. In later stages we learn to appreciate each other's realities as we let our relationship season. That appreciation helps us to seek rewarding ways of being with each other and to experience ourselves as intimate, as caretaking, and as equals.

How We Stop Ourselves from Loving

The words and the feeling "I love you," declares Keyes, usually mean, "When I am with you, things you say and do *help me experience parts of me that I regard as beautiful, capable, and lovable*"—just as I may dislike someone who reminds me of things in me that I dislike (1979, p. 36).

The dark side is that if I don't feel lovable, I'm likely to close myself to loving and feeling loved. I can't give you love unless I can take it in.

On one hand, there are natural individual differences, observable even in infancy, in how readily we extend our affections to others and open ourselves to theirs. On the other hand, painful past experiences and present fears can lead us to restrict the number and kind of loving relationships available to us. Some of us learned to feel unlovable as we grew up. Those old feelings can haunt and hurt us now. Carole Thompson Lentz writes,

> It's like we have this little fort around our heart. And somebody has to . . . prove they're trustworthy—and that they're not going to run away real quick. Then we'll let them into the first courtyard. . . . When you start to realize that you don't need those boundaries . . . you start letting people in much sooner. (in Keyes, 1979, pp. xvi–xvii)

Two kinds of self-defeating behaviors help keep up this "fort" even though that's not our intention. In one, I work hard to put on my best front when I'm attracted to you, hiding everything I think you might not like. If our relationship develops mostly on this basis and then I drop the pretense, you may regard me as deceitful, leading to crisis—and my prophecy that I won't be loved if I reveal my true self is fulfilled. By contrast, when early on I let more of myself be seen, the genuineness that comes through can provide a better foundation for an enduring relationship.

The reverse kind of self-defeating behavior involves challenging you to love me at my worst. "If you can handle that, you can handle anything," such reasoning runs. Unfortunately, with this tack I'm not likely to get into many relationships that have any "later." Here, too, I'm letting you see just one side of me.

You might try this visualization exercise:

Loving Feelings

In your mind's eye, picture an infant, a child, a gentle touch—anything that triggers warm, loving feelings in you. (Even a smiling, well-fed ana-conda will do.) Experience those feelings fully. Notice what happens in your body as well as your mind.

Then feel the part of *yourself* that's like that image. Allow that feeling to spread throughout you. Experience yourself totally as that lovable being.

Do this regularly, at least once each day, until you can remember and call on that feeling fairly easily. Then when you're with another person with whom you want to relate in a warm, caring way, *remember that place in you* and keep it in your awareness. (Adapted from Tessina & Smith, 1980)

Five Kinds of Love

Five types of love are object-centered love, projective love, romantic love, conscious love, and transcendent love. (Like any concept, these categories lie within arbitrary lines, and some of them have elements in common.)

Object-Centered Love.   Love based primarily on the concrete satisfactions that come with loving and being loved is *object centered.* This is the love an infant has for his or her mother and her breasts. The infant *wants* her, and misses her when she's gone.

If, as we grow older, physical satisfactions remain the only source of our feelings for each other, we're apt to be less than satisfied in our love relationship. But object-centered love can begin to involve other ways of loving.

The classic "male chauvinist pig" or "macho" attitude, along with its feminine counterparts, have a strong object-centered component. The priority in our relationship is sexual or status, and I want you to do what I want you to do. When we make love, I'm likely to forget to stay in touch with you. There's little interchange of consciousness, little interplay of loving and caressing.

Such love is possessive. I may try to stop you from growing, changing, or exercising any self-determination when your initiatives don't fit my agenda. I may be reluctant to commit myself even though I insist on your full commitment.

When I want a more deeply caring relationship, I don't stay locked into that "me first" stance. I can be aware that you have your own needs and make space for what you want as well as what I want.

Projective Love.   In my earlier years I fell in love deliciously and painfully so many times! Each new enchantress seemed to embody complete perfection! My underlying process involved finding virtues in her that fit my image of an "ideal other" and then blinding myself to everything that didn't fit.

In *projective love*, I see qualities in you that are missing in me. You may possess these qualities, or I may build some of your characteristics into an elaborate fantasy. You and I almost make contact—but not quite. Todd, for instance, harbored hostility toward his mother that he was never willing to express directly. He married a strong, assertive woman, expecting her to stop his mother from pushing him around. She didn't. When I become aware of my projected needs, I can stop insisting that you fulfill them and start learning to do what I need to do for myself.

In a nurturing love relationship, by contrast, I keep my sense of myself. I give you me as I am, and I'm with you as you are.

Perhaps I'm attracted to someone for her particular kinds of insecurities. That's all right. We all do it. I don't want to pretend that her shaky places don't exist or that she's the incarnation of all truth and virtue, or else she may feel she has to live up to my fantasy. That's a hell of a demand to make of anyone. I'll take you off the pedestal I put you on if you'll take me off the one you put me on. Then maybe we can have a relationship.

A relationship based solely on projective love must come apart. When the images start to crumble under the pressure of reality, we begin to resent each other for being different from "what was promised."

At this point we have some alternatives. One or both of us might be ready to end our relationship. If guilty remorse and confusion leave us afraid to say so directly, we may act so obnoxiously instead that eventually there's no way we'd be willing to stay together longer. We may well finish things off with a new package of projections that portrays the other as just as malicious and terrible as he or she once seemed wonderful.

Alternately, we might recognize what's happening, talk through our feelings, and decide that we've come to a parting place, but still with a measure of caring for each other.

Or we may find that we're both willing to stay together and work on finding nourishing ways to relate as who we are. Then projective love becomes transformed into "conscious love."

Romantic Love.   In *The Natural History of Love*, Morton M. Hunt (1959) relates this tale:

> An anthropologist who lived among the Bemba . . . related . . . an English folk tale about a young prince who climbed glass mountains, crossed chasms, and fought dragons, all to obtain the hand of a maiden he loved. The Bemba were plainly bewildered, but remained silent. Finally an old chief spoke up, voicing the feelings of all present in the simplest of questions. "Why not take another girl?" he asked.

In the Western world, *romantic love*, which involves overwhelming feelings and rituals of adoration, is a strong tradition. It's less so in other parts of the world. In rural India, for example, most marriages are still arranged by a couple's parents, who weigh a variety of factors as they choose a suitable bride or groom.

In our culture, romance is a central theme and the age of initiation is still falling. In the People's Republic of China, by contrast, people are encouraged to delay romantic pursuits until their middle twenties.

In addition to the caring, attachment, and intimacy that social psychologist Zick Rubin (1973) identified as crucial elements of love, Ellen Berscheid and Elaine Walster point out that romantic love also includes physiological arousal (1978). As the one I love comes near, my heart beats more rapidly, my breathing speeds up, my face flushes slightly, and some of my muscles tighten.

Romantic love may fade as quickly as it came—or it may evolve into a gentler, less urgent form. Romantic love includes elements of both object-centered and projective love, and sometimes a measure of conscious love as well.

Corey (1983) identifies several common myths about romantic love:

> *The myth of eternal love: that true love endures forever.*   This myth bypasses the known reality that continuing love requires commitment and work by both people. Our needs and feelings change. Keeping love alive requires adapting to these changes.
> *The myth that love implies constant closeness.*   We need time with ourselves, too. Without it, we feel smothered. Trouble can arise when people differ radically in how much time they like to spend with another and how much alone.
> *The myth that we "fall" in and out of love.*   I have some choice in whether or not to let myself be overwhelmed with emotion when I look at you or think of you. (But there *is* that ecstasy of helpless surrender.)
> *The myth that love is exclusive.*   Each of us has the capacity to feel loving in a variety of different ways toward different people.

The myth that people who love each other never argue or disagree. By following this myth, I can build up poisonous resentment. People in love get as angry as anyone else about some of the things the partner does.

The myth that there is just one true love for each of us. Actually, numerous people separated from their "one true love" by life circumstances have found that they could form an equally deep, if different, relationship with another.

Conscious Love. When I love *consciously,* I remember who I am and love you as you are. I see and hear myself clearly and see and hear you clearly. Conscious love is loving you not only for your specialness, but also for your ordinariness. There comes an ease in our intimacy as we realize that neither of us has to pretend.

Conscious love means loving you with your existing problems and hangups. If you think you need a facelift, a nose job, or training in a school of etiquette to be okay, my love and acceptance includes you with all those anxieties.

Awareness, caring, and trust are important elements of conscious love. I want to feel your caring in concrete ways that nourish me, and to show my caring in concrete ways that nourish you.

The more I can love myself, the more I can love you. The more I take care of my own hangups and conflicts, the more energy I have available for loving others. My reward in loving is as much the way I feel when I love as the love I get back from others.

In our loving, we need closeness and we need space. If you pull me too close for too long, I have mixed feelings: How good it is that you want me so much; how stifling it is to be held so tightly. When I experience your holding me as clutching me, I may be afraid to ask for the space I need, for fear that you'll feel rejected. Yet when you ask me to be your whole world, you're asking me to be more than I am. In his chapter on marriage in *The Prophet,* Gibran writes, "Love one another, but make not a bond of love. . . . Sing and dance together and be joyous, but let each one of you be alone, even as the strings of a lute are alone though they quiver with the same music" (1969, pp. 15–16).

When adults do not threaten to withdraw their love as punishment or grant it only as a reward, they communicate a solid sense of strong and reassuring love.

Transcendent Love. In this state of loving, sometimes called *agape, caritas,* loving kindness, or divine love, we open our hearts toward more than just one person, or a few, and give selflessly and openly to others. In *transcendent love,* I express a deep caring in my acts and attitudes, feeling connected by a common bond to everyone, as in this story told by Jesus:

> The righteous will reply, "Lord, when was it that we saw you hungry and fed you, or thirsty and gave you drink, a stranger and took you home, or naked and clothed you? When did we see you ill or in prison, and came to visit you?" And the King will answer, ". . . Anything you did for one of my brothers here, however humble, you did for me." (Matthew 25:37–40, New English Bible)

One way to feel transcendent love is to be in the presence of someone who radiates such love. Meher Baba declared, "Love is essentially self-communicative; those who do not have it catch it from those who have it. . . . It goes on gathering power and spreading itself until eventually it transforms everyone it touches" (1967, Vol. 1, p. 24).

Transcendent love is the high country of the human spirit, a realm inhabited by saints, mystics, and very unusual ordinary people—like you and me. Those who don't live in that place year-round can visit for an instant, an hour, a day, or longer—and know that it's there and available.

I'd like to know that egoless state, where I am loving rather than lover, more often. On the other hand, if it becomes a "goal to achieve," I'm keeping my egotism involved, which interferes with being there. We can enjoy transcendent love when we experience it without making ourselves unhappy when we don't. As Theresa of Avila reportedly said when asked whether she ever got angry or upset, "What do you think I am, anyway, a saint?"

Styles of Loving

Misunderstandings can occur when we forget that others' *styles* of loving may be different from our own. One person may easily *act* in loving ways toward others but have a hard time putting those feelings into words, while another person may be just the opposite.

We can ask each other for the kinds of expression of love we want. We can initiate actions that are hard for the other to initiate, like reaching toward someone who has a hard time reaching out.

J. A. Lee (1974) describes some different styles of loving. Some people plunge immediately and intensely into love relationships, while others share time and space together until love "just comes naturally," preferring a gentler, more predictable "companionate love" that lacks the complications of intense passion. And often, relationships that begin with wild passion mellow into companionate love. Some people are given to candlelight and roses and laying the world at the feet of the beloved, while others more often love in the style of "a peaceful and enchanting affection . . . without fever, tumult, or folly." Some typically have only one lover at a time, while others tend to be involved in several relationships at once. Some people make love soon after meeting, while others view sex as a deeply intimate act and postpone it until they know each other well. And while some people choose their partners intuitively, others consciously balance the payoffs from various relationships, as in the following newspaper ad: "WIFE WANTED: Frontier farmer, steady, hard-working, good provider, seeks levelheaded wife who is sober, strong, and owns a late-model tractor . . . send pictures of tractor" (Lee, 1974, pp. 43–51; 1976, p. 90).

25

Lasting Relationships

*J*ust as chocolate syrup and spaghetti sauce are fine individually but less desirable when combined, you and I may be perfectly okay as individuals but have a hard time together. Or we may be all right in some areas of our relationship but incompatible when we stumble into certain other areas. The behavior of a couple, or a family, is a *system*—not a simple sum of what its members do. In Gestalt language, the whole is different from the sum of its parts. Ludwig von Bertanlaffy (1969), among others, has worked on developing a body of ideas known as *General System Theory* and applying it to the study of human behavior.

The basic idea of a system is that each part is interrelated with all the others. When one person displays "symptoms" indicating that something is not quite right, it alerts us to look at the system *as a whole*. Indeed, family therapist Murray Bowen refuses to work with a single individual. When a family comes in saying, "The wife has a problem," or, "Our son is having emotional difficulties," Bowen calls that person the *identified patient* or IP. The family's message to the IP is, "If it weren't for you, the family would be okay." Bowen's reply is, "No, it's the whole system," and then proceeds directly to work with the total family to discover what's happening (1965, pp. 214–243). A high proportion of hospitalized patients who have made progress fall right back into the old patterns when returned to their families. In the systems view, the entire family system needs help.

In a couple, each partner tends to label the *other* the IP. "I'm all right—it's *you* who's crazy." Or if I'm obviously not all right, then it's *you* who's to blame for it. In its general form, the statement is, "If only you'd be different, I [we] would be okay," or "I was all right until you came along." I'm accusing you of doing it to me: "If you hadn't snapped at me for not helping you Friday night, then I would have been in a better mood Saturday."

And you respond: "Well, if you'd learn to tell me how you're feeling I'd be more likely to help you, but when you snap at me. . . ."

Each of us is good and right and justified and the other is bad and wrong and unfair. It's a cycle with great energy: We can both end up feeling hurt, guilty, and estranged from each other when what we really wanted was to touch, be close, and let each other know we care.

When I insist, " This isn't fair," and, "You're doing it to me," I surrender my power and responsibility, making myself the helpless, righteous victim. *When I realize that I make myself feel bad, I can learn to stop doing that and start learning to make myself feel good instead.* In any social relationship, the kind of energy that evolves is the shared responsibility of everyone involved.

The recognition and conscious use of the systems concept provides an effective way out of the blaming-and-disowning cycle. This involves two steps.

1. *Remember and state the systems principle:* "Wait a minute—on second thought I guess I played as much a part in that as you did. After all, anything we do involves us both." Find words to say this that fit you. You are using this process to replace the "It's your fault" tape.
2. *Learn to let go:* Even though you've stated that your action was not "the other's fault," you may still *feel* peeved at that person. You help yourself when you quit hanging onto it. Unclench your fists and jaw, let go of the tension in your body, and breathe deeply. If you still feel hurt about what happened, you can mention it in a nonblaming way.

"The idea seems fine," you might object, "but what about situations that really are unbalanced—where one person consistently victimizes the other?"

In fact, there is always collaboration. In order for one person to dominate or exploit the other, the latter must tolerate it. *Both or all are getting something* from what's happening and contribute in some way to keep it going.

In my own life, in my cause-effect mode I take the role of detective, judge, jury, and executioner—or exploited helpless victim. In the systems mode you and I are mutual explorers, adventurers, and discoverers. Choose!

*RULES**

At some point each of us is new at being a spouse, mate, lover, parent, sibling, offspring, employee, or supervisor. Into these relationships we bring *rules* to teach ourselves and others how to be. Rules involve expectations about others and scripts for ourselves. They define how we go about seeking satisfaction in our personal and work relationships. At home, our rules provide a relatively subtle statement of what kinds of responsibilities are assumed and assigned by whom and to whom. At work, the definitions of responsibilities and authority are typically clearer and more explicit. These rules may be called principles, guidelines, paradigms, models, or something else. You probably have your own word. But whatever I call them, they regulate how I can take care of myself and still be in a relationship with you.

---

*We are indebted to Gene Alexander for his valuable insights about family rules, including the "Barton and Cartwright Family Rules."

Some rules change and some don't. Some are more important or more strictly kept than others. Some rules are for all times, all places, all people, and some change depending on the situation. "No screaming at the table" is a rule—until somebody spills hot soup in your lap. Most couples and families share some rules and differ in other rules. For instance:

Barton Family Rules	*Cartwright Family Rules*
Dinner is at six sharp. Children must do chores after dinner.	Dinner is whenever it's ready. Everyone helps after dinner.
Mother makes the rules with Dad's help.	Mother and Dad make the rules together and equally.
If you must cry, cry in your room.	If you cry, get help from someone else.
No cartoons until rooms are clean.	Clean your rooms after cartoons.
If you get angry, do so quietly—don't scream.	If you get angry, get angry, but don't hit anyone.

What are the rules in your relationship of family? Can you make a list and talk about them with your partner, or with other family members?

We end up confused when we try to apply rules learned in the past to all situations in the present and future. When I stop to examine my rules, I need to look not only at who helped me make them, but also at where my rules need to change or be flexible. Are there "rights of appeal"? Are there clear "rights of clarification"? How do I make the statement that says, "This rule worked fine when it was needed, but now it no longer functions and is getting in the way."

Our rules cover what we should talk about and what we shouldn't, what we encourage and what we discourage. If one person doesn't follow the rules of the other people involved, others get frightened, upset, or angry. Sometimes the one who breaks some of the rules is the person who is showing the hurt and pain in the relationship. It happens when children act out the parts, feelings, and ideas that are hidden behind the masks of acceptable behavior that their parents have painstakingly constructed. Then parents get upset at their children for showing parts of themselves that they were supposed to hide.

Some relationships and families have *subcontracts*, or rules we mustn't mention. A subcontract says people are not allowed to discuss the rules, or a particular rule. It is an agreement not to deal with a particular area of relationship and not to mention that agreement. That lets us make an agreement and define some rules without ever having to take responsibility for doing so. For instance, parents may tacitly agree to ignore and deny the growing sexuality of their teenage children. They see a lot of what's going on, but without mentioning it agree never to talk about it.

Subcontracts interfere with our ability to clarify and fulfill our needs. They make it hard to talk about and change rules that need to be changed. We keep many of them outside our awareness. These are the ones most apt to cause us trouble.

Another kind of subcontract states that expressing certain feelings is off limits. Yet another demands that one person be seen in a particular light. Lynn, for example, replaces the assertive solidity she shows in individual counseling with a weepy, pouty Lynn in counseling sessions that include her spouse.

One way we can become aware of our subcontracts is through noticing our own and each other's double messages in which what we do expresses what we're not allowed to say. When Denise and Roger canceled their subcontract to avoid talking about changes in career needs and home expectations, their double messages diminished.

Our rules can help us live comfortably and creatively with each other—*if* we use them consciously and flexibly rather than blindly and rigidly, so that we're using them rather than them using us.

PATTERNS

Knowing something about different patterns of involvement can help us understand our present ways of being and open up a larger horizon of possibilities.

Categories of Relationships

Lynch's (1980) penetrating analysis shows how certain ways of relating can be extremely frustrating to both partners yet at the same time fulfill powerful needs. (The categories of relationships described here are Lynch's, with our addition of acceptance relationships.)

Survival relationships exist when partners are emotionally debilitated and feel that they can't make it on their own. The choice of a partner can be indiscriminate—anyone available will do. The union is a desperately clinging one, threatened by any signs of independence. To be in such a relationship doesn't mean I'm a defective person—I may be able and talented—but that I'm desperate for caring and contact.

Validation relationships exist when one person seeks another's validation of his or her physical attractiveness, sexiness, intelligence, basic worth as a person, and so on. These relationships are appropriate among young people reaching for a sense of their identity. The packaging tends to be important: good looks, sharp clothes, nice car, or whatever is important in your crowd. "These relationships are always a little insecure," says Lynch. "One behavior can be everything—a source of tears and anguish despite everything else the partner has done all week."

Expectancy relationships might also be called "growing up together" or "living out a script" relationships. Lynch calls them "building structure" relationships. Partners seem "just right for each other" in terms of appearance, occupation, and family background. The choice of a partner based predominantly on an external definition of the "perfect couple," however, is hazardous. These relationships tend to become either volatile, endless power struggles or placid, superficial, and committed to the deadly ideal of always looking good while feeling nothing. They easily get stuck in old ruts rather than trying new possibilities.

Acceptance relationships are what most of us traditionally thought we wanted and were getting into: a relationship where partners trust, enjoy, and support each other. Within safe limits, participants are themselves, and they restrain themselves from pushing those limits in ways that may threaten the other's trust, enjoyment, and support.

Individuation/assertion relationships involve acknowledgment and appreciation of each other's differences. Partners are flexible about who does what and actively encourage each other's growth, creativity, and personal interests and directions.

There is probably a higher tolerance for risk and innovation and a greater willingness to test limits.

By working at stating their own needs and hearing their partner's, and at changing their behavior to more effectively provide or allow what the partner needs, couples in other forms of relationships can move into individuation-assertion relationships or acceptance relationships.

Commitments

The transient relationship in which we touch deeply yet expect never to meet again is an exception in a context of relationships that endure. But if we're afraid we'll lose our freedom, or that the relationship will turn bad and we'll be stuck with it, we may hold back from committing to the extent that intimacy requires. From this ambivalence comes the tension of the come-close/stay-back dynamic that brings so much pain.

Commitment is problematic when two people have different understandings of what they're committing themselves to. Some of it comes from conflicting fears and desires—when one side of a person says, "I willingly commit myself to . . . " and another side says, "No dice," and sabotages the commitment the first side made. Commitments can be less frightening, and easier to keep, when both members of a couple explicitly talk through their fears about commitment, and what they are and aren't willing to commit themselves to.

Overloading

> There was a farmer who hauled his produce to market with a horse and wagon. . . . he kept loading more onto the wagon in order to carry the bigger load. One day on his way to the market with a huge load of produce, his horse suddenly collapsed and died. And everyone wondered why the horse, which had been so reliable for so many years, should be suddenly overwhelmed by his task. (Greenwald, 1976, p. 17)

Gestalt therapist Jerry Greenwald maintains that most personal relationships today are like the farmer with his horse. We pile on an ever-growing load of needs and wants and then, when it collapses, question the value of any relationship. Today, the nuclear family (the parents, or a single parent, with a child or children) is called on to perform many of the functions that aunts and uncles, grandparents and neighbors, villagers and friends performed in the old days or in the old country when families stayed in the same place for generations and relatives lived together or nearby. This disintegration of the extended family has led us to develop community and government agencies to serve some of the functions it once served. With the withdrawal of government funding for some of these agencies, the pressure on the nuclear family has become even more intense. So it's important for people to look actively for resources outside their primary relationship, in the form of friends, relatives, community services, church services, or whatever else is available, so they're not trying to do more than they can handle.

The idea that any one person can fill all his or her partner's or children's emotional and intellectual needs is a big source of overloading. Each of us needs different kinds of relationships with people. Your own interpersonal politics with your partner can involve talking about how and when each of you feels overloaded, and what you might do about it so that you aren't too burdened meeting basic needs to have time to enjoy yourself and each other.

ROLES

Different children in a family can have dissimilar personalities and play radically different roles in it. Clearly, no two children are born into the *same* family. There are differences in the relationship between the parents as well as changes in age, health, economic circumstances, and parental attitudes and parenting skills. There are inborn differences in temperament that occur with each child, and differences in the mother's state of mind and hormonal balance while she is carrying each child.

A major contribution to differences among children in a family lies in the varied roles they assume. Each new child, in finding a way to get affection and caring—or at least attention—finds or creates a role that's not already taken, or that can be filled by more than one person. In one family, for instance, a second sister, finding the "good girl" role monopolized by her older sister, might adopt a "nuisance" role to get attention. Another family might have room for two "good girls."

People in a family sometimes have nicknames that denote their roles. Some different nickname roles are:

Wiseguy	Tough guy	Dummy
Devil	Punk	Princess
Brains	Angel	Baby
Tattletale	Hero	Loudmouth
Judge	Policeman	Hermit
Professor	Lamb	

(Alexander, 1982)

What nickname role or roles, if any, do you or other people have in your family? This includes roles that could easily be given such a nickname, even though they weren't.

Some roles feel good and some feel awful. They may change or remain the same. Sometimes even when a person or circumstance changes enough that the roles should change, others keep a person locked into an old role that no longer fits. That can be painful and frustrating—by even though the person is probably colluding with other family members at least a little by staying in that role.

Family Sculpture

Seeing our nonverbal statements of our roles and interaction patterns can expand our perceptions beyond the limits of what I say and what you hear—and vice versa. The process described here is based on the work of Satir and others.

You can do this with your actual family, or with your fellow participants in a class or group. In your own family, with all of you standing near each other, you approach your family members as "lumps of clay," molding each person into the position you perceive him or her to most characteristically take in your family. You may use furniture if you wish; you can have people standing, sitting, or on the floor, touching or not touching. Mold both the individual members and the family as a whole into a human sculpture that effectively expresses your perception of the family.

(One mother who felt "walled off" from her son, for instance, put him on one side of her husband and herself on the other, so that most messages between her and her son were blocked by her husband. She crossed her husband's arms tightly on his chest, placed his head so that he was staring up at a corner of the room, and adjusted the son's posture as if he were trying to make an escape. Then she placed her daughter on one knee, looking upward and tugging at her own skirt, and placed herself wringing her hands and looking disconsolately down at her daughter.)

Your family may discuss your sculpture and how each of you feels in your assigned position. Then each member of the family, in turn, modifies the group structure as he or she sees it, and members comment on that change, until everyone has been the "sculptor."

In a group or class, participants divide into groups about the size of their own families. Then each has a turn to sculpt his or her family, with discussion afterward.

Habits and patterns that suit who I am now can take the place of old ones that no longer do. A woman who has always waited for men to ask her for a date, for instance, might start taking the initiative when she meets men she finds attractive.

It can be very freeing to let go of stereotyped concepts of who has to do what. Recently a storm was coming and, despite a terrible cold, I was all set to go out with pick and shovel to clean out a clogged ditch. I certainly couldn't let my wife do *that*. Asserting herself, she let me know that she was tired of staying indoors with the kids and would much rather go out and work with pick and shovel. And I was relieved that I could stay in the warm house and not exert myself outdoors.

Satir's Communication Scripts

Satir (1972, pp. 64–70) describes five *communication scripts* she often sees people adopt.

A *placater* sends the message, "Calm down—please don't get mad." Whatever you want is okay. As a placater I speak in an ingratiating way, always agreeing, apologizing, and trying to please. My purpose in life is to keep the peace—at any price.

The basic *blamer's* message is, "It's all your fault. If it weren't for you, everything would be all right." My blamer's voice is hard and tight, with clenched muscles, constricted sphincter, and a rigid stance. I stay in charge when I can keep you on the defensive.

As a *computer* I am total rationality. Betraying feeling is exactly that—a betrayal. "He is calm, cool, and collected," writes Satir. "When you are a computer, use the longest words possible. . . . Your voice will naturally go dead [as] you are kept busy choosing the right words. After all, you should never make a mistake" (1972, p. 68).

As a *distractor* I am adept at keeping people's attention away from any sensitive issue. Every response is off the point, going in a different direction from what's happening—or perhaps in several directions at once. If I can keep myself moving fast enough, I won't notice what I'm not noticing.

As a *leveler*, I state simply and directly what I want, feel, and think. I'm hoping for the clarity, trust, and intimacy that allows us to be available to attend, hear, and respond to each other. It's hard work and risky. So is peace.

You can experience these scripts in the exercise that follows with members of your own family or by doing it in a "simulated family" of three to five members in which one person takes the role of father, one of mother, one of a twelve-year-old son, and so on.

Placating, Blaming, Computing, and Distracting

Each of you selects one of these four communication scripts. (If there are more than four people, two can use the same script.) Then make a "statue" in which one of you adopts a physical stance that seems to fit the role. Hold these stances silently, noticing how you feel about yourself and the others.

Then begin to interact, planning some shared activity like a vacation or party, each playing your role fully. After five minutes, *stop*—even in mid-sentence. (Satir suggests using an oven timer, or the group leader can signal when to stop.) Close your eyes, go inside yourself, and notice your physical sensations, your thoughts, and your feelings.

Then open your eyes, tell your partners what you experienced in your role—including how you felt toward them—and listen as they tell you their experiences. If you feel uncomfortable, describe the discomfort.

After that, each of you keeps the same family role, but take new communication scripts—the placater may become the distracter, and so on—and repeat the process. (Adapted from Satir, 1972, pp. 82–86)

In this exercise, notes Satir, some people are at first "revolted by being asked to do openly what they secretly fear they have been doing all along." Actually, if I can recognize and honor these aspects of myself that I may dislike or feel embarrassed about, I become more sensitive to when one of them is taking over. I begin to be able to smile at and even enjoy these sides of me as I develop the ability to move in and out of them. "Oops, there goes my placater again—just *listen* to that eloquent sniveling." In addition, awareness and conscious control can lead to a transformation in the forms these patterns take. A blaming bitchiness that grew out of feeling exploited and powerless, for instance, can turn into effective assertion.

When you were telling your partners how you felt after each five minutes of role playing, you probably came close to leveling. I'm most likely to level with you when my self-esteem is high enough that I'm not afraid you might not like me.

Kantor and Lehr's "Player Parts"

Satir identified scripts as she counseled troubled families. From their study of nontroubled families, Kantor and Lehr (1976, pp. 184–189) have identified inevitable roles that they call *player parts*, which are useful in observing what occurs in other social groups, as well as in the family.

The *mover* initiates an action and establishes the context within which others respond. Other people in the system—the *co-movers*—determine who may and who may not succeed as a mover. "In one family, the mother's . . . need to exalt her boy child led her to disregard and treat as irrelevant the initiating efforts of her brighter girl child."

The *opposer* challenges the mover. He or she may "halt or redirect the action initiated by a mover. . . . He may redirect and teach or may assault and maim." An opposer may reframe the meanings established by the movers, such as interpreting an act that the mover viewed as a gesture of affection as an attempt to control.

A *follower* may support either the mover or the opposer. A follower can remain independent by shifting his or her allegiance, lose all autonomy by becoming completely allied with either the mover or opposer, or support each for different reasons.

A *bystander* may silently witness what goes on, express his or her views privately, or express them in public in ways that do not involve taking sides.

The mover, follower, opposer, and bystander are the family's four main player parts. Three important variations of these deserve special mention. The *manifest mover* is the key person who exercises power and determines decisions, even though others may appear to do so. This person may play any of the four parts to gather data before making a key—often well-timed—move. The *pseudo-bystander* is an opposer or follower who appears to be a bystander but who actually is playing an active part. The *ideal co-mover* moves, opposes, follows, or stands by, flexibly adopting whatever role is needed. Keyes states, "We open the doors of happiness when we let ourselves consciously enjoy playing the roles our life gives us in each moment" (1979, p. 87).

MARRIAGE AND RELATED EVENTS

I am a firm believer that "timing" and being in the
right place at the right time is more important than bells
ringing and the earth moving. When he was ready to
settle down, so was I . . . and so we did.
—Anonymous

Marriage is the hell of false expectations, where both
partners, expecting to be loved, defined and supported,
abdicate responsibility for themselves and accuse the other
of taking away freedom.
                                        —Kathrin Perutz, 1972

The first time you buy a house you see how pretty the
paint is and buy it. The second time you look to see if
the basement has termites. It's the same with men.
                                        —Lupe Velez, 1977

Marriage, in addition to a relationship and a way of living together, is a *public commitment* to maintain a relationship for an indefinite time. It's a special and hopefully a beautiful event, a ceremonial transition to a new stage of life. It can also bring stress of a different kind than occurs in a relationship that either person can end at will. I may have to learn to make my peace with a disliked quality, live with a great deal of aggravation, or enlist my mate's help in dealing with discomfort.

Some partners don't seem to "fit" together in their *personal rhythms.* Someone who meets the world in a slow, deliberate way, assimilating all the information about a matter and letting it percolate before taking action, may find it frustrating to live with a fast-moving, volatile person who acts impulsively and whose mind is in three places at once. Differences like that can seem exciting when people first meet, yet with time can create tension and lead to stress (Luthman, 1972, pp. 101–106). If I try to change your rhythm and send critical messages, we may be headed for trouble. I can deal with such differences more effectively through acknowledging your tempo as yours.

In a successful union we continue to give each other "quality time" as we did in the beginning. Even so, in most cases some of the time we used to spend with each other is now shared with work, relatives, friends, and other interests. When my wife and I were first married, we reserved one day each week to spend together in activities we both enjoyed, regardless of whatever else was going on. We put that time into our appointment book, and nothing else could touch it. When children came, "our day" evolved into "family day." Later, as my wife began feeling overwhelmed with too much of being a housewife and homebody, we took half that day for me to look after the kids and her to have time alone. More recently, we've begun making more explicit time for "dates" alone with each other. At each stage we negotiated the change.

GIVING AND RECEIVING

The following are two scenarios that, while they may appear a little overdrawn, are familiar to most of us. There's no hard data for the effects—just universal hunches.

Julie wanted very much to have a child. When Wendy was born, Julie was generous with her milk, her holding and stroking, and her other ways of caring. Wendy grew and blossomed, and as she received Julie's nourishing care, she learned not only about receiving but also about giving.

Deborah thought she wanted a child, but really didn't. She was always busy with other things, even after Ginny was born. Ginny sensed her mother's distraction and within the first few months of life developed a "basic mistrust." Many years later, Ginny is still haunted by a nagging fear that she "won't get enough." She still has a hard time giving, because she's afraid this would take away from the little she has, and a hard time receiving, because she feels "undeserving."

One response to feeling the way Ginny does is to keep our distance from others. An alternative response is "addiction" to another person's emotional support. I depend on you to take care of my feelings and feel unable to depend on myself emotionally. Without you I feel lost, frightened, or unhappy.

An addictive relationship is inevitably ambivalent. If I'm preoccupied with getting *all* my desires met, I may be somewhat inattentive to *your* wishes. In grasping desperately for what I need, I'm impervious to some of what you need. You probably resent that, even if you also love me. In my proclamations that "I love you so much," the unspoken line is "as long as you're giving me what I want."

Keyes's formula of learning to *prefer* the things we've felt addicted to means learning to emotionally accept whatever is occurring in my life. I don't have to like it. I can still feel angry or unhappy about it. But I *"no longer live with [my] finger stuck on the emotional panic button"* (1979, pp. xvi, 23).

This means developing the emotional self-support of realizing that if I have to, I can make it through by myself even if I don't get all I want from you. By contrast, when I insist on finding everything within myself, I want to look at how I stop myself from obtaining outside support and at what I get out of doing it all by myself.

In any important relationship, there are things I appreciate. If our relationship has any depth, there are also things I resent. In my uneasiness and my fear, I may convince myself that I have no resentments toward you. Actually, telling you my resentments is as much a gift as telling you my appreciations. Sharing these two kinds of feelings opens up communication and leads toward clarity, trust, and communion.

Appreciations and Resentments

With one other person: With your partner, friend, or other person who's important to you, in a situation where you both feel comfortable, face each other. Tell that person all the things you appreciate about his or her behavior, and then all the things you resent. Remember to be as specific as you can.

Then the other person does the same. When you're the listener, beware of the old devil of dextifying—defending, explaining, and justifying. *Don't discuss* what you just said to each other. Later, after you've both had time to reflect, you may want to discuss your thoughts and feelings about what you said.

In a class or group where you've all known one another for some time: You may need two or three hours for the exercise. During that time, each of you seeks out each other person in the group and tells that person what you appreciate and what you resent about his or her behavior, and that person will do the same for you. Your comments don't all have to involve that person's relationship to you or others—some of them may focus on ways he or she is contributing to or inhibiting his or her own development and happiness. Depending on the group size, limit yourself to between five to ten minutes with each person.

This can be an instructive and moving experience to use during the last meeting of a class or group.

If I'm not getting enough of what is essential to me, I'm apt to be greedy in other things, demanding more than I need or more than others want to give. I may be stingy, not giving what I could spare. Depending on what's being asked, and on my own energy and state of mind, giving anything at all can seem painful.

By trying desperately to get, I may push others away and make it even harder for me to get what I need. When I feel too needy, too grabby, people can become frightened. At times like those, I may have to forgo my wants for a while and give the very thing I need to get. Giving it seems to open me to getting it.

Once I was in agony over the crumbling of a love affair. I needed a lot of caring and comforting. A friend came in distraught about events in her life—in no position to listen to me. I pulled myself far enough out of my own pain to listen to her sorrow and frustration. When we'd finished talking, we felt a deep closeness with each other, and I realized that, in some strange way, she had also nourished me.

If I think I have to give something in order to be liked, I'm apt to resent you and take away with one hand while I give with the other. I'm also apt to feel resentful when I accept something I don't want—especially if it seems to carry an obligation. I feel best when I take no more or less than I want to take, and give no more or less than I want to give.

This Hasidic tale is a commentary on the act of overgiving: One day an old, poor Jew lost his prize possession—his snuff box. Sadly walking in the forest, he saw a beautiful goat with long horns that swept the sky, clearly a holy goat. Gently the goat asked him why he was so sad. On being told the reason, the goat invited him to take a piece of his horn and make himself a new snuff box. He did so and it became a curiosity for all the villagers. Under duress he told them where he got the material for the snuff box. One by one they went to the goat and asked for and were given some of the goat's horn. Soon the horns were gone and could no longer sweep the sky so that the stars could shine brightly.

When you take and take, I may start feeling used. Then I need to take care of myself. At the least I need to tell you how I feel and what I want in return. Sometimes it's only your appreciation, but I'd better tell you when I want more. And if I'm not hearing your appreciation and it's important to me, I can tell you that.

On the other hand, my giving feels best to me when I can avoid getting locked into thinking, "What do I get out of it?" or "I'm afraid you're getting more than I am." Loving involves giving because I want to give. "The measure you give is the measure you will receive, with something more besides," said Jesus (Mark 4:24, New English Bible). In such sharing of ourselves and what we have, my giving is receiving, and my receiving is giving. At such times, giving is communion.

26

Sexuality

*Y*ou may or may not know this, but you're probably a *sexualist*—someone who believes that the sex you were born with and the sexually related habits and identifications you've learned influence how you think about things and the way you act. This has little to do with believing that being male or female is better or worse. It has a great deal to do with how you perceive and experience yourself and your life.

CONTEXTS OF SEXUAL BEING

In dealing with garden-variety heterosexuality there are a few things we can say that are probably true no matter where we live.

First, the most obvious function of sexual activity is reproduction—to generate and reconstitute the human family and our personal families. A second function is to convey feelings of love, closeness, and intimacy. A third function is joy, pleasure, and heightened excitement in a relationship: This may have to do with reproduction, or it may not; it may have to do with love, closeness, and intimacy, or it may not. A fourth function is enhancing the ego—to be able to attract, respond, and feel powerful. In our culture especially, to culminate a relationship successfully in sexual play or intercourse can give a powerful boost to our self-esteem. Most of us integrate more than one of these four functions in our sexual relationships.

Sexual Roles

Sexual relationships are heavily influenced by nonsexual activities that define the roles through which we contact others. These role definitions are influenced by the economic structure within which we live, the technology available to us, the social order that governs the patterns of our lives, and our beliefs about all these things.

We can see this in China, where the woman's role is becoming more equal after many centuries during which females were considered almost useless. Now women are more highly valued, and they are expected to make important contributions. As in our own society, there are still inequities, and many people are intensely concerned about them just as we are here. Sometimes while my wife and I were walking in the streets of Beijing, young people asked to walk with us to practice their English. But never was the person who made such a request female. Cultural conventions still require more reticence from women than from men.

Such differences affect the way we meet each other in a sexual relationship. Among them is the attitude of biological determinism that stereotypes the male as the more assertive member of the species. Another is the degree to which we hold "fundamentalist" attitudes about sexual dominance and ways of expressing it.

There are, however, other perspectives: As Alice Duer Miller wrote in 1915,

> Men are too emotional to vote. Their conduct at baseball games and political conventions shows this, while their innate tendency to appeal to force renders them particularly unfit for the task of government. Man's place is in the armory. (in Lewis, 1980, p. 248)

Sexual Wants, Needs, Hopes, and Expectations

Even the most transient of sexual encounters involves some search for a feeling of respect, an experience of security, some excitement and adventure, and a sense of being accepted and valued.

Respect can exist along a continuum from seeking only respect for my prowess to wanting respect as a total person.

Security involves mutual concern. During lovemaking and at our most intimate moments, we are especially vulnerable. We hunger for a sense of security that says, "As lost as I am in you, you'll pay attention to me and keep me safe, and I'll do the same for you."

We go even further when we achieve the sense of acceptance that says, "In this intimate, vulnerable time, you accept me just as I am and I accept you just as you are." That allows us to feel not just the excitement of the hunt and winning the prize, but the playful, intense, and sometimes religious adventure of exploring and being known by another human being to an ultimate degree.

The desire to be accepted and valued, contrasted with the anxiety of loneliness and alienation that is so pervasive in twentieth-century industrial society, heightens our longing for closeness and contact, a longing that often translates into loving and sexual expression. We may confuse sex with intimacy, a special nurturing that includes unconditional love and acceptance. I may appear to be self-sufficient, calm, and aloof when I am actually terribly isolated. But I protect myself so well that I seldom express my loneliness and may not even recognize it. Sex can be a way to contact another person without admitting such vulnerability. We may end up having sex when all we really want is to be held, cuddled, caressed, and comforted.

The sad part of this is that if we consistently sexualize our need for physical contact or our anxiety, fear, anger, or other feelings, we may never find ways to meet directly the needs that they reflect.

By contrast, sexual involvement can accelerate and intensify the knowing and allowing that occurs in a relationship. Our entire self partakes in an ultimate experience of being with a fullness we'd like to feel in other areas of our lives.

Historical and Contemporary Trends in Sexual Behavior

Join me in acknowledging that we have sexual scripts, current or inactive, that include long, emotionally loaded lists of shoulds and prohibitions. Some of the historical reasons for these scripts are evident: Until the advent of effective contraception, intercourse was very likely to lead to conception. Adultery—a member of a married couple having sex with someone else—was strongly proscribed because then a couple wouldn't be certain about the father of the child. Similarly, a woman who was a virgin at marriage was guaranteed not to be carrying another's child, and to be free of venereal disease.

The "double standard," however, allowed a man to dally before marriage, and in most cases if the women involved got pregnant, it was their problem—as often it still is. Many young people found themselves pushed into marriage by hormones and circumstances before they were ready to make a lasting commitment—as some still do.

But today, amid the sexualized hard sell of everything from mouthwash to motorcars, as well as available contraception, women's liberation, and the "new morality," a woman can choose her sexual style much as many men did in the past. A recent *Vogue* article entitled "One-Night Stands—Risky or Fun?" (Frumkes, 1980) points out that now many women openly seek out fleeting affairs and deliberately avoid long-term commitments. As a result of such changing attitudes, there's a wider range of sexual choices available today, from the traditional outlook on sexuality only within marriage at one extreme to Alex Comfort's (1968) comment, "We may eventually come to realize that chastity is no more a virtue than malnutrition" at the other.

But like the old morality, the "new morality" has its problems. One is that people may feel less obligation to support and trust each other. Another is that Hollywood and Madison Avenue images encourage us to chase eroticized visions of the "perfect lover" instead of being with each other as real human beings.

In addition, many women have "caretaking needs" that can go unmet in transient encounters. Helen Gurley Brown mirrors popular attitudes in the foreword to *Cosmopolitan*'s "Love Guide" issue: "What any woman really wants is . . . [not just] an orgasm . . . [but] so much more . . . human, more beautiful . . . more magical . . . more supportive."

But perhaps the "new morality" is already getting old. The recent rapid spread of herpes and Acquired Immune Deficiency Syndrome (AIDS) seems to be causing another swing of the pendulum. Epidemiologists and your physician concur that there are herpes and AIDS epidemics in progress. As a result, some people are becoming more discriminating and less casual about becoming sexually involved.

Sexual Responsibility

In few areas of our behavior are we so inclined to assign the cause of our actions outside ourselves, whether it's fears of pregnancy, disease, or social criticism on one hand or throbbing hormones, the craving for closeness, and pressures from peers on the other. But in reality you're ultimately the one who decides what to do. If you avoid choosing and allow yourself to yield to social pressure, to be seduced, or to drift into making love, that's a choice, too.

Before any act of making love, it's crucial to consider explicitly: "Do I—and we—want this sexual act to result in the conception of a child?"—and, if the answer is "No," to act accordingly.

Lacey, age fifteen, had gone out with Tom several times and they'd been getting increasingly physical. When their kisses and heavy petting finally turned into explosions of passion and desire, she wanted him as desperately as he wanted her.

"Do you—do you have anything?" he stuttered with embarrassment.

"What?"

"Birth control?"

"No."

"Me, neither."

"I didn't think we would . . ."

"Listen—I hear you can't get pregnant your first time . . ."

Lacey discovered to her dismay that you *can* get pregnant the first time. A counselor in a Northern California family planning clinic says, "It seems to be the acknowledgment, 'I am sexually active,' that brings the women in for contraception. She's typically been having intercourse for some time before she starts to think of herself as sexually active."

"With boys," the counselor notes, "there's not the same self-image problem. With them, 'It's cool to have a rubber in your billfold,' even if they never use it. The problem is embarrassment at buying them from the little old lady at the pharmacy. One drugstore put a condom dispenser on the sidewalk in front of the store. It's there 24 hours a day, seven days a week, and a lot of merchandise moves through it.

"There's still a tremendous generation gap," the counselor continued. "In many communities, the kids are already sexually active before the school starts talking about menstruation. When Planned Parenthood started showing movies and providing comic books to communicate with local teens, outraged parents had the program closed down. Now when the kids come in for counseling about an abortion or adoption services, the worried parents quickly change their tune: 'If I'd known she was sexually active, *of course* I'd have let her have contraceptives.' At that point they mean it." But that point is already too late.

The other side of "What will Mom and Dad think?" is how you and I, as Mom and Dad, handle our own children's emerging sexuality. We've got to find a way to handle this normal, healthy, and predictable evolution. One way or another, the Gonad Gavotte will be danced. To pretend it doesn't exist decreases communication with our children, reduces mutual trust, and leaves the guidance of their actions to hearsay, impulse, or ignorance.

A second approach is to tell them what to do according to our own value system. A difficulty here is that young people reaching sexual maturity may use that maturity as part of their rebellion and as a way of declaring their autonomy.

A third way, which is sometimes the hardest but also the most promising, is to tell them we know they'll make their own choices and to emphasize that it's important to listen attentively to their deepest feelings rather than respond to any outside push, and to share with them our own hopes, fears, and available information.

EXCITEMENT AND PERFORMANCE: SOURCES OF PLEASURE AND DYSFUNCTION

Sometimes past conditioning can trigger negative attitudes and physical responses around anything to do with sexuality. And that needs to happen in only one partner for dysfunction to occur and distort the sexual relationship of both.

In *performance anxiety*, a person is afraid of being inadequate, incompetent, and leaving both partners feeling unsatisfied or rejected. Out of that fear grows a pressure to say, "I can," even when at this point, in fact, I can't. So I end up feeling less adequate and more angry, less responsive and more frustrated. The pressure to perform can make us afraid to experiment. Even when performance is successful, if we make sex into a task our sexual relationship can turn into a ritualized and somewhat formal contact where we both feel lonely even as we lie in bed together.

In *pleasure anxiety*, instead of fearing failure to perform I may be afraid that if I experience sexual pleasure, something terrible is happening or is sure to happen.

An urgency for sexual contact appears to be nearly universal under even the most psychologically and physically forbidding circumstances—I have my stories and you have yours. Given that urgency, people seek erotic joining even when communication at its most superficial or distorted is part of the bargain. What emerges, then, out of our passion, anxiety, and insecurity is a marketplace orientation in this act that I would rather experience from a loving place: I offer my product and performance instead of offering myself. If you're skillful enough, I may perform more than once that night. If I'm skillful enough, you may have not just one but many orgasms. Then we can mark our scorecards and go to sleep.

A performance orientation grows out of being *lost in our minds* while making love instead of being *centered in our senses*. Instead of focusing my attention in the tingling warmth and streaming of sensation that the caress of your touch and the warmth of your breath evoke, I'm busy worring about whether I'm doing it right. Instead of sensing how your body responds to mine, I fantasize about how you're responding.

Sex at its best, declares Stanley Keleman, grows out of a pulsation and flow of excitement, being, and self-expression. When I'm worried and anxious, I'm triggering tightness and constriction that interferes with the relaxation and softening that good sex requires. "Satisfaction does not come from a job well done," writes Keleman, "it comes from experiencing deeply" (1975, p. 86).

It's easier to feel and respond when we feel free to explore and experiment. When my wife is amorous and I'm tired, she's the initiator and I'm more passive. Sometimes we switch back and forth between active and passive roles during a single episode of lovemaking. And when one of us wants a little lovin' but wants to be seduced instead of being the initiator, we communicate that.

SEXUAL ENHANCEMENT

Approaches to improving sexual enjoyment are hot items in bookstores and consulting rooms. But sexual activity per se expresses part of a broader, deeper pattern in people's lives and relationships. It speaks of the larger system of attitudes, actions, and expectations of which it's a part.

There are no exact answers for everyone, and no single standard of performance, satisfaction, frequency, or normality against which sexual "success" can be measured. In each of us and in every couple, our sexuality is as unique as our fingerprints and our individual histories.

Whatever else happens in our relationship, we end up dysfunctional when we plug in the formula for "winning." Any therapy focused on sexual dysfunction, no matter what theories underlie it, has to find a way to deal with the relationship of the people involved in terms of these important issues: communication—manipulation, trust—risk—vulnerability, domination—equality, and transparency—(disclosure)—opaqueness (shadows). Each of these represents not a polarity, but a continuum of many possible behaviors and attitudes. In any relationship, how these issues are resolved or not resolved influences the quality of our sexual joys.

Sexual Communication

Many of us, having grown up in families where one of the rules was "Don't talk about sex," assume that the rule applies with our partner, too. Our parents did it but never talked about it, so we think we're supposed to do it but not talk about it.

In addition, some of us believe that asking for what we want and telling how we feel takes the romance out of sex. Or we feel embarrassed about discussing sexual preferences, or afraid that the other person will take our frankness as personal criticism, or that he or she may not want to experiment and innovate.

So we grope in the wordless darkness for each other's unspoken thoughts, feelings, and physical responses. The way you're touching me doesn't feel good but I don't say so. Who am I playing a trick on? Nor do I tell you how I want you to touch me, because if you really love me you "ought to know," or at the very least should remember because I told you once before. Thus we continue, resentful about what we're not getting and guilty about what we may not be giving.

We may withhold questions, issues, or concerns about sex. Elizabeth reports, "After one day of being married I suddenly felt like someone's property. I was expected to have sex whether I wanted it or not. This was stressful and I began to enjoy it less. If our sexual relationship wasn't up to par, I was blamed for it. Sex began to seem like an unpleasant chore—like washing the dishes, something that 'had to be done.' Since I never verbalized this to my husband, he was unaware of my feelings."

In sexuality as elsewhere, I want to be able to say how and what I do and don't enjoy, without setting conditions, without following prescriptions, and certainly without doing it "by the numbers." We can do much of this through signaling, as in moving our partner's hand to a new place. We can listen to each other's sighs of satisfaction and moans of dissatisfaction (as long as we can reliably tell the ecstatic moans from the bored groans). And we can use brief statements like "More gently" or "A little faster" when we need them.

Talking about sexual preferences when we're not making love is often productive. With your own partner, you might find the questionnaire that follows helpful in opening up your sexual communication.

Speaking of Eros

This is a questionnaire for couples. As you answer, accent the positive and remember that it's about behaviors, not attitudes. Each of you fills it out independently; then you discuss your responses.

1. Our erotic dialogues are special and nourishing in the way that we . . .
2. One of the ways you (I) meet my (your) special wants in lovemaking is . . .
3. With all that's good in our sexual relationship, what I want more of from you is . . .
4. Our erotic dialogue can be more elegant through your (my) . . .
5. You are (I am) being most sensitive to me (you) when you (I) . . .
6. I think you are most real with me when you . . .
7. I feel most real with you when you . . .
8. The more you (I) . . . , the more I (you) . . .
9. I have the most fun in our lovemaking when you (I) . . .
10. What I wonder (not worry) most about in our lovemaking is . . .

The most commonly reported sexual problems in therapy are impotence, orgasmic dysfunction, growing disinterest, and premature ejaculation. *Impotence* typically means that a man can't attain or sustain an erection; *orgasmic dysfunction* (formerly called "frigidity") means that a woman consistently fails to have an orgasm; and *premature ejaculation* means the man consistently has an orgasm before his partner.

Problems of impotence include the element of being in our thoughts rather than our senses during the sexual act. Felipe, a twenty-eight-year-old married man, failed to achieve an erection during his first attempt at intercourse, when he was drunk. Subsequently, when intercourse seemed likely, he began to fear that he would be inadequate again. He envisioned his inability to perform, how his wife would respond, and so on. It was a self-fulfilling prophecy: His mind was so involved in catastrophizing that he had little attention left to be excited about making love.

Felipe was encouraged to relax as much as possible, and to experience, moment by moment, what was happening in his body. He and his wife developed some love games that emphasized the process of pleasure rather than the goal of erection and intercourse. It was a good thing they did for each other.

Pacing the Sexual Dance

Many different factors can interfere with anyone's sexual responsiveness, such as fatigue, personal problems, guilt, and resentments toward the partner.

If you've grown up with the idea that having sexual feelings is lewd, unclean, or reprehensible, it's impossible to become a sensuous playmate the first time you have sex. By deliberately replaying those old tapes activated by thoughts about sexual activities, you can be more aware of what you're doing to yourself. You can use the techniques described in Chapter 12 to reframe your thoughts and ultimately your feelings about your sexuality.

Often, a problem of erection or orgasm exists within a larger context: I respond only partially because I don't feel loved or cared for enough or because I feel suppressed, depressed, and oppressed in our relationship. In such cases, the real issue is our willingness to listen to that message—and do something about it.

Bridging the difference between male and female rhythms is something faced by most people—not just the extreme few. Many partners report liking a long period of love play with other areas of their bodies before the sexual organs themselves are stimulated. Such touching, kissing, and caressing can help the slower person become aroused. Learning to find and touch the most sensitive points on a partner's body, partly through exploration of your own body, is part of a loving lover's basic training.

Since women's sexual rhythms are typically slower than men's, a woman tends to need more stroking, hugging, kissing, and other forms of foreplay to excite her to the point where intercourse can elicit orgasm. "To reach orgasm," writes the Boston Women's Health Book Collective (1976), "a woman needs continuous, effective stimulation of the clitoris—by penile thrusting, body pressure, or touching of the clitoral area with a hand or tongue. . . . Most of us need either direct or indirect clitoral stimulation before intercourse, and some of us need direct clitoral manipulation during intercourse." There's the story of the eighty-three-year-old continental rogue receiving a physical exam who, when asked by the doctor to display his sex organ, stuck out his tongue.

In some cases much of the sexual act might involve such stimulation, a woman's lover entering only when she's almost at a climax. Or if she goes into orgasm before being entered, they can rest and then make love again. If her lover is inside her and climaxes before she's ready to, after a brief rest he can stimulate her to climax. Commitment of time, energy, and affection can reduce the probability that either one is left unsatisfied.

There's also something special and magical about an extended union in which we are each engulfed in the other for what seems like a small eternity. One approach to regulating the level of excitement and prolonging the sexual act relies on awareness of breathing and muscular tension. In this kind of sexual dance, male and female partners have somewhat different roles: Hers is to keep herself excited, but avoid pushing him into too much excitement. His is to keep her aroused and keep himself excited enough to stay inside her, but not so much as to tumble into orgasm.

There are several things we can do as part of this process.

> *Signaling.* A simple touch signal, like sudden pressure, may be enough, or just the word "Stop," so the partner knows when to go motionless, or to do something differently to increase the arousal level.

Tension and relaxation. An effective way for a man to reduce arousal level and stop short of an orgasm is to relax the sphincter and buttock muscles. A woman sometimes can increase or decrease her level of arousal by tensing or relaxing pelvic muscles.

Discovering the positions in which you are more likely or less likely to have an orgasm.

Regulating fantasies. You may be able to reduce your arousal by thinking about something unrelated, like oranges or igloos—or orange igloos. Or you may find it more effective, once aroused, to clear your mind and attend totally to your present sensations and your partner's movements. (The "Awareness Continuum" exercise from Chapter 6 can be useful and enjoyable here.) Many people also use sexual fantasies to heighten their arousal.

Breathing. A long, slow sexual act is aided by slow, regular breathing. One enjoyable practice involves the two partners harmonizing their breathing rhythms so that they breathe slowly and in unison. Another is to synchronize movement and breathing. These are aspects of the "yoga of love."

Sensate Focus: Enjoying Sexual Sensuality

When we remember to bring all that we are into our sexual experience rather than making it just an encounter between a penis and a vagina, it can be a larger dialogue to which our history, our experience, our hopes, and our explorations all contribute. An appreciative sensuality that is enjoyable as an event in itself can also enrich the sexual experience.

Here's something you might try:

Sensual Play

This can be done with anyone you might enjoy sensing with. You'll begin with one of you as giver and the other as receiver. As giver, you may touch one hand of the receiver—or, if he or she gives you permission, the hand and forearm. Your aim is to create pleasant sensations for the receiver by means of your touching. After a few minutes, reverse roles.

Then you become giver again, this time touching the other person's face, again with the objective of giving pleasure. Again change roles after a few minutes. Then take a few minutes to discuss what you experienced, including your feelings in response to what the other person did for you.

Masters and Johnson (1970) suggest that sexual partners make time to touch, stroke, caress, and rub each other's bodies *with an explicit agreement of no intercourse at that time.* They call this *sensate focus.* The Boston Women's Health Book Collective (1976) writes,

Set aside a time to enjoy a good meal, snack, or drink together. Undress each other and sit by candlelight with your favorite music. Take turns rubbing each other with oil or lotion. We need to take time to accept pleasures. Tell or show each other what touches please or arouse you. Don't rush into intercourse.

Do this again and again until you both feel relaxed with nudity, with touching, with caressing all parts of your bodies, with talking openly about your feelings, with the giving and getting of pleasure.

The relaxed pleasure of stroking and caressing is its own fulfillment and its own goal. There are no expectations to meet. It can help change the situation when the partners have begun to feel neglected, and reawaken excitement in sexual relationships that have grown routine.

27

Conflict and Negotiation

*T*here will always be times when our interests and wishes differ in areas each of us sees as essential to our well-being. Our challenge is to find sane, wise ways to handle these differences.

Peggy, who has been married for three years, comments, "It was a relief for someone to finally say, 'Conflict in a marriage reflects a relationship that's alive.' Too many times I've been ashamed to acknowledge that Jim and I had an argument. I guess I've been perpetuating the myth that 'happy couples don't fight' because no one thinks we ever get angry with each other."

Gina adds, "After Marty and I have it out, there's reassurance in knowing we can acknowledge such anger with the other and even love that element in our partner."

Conflict exists, suggests social psychologist Morton Deutsch (1973), whenever one person's act prevents, obstructs, or interferes with another person's, or injures that person. Conflict, Deutsch points out, is not the same as competition. In competition, each person seeks the same prize; your victory is my defeat. But conflict can also occur when we agree on what we want to have happen but disagree about how to make it happen. Thus it can occur within a larger cooperative context. On the other hand, competition can occur without conflict. Conflict involves *interfering with* each other's actions. Football and track are both competitive, but football involves conflict and track does not.

Conflicts between two persons, notes Kelley (1979, p. 31) are of two different kinds. Some involve preferences about *individual behaviors.* You might, for instance, want me to nag you less or act less grumpy around the house. Resolving these conflicts involves learning to *exchange* behaviors that are more satisfying to each other.

Other conflicts involve different preferences about our *joint activities*—such as where to go this afternoon, or when and how to have sex. These problems involve *coordinating* our feelings and actions in mutually satisfying ways.

HANDLING CONFLICTS CONSTRUCTIVELY

I'm living dangerously when I try to sweep our differences under the rug and mask potential sources of conflict. This creates an atmosphere where you're not sure what's real and what isn't, and you're likely to be wary and untrusting. But if instead of gunnysacking our conflicts until the next year, meal, or fight, we deal with them constructively and achieve some closure, they're likely to occupy a relatively small place in our relationship. Constructive conflict resolution with one person can improve other relationships, too: If I confront someone with my resentment where it's happening, I'm less likely to misplace my anger onto my mate, my children, my colleagues at work, or my dog.

Sources of Conflict and Support

In a study of young heterosexual couples by Tiggle, Peters and Kelley, the issues that emerged as the most important sources of conflict were the partners'

1. Carelessness, sloppiness, and impulsivity
2. Passivity, lack of confidence, lack of ambition
3. Failure to give appreciation, understanding, and affection
4. Excessive worry, compulsivity, moodiness
5. Leisure time, where and how to live, etc.
6. Inadequate and poor communication
7. Division and fulfillment of responsibility

The things respondents most wanted their partners to *continue* showing were

1. Sex, affection, love, and appreciation
2. Understanding, sensitivity, considerateness, tolerance
3. Encouragement and emotional support
4. Confidence and ambition
5. Sensitive resolution of conflicts about leisure time, where and how to live, etc.
6. Adequate division and fulfillment of responsibility
7. Open and good communication

(in Kelley, 1979, pp. 97–99)

Value and lifestyle differences that can lead to conflict are especially common in countries where people reflect many ethnic and cultural backgrounds. If one partner—or both—views his or her ways as "right" or "good," or better than those of the other person, resentment and tension result.

Ellen, a third generation Irish-American, learned her script well: "Suffer in silence." Jack, a third generation Jewish-American, learned his script well, too: "Blow off the steam." His explosive exchanges with his mother were traumatic for Ellen:

"They never settle anything." Her nonconfronting, avoidant contract with her mother infuriated Jack: "They never settle anything." Learning to appreciate these differences was a major contributor to their well-being.

Many skills and attitudes useful in handling conflicts have been presented in earlier chapters. These include the systems view and approaches to listening, self-disclosure, and assertion. We've also described a host of obstacles to good conflict resolution.

One way of reducing the occasions for extended conflict involves *finding and acknowledging each person's areas of competence, responsibility, and investment*. Left undone, a question of who does what has to be renegotiated or redecided whenever it comes up. When people are clear about authority and responsibility, state Lederer and Jackson, it "does not create a rigid relationship, but a flexibility which is impossible in a chaotic one. It conserves energy and time, leaving room for humor, good cheer, and experimentation" (1968, p. 251). They also suggest that where partners are given to power struggles, they can explicitly *take turns* making decisions.

My wife and I had the opposite problem: Each of us attempted to defer to the other's wishes:

"Either one is all right with me. Which would you prefer?"

"Oh, both are all right. You can decide."

"No, really, I can go with your preference."

"But I genuinely don't care. There must be one you like better."

"Oh, never mind—the movie started ten minutes ago!"

In most cases, neither of us was *totally* impartial. Each of us usually had some small preference, and we learned to ask, "Do you have even the slightest leaning toward either one?" Frequently our "slight leanings" were in the same direction.

Winning and Losing

In a *win-lose* context, one of us loses what the other wins. I seek to take the prize, to force you to capitulate, or to put you down and come out one up. The objective, writes social psychologist Ronald J. Fisher, "is to defeat the adversary to reach your goal. . . . This 'fixed pie' assumption . . . that what one party gains, the other loses . . . [often means that] creative solutions *that might increase the size of the pie* are never even imagined" (1982, p. 592).

There is also, notes Fisher, the time-honored *lose-lose* strategy in which neither you nor I get what we want. I assume that getting what I can is better than losing it all and that confrontation and disagreement are to be avoided at all costs. We then settle for a quickie solution instead of working to find an enduring resolution.

"Splitting the difference" without a fuller exploration can be either win-lose or lose-lose, depending on the situation. This includes lawsuits, divorce trials, and other courtroom settlements. Such settlements seldom meet the criterion that the outcome is the best available for everyone concerned. Jesus recognized that truth and attached great importance to people's resolving their conflicts amicably: "And why can you not judge for yourself what is the right course? While you are going with your opponent to court, make an effort to settle with him while you are still on the way" (Luke 12:59, New English Bible).

The *resolution approach* is "a conscious, systematic attempt to maximize the gains of both parties. . . . The conflict is seen as a mutual problem to be solved rather than as a war to be won or a battle to be avoided" (Fisher, p. 598). *Conflict resolution* as a process leads to mutually satisfactory agreements, with long-term commitments from both—or all—parties. Fisher uses the term *conflict termination* when undesirable outcomes are enforced or accepted in the short term.

To the degree that I live my life win-lose, I can only win by the other person's losing. So even when I win, I have only losers to relate to. Win-lose is a one-up, one-down relationship. If I'm one down, I'm likely to resent the person who's one up. "Go ahead, *be* the winner. *All by yourself.*"

When we play win-lose, the deck is stacked against both of us. Whatever you do, I •can find a way to have you wrong, so I can feel superior or cover up my painful feelings if you win. And since you're likely to resent me when you lose, if you're important to me, that's a loss for me, too. At the level where it counts—the level of loving, caring, trusting, and being good to each other—no one wins a win-lose game. And it doesn't do much for our feelings of security, either.

For most of us, the habits of living win-lose are old and well worn. Through a conflict resolution approach, however, we can find *win-win* solutions. Here are some guidelines toward that end.

Six Ingredients in Resolving Conflicts

1. *Fight clear and clean.* I don't bring up other important but unrelated and distracting subjects like your weight or drinking problem, and you keep away from ancient history that supports your claim to my derelictions. Fighting clean includes two elements:

   a. *Respect. No character assassination or other putdowns.*
   b. *Confining our exchange to the matter at hand.* (An exception: Sometimes lighter comments and digressions can provide "breathers" and help us relax.)

2. *Detach from ego struggles.* Sometimes the substance of my conflict is my insistence on "winning." Then I want to find a way to let go of my position. "Okay. It's no big thing." I especially want to be willing to do this with children, who are involved in a process of defining their identities, in part by disagreeing with someone else. My body tells me when my ego is attached: Clenched teeth as well as tight fists, shoulders, stomach, brows, or sphincter tell me clearly what's at stake. The instant I let go of my position, so long as I don't feel diminished in so doing, I relax.

3. *Breathe.* When I find myself in a conflict, I can notice my breathing. Is it extremely shallow? Am I not breathing at all? Starting to breathe again opens me to hearing both your deeper feelings and my own.

4. *Call a "cease-fire" when appropriate.* In the middle of a fight that's going nowhere and getting nastier—*disengage.* "Wait a minute—I feel lousy with what we're doing. I want to table this for now and come back to it when we're both feeling better."

5. *Nonassaultive humor* can reduce tension. Finding something funny in the situation can help keep a disagreement from becoming a fight or a small conflict from escalating into a large one. I do want to be alert to how I might abuse humor as an avoidance process. I can be very "unfunny" in my denial.

6. *Dialoguing out loud* can be useful—and also a source of comic relief. In the middle of a monologue I might change voices and tell myself, "Listen, know-it-all—she can't get a word in edgewise, so how do you expect to deal with her feelings? Kindly shut up and let her talk." Such overt self-confrontation can be profoundly reassuring to both of us, especially when I follow my directive. Through such statements, I'm sharing with you a broader spectrum of what's happening in me, and moving out of a narrow polarization.

We don't have to resolve all our conflicts. Some are small enough to throw in the garbage can and forget—though if they're not small enough for that, I'll cause myself trouble if I pretend they are: They'll get smellier instead of disappearing.

Other conflicts seem large—until I realize that they're my shadow plays, as I project negative intentions onto another person or group. When I work through my own unfinished business, such projections are less frequent and intrusive.

Today church leaders of a number of faiths, disillusioned at the nuclear threat to humanity and violations of human rights, have begun to show that confrontation can be a manifestation of love rather than a vehicle of hostility.

Our mind-body connections can help us stay in touch with ourselves and each other as we deal with difficult situations. Gestalt therapist Niela Miller Horn (1981) suggests the following exercise:

Centering in Relationships

Sit facing another person whom you don't know very well and with whom you feel some degree of trust. Each of you slowly goes through physical centering (see Chapter 20). Look silently at the other person. *Keep sensing your body.*

Imagine a line that separates you from the other person. Do you tend to lean over into the other person's space as if being sucked into it? Do you tend to lean back, as if withdrawing from the other person, as if being pushed away, or as if to gain a larger view?

Listen for any self-judgments and refute them; you're totally okay. In so doing, you're *creating your own internal cognitive support system.*

Now, each tells the other the kinds of emotional responses, or criticism and judgment, that you have the hardest time handling. Then the other person says those kinds of things to you, in the ways he or she thinks are most likely to "push your buttons" and get you upset. *Your task is to stay physically centered and keep breathing as you listen.* As in meditation, the attitude of your body tends to become an attitude of mind.

After about five minutes, reverse roles and repeat the process.

SOCIAL CONTRACTS

Jean Jacques Rousseau observed in 1762 that every human relationship involves some kind of *contract.* Sometimes it's explicit, as in business. More often it's tacit or implicit: mutually accepted but not stated, or perhaps even unrecognized, or inherent in the nature of the situation.

My wife and I have talked extensively about what we are willing to do for each other, and about the ways in which we want to be sure we keep our own identities. We've written down important agreements that we came to. Whenever one of us becomes dissatisfied with something in our contract, we can bring that item up to *renegotiate*. We can, by mutual consent, change it to fit changes in our lives. When we were getting ready to have our first child, we went through the process again, creating another contract that dealt specifically with what we wanted from each other in regard to our child. It has been a source of support ever since.

Quid pro Quos

A *quid pro quo* is a kind of contract, usually implied rather than explicit. *Quid pro quo* is a Latin phrase that means "something for something"—if you do so-and-so, I'll respond with such-and-such. Through this process, each of us gets something we want. But if people think they've agreed on a set of conditions and one person decides he or she "didn't mean it that way"—look out! The national budget is a well-known result of quid pro quos.

Mutually nourishing quid pro quos take time to develop. Those made quickly are likely to leave too little room for change and to imprison the partners in rigid roles.

Implied and Explicit Contracts

In most cases a relationship, family, or other social institution is better equipped to meet the needs of everyone in it when the expectations and commitments are clear and explicit than when they depend on tacit agreements. As an example of how the latter can cause trouble, parents may subcontract (see Chapter 25) to avoid noticing certain things. When we collude to ignore the things that might cause us pain, we mutually agree to avoid what, paradoxically, we ultimately cannot avoid. When we strive to *define what in fact our contract is,* we're less likely to abide by subcontracts that are destructive.

MAJOR CONFLICT IN RELATIONSHIPS: SEPARATION AND DIVORCE

In 1980, there was one divorce for every two marriages in the United States. Some of those separations could have been avoided had the partners been more effective at resolving conflicts, and some of the unavoidable ones could have been less painful.

Separation or divorce leads to *restructured* or *redesigned* relationships rather than to a total end to contact. Parents who divorce are still the parents of their children and, ironically, are now part of each other's extended families. The enduring bitterness and rancor that so often accompany a divorce can be avoided. In California, mediation has been so successful that in 1981 the California Family Law Act* was enacted, requiring all contested custody cases to go through mediation rather than directly into the adversary proceedings of the courtroom. The American Association for Mediated Divorce, based in California, is an informational network for such media-

*Civil Code, section 4607.

tion services. Parents who choose this service are much more likely to retain an active caring for each other and the children, and often comment that those skills learned in the course of mediation might have salvaged their marriage had they been available to them earlier.

Following a divorce or separation, children can find themselves in either a *single-parent family* or a *blended family*—or perhaps first one and later the other—as well as still being part of the larger restructured family that includes the parent they're not living with at a given time. Both adults and children in such families face the challenge of not closing up and closing off emotionally. When a family restructures, it's crucial to reassure the children that they'll have access to both parents—and to follow through on that, especially during the critical separation period, to reduce fears that one or the other parent might disappear. (You can read "disappear" as "desert.")

In such a restructuring, I need to remember that the conflicts and arguments with the other parent are mine and the children have a right to keep their relationship with him or her unspoiled and intact. Out of my anger at my ex-mate, I can try to form an alliance with the child against the other parent. I want to avoid that for two reasons: First, it poisons the relationship between the child and the other parent and that hurts the child; second, it's likely to cause additional needless conflict.

In addition, in Satir's words, "no one can feel good about himself if he feels he comes from devils and bad people" (1972, p. 191). Even one devil and one angel is only half okay. The statement that's important for a child to hear is that when two parents decide to live apart, it's not because anyone is bad, but because they've decided they can no longer live together without hurting each other too much.

Blended families combine parts of previous families (Satir, 1972, p. 173). An adult with one or more children forms a relationship with another adult, who may or may not also have children. Trouble may arise when members think they "should" feel loving toward all the new members of the blended family—they're likely to feel both guilty and resentful. Things become easier if all concerned follow several principles:

1. Everyone is allowed to have whatever feelings they have. A child doesn't have to love the "new parent," nor a parent love the "new child." Julie, who married Tom after she and her son Davey had lived alone for three years, felt resentful because she wanted Tom to love Davey as she did, and he didn't. Tom was unhappy because Davie was Julie's first priority. When Tom acknowledged Davey as Julie's top priority, but realized that she had plenty of love and time for him, too, and Julie accepted that while Tom loved her deeply, his and Davie's relationship was presently mutually respectful but not more than that, they started living together more comfortably.

2. A stepparent does not have to, and usually cannot, take the place of the absent parent. When adults form a new relationship, states Satir, "the children . . . need to be allowed to keep a place for their original parents, and be helped to find a way to add another parent" (1972, p. 179).

3. The new partner's place is *in* the blended family as a participating member—not standing on the sidelines. A person who remarries may treat his or her own children as "private property" either to "avoid imposing a handicap on the new mate" or for fear that the new partner might not act as desired toward them. Bob was confused by

Tina's attitudes in this area. Her children were "hers," yet she expected Bob to be more assertive in his support for her disciplinary acts. Voicing her concerns and acknowledging her need to "control" went a long way toward resolving this issue.

4. Expectations based on the "ghosts" of past relationships need to be overcome. If my previous partner died or was killed, I may *idealize* that person; no one can ever live up to the standard he or she set. After a divorce, by contrast, the new partner may be expected to be much "better than" the old one—and if he or she isn't, look out.

NEGOTIATION: ATTITUDES AND TACTICS

Currently, effective counseling holds that, when we state explicitly what we want, what we can give easily, and what we have a hard time offering, we have a foundation of clarity and trust for negotiations that stabilize relationships. As we learn to bargain in ways that respect both you and your interests and me and mine, our conflicts become less traumatic, and sometimes even useful.

An effective conflict resolution process includes both an *attitude* and a *method*. The attitude is a willingness to actively try to provide the things that matter most to both of us. As participants in a relationship, we're better off being partly altruistic—acting to maximize our joint outcomes—than being wholly so—acting strictly to maximize the other person's outcomes. We might go to your first-choice event today and my first choice next time (Kelley, 1979, p. 81). If I consistently "make sacrifices" and "do it for your sake," without regard to my own outcomes, I end up feeling frustrated and resentful.

Something of Value

This exercise provides insight into your present negotiation style. It can be done by members of a couple, family, class, or group. First, each person puts something of significant personal value in a container (hat, box, bag, etc.). Then each person draws out an item other than his or her own and attaches a high value to it.

The objective is to get your own item back via negotiations. This may involve direct negotiation when you have B's item and B has yours. It may involve more complex negotiations where B has yours and C has B's item. In the negotiations you will have to describe why your own object is of value to you—and why the object you *now* hold may be of greater value to you.

Notice how you react emotionally during the negotiations. Notice how you use your own skills and how you respond when you're the object of others' processes.

An effective negotiation process, suggest Tessina and Smith (1980, pp. 77–84), usually includes these steps:

1. Define the problem to yourself
2. Agree to negotiate

3. Set the stage
4. State (and explore) wants
5. Negotiate explicitly
6. Confirm decision and restate

This method of negotiation starts with each of us stating what *we* believe we want—even though that may be very different from what the other person wants us to want. It goes on to *exploring all the possibilities* in the situation, so we don't get stuck in the either/or of what you or I asked for and overlook a better option that would maximize our joint outcome. Next, we identify those elements of what we want that mean most to each of us and which mean least. Then we go on to: "I'll give a little here where it's less important to me if you give a little there where it's less important to you." Sometimes that takes the form of "Listen, you really care about this, so today I'm willing to do exactly what you want," so long as I trust that on another occasion you'll do the same for me. Other times it may involve haggling until we hit on something we both consider fair. Finally we restate our agreement so that we're both clear about it.

The process as just described sounds deceptively simple, because it leaves out the complications that make having a-method necessary at all. For instance, I feel surprised and angry at what you want; you respond to my feeling as if it will lead where it led when your parent felt that way; I feel unheard and misunderstood and say some unkind words; these provoke you to think, "Damned if I'll give him what he wants"; I stomp out and slam the door, and both of us wish we'd never mentioned the matter. "Those psychologists said it would be easy!!"

The detailed steps in negotiation are designed to decrease misunderstandings, slow down the fast pace of interaction that leads to erroneous assumptions and regrettable retorts, and help us both get what we want.

If you and another person have a hard time resolving some issues, it's important to move through the following process slowly, one step at a time. Where you resolve matters relatively easily, you can take shortcuts, adding points you've overlooked to your existing process.

Now, step by step:

1. *Define the problem to yourself.* Describe *what you want.* Don't worry about how the other person will respond. Focus on what you *do* want, not what you *don't* want. This moves your process toward being a constructive one and away from being a critical one likely to leave the other person feeling belittled and threatened.

2. *Agree to negotiate.* "I'd like to discuss the way we coordinate our time looking after the kids. Is now a good time, or would later be better?" By being flexible about when we negotiate, notes George Bach (1974; Bach & Wyden, 1970), I avoid "jumping on you" in a way that causes you to feel ambushed. But it's equally important to firmly insist on a commitment to an acceptable time and place, within a day or two. "Okay, if not now, *when?*" "Not getting around to it" can be a way to avoid a request for change. Times that are not good for negotiating are when one or both of us are grumpy, tired, or hassled—or when we're likely to be interrupted.

It's also important to *avoid overloading.* Resolving one item at a time is enough.

3. *Set the stage.* This involves creating a positive frame of mind. It can involve articulating the larger framework of common goals that we share, to establish a cooperative context. It may include reassuring you that I care for you, that I want an

agreement we can both live with, and that I'll talk it through with you until we reach some resolution rather than walking out. It also means identifying my acknowledged feelings of hurt and anger so I don't use them to sabotage you while we negotiate.

4. *State (and explore) wants.* Communication here involves contact and communion. I need to say what I want and feel clearly and specifically, while avoiding trying to dictate how you should behave or dwelling on what you've done in the past. How you should respond to my wants is yet to be negotiated.

When you hear my request, you may explain your actions, agree with my request, reject my complaint, or . . . *My next step is to reflect back your response* and check whether I've reflected correctly: "Did I get that right?"

Then, if your response was an explanation or rejection, *I can assertively repeat my request and incorporate what I just learned from you,* hoping that the latter step helps you feel heard and increases the likelihood that you'll listen to me, too (Scoresby, 1977, pp. 99–100). "Okay, I didn't realize how important it was for you to have that free time this morning. I'd still like to know in advance if you're going to ask me for time on a day when I'm planning to write."

If you're the one asking for change, I need to remember that it's your right to want whatever you want—even if it's not what I want you to want. It's also my job to *accurately hear what you want.* If your request is unclear, I may ask you to clarify it.

5. *Negotiate explicitly.* This is the "horse-trading stage." "I'm willing to . . . if you'll . . . " At this stage it's crucial to assure completed communication. A completed communication consists of the following stages:

a. The first speaker makes a statement.
b. The recipient acknowledges the statement, showing that he or she heard it.
c. The original speaker acknowledges the acknowledgment.

For example,

a. "Then you'll take the kids swimming once a week?"
b. "Either Tuesday or Thursday."
c. "Thanks."

6. *Confirm decision and restate.* This is to make sure we're clear about our agreement. If it's complicated, we should write it down. At least we restate and acknowledge it:
"Then we're agreed: I'll take them swimming on Thursday."
"Right, Thursdays it is."

In negotiating, I want to keep away from using external criteria to measure what I, you, or we do. Citing what the Joneses do is a manipulative ploy rather than a fair bargaining tactic: It's all too easy for me to quote the standard that supports my view.

Whatever the nature, source, and outcome of a conflict, when all else fails, sometimes it helps to recall Samuel Johnson's words: "I dogmatise and am contradicted, and in this conflict of opinions and sentiments I find delight."

28

Work and Community

Work is more than a livelihood. It is a way we can give to others as we take care of ourselves. It is a chance to exercise our initiative and creativity and develop our skills and abilities. It can be a statement of "This is who I am," to ourselves and others. The limits that a white male–dominated society places on women and members of other groups are all the more reprehensible because they deny millions of people the opportunity to experience themselves in these terms.

THE MEANING OF WORK

Freud viewed *lieben und arbeiten*—to love and to work—as central features of human life. Following his lead, British economist E. F. Schumacher contends that we all bear the responsibility to find our own "good work" that helps us to extend our capacities and to express our feeling, caring, and creative sides as well as our practicality. He declares:

> A person's work is undoubtedly one of the most decisive formative influences on . . . character and personality. . . . Business is not there simply to produce goods, it also produces *people,* so that the whole thing becomes a learning process. (1980, pp. 3, 73, 138)

As the movie *Nine to Five* shows, such ideas are becoming more widespread. They represent a sharp break with the past, a shift from the kind of thinking that character-ized the early industrial era. In that older view, human beings are viewed as interchangeable units in a giant production machine. Creative thinking is reversed for the managers and professionals; robotlike obedience is expected of others.

Whenever unemployment is widespread, many job applicants are glad to take jobs they regard as far from ideal. During the recession of the early 1980s, there were lines of applicants even for the jobs of "jumpers" who go inside radioactive nuclear reactors to repair them.

A number of years ago, Erich Fromm and a group of German psychologists known collectively as the *Frankfurt School* began to study the connections between working conditions and the rest of a person's life. They found that not only are the frustrations of a repressive working place often brought home and dumped on the family, but so too is the authoritarian structure of the work environment. A man who is an obedient pawn at work may turn into a dictator at home. In turn, such a family is a training ground for an authoritarian, repressive industrial system, preparing people to function as dutiful cogs (Adorno, Frenkel-Brunswick, Levinson & Sanford, 1950; Fromm, 1955; Horkheimer, 1972; Lasch, 1977; Marcuse, 1964). Authoritarian economics and family structures are poor training for political democracy.

Today impetus for change comes from the top, as in the present interest in "quality circles" and "participative management," and from the bottom, as unions and young people demand more responsive workplaces and more responsible occupational roles. Schumacher (1980, pp. 118–119) encourages these moves, declaring that meaningless work is an abomination. When he asked young people what they wanted and didn't want in their work, he got answers like these:

"Not to be enslaved by machines, bureaucracies, boredom, ugliness."
"I don't want to join the rat race."
"I don't want to become a moron, robot, commuter."
"I don't want to be a fragment of a person."
"I want to deal with people, not masks."
"I want to be able to *care*."
"People matter. Nature matters. Beauty matters. Wholeness matters."
(1980, p. 50)

Such thoughts are not new—just the scale on which they're occurring. Long ago Buddha formulated the principle of *Right Livelihood*, which recognizes that what we do and how we do it shapes who we become. Right Livelihood includes work that's appropriate to our personalities, interests, and abilities, that is valuable to others, and that does not contribute to deceiving, cheating, or harming anyone (Sasdhatissa, 1971). And Right Livelihood means working in ways that respect others and that increase our awareness and our self-respect. In this spirit, religious leaders world-wide have joined in the condemnation of work related to the design, development, and production of nuclear arms.

CHOICES AND CHANGES OF OCCUPATION

The choice of a career, or the decision to change one's occupation—when that's an option—is one of life's important decisions. Besides trying out different kinds of jobs when they first start out in the working world, later on in their lives people go through additional periods of questioning and change regarding their livelihoods. Many women whose early jobs were as mothers and homemakers, for instance, later move into work outside the home, and men and women alike often go through intense self-examination about their work or the lack of it and its meaning in their existence. This questioning may lead to changes in occupation, to involvement in other kinds of work besides the primary job, or to changes in the way we do our work. This frequently occurs between the ages of thirty-five and forty-five, and again during the period just before retirement (Sheehy, 1976).

The technological and social changes of modern society mean that fewer people can expect to hold a single job throughout their working life—if they get a job at all. This development—that lifelong relearning and retraining may become the norm rather than the exception—sometimes has a valuable side effect. The expectation of change can encourage flexibility and reduce the tendency to become imprisoned in rigid habits.

If you're starting out in the job world, or have an option to change from your present occupation to one that suits you better now, Bolles's *What Color Is Your Parachute?* (1981) is a good resource for helping you think through what you want to do. Other useful books are Michelozzi's *Coming Alive from Nine to Five: The Career Search Handbook* (2nd ed., 1984), Weiler's *Reality and Career Planning* (1977), Jackson's *Guerrilla Tactics in the Job Market* (1978), Irish's *Go Hire Yourself an Employer* (1978), and Figler's *The Complete Job Search Handbook* (1979).

If you have a college counseling center available, you can check out their career advising program. Almost all offer tests of personality, interests, and aptitudes and career counseling. If you already have considerable work experience and are considering a change, you might explore whether any occupational exploration workshops are offered in your city.

Interests and Abilities

Career consultant Tom Jackson identifies five career variables: *skills, interests, satisfaction, practicality,* and *willingness to do what's necessary to get the job.* He suggests the following steps to organize these five variables in your own mind.

1. Write down twenty-five activities you like—"trivial" as well as important ones. If that many don't come to mind immediately, think about what you'd do if you had an extended vacation and plenty of money to spend on it.

2. On another piece of paper, list twenty-five things you can do that lead to results you like, or that others compliment you for (you're an amateur pilot, you play the guitar, etc.).

3. Choose five items from each of your two lists. On a new sheet, list five across the top and five down the left side. Their intersections create twenty-five items. Choose ten of these.

4. For each of the ten "combination items" you've just chosen, list three or four related occupational possibilities. If you like traveling and have organizational abilities, for example, you might become a tour organizer or go into the import/export business. This will produce a list of thirty or forty job possibilities.

5. Assign each job possibility an A for maximum satisfaction, a B for moderate satisfaction, or a C for minimum satisfaction. Then evaluate each in terms of how easy it would be to get the job and what extra training or education you would need.

6. Finally, ask yourself whether you're willing to get the training and do whatever else you'd have to do to get the job. If not, cross it out. Then contemplate the options you have left.

7. Get together with three friends or acquaintances who have done the same thing and take fifteen or twenty minutes to discuss the possibilities each of you has ended up with. (Adapted from Jackson, 1978)

The best way to get beyond idealized, glorified views of what a given kind of work is like is to get "hands-on," or direct, experience by finding a job in the area you're interested in, even if it's part time, temporary, low paying, or an unpaid volunteer position. If that option isn't open, you can talk to people in that line of work and find out how it is for them.

Some experimentation and change, when available, is normal. Turnover doesn't mean you've failed: It means you've gained valuable experience and information about what does and doesn't suit you that can be helpful as you select and perform your next job.

People are also finding ways to avoid defining themselves totally in terms of organizational job roles. Through producing useful items or services and exchanging them with others, directly and through *barter networks* in which services and goods are traded with no money changing hands, people are creating alternative economies that offer another kind of perspective on meaningful work.

Traditional ideas about appropriate jobs for men and women can interfere with a full consideration of the possibilities open to us. The United States has gone far toward breaking down such stereotypes and opening up a wider range of options, but not nearly so far as, for example, Israel or the Soviet Union. And we have yet to elect even a woman Vice-President, though such nations as England and India have women heads of state.

Increasingly, women work outside the home at some time in their lives. Part of the notorious difference between men's and women's average incomes is due to discrimination in promotion and pay levels, but another part is due to lower average training levels. Despite higher average grades, fewer women students than men complete their college degrees, and fewer go on to graduate training. Nonetheless, today women and men alike are moving into nontraditional jobs with little or no stigma attached. Such issues are even more pronounced among minority groups.

HOW WE ARE IN WHAT WE DO

No occupation is *the* freeway to happiness. If I'm obsessed with thoughts about how I'd be happy if only I'd gone into some other line of work, I'm probably not doing what I could to make my present work rewarding.

Resenting our work, or pushing too hard, can lead to the kinds of stress reactions described in Chapter 15. In the "workaholic" pattern, a person becomes so immersed in work that he or she finds no time to relax and take it easy. Oddly enough, a workaholic may find little or no satisfaction in the work itself, but only in looking forward to the goal. A true workaholic may feel uneasy about taking time off even during vacations.

Working too intensely for too long, without taking time to relax and replenish our energies, can lead to *burnout,* in which we're not much good either to ourselves or to others. This condition often plagues women who hold down an outside job and also try to do a full-time job as wife and mother. The price of peace of mind and health of body may be leaving the house a little messier than she'd like and involving her family in doing for themselves. This may involve explicit negotiations with her husband or children.

In the course of our work, many of us redefine the nature of our own and others' jobs. The latter is especially true of people in managerial positions. Schumacher speaks of ensuring that every job is worthy of a human being. The model of management or administration that he advocates is like someone holding a cluster of helium-filled balloons by their strings. Each balloon is buoyed up by its own initiative and creativity, and the manager or administrator holds them together and provides guidance. In addition, Schumacher asserts: "A firm is responsible not only to its shareholders but also to its employees, its customers, and the community as a whole" (1980, p. 33). When we adopt that attitude, we acknowledge the workplace as part of the larger social and ecological fabric to which we all belong.

The perspectives of Gestalt and Zen can help us consider how we are in what we do. From a Gestalt viewpoint, we can ask, "To what degree am I a whole person as I do my job here? Which parts of my being do I affirm, and which do I deny? How can I make room for the parts of me that I now leave out and become more fully who I am in what I do?" We can ask those same questions about what we allow and expect of others under our authority.

Zen counsels a directness and simplicity: doing things with care and presence of mind, not leaving undone what should be done, and not doing what's unnecessary. Above all, it counsels using each task, each moment, as a focus of awareness and a vehicle for personal evolution.

HUMAN COMMUNITY

Community is a "place" and it's an attitude: an attitude of respect for the human and natural world in which I live. When I look around me, respect means remembering my sense of wonder. When I create, respect means making something that is beautiful and that will fit into its surroundings in a pleasing way.

With other people, respect means asking, "How can we nurture one another?" It means finding ways to make sure each of us has enough to eat, a warm place to sleep, decent health care, and a worthwhile job to do. It means using our community as a caring agency, and recognizing the impact of the values of the larger social fabric on our immediate and personal communities. We can see this on one hand in a barn raising that contributes to a spirit of mutual assistance, and on the other in attitudes that condone and transmit violence in interpersonal relationships.

Folksinger Ric Masten writes, "Haven't we all stood helplessly in hospital halls? Haven't we all been to the grave together? ... There are streets of people who seem to have it made, but we've all been down in the kitchen, lonely and afraid." In recognizing what we have in common, we don't lose the individuality of you and me. As I see my own heart reflected in your eyes, we can have both the unity we share and the wonder of the uniqueness of each one of us.

THE ECOLOGICAL COMMUNITY

We exist not only within the human community, but also within the larger ecological community that makes human life possible. As living beings we live by the grace of other living beings.

A Navajo who was enrolled in the university decided to drop out and go back to living with his people. "Why?" asked my biologist friend Don Isaac "You're doing so well here!"

The Navajo drew two circles. In each one, he drew a collection of symbols around the inside of the rim: corn, clouds, rain, animal figures, and so on. In the left-hand circle, he put a human figure in the middle. In the right-hand circle, he placed the human figure among the other figures around the inside of the rim, the same size as all the rest.

He pointed to the circle on the left and said: "This is the white man's world." He pointed to the circle on the right and said, "This is the Indian's world. I cannot live in the white man's world any longer."

We need to regain our sense of proportion, our awareness that we are just one strand of the interwoven fabric of life on our earth. This is the great lesson that the American Indian peoples offer us.

Even in the midst of the concrete and asphalt of a city, I can find a park here and there where I can touch the earth. Or at least I can put my hand against a wall and feel the texture of a brick fashioned from red clay.

One afternoon I stood on a high cliff above the sea. A group of seagulls caught the currents of the wind nearby and rode them back and forth, calling out to each other and answering in obvious delight.

That reminded me of a winter day years before when I came upon a group of ducks in a field. As I watched them, the clouds parted and for about two minutes the sky broke into beautiful colors of crimson and gold. One duck looked up, saw it, and started quacking. Then all the rest stopped what they were doing and looked up too, directly at the spot where the light came through the clouds, and started quacking joyfully. When the clouds closed the opening and the sky turned gray again, they turned back to their other activities. Those ducks appreciated the beauty of that moment just as I did, and the seagulls appreciated the joy of their play just as I appreciate the joy of mine.

Naturalist Loren Eiseley says, "I find many versions of myself, with fur and grimaces, surveying my activities from behind leaves and thickets" (1972, p. 161). Eiseley likens humans to the latest bloom on a great tree that stretches backward into the dim recesses of eternity. Each creature is a leaf or a branch on that tree, and the tree is the great stream of life itself.

We have no choice now but to understand the interdependence of all living beings. Our Earth Mother cannot endure our brutality and arrogance forever. Even the timeless seas, which have become our cesspools of last resort, are gravely ill.

Captain Jacques Cousteau, who has spent a lifetime studying the oceanic depths, speaks with alarm of the pollution in the remotest oceans. If we are to survive and prosper, the ethics of ecology must be recognized.

This will cost us something. Cousteau estimates that saving our environment will take an investment of about 6 percent per year of our gross national product—appreciably less than the cost of the credit it takes to keep our economy going. We can afford that. *To pass the earth along to our descendants in a condition no worse than that in which we received it* is probably the most important gift we can give them.

"The world is a sacred vessel, which must not be tampered with or grabbed after," wrote Lao-tzu (1961). In that spirit, we can learn to live with our Earth rather than against it.

References

Abramson, L. Y., Seligman, Martin, & Teasdale, J. D. (1978). Learned helplessness in humans: Critique and reformulation. *Journal of Abnormal Psychology, 87* (1), 49–74.

Adler, Alfred (1964). *The individual psychology of Alfred Adler: A systematic presentation in selections from his writings* (H. L. Ansbacher & R. R. Ansbacher, Eds.). New York: Harper.

Adler, Alfred (1973). *Superiority and social interest.* New York: Viking.

Adorno, T. W., Frenkel-Brunswick, Else, Levinson, Daniel J., & Sanford, R. Nevitt (1950). *The authoritarian personality.* New York: Harper.

Alberti, Robert E., & Emmons, Michael L. (1982). *Your perfect right: A guide to assertive living.* San Luis Obispo, CA: Impact.

Alexander, Gene (1982). Family therapy for children. Unpublished manuscript, San Francisco.

Alinsky, Saul D. (1969). *Reveille for radicals.* New York: Random House.

Alinsky, Saul D. (1972). *Rules for radicals.* New York: Random House.

Allport, Gordon W. (1958). *The nature of prejudice.* Garden City, NY: Doubleday.

Allyon, T., & Azrin, Nathan (1968). *The token economy: A motivational system for therapy and rehabilitation.* New York: Appleton-Century-Crofts.

Anderson, Norman H. (1978). Cognitive algebra: Integration theory applied to social attribution. In L. Berkowitz (Ed.), *Cognitive theories in social psychology.* New York: Academic Press.

Anderson, Walt (1980). *Open secrets: A Western guide to Tibetan Buddhism.* New York: Penguin.

Arkoff, Abe (1980). *Psychology and personal growth* (2nd ed.). Boston: Allyn & Bacon.

Ascher, L. Michael, & Cautela, Joseph R. (1974). An experimental study of covert extinction. *Journal of Behavior Therapy and Experimental Psychiatry, 5* (3-4), 233–238.

Asimov, Isaac (1970). *Foundation.* New York: Avon.

Aurelius, Marcus (1937). *Meditations.* The Harvard Classics. New York: Collier.

Averill, James (1981). Studies of anger and aggression: Implications for theories of emotion. Paper presented at the convention of the American Psychological Association, Los Angeles.

Azrin, Nathan (1967, May). Pain and aggression. *Psychology Today,* pp. 26–33.

Baba, Meher (1967). *Discourses.* San Francisco: Sufism Reoriented.

Bach, George (1974). *Creative aggression: The art of assertive living.* New York: Avon.

Bach, George, & Wyden, Peter (1970). *The intimate enemy: How to fight fair in love and marriage.* New York: Avon.

Baez, Joan (1969). *Daybreak.* New York: Avon.

Bahm, A. J. (1958). *Philosophy of the Buddha.* New York: Capricorn.

Bandler, Richard, & Grinder, John (1975). *The structure of magic.* Palo Alto, CA: Science and Behavior Books.

Bandler, Richard, & Grinder, John (1979). *Frogs into princes.* Moab, UT: Real People Press.

Bandura, Albert (1969). *Principles of behavior modification.* New York: Holt, Rinehart and Winston.

Bandura, Albert (1977). *Social learning theory.* Englewood Cliffs, N.J.: Prentice-Hall.

Bandura, Albert (1982). Self-efficacy mechanisms in human agency. *American Psychologist, 37* (2), 122–147.

Bandura, Albert, & Walters, Richard H. (1959). *Adolescent aggression: A study of the influence of child-training practices and family interrelationships.* New York: Ronald.

Bandura, Albert, & Walters, Richard M. (1963). *Social learning and personality development.* New York: Holt, Rinehart and Winston.

Barron, Frank (1968). *Creativity and personal freedom.* New York: Van Nostrand.

Barron, Frank (1969). *Creative person and creative process.* New York: Holt, Rinehart and Winston.

Beck, Aaron (1972). *Depression: Causes and treatment.* Philadelphia: University of Pennsylvania Press.

Beck, Aaron (1976). *Cognitive therapy and the emotional disorders.* New York: International Universities Press.

Becker, Ernst (1976). *The denial of death.* New York: Macmillan.

Behaviordelia (1973). *An introduction to behavior modification.* Kalamazoo, MI.

Bem, Darryl (1965). An experimental analysis of self-persuasion. *Journal of Experimental Social Psychology, 1,* 199–218.

Bem, Darryl (1967). Self-perception: An alternative interpretation of cognitive dissonance phenomena. *Psychological Review, 74,* 183–200.

Bem, Darryl (1972). Self-perception theory. In L. Berkowitz (Ed.), *Advances in experimental social psychology* (Vol. 6). New York: Academic Press.

Bennett, E. A. (1967). *What Jung really said.* New York: Schocken.

Berkowitz, Leonard (1980). *A survey of social psychology.* New York: Holt, Rinehart and Winston.

Berne, Eric (1961). *Transactional analysis in psychotherapy: A systematic individual and social psychiatry.* New York: Grove Press.

Berne, Eric (1978). *Games people play.* New York: Ballantine.

Berscheid, Ellen, & Walster, Elaine (1978). *A new look at love.* Reading, MA: Addison-Wesley.

Bible, Jerusalem (1971). (Alexander Jones, Ed.) Garden City, NY: Doubleday.

Bible, King James (1974). Nashville, TN: Gideon Bible Society.

Bible, New English (1970). London: Oxford University Press.

Bloomfield, Harold H. (1975). *TM: Discovering inner energy and overcoming stress.* New York: Delacorte.

Bolles, Richard (1981). *What color is your parachute?* Berkeley, CA: Ten Speed Press.

Boston Women's Health Book Collective (1976). *Our bodies, our selves* (2nd ed.). New York: Simon & Schuster.

Boszormenyi-Nagy, Ivan (1965a). A theory of relationships: Experience and transaction. In Ivan Boszormenyi-Nagy & James L. Framo (Eds.), *Intensive family therapy.* New York: Harper & Row.

Boszormenyi-Nagy, Ivan (1965b). Intensive family therapy as process. In Ivan Boszormenyi-Nagy & James L. Framo (Eds.), *Intensive family therapy.* New York: Harper & Row.

Bowen, Murray (1965). Family psychotherapy with schizophrenia in the hospital and in private practice. In Ivan Boszormenyi-Nagy and James L. Framo (Eds.), *Intensive family therapy.* New York: Harper & Row.

Bowen, Murray (1971). The use of family theory in clinical practice. In J. Haley (Ed.), *Changing families.* New York: Grune & Stratton.

Bowen, Murray (1972). *Family therapy in clinical practice.* New York: Aronson.

Bowlby, John (1979). *The making and breaking of affectional bonds* London: Tavistock.

Brehm, Jack, & Cohen, Arthur R. (1962). *Explorations in cognitive dissonance.* New York: Wiley.

Brice, Norman B. (n.d.). Blame is the name of a no-win game. Unpublished paper, Chico State University.

Bruch, M. A. (1975). Influence of model characteristics on psychiatric patients' interview anxiety. *Journal of Abnormal Psychology, 84,* 290–294.

Buber, Martin (1958). *I and thou* (2nd ed.). New York: Scribners.

Buber, Martin, & Glatzer, Nahum N. (1971). *Way of response.* New York: Schocken.

Buddha. See Bahm, 1958; Byles, 1957; Kelen, 1967; Saddhatissa, 1971; Thera, 1962.

Bugenthal, James (1965). *The search for authenticity: An existential-analytic approach to psychotherapy.* New York: Holt, Rinehart and Winston.

Bugenthal, James (1976). *The search for existential identity: Patient-therapist dialogues in humanistic psychotherapy.* San Francisco: Jossey-Bass.

Bugenthal, James (1980). *The search for authenticity: An existential-analytic approach to psychotherapy* (2nd ed.). New York: Holt, Rinehart and Winston.

Bugenthal, James (1981). Address presented at Sonoma State University, Rohnert Park, CA.

Byles, Marie Beuzeville (1957). *Footprints of Gautama the Buddha.* Wheaton, IL: Theosophical Publishing House.

Capra, Fritjof (1977). *The tao of physics.* New York: Bantam.

Castaneda, Carlos (1972). *Journey to Ixtlan: The lessons of Don Juan.* New York: Simon & Schuster.

Cohen, Arthur (1964). *Attitude change and social influence.* New York: Basic Books.

Comfort, Alex (1968, February 18). Reported in *The New York Times.*

Condry, John C. (1981). Experimental approaches to intrinsic motivation: Implications for the use of social control. Paper presented at the meeting of the American Psychological Association, Los Angeles.

Corey, Gerald (1983). *I never knew I had a choice* (2nd ed.). Monterey, CA: Brooks/Cole.

Cousteau, Jacques. Untitled brochure. N.p. Cousteau Society.

Curtis, John D., & Detert, Richard A. (1981). *How to relax: A holistic approach to stress management.* Palo Alto, CA: Mayfield.

Dahms, Alan M. (1972). *Emotional intimacy: Overlooked requirement for survival.* Boulder, CO: Pruett.

Day, Ingeborg (1980, June). What makes you cry. *Ms,* pp. 46–55.

De Bono, Edward (1971). *New think: The use of lateral thinking in the generation of new ideas.* New York: Avon.

Dement, William C. (1976). *Some must watch while some must sleep.* San Francisco: San Francisco Book Co.

Deutsch, Morton (1973). *The resolution of conflict: Constructive and destructive processes.* New Haven, CT: Yale University Press.

Dogen (1971). *A primer of Soto Zen: A translation of Dogen's Shobogenzo Zuimonki* (Reiho Masunaga, Trans.). Honolulu: East-West Center Press.

Dollard, J., Doob, L., Miller, N., Mowrer, O. H., & Sears, R. (1939). *Frustration and aggression.* New Haven: Yale University Press.

Donovan, Marilee, & Pierce, Sandra (1976). *Cancer care nursing.* New York: Appleton-Century-Crofts.

Dreikurs, Rudolf, & Grey, Loren (1968). *Logical consequences: A new approach to discipline.* New York: Hawthorn.

Egan, Gerard (1977). *You and me: The skills of communicating and relating to others.* Monterey, CA: Brooks/Cole.

Egan, Gerard, & Cowan, Michael A. (1980). *Moving into adulthood.* Monterey, CA: Brooks/Cole.

Eiseley, Loren (1972). *The unexpected universe.* New York: Harcourt Brace Jovanovich.

Ellis, Albert (1975). *How to live with a "neurotic."* New York: Crown.

Ellis, Albert, & Grieger, R. (1977). *Handbook of rational emotive therapy.* Berlin and New York: Springer-Verlag.

Ellis, Albert, & Harper, R. A. (1975). *A new guide to rational living.* Englewood Cliffs, NJ: Prentice-Hall.

Epictetus (1937). *The golden sayings of Epictetus* (Hastings Crossley, Trans.). The Harvard Classics. New York: Collier.

Erikson, Erik (1964). *Childhood and society.* New York: Norton.

Estes, William K. (1944). An experimental study of punishment. *Psychological Monographs, 57* (263).

Evans-Wentz, W. Y., Ed. (1960). *Tibetan book of the dead.* London: Oxford University Press.

Eysenck, Hans J. (1968). A theory of the incubation of anxiety/fear responses. *Behavior Research and Therapy, 6,* 309–322.

Faraday, Ann (1981). *Dream power.* New York: Berkley.

Fast, Julius (1971). *Body language.* New York: Pocket Books.

Feifel, Herman (1977). *New meanings of death.* New York: McGraw-Hill.

Fenichel, Otto (1945). *The psychoanalytic theory of neurosis.* New York: Norton.

Feshbach, Seymour (1970). Aggression. In P. H. Mussen (Ed.), *Carmichael's manual of child psychology* (Vol. 2). New York: Viking.

Festinger, Leon (1957). *A theory of cognitive dissonance.* Stanford, CA: Stanford University Press.

Figler, Howard (1979). *The complete job search handbook.* New York: Holt, Rinehart and Winston.

Fisher, Ronald J. (1982). *Social psychology: An applied approach.* New York: St. Martin's.

Fordham, Frieda (1966). *An introduction to Jung's psychology.* Middlesex and New York: Penguin.

French, John R. P., Jr., & Raven, Bertram H. (1959). The bases of social power. In Dorwin Cartwright (Ed.), *Studies in social power* (pp. 150–151). Ann Arbor: Institute for Social Research, University of Michigan.

Freud, Anna (1937). *The ego and the mechanisms of defense.* New York: International Universities Press.

Freud, Sigmund (1938). *The basic writings of Sigmund Freud* (A. A. Brill, Trans., Ed.). New York: Modern Library.

Freud, Sigmund (1959). *Collected papers* (5 vols.; James Strachey, Ed.). New York: Basic Books.

Freud, Sigmund (1967). *Interpretation of dreams* (James Strachey, Trans.). New York: Avon.

Friedman, Mayer, & Rosenman, Ray (1974). *Type A behavior and your heart.* New York: Fawcett.

Fromm, Erich (1955). *The sane society.* New York: Holt, Rinehart and Winston.

Fromm, Erich (1970). *The art of loving.* New York: Bantam.

Fromm, Erich (1971). *Escape from freedom.* New York: Avon.

Frumkes, Lewis Burke (1980, February). One-night stands—risky or fun? *Vogue,* pp. 85–87.

Fujimoto, Roshi Rindo (1961). *The way of Zazen.* Cambridge, MA: Cambridge Buddhist Association.

Funkenstein, D. H., King, S. B., & Drolette, M. (1957). *Mastery of stress.* Cambridge, MA: Harvard University Press.

Gandhi, Mahatma (1960). *All men are brothers.* Ahmedabad: Navajivan.

Gandhi, Mahatma (1965). *Gandhi on non-violence.* New York: New Directions.

Ganley, Anne I. (1981). Address given at "For Better or Worse," conference on wife abuse, Santa Rosa, CA.

Gardner, John (1971). *Self-renewal: The individual and the innovative society.* New York: Harper & Row.

Garfield, Patricia (1976). *Creative dreaming.* New York: Ballantine.

Gaskin, Steve ["Stephen"] (1970). *Monday night class.* Santa Rosa: Book Farm.

Geba, Bruno H. (1973). *Breathe away your tension.* New York: Random House.

Geba, Bruno H. (1974). *Vitality training for older adults.* New York: Random House.

Gendlin, Eugene (1978). *Focusing.* New York: Everest House.

Gibran, Kahlil (1969). *The prophet.* New York: Knopf.

Glasser, William (1965). *Reality therapy: A new approach to psychiatry.* New York: Harper & Row.

Goffman, Erving (1959). *The presentation of self in everyday life.* Garden City, NY: Doubleday.

Goldberg, Philip (1978). *Executive health.* New York: McGraw-Hill.

Goldiamond, Israel (1965). Self-control procedures in personal behavior problems. *Psychological Reports, 17* (3), 851–868. Reprinted in R. Ulrich, T. Stachnik, & J. Mabry (Eds.), *Control of human behavior* (Vol. 1, pp. 115–127). Glenview, IL: Scott, Foresman.

Goldstein, Jeffrey H. (1981). *Social psychology.* New York: Academic Press.

Goldstein, Joseph (1976). *The experience of insight*. Santa Cruz, CA: Unity Press.

Gollin, E. (1954). Forming impressions of personality. *Journal of Personality, 23*, pp. 65–76.

Gottman, John, et al. (1976). *A couple's guide to communication*. Champaign, IL: Research Press.

Greenberg, Rabbi Sidney (1967). *A treasury of the art of living*. Hollywood, CA: Wilshire.

Greenwald, Jerry (1976). *Creative intimacy*. New York: Simon & Schuster.

Gustaitis, Rasa (1969). *Turning on*. New York: Signet.

Haley, Jay (1978). *Problem-solving therapy: New strategies for effective family therapy*. New York: Harper & Row.

Hall, Calvin (1966). *The meaning of dreams*. New York: McGraw-Hill.

Hall, Robert (1975). My life measured out in abandoned words. In John O. Stevens (Ed.), *Gestalt is*. Moab, UT: Real People Press.

Hampden-Turner, Charles (1981). *Maps of the mind*. New York: Macmillan-Collier.

Hampton, Peter J. (1978). The many faces of anger. *Psychology, 15* (1), 35–44.

Harlow, Harry F. (1953). Motivation as a factor in new responses. In *Current theory and research in motivation: A symposium*. Lincoln: University of Nebraska Press.

Harlow, Harry F. (1973). *Learning to love*. St. Louis, MO: Albion Press.

Harris, Thomas A. (1973). *I'm OK—You're OK*. New York: Avon.

Heider, Fritz (1946). Attitudes and cognitive organization. *Journal of Personality, 21*, 107–112.

Heider, Fritz (1958). *The psychology of interpersonal relations*. New York: Wiley.

Hillman, James (1975). *Re-visioning psychology*. New York: Harper & Row.

Hillman, James (1980). Address presented at the convention of the American Psychiatric Association, San Francisco.

Hollander, Edwin P. (1981). *Principles and methods of social psychology* (4th ed.). Oxford and New York: Oxford University Press.

Holmes, Thomas, & Rahe, Richard H. (1967). The social readjustment rating scale. *Journal of Psychosomatic Research, 11*, 213–218.

Horkheimer, Max (1972). *Critical theory*. New York: Seabury.

Horn, Niela Miller (1981). Paper presented at the annual meeting of the Association for Humanistic Psychology, Los Angeles.

Horney, Karen (1945). *Our inner conflicts: A constructive theory of neurosis*. New York: Norton.

Horney, Karen (1950). *Neurosis and human growth*. New York: Norton.

Horowitz, Laurence J. (1966). Parental intervention and behavior modification of under-achievers. Unpublished doctoral dissertation, Stanford University, Stanford, CA.

Houston, John (1981). *The pursuit of happiness*. Glenville, IL: Scott, Foresman.

Hunt, Morton K. (1959). *The natural history of love*. New York: Knopf.

Hupka, Ralph B., Jung, John, & Porteus, Robert (1981). Strategies for impression management in romantic jealousy situations. In Eliot Aronson (Chair), *Exploring sexual jealousy: An interdisciplinary approach*. Symposium presented at the convention of the American Psychological Association, Los Angeles.

Huxley, Aldous (1962). *Island*. New York: Harper & Row.

I Ching. See Wilhelm, Richard, & Baynes, Carl F.

Irish, Richard (1978). *Go hire yourself an employer*. New York: Anchor.

Isbell, Donald, & Nelson, Sally J. (1980). *Understanding and managing stress: A preventative health program*. Internal document, Kaiser Permanente Foundation, Los Angeles.

Jackson, Thomas (1978). *Guerrilla tactics in the job market*. New York: Bantam.

Jacobson, Edmund (1938). *Progressive relaxation*. Chicago: University of Chicago Press.

Jacobson, Edmund (1970). *You must relax*. New York: McGraw-Hill.

Jager, Bernd (1975). Address presented at Sonoma State University, Rohnert Park, CA.

Jakubowski, Patricia, & Lange, Arthur (1978). *The assertive option*. Champaign, IL: Research Press.

Janis, Irving (1971). *Stress and frustration*. New York: Harcourt Brace Jovanovich.

Johnson, Wendell (1946). *People in quandaries: The semantics of personal adjustment*. New York: Harper.

Jones, E. (1964). *Ingratiation: A social psychological analysis*. New York: Appleton-Century-Crofts.

Jones, E. E., & Davis, K. E. (1965). From acts to dispositions. In L. Berkowitz (Ed.), *Advances in experimental social psychology* (Vol. 2). New York: Academic Press.

Jones, E. E., Gergen, K. J., & Davis, K. E. (1962). Some determinants of reactions to being approved or disapproved as a person. *Psychological Monographs, 76*, (2, whole no. 521).

Jourard, Sidney (1968). *Disclosing man to himself*. Princeton, NJ: Van Nostrand.

Jourard, Sidney (1971a). *The transparent self* (2nd ed.). Princeton, NJ: Van Nostrand.

Jourard, Sidney (1971b). *Self-disclosure: An experimental analysis of the transparent self*. New York: Wiley Interscience.

Jourard, Sidney (1975, July). Marriage is for life. *Journal of Marriage and the Family, 199–208*.

Jourard, Sidney, & Landsman, Ted (1980). *The healthy personality*. New York: Macmillan.

Jung, Carl G. (1960–1972). *The collected works of Carl G. Jung* (2nd ed.). Bollingen Series 20. Princeton: Princeton University Press.

Jung, Carl G. (1971). *The portable Jung* (Joseph Campbell, Ed.). New York: Viking.

Jung, Carl G. (1974). *Dreams* (R. F. C. Hull, Trans.). Princeton: Princeton University Press.

Jung, Carl G., Ed. (1968). *Man and his symbols*. New York: Dell.

Kahane, Howard (1976). *Logic and contemporary rhetoric*. Belmont, CA: Wadsworth.

Kantor, David, & Lehr, William (1976). *Inside the family*. New York: Harper & Row.

Katz, Martin, & Sanborn, Ken (1981, Winter). Reported in "Center Currents" column, *East-West Perspectives*, p. 2. Honolulu: East-West Center.

Katz, Stuart, & Burnstein, Eugene (1973). Is an out-of-role act credible to biased observers and does it affect the credibility of neutral acts? Unpublished manuscript, University of Michigan.

Keleman, Stanley (1975). *The human ground: Sexuality, self, and survival*. Palo Alto, CA: Science and Behavior Books.

Keleman, Stanley (1976). *Your body speaks its mind*. New York: Pocket Books.

Kelen, Betty (1969). *Gautama Buddha in life and legend*. New York: Avon.

Kelley, Harold H. (1950). The warm-cold variable in first impressions of persons. *Journal of Personality, 18*, 431–439.

Kelley, Harold H. (1967). Attribution theory in social psychology. In David Levine (Ed.), *Nebraska Symposium on Motivation* (Vol. 15). Lincoln: University of Nebraska Press.

Kelley, Harold H. (1972a). *Causal schemata and the attribution process*. Morristown, NJ: Silver Burdett/General Learning Press.

Kelley, Harold H. (1972b). Attribution in social interaction. In E. E. Jones, D. E. Kanouse, H. H. Kelley, R. E. Nisbett, S. Valins, & B. Wiener (Eds.), *Attribution: Perceiving the causes of behavior*. Morristown, NJ: General Learning Corp.

Kelley, Harold H. (1973). The processes of causal attribution. *American Psychologist, 28*, 107–128.

Kelley, Harold H. (1979). *Personal relationships*. Hillsdale, NJ: Erlbaum.

Kelley, Harold H., & Michela, S. L. (1980). Attribution theory and research. *Annual Review of Psychology, 31*, 457–502.

Kelly, George A. (1964). Man's construction of his alternatives. In Eugene A. Southwell & Michael Merbaum (Eds.), *Personality: Readings in theory and research* (pp. 344–361). Belmont, CA: Wadsworth.

Kelman, Herbert (1974). Attitudes are alive and well and gainfully employed in the sphere of action. *American Psychologist, 29*, 310–335.

Kerr, Carmen (1978). *Sex for women*. New York: Grove Press.

Keyes, Ken (1975). *Handbook for higher consciousness* (5th ed.). St. Mary, KY: Living Love Publications.

Keyes, Ken (1979). *A conscious person's guide to relationships*. St. Mary, KY: Living Love Publications.

Kiechel, Walter III (1981, November 16). Facing up to executive anger. *Fortune*, p. 205.

King, Martin Luther, Jr. (1967). *Where do we go from here: Chaos or community?* New York: Harper & Row.

Knox, R. E., & Inkster, J. A. (1968). Postdecision dissonance at post time. *Journal of Personality and Social Psychology, 8*, 319–323.

Koestler, Arthur (1964). *Action of creation*. New York: Macmillan.

Koffka, Kurt (1967). *Principles of Gestalt psychology*. New York: Harcourt Brace Jovanovich.

Kohler, Wolfgang (1964). *Gestalt psychology: An introduction to new conceptions in modern psychology*. New York: New American Library.

Kopp, Sheldon (1980). *Mirror, mask, and shadow: The risks and rewards of self-acceptance.* New York: Bantam.

Korda, Michael (1981, September). Self-power. *Self,* pp. 69–72.

Korzybski, Alfred (1958). *Science and society: An introduction to non-Aristotelian systems and general semantics* (4th ed.). New York: Institute of General Semantics.

Krantzler, Mel (1979). *Learning to love again.* New York: Bantam.

Krutch, Joseph Wood (1966). *The great chain of life.* New York: Pyramid.

Kübler-Ross, Elisabeth (1974). *Questions and answers on death and dying.* New York: Macmillan.

Kübler-Ross, Elisabeth (1975, March 8). How it feels to die. *Sacramento Union,* UPI release.

Kurtz, Ron, & Prestera, Hector (1976). *The body reveals.* New York: Harper & Row.

Kwong, Jakusho (1975). Address presented at Sonoma State University, Rohnert Park, CA.

Laing, R. D. (1969). *The divided self.* New York: Pantheon.

Laing, R. D. (1971). *Politics of the family.* New York: Basic Books.

Laing, R. D. (1972). *Self and others.* New York: Penguin.

Lakein, Alan (1974). *How to get control of your time and your life.* New York: New American Library.

Lamberth, John, Rappaport, Herbert, & Rappaport, Margaret (1978). *Personality: An introduction.* New York: Knopf.

Lamson, Ralph J. (1982). Building competence: The learned helplessness model of depression; the social learning theory of self-efficacy. Unpublished master's thesis, Sonoma State University, Rohnert Park, CA.

Lange, Arthur, & Jakubowski, Patricia (1976). *Responsible assertive behavior: Cognitive/behavioral procedures for trainers.* Champaign, IL: Research Press.

Lao-tzu (1961). *Tao teh ching* (John C. H. Wu, Trans.; Paul K. J. Sih, Ed.). New York: St. John's University Press.

Lasch, Christopher (1977). *Haven in a heartless world.* New York: Basic Books.

Lazarus, Arnold A. (1971). *Behavior therapy and beyond.* New York: McGraw-Hill.

Lecky, Prescott (1973). *Self-consistency: A theory of personality* (2nd ed.). Hamden, CT: Shoe String Press.

Lederer, William J., & Jackson, Don D. (1968). *The mirages of marriage.* New York: Norton.

Lederman, Janet (1969). *Anger and the rocking chair: Gestalt awareness with children.* New York: Viking.

Lee, Dorothy (1959). *Freedom and culture.* Englewood Cliffs, NJ: Prentice-Hall.

Lee, John Alan (1974, October). The styles of loving. *Psychology Today,* pp. 43–51.

Lee, John Alan (1976). *The colors of love.* Englewood Cliffs, NJ: Prentice-Hall.

Lehner, George F., & Kube, Ella (1964). *The dynamics of personal adjustment.* Englewood Cliffs, NJ: Prentice-Hall.

LeShan, Laurence (1977). *Alternate realities.* New York: Ballantine.

Levi, L. (1968). *Stress: Sources, management and prevention: Medical and psychological aspects of the stress of everyday life.* New York: Liveright.

Lewin, Kurt (1935). *A dynamic theory of personality.* New York: McGraw-Hill.

Lewin, Kurt (1948). *Resolving social conflicts.* New York: Harper.

Lewinsohn, Peter (1982). Depression. In A. S. Bellack, M. Herson, & A. E. Kazdin (Eds.), *International handbook of behavior modification and therapy.* New York: Plenum Press.

Lewis, Alec (1980). *The quotable quotations book.* New York: Crowell.

Liberman, Robert Paul, King, Larry W., De Risi, William J., & McCann, Michael (1975). *Personal effectiveness: Guiding people to assert themselves and improve their social skills.* Champaign, IL: Research Press.

Lidz, Theodore (1963). *The family and human adaptation.* New York: International Universities Press.

Lidz, Theodore, Fleck, Stephen, & Cornelison, Alice R. (1965). *Schizophrenia and the family.* New York: International Universities Press.

Lindner, Robert (1962). *Prescription for rebellion.* New York: Grove Press.

Livingston, Pat (1979). Communications workshop given at "California Renaissance," Association for Humanistic Psychology state convention, Sacramento, CA.

Lowen, Alexander (1976). *Bioenergetics.* New York: Penguin.

Lowy, Samuel (1942). *Foundations of dream interpretation.* London: Kegan Paul.

Luthman, Shirley Gehrke (1972). *Intimacy: The essence of male and female.* San Rafael, CA: Mehitabel & Company.

Luthman, Shirley, & Kirshenbaum, Martin (1974). *The dynamic family.* Palo Alto, CA: Science and Behavior Books.

Lynch, Carmen (1978). Workshop sponsored by Sonoma County Schools. County Administration Center, Santa Rosa, CA.

Lynch, Carmen (1980). Who you're with is where you're at. Workshop given at Sonoma County Library, Santa Rosa, CA.

Mahler, Margaret S., Pine, Fred, & Bergman, Annie (1975). *The psychological birth of the human infant.* New York: Basic Books.

Mao Tse-Tung [Zedong] (1967). *On contradiction.* Peking: Foreign Languages Press.

Marcuse, Herbert (1964). *One-dimensional man.* Boston: Beacon.

Martin, Gary, & Pear, Joseph (1983). *Behavior modification: What it is and how to do it* (2nd ed.). Englewood Cliffs, NJ: Prentice-Hall.

Martin, H. P., & Beezley, P. (1976). Personality of abused children. In H. P. Martin (Ed.), *The abused child.* Cambridge, MA: Ballinger.

Martin, H. P., & Beezley, P. (1977). Behavioral observations of abused children. *Developmental Medicine and Child Neurology, 19* (3), 373–387.

Marx, Martin B., Garrity, Thomas F., & Bowers, Frank R. (1975). The influence of recent life experiences on the health of college freshmen. *Journal of Psychosomatic Research, 19,* p. 97.

Maslow, Abraham (1968). *Toward a psychology of being* (2nd ed.). Princeton, NJ: Van Nostrand.

Maslow, Abraham (1971). *The farther reaches of human nature.* New York: Viking.

Maslow, Abraham (1976). *Religions, values, and peak experiences.* New York: Penguin.

Masters, William H., & Johnson, Virginia E. (1966). *Human sexual response.* New York: Little, Brown.

Masters, William H., & Johnson, Virginia E. (1970, May). Sex and the married woman. *McCall's,* p. 68.

Masters, William H., & Johnson, Virginia E. (1980). *Human sexual inadequacy.* New York: Bantam.

May, Gerald (1980). A pilgrimage of healing: Personal thoughts of a transpersonal psychotherapist. In S. Boorstein (Ed.), *Transpersonal psychotherapy.* Palo Alto, CA: Science and Behavior Books.

May, Rollo (1967). *Man's search for himself.* New York: New American Library.

May, Rollo (1972). *Power and innocence.* New York: Dell.

May, Rollo (1974). *Love and will.* New York: Dell.

May, Rollo (1976). *The courage to create.* New York: Bantam.

Maynard, Joyce (1973). Joyce Maynard on virginity. In *Looking back.* Cited in Alec Lewis (1980), *The quotable quotations book.* New York: Crowell.

McIntire, Roger W. (1970). *For love of children: Behavioral psychology for parents.* Del Mar, CA: CRM Books.

Meher Baba (1967). *Discourses* (6th ed.). San Francisco: Sufism Reoriented.

Meichenbaum, Donald H. (1977). *Cognitive behavior modification.* New York: Plenum Press.

Meichenbaum, Donald H., & Tuck, D. (1976). The cognitive behavioral management of anxiety, anger and pain. In P. Davidson (Ed.), *The behavioral management of anxiety, depression, and pain.* New York: Brunner/Mazel.

Merleau-Ponty, Maurice (1964). *The primacy of perception* (James M. Edie, Ed.). Evanston, IL: Northwestern University Press.

Michelozzi, Betty Neville. *Coming alive from nine to five: The career search handbook* (2nd ed.). Palo Alto, CA: Mayfield, 1984.

Miller, Neal E. (1941). The frustration-aggression hypothesis. *Psychological Review, 48,* 337–342.

Miller, Neal E. (1948). Studies of fear as an acquirable drive, I: Fear as motivation and fear reduction as reinforcement in the learning of new responses. *Journal of Experimental Psychology, 38,* 89–101.

Miller, Neal, & Dollard, John (1941). *Social learning and imitation.* New Haven, CT: Yale University Press.

Minuchin, Salvador (1969). *Families of the slums.* New York: Basic Books.

Missildine, Hugh (1963). *Your inner child of the past.* New York: Simon & Schuster.

Miura, Isshu, & Sasaki, Ruth Fuller (1965). *The Zen koan: Its history and use in Rinzai Zen.* New York: Harcourt Brace Jovanovich.

Morgenstern, Debra (1980, March). Violence—all in the family. *McCall's.*

Moustakas, Clark (1961a). *Creativity and conformity.* Princeton, NJ: Van Nostrand.

Moustakas, Clark (1961b). *Loneliness.* Englewood Cliffs, NJ: Prentice-Hall.

Murphy, Michael (1973). *Golf in the kingdom.* New York: Delta.

Nelson, Sally J., & Isbell, Donald (1978). *Optimizing health and self-care journal.* Internal document, Kaiser Permanente Foundation, Los Angeles.

Nietzsche, Friedrich (1954). *The portable Nietzsche* (Walter Kaufmann, Trans.). New York: Viking.

Nietzsche, Friedrich (1966). *Thus spake Zarathustra* (Walter Kaufmann, Trans.). New York: Viking.

Ornstein, Robert E. (1977). *The psychology of consciousness.* New York: Harcourt Brace Jovanovich.

Overstreet, Bonaro (1971). *Understanding fear in ourselves and others.* New York: Harper & Row.

Peacock, Mary (1980, June). The importance of crying. *Ms.,* p. 45.

Pearson, Leonard (1969). *Death and dying: Current issues in the treatment of the dying person.* New York: Aronson.

Pelletier, Kenneth R. (1977). *Mind as healer, mind as slayer: A holistic approach to preventing stress disorders.* New York: Dell.

Pelletier, Kenneth R. (1978). *Toward a science of consciousness.* New York: Delta.

Perls, Frederick S. [Fritz] (1947). *Ego, hunger, and aggression: The beginning of Gestalt therapy.* New York: Random House.

Perls, Frederick S. [Fritz] (1969a). *Gestalt therapy verbatim.* Moab, UT: Real People Press.

Perls, Fritz (1969b). *In and out the garbage pail.* Moab, UT: Real People Press.

Perls, Fritz (1973). *The Gestalt approach/Eyewitness to therapy.* Palo Alto, CA: Science and Behavior Books.

Perls, Frederick S. [Fritz], Hefferline, Ralph F., & Goodman, Paul (1965). *Gestalt therapy: Excitement and growth in the human personality.* New York: Dell.

Perry, John W. (1962). *The far side of madness.* Englewood Cliffs, NJ: Prentice-Hall.

Peter Pauper Press (1959). *Zen Buddhism: An introduction to Zen.* Mt. Vernon, NY.

Perutz, Kathrin (1972). *Marriage is hell.* New York: Morrow.

Pirsig, Robert M. (1976). *Zen and the art of motorcycle maintenance.* New York: Bantam.

Polster, Miriam (1982). Comments at training workshop, Gestalt Institute of San Diego, San Diego, CA.

Premack, David (1965). Reinforcement theory. In *Nebraska Symposium on Motivation* (Vol. 13 pp. 123–180). Lincoln: University of Nebraska Press.

Prince, George M. (1970). *The practice of creativity: A manual for dynamic group problem solving.* New York: Harper & Row.

Progoff, Ira (1975). *At a journal workshop.* New York: Dialogue House.

Rachman, Stanley J. (1978). *Fear and courage.* San Francisco: Freeman.

Rahe, Richard H. (1972). Subjects' recent life changes and their near-future illness susceptibility. *Advances in Psychosomatic Medicine, 8,* 2–19.

Ram Dass, Baba, & the Lama Foundation (1971). *Be here now.* New York: Harmony.

Raven, Bertram H., & Rubin, Jeffrey (1976). *Social psychology: People in groups.* New York: Wiley.

Reich, Wilhelm (1949). *Character analysis.* New York: Noonday Press.

Reps, Paul, Ed. (1957). *Zen flesh, Zen bones: A collection of Zen and pre-Zen writings.* Garden City, NY: Doubleday.

Resnick, Stella (1975). Gestalt therapy as a meditative practice. In John O. Stevens (Ed.), *Gestalt is.* Moab, UT: Real People Press.

Rimm, David C., & Masters, John (1979). *Behavior therapy: Techniques and empirical findings.* New York: Academic Press.

Rinder, Walter (1973). *Follow your heart.* Millbrae, CA: Celestial Arts.

Ritter, B. (1969). Eliminating excessive fears of the environment through contact desensitization. In J. D. Krumboltz & C. G. Thoreson (Eds.), *Behavioral counseling: Cases and techniques.* New York: Holt, Rinehart and Winston.

Roddenberry, Gene (1982). Address given at King Kamehameha Hotel, Kailua-Kona, Hawaii.

Rogers, Carl (1961). *On becoming a person: A therapist's view of psychotherapy.* Boston: Houghton Mifflin.

Rogers, Carl (1977). *On personal power.* New York: Delacorte.

Rokeach, Milton (1960). *The open and closed mind: Investigations into the nature of belief systems and personality systems.* New York: Basic Books.

Rokeach, Milton (1968). *Beliefs, attitudes, and values.* San Francisco: Jossey-Bass.

Rosenman, Martin (1979). *Loving styles: A guide for increasing intimacy.* Englewood Cliffs, NJ: Prentice-Hall.

Ross, L. (1977). The intuitive psychologist and his shortcomings: Distortions in the attribution process. In L. Berkowitz (Ed.), *Advances in experimental social psychology* (Vol. 10, pp. 173–220). New York: Academic Press.

Ross, L., Greene, S., & House, P. (1977). The "false consensus" effect: An egocentric bias in social perception and attribution processes. *Journal of Experimental Social Psychology, 13,* 279–301.

Rossi, Ernest L. (1972). *Dreams and the growth of personality: Expanding awareness in psychotherapy.* New York: Pergamon.

Rousseau, Jean Jacques (1967). The social contract. In *The social contract and Discourse on the origin of inequality.* New York: Pocket Books.

Rowe, Clarence J. (1980). *An outline of psychiatry.* Dubuque, IA: William C. Brown.

Rubin, Theodore Isaac (1969). *The angry book.* New York: Collier.

Rubin, Zick (1973). *Liking and loving.* New York: Holt, Rinehart and Winston.

Rush, A. John (1978). *Cognitive behavior therapy in managing depression.* BMI Audio Cassettes. New York: Guilford Publications.

Rush, A. John, & Beck, Aaron (1978). Behavior therapy in adults with affective disorders. In M. Herson & S. Bellack (Eds.), *Behavior therapy in the psychiatric setting.* Baltimore, MD: Williams & Wilkins.

Russell, Bertrand (1930). *The conquest of happiness.* New York: Liveright.

Saddhatissa, H. (1971). *The Buddha's way.* New York: Braziller.

Sampson, Edward E. (1971). *Social psychology and contemporary society.* New York: Wiley.

Sartre, Jean Paul (1967). *Essays in existentialism.* Secaucus, NJ: Citadel Press.

Satir, Virginia (1972). *Peoplemaking.* Palo Alto, CA: Science and Behavior Books.

Schaffer, Laurence F., & Shoben, Edward J., Jr. (1956). *The psychology of adjustment* (2nd ed.). Boston: Houghton-Mifflin.

Schumacher, E. F., with Dillingham, Peter N. (1980). *Good work.* New York: Harper.

Scoresby, A. L. (1977). *The marriage dialogue.* Reading, MA: Addison-Wesley.

Sears, Robert R. (1941). Non-aggressive responses to frustration. *Psychological Review, 48,* 343–346.

Seligman, Martin E. P. (1971). Phobias and preparedness. *Behavior Therapy, 2,* 307–320.

Seligman, Martin E. P. (1975). *Helplessness: On depression, development, and death.* San Francisco: Freeman.

Selye, Hans (1974). *Stress without distress.* New York: New American Library.

Selye, Hans (1976). *The stress of life.* New York: McGraw-Hill.

Seton, Ernest T., & Seton, Julia M. (1966). *The gospel of the red man.* Santa Fe, NM: Seton Village.

Shah, Idries (1970a). *Tales of the dervishes.* New York: Dutton.

Shah, Idries (1970b). *The way of the Sufi.* New York: Dutton.

Shah, Idries (1972). *Caravan of dreams.* Baltimore, MD: Penguin.

Shapiro, Sam (1982). A vision of transpersonal psychology. *Psychologia, 25,* 195–204.

Sheehy, Gail (1976). *Passages.* New York: Dutton.

Simon, Sidney B., Howe, Leland W., & Kirshenbaum, Howard (1972). *Values clarification: A handbook of practical strategies for teachers and students.* New York: Hart.

Singer, Margaret, & Wynne, L. C. (1965). Thought disorder and the family relations of schizophrenics: IV: Results and implications. *Archives of General Psychiatry, 12,* 201–212.

Skinner, B. F. (1953). *Science and human behavior.* New York: Macmillan.

Smith, Manuel J. (1975). *When I say no, I feel guilty.* New York: Bantam.

Solomon, R. L., & Wynne, L. C. (1953). Traumatic avoidance learning: Acquisition in normal dogs. *Psychological Monographs, 67,* 354.

Solomon, R. L., & Wynne, L. C. (1954). Traumatic avoidance learning: The principles of anxiety conservation and partial irreversibility. *Psychological Review, 61,* 353–385.

Springer, Ann Murphy (1981, December 20). Quoted in: Taking the stress out of Christmas. *Santa Rosa Press Democrat.*

Stevens, Barry (1975). Voids, voids, noddings. In John O. Stevens (Ed.), *Gestalt is.* Moab, UT: Real People Press.

Stevens, John O. (1971). *Awareness: Exploring, experimenting, experiencing.* Moab, UT: Real People Press.

Stewart, Kilton (1954). *Pygmies and dream giants.* New York: Norton.

Storm, Hyemeyohsts (1972). *Seven arrows.* New York: Ballantine.

Suzuki, Daisetz Taitaro (1960). *Manual of Zen Buddhism.* New York: Grove Press.

Suzuki, Daisetz Taitaro, Fromm, Erich, & DeMartino, Richard (1960). *Zen Buddhism and psychoanalysis.* New York: Harper.

Suzuki, Shunryu (1970). *Zen mind, beginner's mind* (Trudy Dixon, Ed.). Tokyo and New York: Weatherhill.

Tappan, Gordon (1974). Address presented at Sonoma State University, Rohnert Park, CA.

Tappan, Gordon (1980). Address presented at Sonoma State University, Rohnert Park, CA.

Tavris, Carol (1983). *The anatomy of anger.* New York: Simon & Schuster.

Tessina, Tina, & Smith, Riley K. (1980). *How to be a couple and still be free.* North Hollywood, CA: Newcastle.

Tharp, Roland G., & Wetzel, Ralph J. (1969). *Behavior modification in the natural environment.* New York and London: Academic Press.

Thera, Nyanaponika (1962). *The heart of Buddhist meditation.* New York: Weiser.

Thoreau, Henry David (1960). *Thoreau on man and nature.* Mt. Vernon, NY: Peter Pauper Press.

Thoreau, Henry David (1971). *Walden, and other writings* (Joseph Wood Krutch, Ed.). New York: Bantam.

Tinbergen, Nikolas (1974). Etiology and stress diseases. *Science, 185,* 26.

Ullman, Montague, & Zimmerman, Nan (1979). *Working with dreams.* New York: Delacorte.

Upanishads, the breath of the eternal (1957). (Swami Prabhavenanda & Frederick Manchester, Trans.) New York: New American Library.

Van Dusen, Wilson (1972). *The natural depth in man.* New York: Random House/Bookworks.

Van Dusen, Wilson (1975). Wu Wei, No-mind, and the fertile void. In John O. Stevens (Ed.), *Gestalt is.* Moab, UT: Real People Press.

Van Nuys, David (1975, April). Second thoughts—dealing with anger: Detachment or denial? *Human Behavior,* pp. 14–15.

Velez, Lupe (1977). Quoted in Leta Clark (Ed.), *Women, women, women.* Cited in Alec Lewis (1980), *The quotable quotations book.* New York: Crowell.

von Bertanlaffy, Ludwig (1969). *General system theory: Essays on its foundation and development* (Rev. ed.). New York: Braziller.

von Franz, Marie Louise (1968). The process of individuation. In Carl G. Jung (Ed.), *Man and his symbols.* New York: Dell.

von Franz, Marie Louise (1979). *Jung's typology.* Dallas, TX: Spring Publications.

Walker, James L. (1971). *Body and soul.* Nashville, TN: Abingdon.

Watson, David, & Tharp, Roland (1981). *Self-directed behavior: Self-modification for personal adjustment* (3rd ed.). Monterey, CA: Brooks/Cole.

Watson, John B. (1924). *Psychology from the standpoint of a behaviorist* (2nd ed.). Philadelphia, PA: Lippincott.

Watson, John B. (1925). *Behaviorism.* New York: Norton.

Watts, Alan (1968). *The wisdom of insecurity.* New York: Random House.

Watzlawick, Paul, Beavin, Janet Helmick, & Jackson, Don D. (1967). *Pragmatics of human communication: A study of interactional patterns, pathologies, and paradoxes.* New York: Norton.

Watzlawick, Paul, Weakland, John M., & Fisch, Richard (1974). *Change: Principles of problem formation and problem resolution.* New York: Norton.

Way, L. (1950). *Adler's place in psychology.* London: George Allen & Unwin.

Webster's New World Dictionary of the American Language (1966). New York: World.

Weiler, Nicholas W. (1977). *Reality and career planning.* Reading, MA: Addison-Wesley.

Wertheimer, Max (1978). *Productive thinking.* Westport, CT: Greenwood Press.

White, Robert W. (1972). *The enterprise of living.* New York: Holt, Rinehart and Winston.

Wiessler, David A. (1984, January 2). Language takes a turn for "plusungood." *U.S. News and World Report,* p. 95.

Wild, John (1955). *The challenge of existentialism.* Bloomington, IN: Indiana University Press.

Wilhelm, Richard. (Trans.) (1956). *The secret of the golden flower: A Chinese book of life.* New York: Harcourt, Brace and World.

Wilhelm, Richard, & Baynes, Carl F. (Trans.) (1967). *I Ching, or Book of changes* (3rd ed.). Princeton, NJ: Princeton University Press.

Wolpe, Joseph (1982). *The practice of behavior therapy* (3rd ed.). New York: Pergamon.

Wynne, L. C. (1965). Some indications and contraindications for exploratory family therapy. In Ivan Boszormenyi-Nagy & James L. Framo (Eds.), *Intensive family therapy,* pp. 289–322. New York: Harper & Row.

Wynne, L. C., Ryckoff, I., Day, J., & Hirsch, S. (1958). Pseudomutuality in the family relations of schizophrenics. *Psychiatry, 21* (205).

Yankelovich, Daniel (1981). New rules in American life: Searching for self-fulfillment in a world turned upside down. *Psychology Today, 15* (4).

Yates, A. J. (1958). The application of learning theory to the treatment of tics. *Journal of Abnormal and Social Psychology, 56,* 175–182.

Yogi, Maharishi Mahesh (1975). *Transcendental meditation.* New York: New American Library.

Zajonc, Robert B. (1960). The process of cognitive tuning in communication. *Journal of Abnormal and Social Psychology, 61,* 159–168.

Zimbardo, Philip (1978). *Shyness.* New York: Harcourt Brace Jovanovich.

Index

Choice (*continued*)
and dissonance, 214–15
effects of environment on, 44–45
guidance of, by reality, 199
removing obstacles to, 50
self-definition through, 45–46
in sexual behavior, 319–21
and stress, 185
subjects v. objects and, 47–49
Christianity
and aggression, 156, 157
and fear, 133
and repentance, 260
Chronic anxiety, 135
Chronic stress, 184
CIA, 132
Clairvoyant dreams, 236–37
Cliché layer of personality, 169
Closed questions, 92
Close Encounters (exercise), 294
Cocaine, 249
Coercive power, 106
Cognitive and Active Valuing (exercise), 220
Cognitive consistency, 213–14
Cognitive dissonance, 214–15
Cognitive intimacy, 294
Cognitive meaning, 202
Cohen, Arthur R., 89, 214
Collective unconscious, 240
Colonialism, 158
Comfort, Alex, 319
Coming Alive from Nine to Five: The Career Search Handbook (Michelozzi), 339
Commitments
fear of, 309
of marriage, 314
overloading of, 309–10
and values, 219–20
Communication. *See also* Dialogue, internal; Listening; Media, communications; Talking
anger as, 147, 149
attention in, 59, 61
in conflict resolution, 336
emotional, 295, 296
nonverbal, 176–79
openness in, 78–79
sexual, 322–23, 325–26
surface v. deep structure of, 90–91
trust in, 76
Communication scripts, 311–13

Communion, 295, 297, 315, 316
Community, 341–43
Co-movers, 313
Compassion and trust, 76
Compensation, 162
Competence, 211–12, 267–68
Complaints, 102–3, 289
Complementary models, 264
The Complete Job Search Handbook (Figler), 339
Complexes, 124–25
physical manifestations of, 181
Compulsion, 162–63
Compulsive control, 106
Computer (role), 312
Concentration, 251, 254, 255
Concepts, formation of, 198–202
Concrete thought, 200–202
Conditioning, 259, 269–81
Condry, John, 281
Confirmation, 27
Conflicts, 168. *See also* Disagreements
body-mind, 181
evocation of, by dreams, 235, 236, 237, 243
interpersonal, 327–36
Confluence, 27
Conformity and adjustment, 5
Confrontation, 112–13
of death, 145–46
of domestic violence, 157–58
of fear/anxiety, 136, 137
of unfinished business, 226
Confusion, 168, 294–95, 296
Conscious love, 303
Consciousness, 197–98
alteration of, through meditation, 250–56
experience of, 245–46, 248–49
and intention, 47
obstruction of, 247–49
spontaneity of, 56–57, 58
transpersonal, 249–50
Consensus, rule of, 81
Consistency, rule of, 81–82
Contact, 27. *See also* Intimacy
and happiness, 171
physical, 174–76
Contemplation, 244, 254–55
Content messages, 97
Contraception, 319, 320
Contracts, 289, 331–32
Control
contrasted with power, 106
disguised, 107

of environmental stimuli, 279–80, 282–83
of future, 230
and stress, 185
as substitute for anger, 150
Conversation. *See* Communication; Dialogue; Listening; Talking
Coping models, 264–65
Corey, Gerald, 302–3
Correspondence and attribution, 81
Cosmopolitan, 319
Counter experience, 222
Counting Judgments (exercise), 17
Counting meditation, 254, 255
Cousteau, Jacques, 343
Cowan, Michael A., 69
"Crazy times," 188
Creativity, 206–7
and cultivation of personality, 36, 38
in work, 337–38
Criticism. *See* Evaluation; Judgments
Cross-complaints, 103
Crossroads (exercise), 231
Crow, the, 40
Crying, 120, 123–24
as disguise, 150
and emotional pain, 132
and grief, 144
Cues, 279–80
Curiosity, 266–67. *See also* Interest
Curtis, John D., 184, 185

Dahms, Alan M., 294
Dark Ages, 157
Davis, K. E., 81
Day, J., 123
Daydreams, 55, 56–57, 163
Death
and anxiety, 136
confrontation of, 145–46
grieving over, 143–44
imminence of, 232–33
and terminal illness, 144–45
Death layer of personality, 169–70
De Bono, Edward, 206
Decision-making. *See* Choice
Deep structure of communication
definition of, 90–91
explication of, 91–104

response to, 113–14
of self, 15–17
snap, 95
types of, 13
Jung, Carl G., 24, 33, 71
  on complexes, 124
  on dreams, 235, 236, 239,
    240, 243, 244
  on personality, 36–38, 40
Jung, John, 166
Justifying, 165, 166, 214, 215
Just One Thing at a Time (exercise), 59–60

Kahane, Howard, 202, 203
Kaiser-Permanente medical organization, 182
Kantor, David, 313
Karma, 42
Katz, Martin, 81, 246
Keleman, Stanley
  on blocking, 182
  on nonverbal messages, 177,
    179
  on sexual excitement, 321
  on touch, 175
Kelley, Harold H., 47, 87
  on interpersonal conflict, 327,
    328
  on interpretation of behavior,
    81
  on intimacy, 296
  on negotiation, 334
Kelly, Gene, 39
Kelly, George A., 46
Kelman, Herbert, 213
Keyes, Ken, 300
  on addiction, 172
  on emotional addiction, 315
  on interpersonal relationships,
    67
  on love, 299
  on roles, 313
Kiechel, Walter, III, 150
Kierkegaard, Sören, 22
King, Larry W., 115–16
King, Martin Luther, Jr., 158
King, S. B., 185
Kirschenbaum, Martin, 18–19,
  46
Kirshenbaum, Howard, 219
Knowledge
  and confirmation of fears, 132,
    142–43
  contrasted with awareness, 53–
    54

disclosure of, in confrontation,
  112
incompleteness of, in prejudice,
  215–16
and interpretation of behavior,
  87, 88–89
openness to, 208–9
selective, 214–15
and wisdom, 9–10
Knox, R. E., 214
Koestler, Arthur, 206
Kopp, Sheldon, 197
Korda, Michael, 106
Korzybski, Alfred, 200, 201, 247
Krantzler, Mel, 73
Krutch, Joseph Wood, 120
Kübler-Ross, Elisabeth, 143, 146
Kurtz, Ron, 179
Kwong, Jakusho, 172

Laing, R. D., 24, 27, 28, 29, 183
Lakein, Alan, 229–30
Lamson, Ralph J., 268
Lange, Arthur, 109–10, 111, 114
Language
  distancing, 87–88
  as representation of reality,
    200–202
Lao Tzu, 9, 343
Lasch, Christopher, 338
Lateral thinking, 206–7
Laughter, 120, 256
  and joy, 172–73
  and pain, 132, 173
Lazarus, Arnold, 217
Learned helplessness, 140–41,
  268
Learning
  affective, 167
  effectiveness in, 267–68
  effect of fear on, 132
  of intimacy, 296–97
  intrinsic motivation of, 280–81
  observational, 264–65
  and respect for authenticity,
    29–30
Learning to Love Again (Krantz-
  ler), 73
Lecky, Prescott, 210
Lederer, William J., 76, 103, 107,
  329
Lee, Dorothy, 29
Lee, J. A., 304
Legitimate power, 107
Lehr, William, 313
Lentz, Carole Thompson, 300
Le Shan, Laurence, 247

Leveler, 312
Levels of Feeling (exercise), 124
Levi, L., 185
Lewin, Kurt, 168, 214
Lewinsohn, Peter, 140
Lewis, Alec, 318
Liberman, Robert Paul, 115–16
Lidz, Theodore, 86, 264
Life
  absurdity of, 172, 173
  cyclical nature of, 232
  enjoyment of, 11, 172–73
  implications of death for, 145–
    46, 232–33
Life events
  exploration of, 22–23
  exercise for, 23
  and stress, 184, 185–86
Limits
  on change, 261, 262
  in relationships, 308–9
Lindner, Robert, 5
Linear thinking, 206
Listening. *See also* Communication
  obstacles to, 94–96, 99
  and projection, 84
  reflective, 98–100, 113, 115
  role of intention in, 97–98
Livingston, Pat, 96, 99, 115
Logic
  defective, 203–4
  definition of, 202–3
  of dreams, 239
  paradoxical, 206
Loneliness, 22. *See also* Aloneness
  definition of, 68
  forms of, 68–69
  responses to, 69–70
  and sexual contact, 318, 321
Lose-lose strategy, 329
Loss, in grief, 143–44
Love
  as disguise for fear, 133
  expression of, 127
  and giving, 316
  mutuality in, 73, 74
  need for, 299
  and need for solitude, 71
  obstacles to, 299–300
  projection of, 82, 301–2
  styles of, 304
  types of, 300–304
  withdrawal of, 287
Lovemaking, 301, 304, 318,
  321–26
Loving Feelings (exercise), 300

for feelings, 122–23
as repudiation of dependency, 43
sexual, 320–21
and social environment, 44–45
and stress, 185
Retroflection, 150, 163
Reviewing Your Scripts (exercise), 25–26
Reward power, 106
Rewards
and behavioral change, 270–79 *passim*
deprivation of, 140
incremental, 277–78
and learning, 265
and motivation, 281
Right Livelihood, 338
Rilke, Rainer Maria, 74
Risk-taking, 231, 262, 293, 294
Ritter, B., 139
Roddenberry, Gene, 245
Rogers, Carl, 5, 30
on expression of feelings, 128
on listening, 98
on power, 106
on value formation, 219
Rokeach, Milton, 208
Roles
and authenticity, 24–26
dependent v. responsible, 43
family, 310–13
imitation of, 139–40, 264–65
and inauthenticity, 28
and personality, 33, 38–40
playing, 87, 265–66
sexual, 317–18
as source of power, 107
subject v. object, 72–73
work, 340
Roles and games layer of personality, 169
Romantic love, 302–3
Rosenman, Martin, 76
Rosenman, Ray, 187
Roshi, Fujimoto, 251
Ross, L., 87
Rossi, Ernest L., 236, 240, 241
Rousseau, Jean Jacques, 331
Rowe, Clarence J., 134–35
Rubin, Jeffrey, 75, 107
Rubin, Zick, 302
Rules, 306–8
Rush, A. John, 142
Russell, Bertrand, 223
Ryckoff, I., 123

Saadi of Shiraz, Sheikh, 165
Sabotage, 129
Sadhatissa, H., 338
Sampson, Edward E., 215–16
Sanborn, Ken, 246
Sandperl, Ira, 233
Sanford, R. Nevitt, 338
San Francisco, 174
Sarcasm, 91, 149
Sartre, Jean-Paul, 43, 45, 47
Sasaki, Ruth Fuller, 9, 198
Satir, Virginia, 24, 298
on appreciation of differences, 74
on divorces, 333
on roles, 310–13
Scapegoating, 216
Schaffer, Laurence F., 4
Schizophrenia, 27, 62
Schumacher, E. F., 337, 338, 341
Scoresby, A. L., 78, 103, 104, 336
Scripts, 25–26, 311–13, 319. *See also* Characters; Roles
Sears, Robert R., 155
Secondary reinforcement, 271–72
Secret of the Golden Flower, The, 189
Secrets (exercise), 133
Seeing like a Child (exercise), 298
Self-acceptance and awareness, 56
Self-assessment, 7–8
Self-consciousness, 54
and projection, 84–85
Self-definition. *See also* Identity; Individuation
through action, 45–46, 48–49
through experience, 46
Self-depreciation, 15–17, 33. *See also* Depreciative judgments
exercise for exploring, 15
Self-determination, 21–22, 105–6
exercise for, 8
and mutuality, 77
and transcendence of barriers, 8–9
Self-disclosure, 77–79, 111, 126–27
Self-esteem, 12–13
and assertion, 108, 109
and interpersonal relationships, 67
and judgments, 14
and learning, 267–68

and punishment, 287
and resolution of complexes, 125
Self-Esteem Estimator, The (exercise), 12–13
Self-fulfillment, mystique of, 5–6
Self-glorification, 32–33
Self-image
definition of, 209–10
idealization of, 210
inferiority/superiority in, 210–11
protection of, 163, 164–65
success/failure and, 211–13
Self-justification, 87, 165, 166, 214, 215
Self-knowledge, development of, 6. *See also* Awareness; Knowledge
Self-monitoring, 187, 263
Self-pity, 142
Self-righteous anger, 151
Self-sacrifice, 108
and conflict resolution, 334
Self-support, 67, 73, 74, 315
Seligman, Martin, 140–41, 268
Selves, personal v. social, 24–25
Selye, Hans, 182, 183–84
Senoi, the, 234, 241
Sensuality, sexual, 321, 325–26
Sensual Play (exercise), 325
Separation
at death, 143–44
loneliness of, 69
in marriage, 332–33
Seton, Ernest T., 4
Seton, Julia M., 4
Seven Arrows (Storm), 34, 40
Sexuality
enhancement of, 322–26
excitement in, 318, 321–22, 324–25
functions of, 317, 318–19
performance in, 321, 323
responsibility in, 320–21
and social mores, 319
and social roles, 317–18
Shadow, the, 33–34
projection of, onto others, 82–83
Shah, Idries, 165, 223, 230, 246
Shamanism, 209
Shame, 148
Shaping, 277–78, 280
Shapiro, Sam, 249, 250
Sheehy, Gail, 339
Shiatsu massage, 191